Praise for *Windows System Programming, Third Edition*

"If you're a systems-level 32-bit or 64-bit Windows [developer], whether using the Windows API directly or via .NET interop, you'll definitely want to take a look at this update to Johnson Hart's well-respected and well-loved book. Johnson starts with Windows history and cultural issues and moves through basic and advanced system services in a thoughtful, thorough manner. If Mr. Rogers wrote a book with David Cutler, this is what they'd come up with."
   —**Chris Sells,** Longhorn Content Strategist,
   Microsoft Corporation

"While focusing on UNIX developers that are looking to augment their skills or simply jump ship, *Windows System Programming, Third Edition* is a book that even some seasoned systems-level Windows developers will undoubtedly find useful. This is not your average bland GUI treatise; Hart takes you down to the metal, explains all the relevant concepts clearly and in-depth, and gives you an extensive library of high-quality code examples that can be easily adapted for your own larger applications. Even if you've created server applications before, *Windows System Programming* will teach you new tricks, shed new light on concepts you thought you'd mastered, and offer new strategies for creating robust and secure solutions."
   —**Klaus H. Probst,** Senior Architect,
   Spherion Technology Services; Microsoft MVP

"This book is quite easy to follow; there are clear explanations of everything. Even the explanation of the standards is readable! For a developer not familiar with developing with Windows, Hart's book also provides basic information on where Windows was and where it is today, plus a great explanation of how it is different from Posix and Unix."
   —**Eric Landes,** Microsoft MVP,
   www.aspalliance.com/corporatecoder

"Even advanced developers will always need to have a book like this one on hand when the abstractions of a platform like .NET are inadequate or when they need to know more about how .NET is implemented. And the focus on low-level programming (specifically memory management and IO) and other non-GUI topics makes it stand out as superior among other Windows programming books. In keeping the GUI focus to a minimum, Hart's book is able to be comprehensive on the topics contained within."
   —**Michael Davidson,** IT Analyst

Windows System Programming
Third Edition

Windows System Programming
Third Edition

Johnson M. Hart

✦✦Addison-Wesley

Boston • San Francisco • New York • Toronto • Montreal
London • Munich • Paris • Madrid
Capetown • Sydney • Tokyo • Singapore • Mexico City

The publisher offers excellent discounts on this book when ordered in quantity for bulk purchases or special sales, which may include electronic versions and/or custom covers and content particular to your business, training goals, marketing focus, and branding interests. For more information, please contact:

    U.S. Corporate and Government Sales
    (800) 382-3419
    corpsales@pearsontechgroup.com

For sales outside of the U.S., please contact:

    International Sales
    international@pearsoned.com

Visit us on the Web: www.awprofessional.com

Library of Congress Cataloging-in-Publication Data
Hart, Johnson M., 1944-
  Windows system programming / Johnson M. Hart.—3rd ed.
    p. cm.
  Includes bibliographical references and index.
  ISBN 0-321-25619-0 (hardback : alk. paper
  1. Application software—Development. 2. Microsoft Win32. 3. Microsoft Windows
(Computer file) I. Title

  QA76.76.A65H474 2004
  005.4'3—dc22   2004017402

ISBN: 0-321-25619-0
Text printed in the United States on recycled paper at Courier in Westford, Massachusetts.
Second printing, April 2005

Contents

Chapter 5   Memory Management, Memory-Mapped Files, and DLLs   119

Chapter 6   Process Management   163

Chapter 9   **Synchronization Performance Impact and Guidelines   265**

Chapter 10   **Advanced Thread Synchronization   281**

Figures

Tables

Programs

Preface

This book describes application development using the Microsoft Windows Application Programming Interface (API), concentrating on the core system services, including the file system, process and thread management, interprocess communication, network programming, and synchronization. User interfaces, internals, and I/O drivers, although important and interesting topics, are beyond the book's scope. The examples concentrate on realistic scenarios, and in many cases the examples can be used as the foundations for real applications.

The Win32/Win64 API, or the Windows API, is supported by Microsoft's family of 32-bit and 64-bit operating systems, which currently consists of Windows XP, Windows 2000, and Windows 2003. Older Windows family members include Windows NT, Me, 98, and 95; these systems are considered obsolete, but they will run many of the example programs. Migration issues from Win32 to the emerging Win64 are discussed as required. Win64, supported as a 64-bit interface on some versions of Windows 2003 and XP, is nearly identical to Win32.

There is no doubt that the Windows API is an important factor for application development, in many cases replacing the POSIX API, supported by UNIX and Linux, as the preferred, or at least peer, API for applications targeted at desktop and server systems. Therefore, many experienced programmers will want to learn the Windows API quickly, and this book is designed to help them do so.

The first objectives are to explain what Windows is, show how to use it in realistic situations, and do so as quickly as possible without burdening the reader with unnecessary detail. This book is, therefore, not a reference guide, but it explains the central features of the most important functions and shows how to use them in practical programming situations. Equipped with this knowledge, the reader will be able to use the comprehensive Microsoft reference documentation to explore details, advanced options, and the more obscure functions as requirements or interests dictate. I have found the Windows API easy to learn using this approach, and I have greatly enjoyed developing Windows programs, despite occasional frustration. This enthusiasm will show through at times, as it should. This does not mean that I feel that Windows is necessarily better than other operating system (OS) APIs, but it certainly has many attractive features.

Many Windows books spend a great deal of time explaining how processes, virtual memory, interprocess communication, and preemptive scheduling work without showing how to use them in realistic situations. A programmer experienced in UNIX, Linux, IBM MVS, OpenVMS, or another OS will be familiar with these concepts and will be impatient to find out how they are implemented in Windows. Most Windows books also spend a great deal of space on user interface programming. This book avoids the user interface, beyond discussing simple character-based console I/O, in the interest of concentrating on the important core features.

The book takes the point of view that Windows is just an OS API, providing a well-understood set of features. Many programmers, regardless of experience level, need to learn Windows quickly, and an understanding of Windows is invaluable in discussing subjects such as Microsoft's Component Object Model (COM). The Windows systems, when compared with other systems, have good, bad, and average features and quality. The purpose of this book is to show how to use those features efficiently and in realistic situations to develop useful, high-quality, and high-performance applications.

Audience

- Anyone who wants to learn about Windows application development quickly, regardless of previous experience.

- Programmers and software engineers who must port existing applications, often in UNIX, to Windows for operation on any of the Windows platforms. The book contains many comparisons among Windows, UNIX, and standard C library functions and programming models. All common UNIX functionality, including process management, synchronization, file systems, and interprocess communication, is covered in Windows terms.

- Readers starting new projects who are not constrained by the need to port existing code. Many aspects of program design and implementation are covered, and Windows functions are used to create useful applications and to solve common programming problems.

- Programmers using COM and .NET Framework, who will find much of the information here helpful in understanding dynamic link libraries (DLLs), thread usage and models, interfaces, and synchronization.

- Computer science students at the upper-class undergraduate or beginning graduate level in courses covering systems programming or application development. This book will also be useful to those who are learning multithreaded programming or need to build networked applications. This book would be a useful complementary text to a book such as W. Richard Stevens' *Advanced Programming in the UNIX Environment* (see the Bibliography) so that students could compare Windows and UNIX. Students in OS courses will find this book to be a useful supplement as it illustrates how a commercially important OS provides essential OS functionality.

The only other assumption, implicit in all the others, is a knowledge of C programming.

Changes in the Third Edition

The third edition presents extensive new material along with significant updating and reorganization of the first and second editions. Objectives of the third edition include the following

- Cover important new features of Windows XP, 2000, and 2003 along with Win64 migration.

- Make obsolete Windows 95, 98, and Me (the "Windows 9x" family), since Windows XP is now provided with personal systems and Windows 9x limitations are no longer relevant.[1] Program examples freely exploit features found only in current Windows versions, even though some programs will not operate on Windows 9x.

- Provide enhanced coverage of threads and synchronization, including performance, scalability, and reliability considerations. Chapter 9 is new, as are some examples in Chapter 10.

- Emphasize the increasingly important role and new features of Windows 2000 and 2003 in running high-performance, scalable, multithreaded server applications.

- Study performance implications of different program designs, especially in multithreaded programs with synchronization and when running on symmetric multiprocessor (SMP) systems.

- Incorporate reader and student feedback to fix defects, improve explanations, improve the organization, and address numerous details, large and small.

Organization

Chapters are organized topically so that the features required in even a single-threaded application are covered first, followed by process and thread management features, and finally network programming in a multithreaded environment. This organization allows the reader to advance logically from file systems to memory management and file mapping, and then to processes, threads, and synchronization, followed by interprocess and network communication and security. This organization also allows the examples to evolve in a natural way, much as a developer might create a simple prototype and then add additional capability. The advanced features, such as asynchronous I/O and security, appear last.

---

[1] Nonetheless, features that do not apply to Windows 9x are noted as appropriate.

Within each chapter, after introducing the functionality area, such as process management or memory-mapped files, we discuss important Windows functions and their relationships in detail. Illustrative examples follow. Within the text, only essential parts of programs are listed; complete programs and the required include files, utility functions, and the like are in Appendix A or on the book's Web site (http://www.awprofessional.com/titles/0321256190). Throughout, we identify those features supported only by current Windows versions (XP, 2000, and 2003) but not by earlier versions such as Windows 9x and NT, which do not implement many advanced features. Each chapter suggests related additional reading and gives some exercises. Many exercises address interesting and important issues that did not fit within the normal text, and others allow the reader to explore advanced or specialized topics.

Chapter 1 is a high-level introduction to the Windows OS family and Windows. A simple example program shows the basic elements of Windows programming style and lays the foundation for more advanced Windows features. Win64 and migration issues are introduced in Chapter 1, described extensively in Chapter 16, and included throughout the book as required.

Chapters 2 and 3 deal with file systems, console I/O, file locking, and directory management. Unicode, the extended character set used by Windows, is also introduced in Chapter 2. Examples include sequential and direct file processing, directory traversal, and file archiving. Chapter 3 ends with a discussion of registry management programming, which is similar in many ways to file and directory management.

Chapter 4 introduces Windows' exception handling, including Structured Exception Handling (SEH), which will be used extensively throughout the book. Many books defer SEH to later chapters, but by introducing it early, we will be able to use SEH throughout and thus simplify some programming tasks and improve quality. Vectored exception handling, a newer feature, is also described.

Chapter 5 treats Windows' memory management and shows how to use memory-mapped files both to simplify programming and to improve performance. This chapter also covers DLLs.

Chapter 6 introduces Windows' processes, process management, and simple process synchronization. Chapter 7 then describes thread management in similar terms. Examples in each chapter show the many benefits, including program simplicity and performance, of threads and processes.

Chapters 8, 9, and 10 provide an extended, in-depth treatment of Windows' thread synchronization, one of Windows' strong features. Synchronization is a complex topic, and these chapters use extended examples and well-understood models to help readers obtain the programming and performance benefits of threads while avoiding many of the pitfalls. New material covers performance and scalability issues, which are important when building server-based applications, including those that will run on SMP systems.

Chapters 11 and 12 are concerned with interprocess and interthread communication and networking. Chapter 11 concentrates on the features that are properly part of Windows—namely, anonymous pipes, named pipes, and mailslots. Chapter 12 discusses Windows Sockets, which allow interoperability with non-Windows systems using industry-standard protocols, primarily TCP/IP. Windows Sockets, while not strictly part of the Windows API, provide for network and Internet communication and interoperability, and the subject matter is consistent with the rest of the book. A multithreaded client/server system illustrates how to use interprocess communication along with threads.

Chapter 13 describes how Windows allows server applications, such as the ones created in Chapters 11 and 12, to be converted to Windows Services that can be managed as background servers. Some small programming changes will turn the servers into services.

Chapter 14 shows how to perform asynchronous I/O using overlapped I/O with events and completion routines. You can achieve much the same thing with threads, so examples compare the different solutions for simplicity and performance. The closely related I/O completion ports are, however, necessary for scalable multithreaded servers, so this feature is illustrated with the servers created in earlier chapters. Waitable timers, which require concepts introduced earlier in the chapter, are also described.

Chapter 15 explains Windows' object security, showing, in an example, how to emulate UNIX-style file permissions. Additional examples shows how to secure processes, threads, and named pipes. Security upgrades can then be applied to the earlier examples as appropriate.

Chapter 16 concludes with a description of Win64 programming issues and how to assure that code is portable to Win64. An earlier example is then ported to Win64.

There are three appendixes. Appendix A describes the programs provided on the book's Web site and how to use them. Appendix B contains several tables that compare Windows functions with their counterparts in UNIX and the Standard C library. Appendix C compares the performance of alternative implementations of some of the examples in the text so that you can gauge the trade-offs between Windows features, both basic and advanced, and the C library.

UNIX and C Library Notes and Tables

Within the text at appropriate points, we contrast Windows style and functionality with the comparable UNIX (and Linux) and ANSI Standard C library features. As mentioned, Appendix B presents tables listing these comparable functions. This information is included because many readers are familiar with UNIX and are interested in the comparisons between the two systems. Readers without a

UNIX background should feel free to skip those paragraphs in the text, which are indented and set in a smaller font.

Examples

The examples are designed for the following tasks:

- Illustrate common, representative, and useful applications of the Windows functions.

- Correspond to real programming situations encountered in program development, consulting, and teaching. Some of my clients and course participants have used the code examples as the bases for their own systems. During my consulting activities, I frequently encounter code that is similar to that used in the examples, and on several occasions I have seen code taken directly from the first or second edition of this book. (Feel free to do so yourself; an acknowledgment in your documentation would be greatly appreciated.) Frequently, this code occurs as part of COM or C++ objects. The examples, subject to time and space constraints, are "real-world" examples and solve "real-world" problems.

- Emphasize how the functions actually behave and interact, which is not always as you might first expect after reading the documentation. Throughout this book, the text and the examples concentrate on interactions between functions rather than the functions themselves.

- Grow and expand, adding new capability to a previous solution in an easy and natural manner and exploring alternative implementation techniques.

- In the earlier chapters, many examples implement UNIX commands, such as `ls`, `touch`, `chmod`, and `sort`, showing the Windows functions in a familiar context while creating a useful set of utilities.[2] Different implementations of the same command will also give us an easy way to compare performance benefits available with advanced Windows features. Appendix C contains the results of these performance tests.

Examples in the early chapters are usually short, but the later chapters present longer examples when appropriate.

---

[2] Several commercial and open source products provide complete sets of UNIX utilities; there is no intent to supplement them. These examples, although useful, are primarily intended to illustrate the use of Windows features. A reader who is not familiar with UNIX should not, however, have any difficulty understanding the programs or their functionality.

Exercises at the end of each chapter suggest alternative designs, subjects for investigation, and additional functionality that is important but beyond the book's scope. Some exercises are easy, and a few are very challenging. Frequently, clearly labeled defective solutions are provided, because fixing the bugs is an excellent way to sharpen skills.

All examples have been debugged and tested under Windows XP, 2000, and 2003. Where appropriate, they have been tested under Windows 9x and NT. Although the bulk of the development was performed on single-processor, Intel-based systems, most programs were also tested on multiprocessor systems. The client/server applications have been tested using multiple clients simultaneously interacting with a server. Nonetheless, there is no guarantee or assurance of program correctness, completeness, or fitness for any purpose. Undoubtedly, even the simplest examples contain defects or will fail under some conditions; such is the fate of nearly all software. I will, however, gratefully appreciate any messages regarding program defects—and, better still, fixes.

The Web Site

The book's Web site (http://www.awprofessional.com/titles/0321256190) contains a downloadable file with complete code and projects for all the book's examples, a number of exercise solutions, alternative implementations of some of the examples, instructions, and performance evaluation tests. This material will be updated periodically to include new material and corrections.

My personal Web site (http://world.std.com/~jmhart/windows.htm) contains book errata, along with additional examples, reader contributions, additional explanations, and much more. PowerPoint slides are also included and can be used for noncommercial instructional purposes. These slides have been used numerous times in professional training courses, and they are also suitable for use in college courses.

The material will be updated as required when defects are fixed and as reader input is received. If you encounter any difficulties with the programs or any material in the book, check these locations first because there may already be a fix or explanation. If that does not answer your question, feel free to send e-mail to jmhart@world.std.com.

Acknowledgments

Numerous people have provided assistance, advice, and encouragement during the preparation of the third edition, and readers have provided many important ideas and corrections. The author's Web site acknowledges the significant contributions that have found their way into the third edition, and the first two editions acknowledge earlier valuable contributions. In addition several recent reviewers—Vagif Abilov, Bill Draper, Horst D. Clausen, Michael Davidson, Daniel Jiang, Eric Landes, Klaus H. Probst, and Douglas Reilly—have gone above and beyond the call of duty to read the early drafts and to provide excellent and detailed feedback; their recommendations and advice are greatly appreciated, and I only hope that I've done justice to their hard work. My friends and colleagues at ArrAy Inc. also deserve a note of special thanks; I've learned a lot from them.

Anne H. Smith, the compositor, has used her skill, persistence, and patience to prepare the book for publication; the book simply would not have been possible without her assistance. Elissa Armour, the compositor for the first two editions, laid the groundwork for this edition and facilitated a smooth transition.

Chrysta Meadowbrooke, the copyeditor, made significant contributions to the book's accuracy, clarity, and conciseness. Her careful manuscript reading, incisive questions, and insight helped flush out many issues, large and small.

The staff at Addison-Wesley Professional has exhibited the professionalism and expertise that make an author's work a pleasure. Stephane Nakib, the editor, and Karen Gettman, the Editor-in-Chief, have worked with the project from the beginning, urging me on, making sure that no barriers get in the way, and assuring that hardly any schedules are slipped. Ebony Haight, the editorial assistant, has managed the process throughout, and the production team of John Fuller and Patrick Cash-Peterson, the Production Coordinator, has made the production process seem almost simple.

The book is dedicated, with love, to Bob and Elizabeth.

Johnson (John) M. Hart
jmhart@world.std.com
August 2004

1 | Getting Started with Win32 and Win64

This chapter introduces the Microsoft Windows operating system (OS) family and the Win32 Application Programming Interface (API) used by all family members. There is also a brief description of the newer 64-bit Win64 API, and migration and portability between Win32 and Win64 are discussed as required. For convenience, we will speak mainly of Windows and the Windows API. In general, Win32 and Win64 will be mentioned only when there is an important distinction. The context will help distinguish between Windows as an OS and Windows as an API for application development.

The Windows API, like any other OS API, has its own set of conventions and programming techniques, which are driven by the Windows philosophy. A simple file copy example introduces the Windows programming style, and this same style is used for file management, process and memory management, and advanced features such as thread synchronization. The example is also shown coded using the Standard C library in order to contrast Windows with more familiar programming styles.

The first step is to review the basic features that any modern OS must provide and, from there, to learn how to use these features in Windows.

Operating System Essentials

Windows makes core OS features available on systems as diverse as cell phones, handheld devices, laptop PCs, and enterprise servers. OS features can be described by considering the most important resources that a modern OS manages.

- **Memory**. The OS manages a large, flat, virtual memory address space and transparently moves information between physical memory and disk and other secondary storage.

- **File systems**. The OS manages a named file space and provides both direct and sequential access as well as directory and file management. Most systems have a hierarchical name space.

- **Resource naming and location**. File naming allows for long, descriptive names, and the naming scheme is extended to objects such as devices, synchronization, and interprocess communication objects. The OS also locates and manages access to named objects.

- **Multitasking**. The OS must manage processes, threads, and other units of independent, asynchronous execution. Tasks can be preempted and scheduled according to dynamically determined priorities.

- **Communication and synchronization**. The OS manages task-to-task communication and synchronization within single systems as well as communication between networked systems and with the Internet.

- **Security and protection**. The OS provides flexible mechanisms to protect resources from unauthorized and accidental access and corruption.

The Microsoft Windows Win32/Win64 API supports all these OS features and more and makes them available on a range of Windows versions, some of which are becoming obsolete and some of which support only a subset of the full API.

Windows Evolution

The Windows API is supported on several Windows versions. Having several distinct Windows versions can be confusing, but from the programmer's perspective, they are similar. In particular, they all support subsets of the *identical* Windows API. Programs developed for one system can, with considerable ease, run on another, resulting in source and, in most cases, binary portability.

New Windows versions have added small amounts of new API functionality, although the API has been remarkably stable since the beginning. Major themes in Windows evolution include the following.

- **Scalability**. Newer versions run on a wider range of systems, up to enterprise servers with large memories and storage systems.

- **Integration**. Each new release integrates additional technology, such as multimedia, wireless networking, Web Services, and plug-and-play capability. This technology is, in general, out of scope for this book.

- **Ease of use**. Improved graphical desktop appearance and ease of use are readily apparent with each release.

- **Enhanced API**. Important API enhancements have been added over time. The API is the central topic of this book.

Windows Versions

Windows, in an evolving series of versions, has been used since 1993. The following important versions are listed on the Microsoft Web site at the time of this writing.

- **Windows XP**, including the Home, Professional, and other editions, is targeted at the individual user. Most commercial PCs sold today, including laptops and notebooks, come with an appropriate version of Windows XP preinstalled. The differences between the versions are generally not important in this book.

- **Windows Server 2003**, targeted at enterprise and server applications, has Small Business Server, Storage Server 2003, and other product editions. Systems running Windows 2003 ("Server" will be omitted from now on) frequently use symmetric multiprocessing (SMP) with multiple independent processors. New 64-bit applications, requiring Win64, are emerging primarily on Windows 2003 systems.

- **Windows 2000**, available in Professional and several Server editions, is still commonly used on both personal and server systems. Over time, Windows XP and future Windows versions will supplant Windows 2000, which is no longer sold.

- **Windows Embedded**, **Windows CE**, **Tablet PC**, and **Windows Mobile** are specialized Windows versions targeted at smaller systems, such as palmtops and embedded processors, and provide large subsets of Windows features.

Obsolete Previous Windows Versions

Earlier Windows versions, while no longer offered or supported by Microsoft, are still in use and will run many, but not all, of the examples discussed in this book. The older versions include those listed here.

- **Windows NT** 3.5, 3.5.1, and 4.0 are the predecessors of current NT versions and date back to 1993; Windows NT Version 4.0 Service Pack 3 (SP 3) was the most popular version. NT was originally targeted at servers and professional users, with Windows 9x (see the next bullet) sold for personal and office use. Windows 2000 was originally referred to as NT Version 5.0, and many users still simply use the terms Windows NT or NT5 when speaking of Windows 2000, 2003, and XP. Nearly all the programs in this book will operate correctly, if suboptimally, on Version 4.0; however, there are important exceptions, especially in the later chapters.

- **Windows 95**, **Windows 98**, and **Windows Me** (or simply **Windows 9x**, because the distinction is rarely important) were primarily desktop and laptop OSs lacking, among other things, the NT security features. Windows XP replaces these systems and combines their features with those of NT. Many but not all of the programs, especially in the earlier chapters, will operate correctly on Windows 9x.

Further back, Windows 3.1, a 16-bit OS, was dominant on personal systems before the Windows 95 introduction, and its graphical user interface (GUI) was a predecessor to the modern Windows GUI. The API, however, did not support many of the essential OS features, such as true multitasking, memory management, and security.

Going further back to the late 1980s, it is possible to identify DOS as the original "IBM PC" OS. DOS had only a simple command line interface, and DOS commands are still used. In fact, most of the book's examples are written as command line programs, so they can be run under the command prompt, and some DOS batch files are provided to run performance tests.

Windows NT 5.x

Windows 2000, XP, and 2003 are collectively referred to as NT Version 5.x or simply NT5. All three use Version 5 of the Windows NT kernel, although the minor version (the "x" in "5.x") may vary. For example, Windows XP uses kernel Version NT 5.1.

While many programs will run on earlier versions, in general we will assume NT5, which provides some features not found in earlier versions. This is a safe assumption as any new Windows system will have NT5, and the assumption will allow us to take advantage of some advanced features. Many older systems, however, may still be running an earlier NT version or Windows 9x, so, on start-up, the sample programs will test the Windows version number and terminate with an error message if necessary.

The Microsoft API documentation states the version requirements, given in terms of NT, Windows (meaning 9x in this context), CE, and other requirements. Check the documentation if there is any doubt about an API function's operation on a particular Windows version.

Other Windows Programming Interfaces

Windows (by which we mean the Win32 and Win64 API as well as NT5, unless otherwise noted) is capable of supporting other "subsystem" environments, although this feature is rarely used and is not relevant to this book. The NT OS kernel is truly protected from applications. Windows is only one of several possible environments. A POSIX subsystem is part of a resource kit from Microsoft, and open source POSIX subsystems are also available.

Processor Support

Windows can support different underlying processor and system architectures and has a Hardware Abstraction Layer (HAL) to enable porting to different processor architectures, although this is not a direct concern for the application developer.

Windows runs primarily on the Intel x86 processor family, whose current members include Pentium and Xeon, and previously the 486. Compatible Advanced Micro Devices (AMD) processors are common. Furthermore, Windows was designed to be processor independent. Most importantly, Windows 2003 is supported on the Intel Itanium, a new 64-bit architecture radically different from the classic x86 architecture.

Other examples, past and present, of the architectural independence of Windows include the following.

- Windows CE runs on a variety of non-x86 processors.

- Windows NT was originally supported on the Digital Equipment Corporation (since acquired by Compaq and then HP) Alpha processor.

- The AMD Athlon 64 and Opteron 64-bit (AMD64) processors provide a 64-bit extension of the x86 architecture, which is a different approach than that used in the Itanium architecture.

- Intel's recently announced 32/64-bit processors will be 64-bit x86 extensions.

The Windows Market Role

Windows is hardly unique in its ability to provide essential functionality on several platforms. After all, numerous proprietary and open OSs have these features, and UNIX[1] and Linux have long been available on a wide range of systems. There are, however, significant advantages, both business and technical, to using Windows and to developing Windows applications.

- Windows dominates the market, especially on the desktop, and has done so for many years with no change in sight.[2] Therefore, Windows applications have a large target market, numbering in the tens of millions and dwarfing other desktop systems, including UNIX, Linux, and Macintosh.

- The market dominance of the Windows OSs means that applications and software development and integration tools are widely and inexpensively available for Windows. Furthermore, innovations often appear first on Windows systems.

- Windows applications can use a GUI familiar to tens of millions of users, and many Windows applications are customized or "localized" for the language and user interface requirements of users throughout the world.

- SMP systems are also supported by Windows. Windows is not confined to the desktop; it can support departmental and enterprise servers and high-performance workstations.[3]

- Windows (although not Windows 9x and CE) is certified at the National Security Agency (NSA) C2 security level.

- Most OSs, other than UNIX, Linux, and Windows, are proprietary to systems from a single vendor.

- The Windows OSs have many features not available in standard UNIX, although they may be available in some UNIX implementations. C2-level security and NT Services are two examples.

---

[1] UNIX comments always apply to Linux as well as to any other system that supports the POSIX API.

[2] Linux is occasionally mentioned as a threat to Windows' dominance, primarily as a server but also for personal applications. While extremely interesting, speculation regarding future developments, much less the comparative merits of Linux and Windows, is out of scope for this book.

[3] The range of Windows host systems can be appreciated by considering that programs in this book have been tested on systems spanning from an obsolete 486 system with 16MB of RAM to a four-processor, 8GB RAM, 2GHz Xeon-based enterprise server.

Windows provides modern OS functionality and can run applications ranging from word processors and e-mail to enterprise integration systems and large database servers. Furthermore, Windows platforms scale from the desktop to the enterprise. Decisions to develop Windows applications are driven by both technical features and business requirements.

Windows, Standards, and Open Systems

This book is about developing applications using the Windows API. For a programmer coming from UNIX and open systems, it is natural to ask, "Is Windows open?" "Is Windows an industry standard?" "Is Windows just another proprietary API?" The answers depend very much on the definitions of *open*, *industry standard*, and *proprietary*, as well as on the benefits expected from open systems.

The Windows API is totally different from the POSIX standard API supported by Linux and UNIX. Windows does not conform to the X/Open standard or any other open industry standards formulated by standards bodies or industry consortia.

Windows is controlled by one vendor. Although Microsoft solicits industry input and feedback, it remains the sole arbiter and implementer. This means that the user receives many of the benefits that open standards are intended to provide as well as other advantages.

- Uniform implementations reach the market quickly.

- There are no proprietary "improvements" or "extensions" to baffle the programmer, although the small differences among the various Windows platforms must be considered.

- One vendor has defined and implemented competent OS products with all the required capabilities. Applications developers add value at a higher level.

- The underlying hardware platform is open. Developers can select from numerous platform vendors.

Arguments will continue to rage about whether this situation is beneficial or harmful to users and the computer industry as a whole. This book will not settle the argument; it is merely intended to help application developers come up to speed quickly with Windows.

Windows systems do support many essential standards. For example, Windows supports the Standard C and C++ libraries and a wide array of open interoperability standards. Thus, Windows Sockets provide a standard networked programming interface for access to TCP/IP and other networking protocols, allowing Internet access and interoperability with non-Windows systems. The same is true with Remote Procedure Calls (RPCs).[4] Diverse systems can communicate with high-level database management system (DBMS) protocols using Structured Query Language (SQL). Finally, Internet support with Web and other servers is part of the total Windows offering. The key standards, such as TCP/IP, are supported by Windows, and many valuable options, including X Windows clients and servers, are available at reasonable cost in an active market of Windows solution suppliers.

In summary, Windows supports the essential interoperability standards, and, while the core API is proprietary, it is available cost-effectively on a wide variety of systems.

Compatibility Libraries

Compatibility libraries are available but are rarely used. There are two possibilities.

- A Windows compatibility library, such as the Wine open source Windows emulator, can be hosted on UNIX, Linux, Macintosh, or some other system, allowing source code portability from Windows.

- A POSIX compatibility library can be hosted on top of the Windows subsystem using Microsoft's Windows Resource Kit and open source code. Microsoft's Visual C++ development environment includes a very limited compatibility library.

Thus, it is possible, but rare, to select one API and host portable applications on Windows, POSIX, or even Macintosh systems.

Windows Principles

It is helpful to keep in mind some basic Windows principles. The Windows API is different in many ways, both large and small, from other APIs such as the POSIX API familiar to UNIX and Linux programmers. Although Windows is not inherently difficult, it requires some changes in coding style and technique.

Here are some of the major characteristics of Windows, which will become much more familiar as you read through the book.

---

[4] Windows Sockets and RPCs are not properly part of Windows, but sockets are described in this book because they relate directly to the general subject matter and approach.

Many system resources are represented as a *kernel object* identified and referenced by a *handle*. These handles are comparable to UNIX file descriptors and process IDs.[5]

- Kernel objects must be manipulated by Windows APIs. There are no "back doors." This arrangement is consistent with the data abstraction principles of object-oriented programming, although Windows is not object-oriented.

- Objects include files, processes, threads, pipes for interprocess communication, memory mapping, events, and many more. Objects have security attributes.

- Windows is a rich and flexible interface. First, it contains many functions that perform the same or similar operations; in particular, convenience functions combine common sequences of function calls into one function (`CopyFile` is one such convenience function, and it is used in an example later in the chapter.) Second, a given function will often have numerous parameters and flags, many of which can normally be ignored. This book concentrates on the most important functions and options rather than being encyclopedic.

- Windows offers numerous synchronization and communication mechanisms tailored for different requirements.

- The Windows thread is the basic unit of execution. A process can contain one or more threads.

- Windows function names are long and descriptive. The following function names illustrate function name conventions as well as Windows' variety:

      WaitForSingleObject

      WaitForSingleObjectEx

      WaitForMultipleObjects

      WaitNamedPipe

In addition to these features, there are a few conventions for type names.

- The names for predefined data types, required by the API, are in uppercase and are also descriptive. The following typical types occur frequently:

      BOOL (defined as a 32-bit object for storing a single logical value)

      HANDLE

---

[5] These handles are similar to but not the same as the HWND and HDC handles used in Windows GUI programming.

DWORD (the ubiquitous 32-bit unsigned integer)

LPTSTR (a string pointer of either 8-bit or 16-bit characters)

LPSECURITY_ATTRIBUTES

Many other data types will be introduced as required.

- The predefined types avoid the * operator and make distinctions such as differentiating LPTSTR (defined as TCHAR *) from LPCTSTR (defined as const TCHAR *). *Note*: TCHAR may be a normal char or a two-byte wchar_t.

- Variable names, at least in function prototypes, also have conventions. For example, lpszFileName might be a "long pointer to a zero-terminated string" representing a file name. This is the so-called Hungarian notation, which this book does not generally use for program variables. Similarly, dwAccess is a double word (32 bits) containing file access flags; "dw" denotes flags in a double word.

Note: It is informative to look at the system include files where the functions, constants, flags, error codes, and so on are defined. Many interesting files, such as the following, are part of the Microsoft Visual C++ environment and are normally installed in the Program Files\Microsoft Visual Studio .NET\Vc7\ PlatformSDK\Include directory (or, on VC++ version 6.0, Program Files\ Microsoft Visual Studio\VC98\Include):

WINDOWS.H (this file brings in all the others)

WINNT.H

WINBASE.H

Finally, even though the original Win32 API was created from scratch, it was designed to be backward-compatible with the Windows 3.1 Win16 API. This has several effects that annoy programmers.

- There are anachronisms in types, such as LPTSTR and LPDWORD, which refer to the "long pointer" that is simply a 32-bit or 64-bit pointer. There is no need for any other pointer type. At other times, the "long" is omitted, and LPVOID and PVOID are equivalent.[6]

---

[6] The include files contain types, such as PVOID, without the prefix, but the examples conform to the usage in many other books and the Microsoft documentation.

- "WIN32" sometimes appears in macro names, such as WIN32_FIND_DATA, even though the macro is also used with Win64.

- The former requirement, no longer relevant, for backward compatibility means that numerous 16-bit functions are never used in this book, even though they might seem important. OpenFile is such a function; always use CreateFile to open an existing file.

Getting Ready for Win64

Win64, which is supported (at the time of writing) by Windows XP and 2003 on AMD's AMD64 (Opteron and Athlon 64) processor family and Intel's Itanium processor family (previously known by code names such as Merced, McKinley, Madison, and IA-64), will be an increasingly important factor in the building of large applications. The essential difference between Win32 and Win64 is the size of pointer variables (64 bits in Win64) and the size of virtual address space.

Throughout this book, Win64 migration is discussed as appropriate, and the programs are built so that a simple compiler switch will enable you to build the programs as Win64 applications. The example program projects on the book's Web site are set up to generate 64-bit migration warnings, and most (but not all) warning situations have been eliminated from the code.

Most of the differences, from a programming point of view, concern the size of pointers and careful avoidance of the assumption that a pointer and an integer (LONG, DWORD, and so on) are of the same length. Thus, the types DWORD32 and DWORD64 are defined so that you explicitly control variable size. Two other types, POINTER_32 and POINTER_64, control pointer size.

With a little care, you will find that it is fairly simple to ensure that your programs will run under either Win32 or Win64, and, in general, we will continue to use Windows, or sometimes Win32, to refer to the API. Chapter 16 provides more information on Win64, including information on source and binary compatibility issues.

UNIX and Linux programmers will find some interesting differences in Windows. For example, Windows HANDLEs are "opaque." They are not integers allocated in sequential order. Thus, the fact that 0, 1, and 2 are special file descriptor values, which is important to some UNIX programs, has no analogy in Windows.

Many of the distinctions between, say, process IDs and file descriptors go away. Windows simply uses a HANDLE for both. Many important functions treat file, process, event, pipe, and other handles identically.

UNIX programmers familiar with short, lowercase function and parameter names will need to adjust to the more verbose Windows style. The Windows style is closer to that of HP (formerly DEC and Compaq); OpenVMS and OpenVMS programmers will find many familiar features. One reason for the similarity to OpenVMS is that the original VMS architect, David Cutler, assumed a similar role with NT and Windows.

Critical distinctions are made with such familiar concepts as processes. Windows processes do not, for example, have parent-child relationships, although Windows processes can be organized into job objects.

Finally, Windows text files represent the end-of-line sequence with **CR—LF** rather than with **LF** as in UNIX.

The Standard C Library: When to Use It for File Processing

Despite Windows' unique features, it is still possible to achieve most file processing (the subject of Chapters 2 and 3) by using the familiar C programming language and its ANSI Standard C library. The C library (the adjectives ANSI and Standard are often omitted) also contains numerous indispensable functions that do not correspond to Windows system calls, such as <string.h>, <stdlib.h>, <signal.h>, formatted I/O functions, and character I/O functions. Other functions, however, correspond closely to system calls, such as the fopen and fread functions in <stdio.h>.

When is the C library adequate, and when is it necessary to use native Windows file management system calls? This same question could be asked about using C++ I/O streams or the system I/O provided within .NET. There is no easy answer, but portability to non-Windows platforms is a consideration in favor of the C library or C++ I/O streams if an application needs only file processing and not, for example, process management or other Windows capabilities. However, many programmers have formulated guidelines as to when the C library is or is not adequate, and these same guidelines should apply to Windows. In addition, given the increased power, performance potential, and flexibility provided by Windows, it is often convenient or even necessary to go beyond the C library, as we will see starting as early as Chapter 3. Windows file processing features not available with the C library include file locking, memory mapping (required for memory sharing), asynchronous I/O, random access to very long files (more than 4GB in length), and interprocess communication.

The C library file management functions are often adequate for simple programs. With the C library, it is possible to write portable applications without learning Windows, but options will be limited. For example, Chapter 5 exploits memory-mapped files for performance and programming convenience, and this functionality is not included in the C library.

What You Need to Use This Book

Here is what you will need to build and run the examples in this chapter and the rest of the book.

First, of course, it is helpful to bring your knowledge of applications development; knowledge of C programming is assumed. Before you tackle the exercises and examples, however, you will need some basic hardware and software.

- A system running Windows.

- A C compiler and development system, such as Microsoft Visual Studio .NET or Microsoft Visual C++ Version 6.0. Other vendors also supply development systems, and although none have been tested with the examples, several readers have mentioned using other development systems successfully with only minor adjustments. Appendix A also mentions using open source tools. *Note*: We will concentrate on developing Windows console applications and will not truly exploit the full powers of Microsoft Visual Studio .NET.

- Enough RAM and disk space for program development. Nearly any commercially available system will have more than enough memory, disk space, and processing power to run all the example programs as well as the development system, but check the requirements for the development system.[7]

- A CD-ROM drive, on either the system or the network, to install the development system.

- The on-line documentation, such as that provided with Microsoft Visual C++. It is recommended that you install this documentation on your disk because you will access it frequently. You can also access the information on the Microsoft Web site.

Example: A Simple Sequential File Copy

The following sections show short example programs implementing a simple sequential file copy program in three different ways:

---

[7] The rapid pace of improvements in cost and performance is illustrated by recalling that in 1997 the first edition of this book specified, without embarrassment or apology, 16MB of RAM and 256MB of disk space. This third edition of the book is being written on a laptop costing less than $1,000, with more than 10 times the RAM (the RAM space exceeds the previously required disk space), 100 times the disk space, and a processor running 50 times as fast as the one used when starting the first edition on a $2,500 PC.

1. Using the Standard C library

2. Using Windows

3. Using a single Windows convenience function, `CopyFile`

In addition to showing contrasting programming models, these examples show the capabilities and limitations of the C library and Windows. Alternative implementations will enhance the program to improve performance and increase flexibility.

Sequential file processing is the simplest, most common, and most essential capability of any file system, and nearly any large program processes at least some files sequentially. Therefore, a simple file processing program is a good way to introduce Windows and its conventions.

File copying, often with updating, and the merging of sorted files are common forms of sequential processing. Compilers and text processing tools are examples of other applications that access files sequentially.

Although sequential file processing is conceptually simple, efficient processing that attains optimal speed can be much more difficult to achieve. It can require overlapped I/O, memory mapping, threads, or other techniques.

Simple file copying is not very interesting by itself, but comparing programs gives us a quick way to contrast different systems and to introduce Windows. The following examples implement a limited version of the UNIX `cp` command, copying one file to another, where the file names are specified on the command line. Error checking is minimal, and existing files are simply overwritten. Subsequent Windows implementations of this and other programs will address these and other shortcomings. *Note*: A UNIX implementation is included on the book's Web site.

File Copying with the Standard C Library

As illustrated in Program 1–1, the Standard C library supports stream `FILE` I/O objects that are similar to, although not as general as, the Windows `HANDLE` objects shown in Program 1–2.

Program 1–1   `cpC`: File Copying with the C Library

```
/* Chapter 1. Basic cp file copy program.
   C library Implementation. */
/* cp file1 file2: Copy file1 to file2. */

#include <stdio.h>
#include <errno.h>
#define BUF_SIZE 256
```

```c
int main (int argc, char *argv [])
{
    FILE *in_file, *out_file;
    char rec [BUF_SIZE];
    size_t bytes_in, bytes_out;
    if (argc != 3) {
        printf ("Usage: cpC file1 file2\n");
        return 1;
    }
    in_file = fopen (argv [1], "rb");
    if (in_file == NULL) {
        perror (argv [1]);
        return 2;
    }
    out_file = fopen (argv [2], "wb");
    if (out_file == NULL) {
        perror (argv [2]);
        return 3;
    }

    /* Process the input file a record at a time. */
    while ((bytes_in = fread (rec, 1, BUF_SIZE, in_file)) > 0) {
        bytes_out = fwrite (rec, 1, bytes_in, out_file);
        if (bytes_out != bytes_in) {
            perror ("Fatal write error.");
            return 4;
        }
    }
    fclose (in_file);
    fclose (out_file);
    return 0;
}
```

This simple example clearly illustrates some common programming assumptions and conventions that do not always apply with Windows.

1. Open file objects are identified by pointers to FILE structures (UNIX uses integer file descriptors). NULL indicates an invalid value. The pointers are, in effect, a form of handle to the open file object.

2. The call to fopen specifies whether the file is to be treated as a text file or a binary file. Text files contain system-specific character sequences to indicate situations such as an end of line. On many systems, including Windows, I/O operations on a text file convert between the end-of-line character sequence and the null character that C interprets as the end of a string. In the example, both files are opened in binary mode.

3. Errors are diagnosed with `perror`, which, in turn, accesses the global variable `errno` to obtain information about the function call failure. Alternatively, the `ferror` function could be used to return an error code that is associated with the `FILE` rather than the system.

4. The `fread` and `fwrite` functions directly return the number of bytes processed, rather than return the value in an argument, and this arrangement is essential to the program logic. A successful read is indicated by a non-negative value, and 0 indicates an end of file.

5. The `fclose` function applies only to `FILE` objects (a similar statement applies to UNIX file descriptors).

6. The I/O is synchronous so that the program must wait for the I/O operation to complete before proceeding.

7. The C library `printf` I/O function is useful for error messages and occurs even in the initial Windows example.

The C library implementation has the advantage of portability to UNIX, Windows, and other systems that support ANSI C. Furthermore, as shown in Appendix C, C library performance for sequential I/O is competitive with alternative implementations. Nonetheless, programs are still constrained to synchronous I/O operations, although this constraint will be lifted somewhat when using Windows threads (starting in Chapter 7).

C library file processing programs, like their UNIX equivalents, are able to perform random access file operations (using `fseek` or, in the case of text files, `fsetpos` and `fgetpos`), but that is the limit of sophistication of Standard C library file I/O. *Note*: Visual C++ does provide nonstandard extensions that support, for example, file locking. Finally, the C library cannot control file security.

In summary, if simple synchronous file or console I/O is all that is needed, then use the C library to write portable programs that will run under Windows.

File Copying with Windows

Program 1–2 shows the same program using the Windows API, and the same basic techniques, style, and conventions will be used throughout this book.

Program 1–2   `cpW`: File Copying with Windows, First Implementation

```
/* Chapter 1. Basic cp file copy program. Windows Implementation. */
/* cpW file1 file2: Copy file1 to file2. */

#include <windows.h>
#include <stdio.h>
```

```
#define BUF_SIZE 256
int main (int argc, LPTSTR argv [])
{
    HANDLE hIn, hOut;
    DWORD nIn, nOut;
    CHAR Buffer [BUF_SIZE];

    if (argc != 3) {
        printf ("Usage: cpW file1 file2\n");
        return 1;
    }
    hIn = CreateFile (argv [1], GENERIC_READ, 0, NULL,
            OPEN_EXISTING, 0, NULL);
    if (hIn == INVALID_HANDLE_VALUE) {
        printf ("Cannot open input file. Error: %x\n",
                GetLastError ());
        return 2;
    }
    hOut = CreateFile (argv [2], GENERIC_WRITE, 0, NULL,
            CREATE_ALWAYS, FILE_ATTRIBUTE_NORMAL, NULL);
    if (hOut == INVALID_HANDLE_VALUE) {
        printf ("Cannot open output file. Error: %x\n",
                GetLastError ());
        return 3;
    }
    while (ReadFile (hIn, Buffer, BUF_SIZE, &nIn, NULL) && nIn > 0) {
        WriteFile (hOut, Buffer, nIn, &nOut, NULL);
        if (nIn != nOut) {
            printf ("Fatal write error: %x\n", GetLastError ());
            return 4;
        }
    }
    CloseHandle (hIn);
    CloseHandle (hOut);
    return 0;
}
```

This simple example illustrates some Windows programming features that Chapter 2 will start to explain in detail.

1. <windows.h> is always included and contains all Windows function definitions and data types.[8]

---

[8] Appendix A shows how to exclude unwanted definitions to expedite compilations and save disk space.

2. All Windows objects are identified by variables of type `HANDLE`, and a single generic `CloseHandle` function applies to most objects.

3. It is recommended that all open handles be closed when they are no longer required so as to free resources. However, the handles will be closed automatically by the OS when a process exits, and the OS will destroy an object and free its resources, as appropriate, if there are no remaining handles referring to the object. (*Note*: Files are generally not destroyed in this way.)

4. Windows defines numerous symbolic constants and flags. Their names are usually quite long and often describe their purposes. `INVALID_HANDLE_VALUE` and `GENERIC_READ` are typical.

5. Functions such as `ReadFile` and `WriteFile` return Boolean values rather than byte counts, which are arguments. This alters the loop logic slightly.[9] The end of file is detected by a zero byte count and is not a failure.

6. System error codes, as `DWORD`s, can be obtained at any point through `GetLastError`. Program 2–2 shows how to obtain Windows-generated textual error messages.

7. Windows NT has a more powerful security system, described in Chapter 15. The output file in this example is not secured.

8. Functions such as `CreateFile` have a rich set of options, and the example uses default values.

File Copying with a Windows Convenience Function

Windows has a number of convenience functions that combine several functions to perform a common task. These convenience functions can also improve performance in some cases (see Appendix C). `CopyFile`, for example, greatly simplifies the file copy program (Program 1–3). Among other things, there is no need to be concerned with the appropriate buffer size, which was arbitrarily set to 256 in the two preceding programs.

Program 1–3   `cpCF`: File Copying with a Windows Convenience Function

```
/* Chapter 1. Basic cp file copy program. Windows implementation
   using CopyFile for convenience and improved performance. */
/* cpCF file1 file2: Copy file1 to file2. */
```

---

[9] Notice that the loop logic depends on ANSI C's left-to-right evaluation of logical "and" (`&&`) and logical "or" (`||`) operations.

```
#include <windows.h>
#include <stdio.h>

int main (int argc, LPTSTR argv [])
{
    if (argc != 3) {
        printf ("Usage: cpCF file1 file2\n");
        return 1;
    }
    if (!CopyFile (argv [1], argv [2], FALSE)) {
        printf ("CopyFile Error: %x\n", GetLastError ());
        return 2;
    }
    return 0;
}
```

Summary

The introductory examples, three simple file copy programs, illustrate many of the differences between C library and Windows programs. Appendix C shows some of the performance differences among the various implementations. The Windows examples clearly illustrate Windows programming style and conventions but only hint at the functionality available to Windows programmers.

Windows NT5 (XP, 2000, and 2003) systems are the target platforms for this book and its examples. Nonetheless, much of the book applies to earlier NT versions and Windows 9x (95, 98, and Me).

Looking Ahead

Chapters 2 and 3 take a much more extensive look at I/O and the file system. Topics include console I/O, ASCII and Unicode character processing, file and directory management, file attributes, and advanced options, as well as registry programming. These two chapters develop the basic techniques and lay the groundwork for the rest of the book.

Additional Reading

Publication information about the following books is listed in the bibliography.

Win32

Win32 System Services, by Marshall Brain and Ron Reeves, and *Programming Applications for Microsoft Windows* (formerly *Advanced Windows* in earlier editions), by Jeffrey Richter, are two of the available books covering Win32 programming subjects from varying perspectives. Many of the available books have not been updated to cover advances since Windows 95 or Windows NT, however.

The hypertext on-line help available with Microsoft Visual C++ documents every function, and the same information is available from the Microsoft home page, http://www.microsoft.com, which also contains a number of technical papers covering different Windows subjects. Start with the MSDN (Microsoft Developer's Network) section and search for any topic of interest. You'll find a variety of white papers, product descriptions, sample code, and other useful information.

Win64

Few books discuss Win64, but you can find a wealth of material on the Microsoft home page. See Chapter 16 for more information.

Windows NT Architecture and Windows NT History

Inside Windows 2000, by David Solomon and Mark Russinovich, is for the reader who wants to know more about Windows design objectives or who wants to understand the underlying architecture. The book discusses objects, processes, threads, virtual memory, the kernel, and I/O subsystems. It does not, however, discuss the actual API functions or Windows 9x and CE. You may want to refer to Solomon and Russinovich as you read this book. Also note the earlier books by Helen Custer and Solomon that preceded this book and provide important historical insight into NT evolution.

UNIX

Advanced Programming in the UNIX Environment, by the late W. Richard Stevens, discusses UNIX in much the same terms in which this book discusses Windows. Stevens remains the standard reference on UNIX features, but the book does not discuss threads. UNIX standardization has progressed, but the Stevens book offers a convenient working definition of what UNIX, as well as Linux, provides. This book also contrasts C library file I/O with UNIX I/O, and this discussion is relevant to Windows.

If you are interested in OS comparisons and an in-depth UNIX discussion, *The Art of UNIX Programming*, by Eric S. Raymond, is essential and fascinating reading, although many Windows users may find the discussion slightly biased.

Windows GUI Programming

Windows user interfaces are not covered here. See Brent Rector and Joseph M. Newcomer, *Win32 Programming*, and Charles Petzold, *Programming Windows, Fifth Edition*.

Operating Systems Theory

There are many good texts on general OS theory. *Operating System Concepts*, by Abraham Silberschatz et al., is one of the more popular.

The ANSI Standard C Library

The Standard C Library, by P. J. Plauger, is a comprehensive guide. For a quick overview, *The C Programming Language*, by Brian W. Kernighan and Dennis M. Ritchie, lists and explains the complete library, and this book remains the classic book on C. These books can be used to help decide whether the C library is adequate for your file processing requirements.

Windows CE

SAMS Teach Yourself Windows CE Programming in 24 Hours, by Jason P. Nottingham, Steven Makofsky, and Andrew Tucker, is recommended for those who wish to apply the material in this book to Windows CE.

Windows Emulation on UNIX

See http://www.winehq.com for information and downloads for Wine, an open source Windows API emulation on top of UNIX and X.

Exercises

1–1. Compile, build, and execute the three file copy programs. Other possibilities include using UNIX compatibility libraries, including the Microsoft Visual C++ library (a program using this library is included on the book's Web site). *Note*: All source code is included on the Web site. Appendix A gives some brief notes on getting started with the Web site code using Microsoft Visual Studio .NET or Visual C++ 6.0.

1–2. Become familiar with a development environment, such as Microsoft Visual Studio .NET or Visual C++. In particular, learn how to build console applications. Also experiment with the debugger on the programs in this chapter. Appendix A will get you started, and you will find extensive information on the Microsoft Web site and with the development environment's documentation.

1–3. Windows uses the carriage return–line feed (CR–LF) sequence to denote an end of line. Determine the effect on Program 1–1 if the input file is opened in binary mode and the output file in text mode, and conversely. What is the effect under UNIX or some other system?

1–4. Time the file copy programs on any large file. Obtain data for as many of the combinations as possible and compare the results. Needless to say, performance depends on many factors, but, by keeping other system parameters the same, it is possible to get helpful comparisons between the implementations. *Suggestion*: Tabulate the results in a spreadsheet to facilitate analysis. Chapter 6 contains a program for timing programs, and Appendix C gives some experimental results.

2 | Using the Windows File System and Character I/O

The file system and simple terminal I/O are often the first OS features that the developer encounters on any system. Early PC OSs such as MS-DOS did little more than manage files and terminal (or *console*) I/O, and these resources are also central features of nearly every OS.

Files are essential for the long-term storage of data and programs and are the simplest form of program-to-program communication. Furthermore, many aspects of the file system model apply to interprocess and network communication.

The file copy programs in Chapter 1 introduced the four essential sequential file processing functions:

    CreateFile   WriteFile

    ReadFile   CloseHandle

This chapter explains these and other related functions and also describes character processing and console I/O functions in detail. First, it is necessary to say a few words about the various file systems available and their principal characteristics. In the process, we'll show how to use Unicode wide characters for internationalization. The chapter concludes with an introduction to Windows file and directory management.

The Windows File Systems

Windows supports four file systems on directly attached devices, but only the first is important throughout the book as it is Microsoft's primary, full-functionality file system.

1. The *NT* file system (NTFS) is a modern file system supporting long file names, security, fault tolerance, encryption, compression, extended attributes, and support for very large files and volumes. Note that diskettes do not support NTFS and that Windows 9x also does not support NTFS.

2. The *File Allocation Table* (FAT and FAT32) file systems descend from the original MS-DOS and Windows 3.1 FAT (or FAT16) file systems. FAT32 was introduced with Windows 98 to support larger disk drives and other enhancements, and the term FAT will refer to both versions. FAT does not support Windows security, among other limitations. The FAT file system is the only one available on diskettes and Windows 9x disks (other than CD-ROMs). TFAT is a transaction-oriented version used with Windows CE. FAT is increasingly obsolete and is most frequently seen on older systems, particularly ones that have been upgraded from Windows 9x without selecting the option to convert existing file system drives.

3. The *CD-ROM* file system (CDFS), as the name implies, is for accessing information provided on CD-ROMs. CDFS is compliant with the ISO 9660 standard.

4. The *Universal Disk Format* (UDF) supports DVD drives and will ultimately supplant CDFS. Read-write support is available with XP, but Windows 2000 just provides read-only support for UDF.

Windows provides both client and server support for distributed file systems, such as the Networked File System (NFS) and Common Internet File System (CIFS); servers normally use NTFS. Windows 2000 and 2003 provide extensive support for storage area networks (SANs) and emerging storage technologies, such as IP storage. Windows also allows the development of custom file systems, which also support the same file access API covered in this chapter and in Chapter 3.

All the file systems are accessed in the same way, sometimes with limitations. For example, only NTFS supports security. This book will point out features unique to NTFS as appropriate, but, in general, assume NTFS.

The format of a file system (FAT, NTFS, or custom), as a disk volume or partition, is determined when a disk is partitioned.

File Naming

Windows supports hierarchical file naming, but there are a few subtle distinctions for the UNIX user and basic rules for everyone.

- The full pathname of a disk file starts with a drive name, such as A: or C:. The A: and B: drives are normally diskette drives, and C:, D:, and so on are hard discs and CD-ROMs. Network drives are usually designated by letters that fall later in the alphabet, such as H: and K:. *Note*: CE does not support drive letters.

- Alternatively, a full pathname, or Universal Naming Code (UNC), can start with a double backslash (\\), indicating the global root, followed by a server name and a *share name* to indicate a path on a network file server. The first part of the pathname, then, is \\servername\sharename.

- The pathname *separator* is the backslash (\), although the forward slash (/) can be used in API parameters, which is more convenient in C.

- Directory and file names cannot contain any of the ASCII characters with values in the range 1–31 or any of these characters:

    <   >   :   " | ?   *   \   /

    Names can contain blanks. However, when using file names with blanks on a command line, be sure to put each file name in quotes so that the name is not interpreted as naming two distinct files.

- Directory and file names are *case-insensitive*, but they are also *case-retaining*, so that if the creation name is MyFile, the file name will show up as it was created, but the file can also be accessed with the name myFILE.

- File and directory names can be as many as 255 characters long, and path-names are limited to MAX_PATH characters (currently 260).

- A period (.) separates a file's name from its extension, and extensions (usually two or three characters after the rightmost period in the file name) conventionally indicate the file's type. Thus, atou.EXE would be an executable file, and atou.C would be a C language source file. File names can contain multiple periods.

    A single period (.) and two periods (..), as directory names, indicate the current directory and its parent, respectively.

With this introduction, it is now time to learn more about the Windows functions introduced in Chapter 1.

Opening, Reading, Writing, and Closing Files

The first Windows function described in detail is CreateFile. It is used for opening existing files and creating new ones. This and other functions are described first by showing the function prototype and then by describing the parameters and operation.

Creating and Opening Files

This is the first Windows function, so it is described in some detail; later descriptions will frequently be much more streamlined. Nonetheless, CreateFile has numerous options not described here; this additional detail can always be found in the on-line help.

The simplest use of CreateFile is illustrated in Chapter 1's introductory Windows program (Program 1–2), in which there are two calls that rely on default values for dwShareMode, lpSecurityAttributes, and hTemplateFile. dwAccess is either GENERIC_READ or GENERIC_WRITE.

```
HANDLE CreateFile (
    LPCTSTR lpName,
    DWORD dwAccess,
    DWORD dwShareMode,
    LPSECURITY_ATTRIBUTES lpSecurityAttributes,
    DWORD dwCreate,
    DWORD dwAttrsAndFlags,
    HANDLE hTemplateFile)

Return: A HANDLE to an open file object, or
    INVALID_HANDLE_VALUE in case of failure.
```

Parameters

The parameter names illustrate some Windows conventions. The prefix dw is used when a DWORD (32 bits, unsigned) contains flags or numerical values, such as counts, and lpsz (long pointer to a zero-terminated string), or, more simply, lp, is for pathnames and other strings, although the Microsoft documentation is not entirely consistent. At times, you need to use common sense or read the documentation carefully to determine the correct data types.

lpName is a pointer to the null-terminated string that names the file, pipe, or other named object to open or create. The pathname is normally limited to

MAX_PATH (260) characters, but Windows NT can circumvent this restriction if the pathname is prefixed with \\?\ to allow for very long pathnames (as long as 32K). The prefix is not part of the name. The LPCTSTR data type will be explained in an upcoming section; just regard it as a string data type for now.

dwAccess specifies the read and write access, using GENERIC_READ and GENERIC_WRITE. Flag values such as READ and WRITE do not exist. The GENERIC_ prefix may seem redundant, but it is required to conform with the macro names in the Window header file, WINNT.H. Numerous other constant names may seem longer than necessary.

These values can be combined with a bit-wise "or" operator (|), so to open a file for read and write access, use the following:

```
GENERIC_READ | GENERIC_WRITE
```

dwShareMode is a bit-wise "or" combination of the following:

- 0—The file cannot be shared. Furthermore, not even this process can open a second handle on this file. (Uppercase HANDLE is used only when it is important to emphasize the data type.)

- FILE_SHARE_READ—Other processes, including the one making this call, can open this file for concurrent read access.

- FILE_SHARE_WRITE—This allows concurrent writing to the file.

By using locks or other mechanisms, the programmer must take care to prevent concurrent updates to the same file location. Chapter 3 covers this in more detail.

lpSecurityAttributes points to a SECURITY_ATTRIBUTES structure. Use NULL values with CreateFile and all other functions for now; security is treated in Chapter 15.

dwCreate specifies whether to create a new file, whether to overwrite an existing file, and so on. The individual values can be combined with the C bit-wise "or" operator.

- CREATE_NEW—Fail if the specified file already exists; otherwise, create a new file.

- CREATE_ALWAYS—An existing file will be overwritten.

- OPEN_EXISTING—Fail if the file does not exist.

- OPEN_ALWAYS—Open the file, creating it if it does not exist.

- TRUNCATE_EXISTING—The file length will be set to zero. dwCreate must specify at least GENERIC_WRITE access. If the specified file exists, all contents are destroyed. If the file does not exist, the function still succeeds, unlike CREATE_NEW.

dwAttrsAndFlags specifies file attributes and flags. There are 16 flags and attributes. Attributes are characteristics of the file, as opposed to the open HANDLE, and are ignored when an existing file is opened. Here are some of the more important flag values.

- FILE_ATTRIBUTE_NORMAL—This attribute can be used only when no other attributes are set (flags can be set, however).

- FILE_ATTRIBUTE_READONLY—Applications can neither write to nor delete the file.

- FILE_FLAG_DELETE_ON_CLOSE—This is useful for temporary files. The file is deleted when the last open HANDLE is closed.

- FILE_FLAG_OVERLAPPED—This attribute flag is important for asynchronous I/O, which is described in Chapter 14.

Several additional flags also specify how a file is processed and help the Windows implementation optimize performance and file integrity.

- FILE_FLAG_WRITE_THROUGH—Intermediate caches are written through directly to the file on disk.

- FILE_FLAG_NO_BUFFERING—There is no intermediate buffering or caching, and data transfers occur directly to and from the program's data buffers specified in the ReadFile and WriteFile calls (described in upcoming subsections). Accordingly, the buffers are required to be on sector boundaries, and complete sectors must be transferred. Use the GetDiskFreeSpace function to determine the sector size when using this flag.

- FILE_FLAG_RANDOM_ACCESS—The file is intended for random access, and Windows will attempt to optimize file caching.

- FILE_FLAG_SEQUENTIAL_SCAN—The file is for sequential access, and Windows will optimize caching accordingly. These last two access modes are not enforced.

hTemplateFile is the handle of an open GENERIC_READ file that specifies extended attributes to apply to a newly created file, ignoring dwAttrsAndFlags. Normally, this parameter is NULL. hTemplateFile is ignored when an existing file is opened. This parameter can be used to set the attributes of a new file to be the same as those of an existing file.

The two `CreateFile` instances in Program 1–2 use default values extensively and are as simple as possible but still appropriate for the task. It could be beneficial to use `FILE_FLAG_SEQUENTIAL_SCAN` in both cases. (Exercise 2–3 explores this option, and Appendix C shows the performance results.)

Notice that if the file share attributes and security permit it, there can be numerous open handles on a given file. The open handles can be owned by the same process or by different processes. (Chapter 6 describes process management.)

Windows 2003 Server provides the `ReOpenFile` function that returns a new handle with different flags, access rights, and so on than the original handle, although the new rights cannot conflict with those of the existing handle.

Closing Files

One all-purpose function closes and invalidates handles and releases system resources for nearly all objects. Exceptions will be noted. Closing a handle also decrements the object's handle reference count so that nonpersistent objects such as temporary files and events can be deleted. The system will close all open handles on exit, but it is still good practice for programs to close their handles before terminating.

Closing an invalid handle or closing the same handle twice will cause an exception (Chapter 4 discusses exceptions and exception handling). It is not necessary or appropriate to close standard device handles, which are discussed later in this chapter in the section entitled Standard Devices and Console I/O.

```
BOOL CloseHandle (HANDLE hObject)
```

Return: `TRUE` if the function succeeds; `FALSE` otherwise.

The comparable UNIX functions are different in a number of ways. The UNIX open function returns an integer file descriptor rather than a handle, and it specifies access, sharing, create options, and the attributes and flags in the single-integer `oflag` parameter. The options overlap, with Windows providing a richer set.

There is no UNIX equivalent to `dwShareMode`. UNIX files are always shareable.

Both systems use security information when creating a new file. In UNIX, the `mode` argument specifies the familiar user, group, and other file permissions.

`close` is comparable to `CloseHandle`, but it is not general purpose.

The C library <stdio.h> functions use FILE objects, which are comparable to handles (for disk files, terminals, tapes, and other devices) connected to streams. The fopen mode parameter specifies whether the file data is to be treated as binary or text. There is a set of options for read-only, update, append at the end, and so on. freopen allows FILE reuse without closing it first. Security permissions cannot be set with the Standard C library.

fclose closes a FILE. Most stdio FILE-related functions have the f prefix.

Reading Files

```
BOOL ReadFile (
    HANDLE hFile,
    LPVOID lpBuffer,
    DWORD nNumberOfBytesToRead,
    LPDWORD lpNumberOfBytesRead,
    LPOVERLAPPED lpOverlapped)
```

Return: TRUE if the read succeeds (even if no bytes were read due to an attempt to read past the end of file).

Assume, until Chapter 14, that the file handle does *not* have the FILE_FLAG_OVERLAPPED option set in dwAttrsAndFlags. ReadFile, then, starts at the current file position (for the handle) and advances the position by the number of bytes transferred.

The function fails, returning FALSE, if the handle or any other parameters are invalid. The function does not fail if the file handle is positioned at the end of file; instead, the number of bytes read (*lpNumberOfBytesRead) is set to 0.

Parameters

Because of the long variable names and the natural arrangement of the parameters, they are largely self-explanatory. Nonetheless, here are some brief explanations.

hFile is a file handle with GENERIC_READ access. lpBuffer points to the memory buffer to receive the input data. nNumberOfBytesToRead is the number of bytes to read from the file.

lpNumberOfBytesRead points to the actual number of bytes read by the ReadFile call. This value can be zero if the handle is positioned at the end of file or there is an error, and message-mode named pipes (Chapter 11) allow a zero-length message.

lpOverlapped points to an OVERLAPPED structure (Chapters 3 and 14). Use NULL for now.

Writing Files

```
BOOL WriteFile (
    HANDLE hFile,
    LPCVOID lpBuffer,
    DWORD nNumberOfBytesToWrite,
    LPDWORD lpNumberOfBytesWritten,
    LPOVERLAPPED lpOverlapped)

Return: TRUE if the function succeeds; FALSE otherwise.
```

The parameters are familiar by now. Notice that a successful write does not ensure that the data actually is written through to the disk unless FILE_FLAG_WRITE_THROUGH is specified with CreateFile. If the handle is positioned at the file end, Windows will extend the length of an existing file.

ReadFileGather and WriteFileGather allow you to read and write using a collection of buffers of different sizes.

UNIX read and write are the comparable functions, and the programmer supplies a file descriptor, buffer, and byte count. The functions return the number of bytes actually transferred. A value of 0 on read indicates the end of file; −1 indicates an error. Windows, by contrast, requires a separate transfer count and returns Boolean values to indicate success or failure.

The functions in both systems are general purpose and can read from files, terminals, tapes, pipes, and so on.

The Standard C library fread and fwrite binary I/O functions use object size and object count rather than a single byte count as in UNIX and Windows. A short transfer could be caused by either an end of file or an error; test explicitly with ferror or feof. The library provides a full set of text-oriented functions, such as fgetc and fputc, that do not exist outside the C library in either OS.

Interlude: Unicode and Generic Characters

Before proceeding, it is necessary to explain briefly how Windows processes characters and differentiates between 8- and 16-bit characters and generic characters. The topic is a large one and beyond the book's scope, so we only provide the minimum detail required, rather than a complete chapter.

Windows supports standard 8-bit characters (type char or CHAR) and (except on Windows 9x) wide 16-bit characters (WCHAR, which is defined to be the C wchar_t type). The Microsoft documentation refers to the 8-bit character set as ASCII, but it is actually the Latin-1 character set; for convenience, in this discussion we use ASCII too. The wide character support that Windows provides using the Unicode UTF-16 encoding is capable of representing symbols and letters in all major languages, including English, French, Spanish, German, Japanese, and Chinese, using the Unicode representation.

Here are the steps commonly used to write a generic Windows application that can be built to use either Unicode (UTF-16, as opposed to UCS-4, for example) or 8-bit ASCII characters.

1. Define all characters and strings using the generic types TCHAR, LPTSTR, and LPCTSTR.

2. Include the definitions #define UNICODE and #define _UNICODE in all source modules to get Unicode wide characters (ANSI C wchar_t); otherwise, with UNICODE and _UNICODE undefined, TCHAR will be equivalent to CHAR (ANSI C char). The definition must precede the #include <windows.h> statement and is frequently defined on the compiler command line. The first preprocessor variable controls the Windows function definitions, and the second variable controls the C library.

3. Character buffer lengths—as used, for example, in ReadFile—can be calculated using sizeof (TCHAR).

4. Use the collection of generic C library string and character I/O functions in <tchar.h>. Available representative functions are _fgettc, _itot (for itoa), _stprintf (for sprintf), _tstcpy (for strcpy), _ttoi, _totupper, _totlower, and _tprintf.[1] See the on-line help for a complete and extensive list. All these definitions depend on _UNICODE. This collection is not complete. memchr is an example of a function without a wide character implementation. New versions are provided as required.

---

[1] The underscore character (_) indicates that a function or keyword is provided by Microsoft C, and the letters t and T denote a generic character. Other development systems provide similar capability but may use different names or keywords.

5. Constant strings should be in one of three forms. Use these conventions for single characters as well. The first two forms are ANSI C; the third—the _T macro (equivalently, TEXT and _TEXT)—is supplied with the Microsoft C compiler.

```
"This string uses 8-bit characters"

L"This string uses 16-bit characters"

_T ("This string uses generic characters")
```

6. Include <tchar.h> after <windows.h> to get required definitions for text macros and generic C library functions.

Windows uses Unicode 16-bit characters (UTF-16 encoding) throughout, and NTFS file names and pathnames are represented internally in Unicode. If the UNICODE macro is defined, wide character strings are required by Windows calls; otherwise, 8-bit character strings are converted to wide characters. If the program is to run under Windows 9x, which is not a Unicode system, *do not* define the UNICODE and _UNICODE macros. Under NT and CE, the definition is optional unless the executable is to run under Windows 9x as well.

All future program examples will use TCHAR instead of the normal char for characters and character strings unless there is a clear reason to deal with individual 8-bit characters. Similarly, the type LPTSTR indicates a pointer to a generic string, and LPCTSTR indicates, in addition, a constant string. At times, this choice will add some clutter to the programs, but it is the only choice that allows the flexibility necessary to develop and test applications in either Unicode or 8-bit character form so that the program can be easily converted to Unicode at a later date. Furthermore, this choice is consistent with common, if not universal, industry practice.

It is worthwhile to examine the system include files to see how TCHAR and the system function interfaces are defined and how they depend on whether or not UNICODE and _UNICODE are defined. A typical entry is of the following form:

```
#ifdef UNICODE
#define TCHAR WCHAR
#else
#define TCHAR CHAR
#endif
```

Alternative Generic String Processing Functions

String comparisons can use lstrcmp and lstrcmpi rather than the generic _tcscmp and _tcscmpi to account for the specific language and region, or *locale*, at run time and also to perform *word* rather than *string* comparisons.[2] String comparisons simply compare the numerical values of the characters, whereas word comparisons consider locale-specific word order. The two methods can give opposite results for string pairs such as *coop/co-op* and *were/we're*.

There is also a group of Windows functions for dealing with Unicode characters and strings. These functions handle local characteristics transparently. Typical functions are `CharUpper`, which can operate on strings as well as individual characters, and `IsCharAlphaNumeric`. Other string functions include `CompareString` (which is locale-specific) and `MultiByteToWideChar`. Multibyte characters in Windows 3.1 and 9x extend the 8-bit character set to allow double bytes to represent character sets for languages of the Far East. The generic C library functions (`_tprintf` and the like) and the Windows functions (`CharUpper` and the like) will both appear in upcoming examples to demonstrate their use. Examples in later chapters will rely mostly on the generic C library.

The Generic Main Function

The C main function, with its argument list (`argv [ ]`), should be replaced by the macro `_tmain`. The macro expands to either `main` or `wmain` depending on the `_UNICODE` definition. `_tmain` is defined in `<tchar.h>`, which must be included after `<windows.h>`. A typical main program heading, then, would look like this:

```
#include <windows.h>
#include <tchar.h>
int _tmain (int argc, LPTSTR argv [])
{
    . . .
}
```

The Microsoft C `_tmain` function also supports a third parameter for environment strings. This nonstandard extension is also common in UNIX.

Function Definitions

A function such as `CreateFile` is defined through a preprocessor macro as `CreateFileA` when UNICODE is not defined and as `CreateFileW` when UNICODE is defined. The definitions also describe the string parameters as 8-bit or wide character strings. Consequently, compilers will report a source code error, such as

---

[2] Historically, the l prefix was used to indicate a long pointer to the character string parameters.

an illegal parameter to `CreateFile`, as an error in the use of `CreateFileA` or
`CreateFileW`.

Unicode Strategies

A programmer who is starting a Windows project, either to develop new code or to
port existing code, can select from four strategies, based on project requirements.

1. **8-bit only**. Ignore Unicode and continue to use the `char` (or `CHAR`) data type
   and the Standard C library for functions such as `printf`, `atoi`, and `strcmp`.

2. **8-bit but Unicode enabled**. Follow the earlier guidelines for a generic application, but do not define the two Unicode preprocessor variables. The example
   programs generally use this strategy.

3. **Unicode only**. Follow the generic guidelines, but define the two preprocessor
   variables. Alternatively, use wide characters and the wide character functions
   exclusively. The resulting programs will not run properly under Windows 9x.

4. **Unicode and 8-bit**. The program includes both Unicode and ASCII code and
   decides at run time which code to execute, based on a run-time switch or other
   factors.

As mentioned previously, writing generic code, while requiring extra effort
and creating awkward-looking code, allows the programmer to maintain
maximum flexibility.

The locale can be set at run time. Program 2–2 shows how the language for
error messages is specified.

The POSIX XPG4 internationalization standard, provided by many UNIX
vendors, is considerably different from Unicode. Among other things, characters
can be represented by 4 bytes, 2 bytes, or 1 byte, depending on the context, locale,
and so on.

Microsoft C implements the Standard C library functions, and there are generic
versions. Thus, there is a `_tsetlocale` function in `<wchar.h>`. Windows NT
uses Unicode characters, and Windows 9x uses the same multibyte characters (a
mix of 8- and 16-bit characters) used by Windows 3.1.

Standard Devices and Console I/O

Like UNIX, Windows has three standard devices for input, output, and error
reporting. UNIX uses well-known values for the file descriptors (0, 1, and 2), but

Windows requires handles and provides a function to obtain them for the standard devices.

```
HANDLE GetStdHandle (DWORD nStdHandle)
```

Return: A valid handle if the function succeeds;
   `INVALID_HANDLE_VALUE` otherwise.

Parameters

`nStdHandle` must have one of these values:

- `STD_INPUT_HANDLE`
- `STD_OUTPUT_HANDLE`
- `STD_ERROR_HANDLE`

The standard device assignments are normally the console and the keyboard. Standard I/O can be redirected.

`GetStdHandle` does not create a new or duplicate handle on a standard device. Successive calls with the same device argument return the same handle value. Closing a standard device handle makes the device unavailable for future use. For this reason, the examples often obtain a standard device handle but do not close it.

```
BOOL SetStdHandle (
    DWORD nStdHandle,
    HANDLE hHandle)
```

Return: `TRUE` or `FALSE` indicating success or failure.

Parameters

In `SetStdHandle`, `nStdHandle` has the same possible values as in `GetStdHandle`. `hHandle` specifies an open file that is to be the standard device.

One method for redirecting standard I/O within a process is to use `SetStdHandle` followed by `GetStdHandle`. The resulting handle is used in subsequent I/O operations.

There are two reserved pathnames for console input (the keyboard) and console output: "CONIN$" and "CONOUT$". Initially, standard input, output, and error are assigned to the console. It is possible to use the console regardless of any redirection to these standard devices; just open handles to "CONIN$" or "CONOUT$" using CreateFile.

UNIX standard I/O redirection can be done in one of three ways (see Stevens [1992, pp. 61–64]).

The first method is indirect and relies on the fact that the dup function returns the lowest numbered available file descriptor. Suppose you wish to reassign standard input (file descriptor 0) to an open file description, fd_redirect. It is possible to write this code:

```
close (STDIN_FILENO);

dup (fd_redirect);
```

The second method uses dup2, and the third uses F_DUPFD on the cryptic and overloaded fcntl function.

Console I/O can be performed with ReadFile and WriteFile, but it is simpler to use the specific console I/O functions, ReadConsole and WriteConsole. The principal advantages are that these functions process generic characters (TCHAR) rather than bytes, and they also process characters according to the console mode, which is set with the SetConsoleMode function.

```
BOOL SetConsoleMode (
    HANDLE hConsoleHandle,
    DWORD fdevMode)
```

Return: TRUE if and only if the function succeeds.

Parameters

hConsoleHandle identifies a console input or screen buffer, which must have GENERIC_WRITE access even if it is an input-only device.

fdevMode specifies how characters are processed. Each flag name indicates whether the flag applies to console input or output. Five commonly used flags are listed here; they are all enabled by default.

- ENABLE_LINE_INPUT—A read function (ReadConsole) returns when a carriage return character is encountered.

- ENABLE_ECHO_INPUT—Characters are echoed to the screen as they are read.

- ENABLE_PROCESSED_INPUT—This flag causes the system to process backspace, carriage return, and line feed characters.

- ENABLE_PROCESSED_OUTPUT—This flag causes the system to process backspace, tab, bell, carriage return, and line feed characters.

- ENABLE_WRAP_AT_EOL_OUTPUT—Line wrap is enabled for both normal and echoed output.

If SetConsoleMode fails, the mode is unchanged and the function returns FALSE. GetLastError will, as is always the case, return the error code number.

The ReadConsole and WriteConsole functions are similar to ReadFile and WriteFile.

```
BOOL ReadConsole (HANDLE hConsoleInput,
    LPVOID lpBuffer,
    DWORD cchToRead,
    LPDWORD lpcchRead,
    LPVOID lpReserved)
```

Return: TRUE if and only if the read succeeds.

The parameters are nearly the same as with ReadFile. The two length parameters are in terms of generic characters rather than bytes, and lpReserved must be NULL. Never use any of the reserved fields that occur in some functions. WriteConsole is now self-explanatory. The next example shows how to use ReadConsole and WriteConsole with generic strings and how to take advantage of the console mode.

A process can have only one console at a time. Applications such as the ones developed so far are normally initialized with a console. In many cases, such as a server or GUI application, however, you may need a console to display status or debugging information. There are two simple parameterless functions for this purpose.

```
BOOL FreeConsole (VOID)

BOOL AllocConsole (VOID)
```

FreeConsole detaches a process from its console. Calling AllocConsole then creates a new one associated with the process's standard input, output, and error handles. AllocConsole will fail if the process already has a console; to avoid this problem, precede the call with FreeConsole.

Note: Windows GUI applications do not have a default console and must allocate one before using functions such as WriteConsole or printf to display on a console. It's also possible that server processes may not have a console. Chapter 6 shows how a process can be created without a console.

There are numerous other console I/O functions for specifying cursor position, screen attributes (such as color), and so on. This book's approach is to use only those functions needed to get the examples to work and not to wander further than necessary into user interfaces. Additional functions will be easy for you to learn from the reference material after you see the examples.

For historical reasons, Windows is not terminal- and console-oriented in the way that UNIX is, and not all the UNIX terminal functionality is replicated by Windows. Stevens (1992) dedicates a chapter to UNIX terminal I/O (Chapter 11) and one to pseudo terminals (Chapter 19).

Serious Windows user interfaces are, of course, graphical, with mouse as well as keyboard input. The GUI is outside the scope of this book, but everything we discuss works within a GUI application.

Example: Printing and Prompting

The ConsolePrompt function, which appears in Program 2–1, is a useful utility that prompts the user with a specified message and then returns the user's response. There is an option to suppress the response echo. The function uses the console I/O functions and generic characters. PrintStrings and PrintMsg are the other entries in this module; they can use any handle but are normally used with standard output or error handles. The first function allows a variable-length argument list, whereas the second one allows just one string and is for convenience only. PrintStrings uses the va_start, va_arg, and va_end functions in the Standard C library to process the variable-length argument list.

Example programs will use these functions and the generic C library functions as convenient. *Note*: The code on the book's Web site is thoroughly commented and documented. Within the book, most of the comments are omitted for brevity and to concentrate on Windows usage.

This example also introduces an include file developed for the programs in the book. The file, Envirmnt.h (listed in Appendix A and provided on the Web site), contains the UNICODE and _UNICODE definitions (the definitions are commented out; remove the comment characters to build a Unicode application) and related preprocessor variables to specify the environment. The header files on the Web site also define additional modifiers to import or export the function names and to assure that the functions use the proper calling conventions.

Program 2–1   `PrintMsg`: Console Prompt and Print Utility Functions

```
/* PrintMsg.c: ConsolePrompt, PrintStrings, PrintMsg */

#include "Envirmnt.h" /* #define or #undef UNICODE here. */
#include <windows.h>
#include <stdarg.h>

BOOL PrintStrings (HANDLE hOut, ...)

/* Write the messages to the output handle. */
{
    DWORD MsgLen, Count;
    LPCTSTR pMsg;
    va_list pMsgList; /* Current message string. */
    va_start (pMsgList, hOut); /* Start processing messages. */
    while ((pMsg = va_arg (pMsgList, LPCTSTR)) != NULL) {
        MsgLen = _tcslen (pMsg);
            /* WriteConsole succeeds only for console handles. */
        if (!WriteConsole (hOut, pMsg, MsgLen, &Count, NULL)
                /* Call WriteFile only if WriteConsole fails. */
            && !WriteFile (hOut, pMsg, MsgLen * sizeof (TCHAR),
                &Count, NULL))
            return FALSE;
    }
    va_end (pMsgList);
    return TRUE;
}

BOOL PrintMsg (HANDLE hOut, LPCTSTR pMsg)

/* Single message version of PrintStrings. */
{
    return PrintStrings (hOut, pMsg, NULL);
}

BOOL ConsolePrompt (LPCTSTR pPromptMsg, LPTSTR pResponse,
        DWORD MaxTchar, BOOL Echo)

/* Prompt the user at the console and get a response. */
{
    HANDLE hStdIn, hStdOut;
    DWORD TcharIn, EchoFlag;
    BOOL Success;
```

```
hStdIn = CreateFile (_T ("CONIN$"),
        GENERIC_READ | GENERIC_WRITE, 0,
        NULL, OPEN_ALWAYS, FILE_ATTRIBUTE_NORMAL, NULL);
hStdOut = CreateFile (_T ("CONOUT$"), GENERIC_WRITE, 0,
        NULL, OPEN_ALWAYS, FILE_ATTRIBUTE_NORMAL, NULL);
EchoFlag = Echo ? ENABLE_ECHO_INPUT : 0;
Success =
        SetConsoleMode (hStdIn, ENABLE_LINE_INPUT |
            EchoFlag | ENABLE_PROCESSED_INPUT)
        && SetConsoleMode (hStdOut,
            ENABLE_WRAP_AT_EOL_OUTPUT | ENABLE_PROCESSED_OUTPUT)
        && PrintStrings (hStdOut, pPromptMsg, NULL)
        && ReadConsole (hStdIn, pResponse,
            MaxTchar, &TcharIn, NULL);
if (Success) pResponse [TcharIn - 2] = '\0';
CloseHandle (hStdIn);
CloseHandle (hStdOut);
return Success;
}
```

Notice that `ConsolePrompt` returns a Boolean success indicator, exploiting ANSI C's guaranteed left-to-right "short circuit" evaluation of logical "and" operators (`&&`) where evaluation stops on encountering the first `FALSE`. This coding style may appear compact, but it has the advantage of presenting the system calls in a clear, sequential order without the clutter of numerous conditional statements. Furthermore, `GetLastError` will return the error from the function that failed. Windows' Boolean return values (for many functions) encourage the technique.

The function does not report an error; the calling program can do this if necessary.

The code exploits the documented fact that `WriteConsole` fails if the handle is redirected to something other than a console handle. Therefore, it is not necessary to interrogate the handle properties. The function will take advantage of the console mode when the handle is attached to a console.

Also, `ReadConsole` returns a carriage return and line feed, so the last step is to insert a null character in the proper location over the carriage return.

Example: Error Processing

Program 1–2 showed some rudimentary error processing, obtaining the `DWORD` error number with the `GetLastError` function. A function call, rather than a global error number, such as the UNIX `errno`, ensures that system errors can be unique to the threads (Chapter 7) that share data storage.

The function `FormatMessage` turns the message number into a meaningful message, in English or one of many other languages, returning the message length.

Program 2–2 shows a useful general-purpose error-processing function, `ReportError`, which is similar to the C library `perror` and to `err_sys`, `err_ret`, and other functions in Stevens (1992, pp. 682ff). `ReportError` prints a message specified in the first argument and will terminate with an exit code or return, depending on the value of the second argument. The third argument determines whether the system error message should be displayed.

Notice the arguments to `FormatMessage`. The value returned by `GetLastError` is used as one parameter, and a flag indicates that the message is to be generated by the system. The generated message is stored in a buffer allocated by the function, and the address is returned in a parameter. There are several other parameters with default values. The language for the message can be set at either compile time or run time. `FormatMessage` will not be used again in this book, so there is no further explanation in the text.

`ReportError` can simplify error processing and will be used in nearly all subsequent examples. Chapter 4 modifies this function to generate exceptions.

Program 2–2 introduces the include file `EvryThng.h`. As the name implies, this file includes `<windows.h>`, `Envirmnt.h`, and the other include files explicitly shown in Program 2–1. It also defines commonly used functions, such as `PrintMsg`, `PrintStrings`, and `ReportError` itself. All subsequent examples will use this single include file, which is listed in Appendix A.

Notice the call to the function `HeapFree` near the end of the program. This function will be explained in Chapter 5.

Program 2–2   `ReportError` for Reporting System Call Errors

```
#include "EvryThng.h"
VOID ReportError (LPCTSTR UserMessage, DWORD ExitCode,
      BOOL PrintErrorMsg)

/* General-purpose function for reporting system errors. */
{
    DWORD eMsgLen, LastErr = GetLastError ();
    LPTSTR lpvSysMsg;
    HANDLE hStdErr = GetStdHandle (STD_ERROR_HANDLE);
    PrintMsg (hStdErr, UserMessage);
    if (PrintErrorMsg) {
        eMsgLen = FormatMessage
                (FORMAT_MESSAGE_ALLOCATE_BUFFER |
                FORMAT_MESSAGE_FROM_SYSTEM, NULL, LastErr,
                MAKELANGID (LANG_NEUTRAL, SUBLANG_DEFAULT),
                (LPTSTR) &lpvSysMsg, 0, NULL);
```

```
        PrintStrings (hStdErr, _T ("\n"), lpvSysMsg,
                _T ("\n"), NULL);
        /* Free the memory block containing the error message. */
        HeapFree (GetProcessHeap (), 0, lpvSysMsg); /* See Ch. 5. */
    }
    if (ExitCode > 0)
        ExitProcess (ExitCode);
    else
        return;
}
```

Example: Copying Multiple Files to Standard Output

Program 2–3 illustrates standard I/O and extensive error checking as well as user interaction. This program is a limited implementation of the UNIX `cat` command, which copies one or more specified files—or standard input if no files are specified—to standard output.

Program 2–3 includes complete error handling. The error checking is omitted or minimized in most other programs, but the Web site contains the complete programs with extensive error checking and documentation. Also, notice the `Options` function (listed in Appendix A), which is called at the start of the program. This function, included on the Web site and used throughout the book, evaluates command line option flags and returns the `argv` index of the first file name. Use `Options` in much the same way as `getopt` is used in many UNIX programs.

Program 2–3   `cat`: File Concatenation to Standard Output

```
/* Chapter 2. cat. */
/* cat [options] [files] Only the -s option, which suppresses error
   reporting if one of the files does not exist. */

#include "EvryThng.h"
#define BUF_SIZE 0x200

static VOID CatFile (HANDLE, HANDLE);
int _tmain (int argc, LPTSTR argv [])
{
    HANDLE hInFile, hStdIn = GetStdHandle (STD_INPUT_HANDLE);
    HANDLE hStdOut = GetStdHandle (STD_OUTPUT_HANDLE);
    BOOL DashS;
    int iArg, iFirstFile;

    /* DashS will be set only if "-s" is on the command line. */
    /* iFirstFile is the argv [] index of the first input file. */
```

```
    iFirstFile = Options (argc, argv, _T ("s"), &DashS, NULL);
    if (iFirstFile == argc) { /* No input files in arg list. */
                             /* Use standard input. */
        CatFile (hStdIn, hStdOut);
        return 0;
    }
/* Process each input file. */
    for (iArg = iFirstFile; iArg < argc; iArg++) {
        hInFile = CreateFile (argv [iArg], GENERIC_READ,
            0, NULL, OPEN_EXISTING, FILE_ATTRIBUTE_NORMAL, NULL);
        if (hInFile == INVALID_HANDLE_VALUE && !DashS)
            ReportError (_T ("Cat file open Error"), 1, TRUE);
        CatFile (hInFile, hStdOut);
        CloseHandle (hInFile);
    }
    return 0;
}

/* Function that does the work:
/* read input data and copy it to standard output. */
static VOID CatFile (HANDLE hInFile, HANDLE hOutFile)
{
    DWORD nIn, nOut;
    BYTE Buffer [BUF_SIZE];
    while (ReadFile (hInFile, Buffer, BUF_SIZE, &nIn, NULL)
            && (nIn != 0)
            && WriteFile (hOutFile, Buffer, nIn, &nOut, NULL));
    return;
}
```

Example: ASCII to Unicode Conversion

Program 2–4 builds on Program 1–3, which used the `CopyFile` convenience function. File copying is familiar by now, so this example also converts a file to Unicode, assuming it is ASCII; there is no test. The program also includes some error reporting and an option to suppress replacement of an existing file, and it replaces the final call to `CopyFile` with a new function that performs the ASCII to Unicode file conversion.

This program is concerned mostly with ensuring that the conversion can take place successfully. The operation is captured in a single function call at the end. This boilerplate, similar to that in the previous program, will be used again in the future but will not be repeated in the text.

Notice the call to `_taccess`, which tests the file's existence. This is a generic version of the `access` function, which is in the UNIX library but is not part of the Standard C library. It is defined in `<io.h>`. More precisely, `_taccess` tests to see whether the file is accessible according to the mode in the second parameter. A value of 0 tests for existence, 2 for write permission, 4 for read permission, and 6 for read-write permission (these values are not directly related to the Windows access values, such as GENERIC_READ). The alternative to test for the file's existence would be to open a handle with CreateFile and then close the handle after a validity test.

Program 2–4 atou: File Conversion with Error Reporting

```
/* Chapter 2. atou -- ASCII to Unicode file copy. */

#include "EvryThng.h"

BOOL Asc2Un (LPCTSTR, LPCTSTR, BOOL);
int _tmain (int argc, LPTSTR argv [])
{
    DWORD LocFileIn, LocFileOut;
    BOOL DashI = FALSE;
    TCHAR YNResp [3] = _T ("y");

/* Get the command line options and the index of the input file. */
    LocFileIn = Options (argc, argv, _T ("i"), &DashI, NULL);
    LocFileOut = LocFileIn + 1;

    if (DashI) { /* Does output file exist? */
        /* Generic version of access function to test existence. */
        if (_taccess (argv [LocFileOut], 0) == 0) {
            _tprintf (_T ("Overwrite existing file? [y/n]"));
            _tscanf (_T ("%s"), &YNResp);
            if (lstrcmp (CharLower (YNResp), YES) != 0)
                ReportError (_T ("Will not overwrite"), 4, FALSE);
        }
    }
    /* This function is modeled on CopyFile. */
    Asc2Un (argv [LocFileIn], argv [LocFileOut], FALSE);
    return 0;
}
```

Program 2–5 is the conversion function Asc2Un called by Program 2–4.

Program 2–5 Asc2Un Function

```
#include "EvryThng.h"
#define BUF_SIZE 256

BOOL Asc2Un (LPCTSTR fIn, LPCTSTR fOut, BOOL bFailIfExists)
```

```
/* ASCII to Unicode file copy function.
   Behavior is modeled after CopyFile. */
{
   HANDLE hIn, hOut;
   DWORD dwOut, nIn, nOut, iCopy;
   CHAR aBuffer [BUF_SIZE];
   WCHAR uBuffer [BUF_SIZE];
   BOOL WriteOK = TRUE;

   hIn = CreateFile (fIn, GENERIC_READ, 0, NULL,
         OPEN_EXISTING, FILE_ATTRIBUTE_NORMAL, NULL);

   /* Determine CreateFile action if output file already exists. */
   dwOut = bFailIfExists ? CREATE_NEW : CREATE_ALWAYS;
   hOut = CreateFile (fOut, GENERIC_WRITE, 0, NULL,
         dwOut, FILE_ATTRIBUTE_NORMAL, NULL);
   while (ReadFile (hIn, aBuffer, BUF_SIZE, &nIn, NULL)
         && nIn > 0 && WriteOK) {
      for (iCopy = 0; iCopy < nIn; iCopy++)
         /* Convert each character. */
         uBuffer [iCopy] = (WCHAR) aBuffer [iCopy];
      WriteOK = WriteFile (hOut, uBuffer, 2 * nIn, &nOut, NULL);
   }
   CloseHandle (hIn);
   CloseHandle (hOut);
   return WriteOK;
}
```

Performance

Appendix C shows that the performance of the file conversion program can be improved by using such techniques as providing a larger buffer and by specifying FILE_FLAG_SEQUENTIAL_SCAN with CreateFile. Appendix C also contrasts performance on NTFS and distributed file systems.

File and Directory Management

This section introduces the basic functions for file and directory management.

File Management

Windows provides a number of functions, which are generally straightforward, to manage files. The following functions delete, copy, and rename files. There is also a function to create temporary file names.

Delete files by specifying the file names. Recall that all absolute pathnames start with a drive letter or a server name. In general it is not possible to delete an open file (it is possible in Windows 9x and UNIX); attempting to do so will result in an error. This limitation can be beneficial as it can prevent an open file from being deleted inadvertently.

```
BOOL DeleteFile (LPCTSTR lpFileName)
```

Copy an entire file using a single function.

```
BOOL CopyFile (
    LPCTSTR lpExistingFileName,
    LPCTSTR lpNewFileName,
    BOOL fFailIfExists)
```

`CopyFile` copies the named existing file and assigns the specified new name to the copy. If a file with the new name already exists, it will be replaced only if `fFailIfExists` is FALSE.

Under NT5, it is possible to create a hard link between two files with the `CreateHardLink` function, which is similar to a UNIX hard link. With a hard link, a file can have two separate names. Note that there is only one file, so a change to the file will be available regardless of which name was used to open the file.

```
BOOL CreateHardLink (
    LPCTSTR lpFileName,
    LPCTSTR lpExistingFileName,
    BOOL lpSecurityAttributes)
```

The first two arguments, while in the opposite order, are used as in `CopyFile`. The two file names, the new name and the existing name, must occur in the same file system volume, but they can be in different directories. The security attributes, if any, apply to the new file name.

Close examination of Microsoft documentation shows a "number of links" member field in the `BY_HANDLE_FILE_INFO` structure, and this link count is used to determine whether or not a file can be deleted. `DeleteFile` removes the name from the file system directory, but the actual file cannot be deleted until the "number of links" count reaches `0`.

There is no soft link, although shortcuts are supported by the Windows shells, which interpret the file contents to locate the actual file, but not by Windows. Shortcuts provide soft link-like features, but only to shell users.

A pair of functions is available to rename, or "move," a file. These functions also work for directories. (`DeleteFile` and `CopyFile` are restricted to files.)

```
BOOL MoveFile (
    LPCTSTR lpExistingFileName,
    LPCTSTR lpNewFileName)

BOOL MoveFileEx (
    LPCTSTR lpExistingFileName,
    LPCTSTR lpNewFileName,
    DWORD dwFlags)
```

`MoveFile` fails if the new file already exists; use `MoveFileEx` for existing files. Note the `Ex` suffix is commonly used to create an enhanced version of an existing function in order to provide additional functionality.

Parameters

`lpExistingFileName` specifies the name of the existing file *or* directory.

`lpNewFileName` specifies the new file or directory name, which cannot already exist in the case of `MoveFile`. A new file can be on a different file system or drive, but new directories must be on the same drive. If `NULL`, the existing file is deleted.

`dwFlags` specifies options as follows:

- `MOVEFILE_REPLACE_EXISTING`—Use this option to replace an existing file.

- `MOVEFILE_WRITETHROUGH`—Use this option to ensure that the function does not return until the copied file is flushed through to the disk.

- `MOVEFILE_COPY_ALLOWED`—When the new file is on a different volume, the move is achieved with a `CopyFile` followed by a `DeleteFile`.

- `MOVEFILE_DELAY_UNTIL_REBOOT`—This flag, which cannot be used in conjunction with `MOVEFILE_COPY_ALLOWED`, is restricted to administrators and ensures that the file move does not take effect until the system restarts.

There are a couple of important limitations when you're moving (renaming) files.

- Windows 9x does not implement `MoveFileEx`; you must perform a `CopyFile` followed by a `DeleteFile`. This means that two copies will exist temporarily, which could be a problem with a nearly full disk or a large file. The effect on file time attributes is different from that of a true move.

- Wildcards are not allowed in file or directory names. Specify the actual name.

UNIX pathnames do not include a drive or server name; the slash indicates the system root. The Microsoft C library file functions also support drive names as required by the underlying Windows file naming.

UNIX does not have a function to copy files directly. Instead, you must write a small program or `system( )` to execute the cp command.

`unlink` is the UNIX equivalent of `DeleteFile` except that `unlink` can also delete directories.

`rename` and `remove` are in the C library, and `rename` will fail when attempting to move a file to an existing file name or a directory to a directory that is not empty. A new directory can exist if it is empty.

Directory Management

Creating or deleting a directory involves a pair of simple functions.

```
BOOL CreateDirectory (
    LPCTSTR lpPathName,
    LPSECURITY_ATTRIBUTES lpSecurityAttributes)

BOOL RemoveDirectory (LPCTSTR lpPathName)
```

lpPathName points to a null-terminated string with the name of the directory that is to be created or deleted. The security attributes, as with other functions, should be NULL for the time being; Chapter 15 describes file and object security. Only an empty directory can be removed.

A process has a current, or working, directory, just as in UNIX. Furthermore, each individual drive keeps a working directory. The programmer can both get and set the current directory. The first function sets the directory.

```
BOOL SetCurrentDirectory (LPCTSTR lpPathName)
```

lpPathName is the path to the new current directory. It can be a relative path or a fully qualified path starting with either a drive letter and colon, such as D:, or a UNC name (such as \\ACCTG_SERVER\PUBLIC).

If the directory path is simply a drive name (such as A: or C:), the working directory becomes the working directory on the specified drive. For example, if the working directories are set in the sequence

```
C:\MSDEV
INCLUDE
A:\MEMOS\TODO
C:
```

then the resulting working directory will be

```
C:\MSDEV\INCLUDE
```

The next function returns the fully qualified pathname into a buffer provided by the programmer.

```
DWORD GetCurrentDirectory (DWORD cchCurDir,
    LPTSTR lpCurDir)
```

Return: The string length of the returned pathname, or the
    required buffer size if the buffer is not large enough; zero if the
    function fails.

cchCurDir is the character (not byte) length of the buffer for the directory name. The length must allow for the terminating null character. lpCurDir points to the buffer to receive the pathname string.

Notice that if the buffer is too small for the pathname, the return value tells how large the buffer should be. Therefore, the test for function failure should test both for zero and for the result being larger than the cchCurDir argument.

This method of returning strings and their lengths is common in Windows and must be handled carefully. Program 2–6 illustrates a typical code fragment that performs the logic. Similar logic occurs in other examples. The method is not always consistent, however. Some functions return a Boolean, and the length parameter is used twice; it is set with the length of the buffer before the call, and the function changes the value. LookupAccountName in Chapter 15 is one of many examples.

An alternative approach, illustrated with the GetFileSecurity function in Program 15–4, is to make two function calls with a buffer memory allocation in between. The first call gets the string length, which is used in the memory allocation. The second call gets the actual string. The simplest approach in this case is to allocate a string holding MAX_PATH characters.

Example: Printing the Current Directory

Program 2–6 implements a version of the UNIX command pwd. The MAX_PATH value is used to size the buffer, but an error test is still included to illustrate GetCurrentDirectory.

Program 2–6   pwd: Printing the Current Directory

```
/* Chapter 2. pwd -- Print working directory. */

#include "EvryThng.h"
#define DIRNAME_LEN MAX_PATH + 2

int _tmain (int argc, LPTSTR argv [])
{
    TCHAR pwdBuffer [DIRNAME_LEN];
    DWORD LenCurDir;

    LenCurDir = GetCurrentDirectory (DIRNAME_LEN, pwdBuffer);

    if (LenCurDir == 0) ReportError
        (_T ("Failure getting pathname."), 1, TRUE);
    if (LenCurDir > DIRNAME_LEN)
        ReportError (_T ("Pathname is too long."), 2, FALSE);
```

```
        PrintMsg (GetStdHandle (STD_OUTPUT_HANDLE), pwdBuffer);
        return 0;
}
```

Summary

Windows supports a complete set of functions for processing and managing files and directories, along with character processing functions. In addition, you can write portable, generic applications that can be built for either ASCII or Unicode operation.

The Windows functions resemble their UNIX and C library counterparts in many ways, but the differences are also apparent. Appendix B contains a table showing the Windows, UNIX, and C library functions, noting how they correspond and pointing out some of the significant differences.

Looking Ahead

The next step, in Chapter 3, is to discuss direct file access and to learn how to deal with file and directory attributes such as file length and time stamps. Chapter 3 also shows how to process directories and ends with a discussion of the registry management API, which is similar to the directory management API.

Additional Reading

NTFS and Windows Storage

Inside Windows Storage, by Dilip Naik, is a comprehensive discussion of the complete range of Windows storage options including directly attached and network attached storage. Recent developments, enhancements, and performance improvements, along with internal implementation details, are all described.

Inside the Windows NT File System, by Helen Custer, is a short monograph describing the goals and implementation of NTFS. This information is helpful in both this chapter and the next.

Unicode

Developing International Applications for Windows 95 and Windows NT, by Nadine Kano, shows how to use Unicode in practice, with guidelines, international standards, and culture-specific issues.

The Microsoft home page has several helpful articles on Unicode. "Unicode Support in Win32" is the basic paper; a search will turn up others.

UNIX

Stevens (1992) covers UNIX files and directories in Chapters 3 and 4 and terminal I/O in Chapter 11.

UNIX in a Nutshell, by Daniel Gilly et al., is a useful quick reference on the UNIX commands.

Exercises

2–1. Write a short program to test the generic versions of `printf` and `scanf`.

2–2. Modify the `CatFile` function in Program 2–3 so that it uses `WriteConsole` rather than `WriteFile` when the standard output handle is associated with a console.

2–3. `CreateFile` allows you to specify file access characteristics so as to enhance performance. `FILE_FLAG_SEQUENTIAL_SCAN` is an example. Use this flag in Program 2–5 and determine whether there is a performance improvement for large files. Appendix C shows results on several systems. Also try `FILE_FLAG_NO_BUFFERING`.

2–4. Determine whether there are detectable performance differences between the FAT and NTFS file systems when using `atou` to convert large files.

2–5. Run Program 2–4 with and without `UNICODE` defined. What is the effect, if any? If you have access to a Windows 9x system, determine whether or not the programs function properly on that system.

2–6. Compare the information provided by `perror` (in the C library) and `ReportError` for common errors such as opening a nonexistent file.

2–7. Test the `ConsolePrompt` (Program 2–1) function's suppression of keyboard echo by using it to ask the user to enter and confirm a password.

2–8. Determine what happens when performing console output with a mixture of generic C library and Windows `WriteFile` or `WriteConsole` calls. What is the explanation?

2–9. Write a program that sorts an array of Unicode strings. Determine the difference between the word and string sorts by using `lstrcmp` and `_tcscmp`. Does `lstrlen` produce different results from those of `_tcslen`? The remarks under the `CompareString` function entry in the Microsoft online help are useful.

2–10. Extend the `Options` function implementation so that it will report an error if the command line option string contains any characters not in the list of permitted options in the function's `OptionString` parameter.

2–11. Appendix C provides performance data for file copying and `atou` conversion using different program implementations and on different file systems. Investigate performance with the test programs on systems available to you. Also, if possible, investigate performance using networked file systems, SANs, and so on to understand the impact of various storage architectures when performing sequential file access.

3 | Advanced File and Directory Processing, and the Registry

File systems provide more than sequential processing; they must also provide direct access, file locking, directory processing, and file attribute management. Starting with direct file access, which is required by database, file management, and many other systems, this chapter shows how to manage file pointers to access files at any location. In particular, it is necessary to show how to use Windows' 64-bit file pointers, because the NTFS can support huge files.

The next step is to show how to scan directory contents and how to manage and interpret file attributes, such as time stamps, access, and size. Finally, file locking protects files from concurrent modification by more than one process.

The final topic is the Windows registry, a centralized database that contains configuration information for applications and for the system itself. Registry access functions and program structure are similar to the file and directory management functions, as shown by the final program example, so this short topic is included at the chapter's end rather than creating a separate chapter for it.

The 64-Bit File System

Win32 and Win64, with the NTFS, support 64-bit file addresses so that files can, in principle, be as long as 2^{64} bytes.

The 2^{32}-byte length limit of 32-bit file systems constrains file lengths to 4GB (4×10^9 bytes). This limit is a serious constraint with some applications, including large database and multimedia systems, so any complete modern OS must support much larger files. Files larger than 4GB are sometimes called *huge files*.

Needless to say, many applications will never need huge files, so, for many programmers, 32-bit file addresses will be adequate for years to come. It is, however, a good idea to start working with 64-bit addresses from the beginning of a new development project, given the rapid pace of technical change and disk capacity growth,[1] cost improvements, and application requirements.

Win32, despite the 64-bit file addresses and the support for huge files, is still a 32-bit OS API because of its 32-bit memory addressing, as discussed in Chapter 5; Win64 is required for 64-bit memory addresses.

File Pointers

Windows, just like UNIX, the C library, and nearly every other OS, maintains a *file pointer* with each open file handle, indicating the current byte location in the file. The next `WriteFile` or `ReadFile` operation will start transferring data sequentially to or from that location and increment the file pointer by the number of bytes transferred. Opening the file with `CreateFile` sets the pointer to zero, indicating the start of the file, and the handle's pointer is advanced with each successive read or write. The crucial operation required for direct file access is the ability to set the file pointer to an arbitrary value, using `SetFilePointer`.

`SetFilePointer` shows, for the first time, how Windows handles the 64-bit NTFS. The techniques are not always pretty with this function, and `SetFilePointer` is easiest to use with small files.

```
DWORD SetFilePointer (
    HANDLE hFile,
    LONG lDistanceToMove,
    PLONG lpDistanceToMoveHigh,
    DWORD dwMoveMethod)
```

Return: The low-order `DWORD` (unsigned) of the new file pointer. The high-order portion of the new file pointer goes to the `DWORD` indicated by `lpDistanceToMoveHigh` (if non-`NULL`). In case of error, the return value is `0xFFFFFFFF`.

---

[1] At the time this is being written, even inexpensive laptop systems contain 40GB or more of disk capacity, so files larger than 4GB are possible and sometimes necessary, even on small systems.

Parameters

`hFile` is the handle of an open file with read or write access (or both).

`lDistanceToMove` is the 32-bit `LONG` *signed* distance to move or *unsigned* file position, depending on the value of `dwMoveMethod`.

`lpDistanceToMoveHigh` points to the high-order portion of the move distance. If this value is `NULL`, the function can operate only on files whose length is limited to 2^{32}–2. This parameter is also used to receive the high-order return value of the file pointer.[2] The low-order portion is the function's return value.

`dwMoveMethod` specifies one of three move modes.

- `FILE_BEGIN`: Position the file pointer from the start of the file, interpreting `DistanceToMove` as *unsigned*.

- `FILE_CURRENT`: Move the pointer forward or backward from the current position, interpreting `DistanceToMove` as *signed*. Positive is forward.

- `FILE_END`: Position the pointer backward or forward from the end of file.

It is possible to use this function to obtain the file length by specifying a zero-length move from the end of file.

The method of representing 64-bit file positions causes complexities because the function return can represent both a file position and an error code. For example, suppose that the actual position is location 2^{32}–1 (that is, `0xFFFFFFFF`) and that the call also specifies the high-order move distance. Invoke `GetLastError` to determine whether the return value is a valid file position or whether the function failed, in which case the return value would not be `NO_ERROR`. This explains why file lengths are limited to 2^{32}–2 when the high-order component is omitted.

Another confusing factor is that the high- and low-order components are separated and treated differently. The low-order address is treated as a call by value and returned by the function, whereas the high-order address is a call by reference and is both input and output.

Fortunately, 32-bit file addresses are sufficient for most programming tasks. Nonetheless, the programming examples take the long view and "do it right" using 64-bit arithmetic.

64-Bit Arithmetic

It is not difficult to perform the 64-bit file pointer arithmetic, and our example programs use Microsoft C's `LARGE_INTEGER` 64-bit data type, which is a union of

---

[2] Windows is not consistent, as can be seen by comparing `SetFilePointer` with `GetCurrentDirectory`. In some cases, distinct input and output parameters are used.

a LONGLONG (called QuadPart) and two 32-bit quantities (LowPart, a DWORD, and HighPart, a LONG). LONGLONG supports all the arithmetic operations. There is also a ULONGLONG, which is unsigned.

---

lseek (in UNIX) and fseek (in the C library) are similar to SetFilePointer. Both systems also advance the file position during read and write operations.

Specifying File Position with an Overlapped Structure

Windows provides another way to set the file position that does not require SetFilePointer. Recall that the final parameter to both ReadFile and WriteFile is the address of an overlapped structure, and this value has always been NULL in the previous examples. Two members of this structure are Offset and OffsetHigh. You can set the appropriate values in an overlapped structure, and the I/O operation can start at the specified location. The file pointer is changed to point past the last byte transferred, but the overlapped structure values are not changed. The overlapped structure also has a handle member, hEvent, that must be set to NULL. *Note*: This technique will not work with Windows 9x as the overlapped pointer must be NULL when processing files.

Caution: Even though this example uses an overlapped structure, this is not overlapped I/O, which is covered in Chapter 14.

The overlapped structure is especially convenient when updating a file record, as illustrated in the following code fragment; otherwise, separate SetFile-Pointer calls would be required before the ReadFile and WriteFile calls. The hEvent field is the last of five fields, as is shown in the initialization statement. The LARGE_INTEGER data type is used to compute the file position.

```
OVERLAPPED ov = { 0, 0, 0, 0, NULL };
RECORD r; /* Definition not shown
          but it includes the RefCount field. */
LONGLONG n;
LARGE_INGETER FilePos;
DWORD nRead, nWrite;
...
/* Update the reference count in the nth record. */
FilePos.QuadPart = n * sizeof (RECORD);
ov.Offset = FilePos.LowPart;
ov.OffsetHigh = FilePos.HighPart;
ReadFile (hFile, r, sizeof (RECORD), &nRead, &ov);
r.RefCount++; /* Update the record. */
WriteFile (hFile, r, sizeof (RECORD), &nWrite, &ov);
```

If the file handle was created with the `FILE_FLAG_NO_BUFFERING` `CreateFile` flag, then both the file position and the record size (byte count) must be multiples of the disk volume's sector size. Physical disk information, including sector size, is returned by `GetDiskFreeSpace`.

Overlapped structures will be used again later in this chapter to specify file lock regions and in Chapter 14 for asynchronous I/O and direct file access.

Getting the File Size

Determine a file's size by positioning 0 bytes from the end and using the file pointer value returned by `SetFilePointer`. Alternatively, you can use a specific function, `GetFileSize`, for this purpose.

```
DWORD GetFileSize (
    HANDLE hFile,
    LPDWORD lpFileSizeHigh)
```

Return: The low-order component of the file size. `0xFFFFFFFF` indicates a possible error; check `GetLastError`.

Notice that the length is returned in much the same manner that `SetFilePointer` returns the actual file pointer.

`GetFileSize` and `GetFileSizeEx` (which returns the 64-bit size in a single data item) require that the file have an open handle. It is also possible to obtain the length by name. `GetCompressedFileSize` returns the size of the compressed file, and `FindFirstFile`, discussed in the upcoming File Attributes and Directory Processing section, gives the exact size of a named file.

Setting the File Size, File Initialization, and Sparse Files

The `SetEndOfFile` function resizes the file using the current value of the file pointer to determine the length. A file can be extended or truncated. With extension, the contents of the extended region are not defined. The file will actually consume the disk space and user space quotas, unless the file is a sparse file. Files can also be compressed to consume less space. Exercise 3–1 explores this topic.

`SetEndOfFile` sets the physical end of file. Before setting the physical end, which can be time consuming as data is written to fill the file, you can also set the logical end of file with `SetFileValidData`. This function defines that part of the file in which you currently expect to have valid data, saving time when you set the physical end. The file's *tail* is the portion between the logical and physical ends, and the tail can be shortened by writing data past the logical end or with another call to `SetFileValidData`.

With sparse files, which were introduced with Windows 2000, disk space is consumed only as data is written. A file, directory, or volume can be specified to be sparse by the administrator. Also, the `DeviceIoControl` function can use the `FSCTL_SET_SPARSE` flag to specify that an existing file is sparse. Program 3–1 will illustrate a situation where a sparse file can be used conveniently. `SetValidFileData` does not apply to sparse files.

A FAT file is *not* initialized to all zeros automatically. The file contents, according to the Microsoft documentation, are not predictable; experiments confirm this. Therefore, applications must initialize the file with a series of `WriteFile` operations if initialization is required for correct operation. An NTFS file will be initialized because C2 security, which Windows provides, requires that contents of a deleted file not be readable.

Notice that the `SetEndOfFile` call is not the only way to extend a file. You can also extend a file using many successive write operations, but this will result in more fragmented file allocation; `SetEndOfFile` allows the OS to allocate larger contiguous disk units.

Example: Random Record Updates

Program 3–1, `RecordAccess`, maintains a fixed-size file of fixed-size records. The file header contains the number of nonempty records in the file along with the file record capacity. The user can interactively read, write (update), and delete records, which contain time stamps, a text string, and a count to indicate how many times the record has been modified. A simple and realistic extension would be to add a key to the record structure and locate records in the file by applying a hash function to the key value.

The program demonstrates file positioning to a specified record and shows how to perform 64-bit arithmetic using Microsoft C's `LARGE_INTEGER` data type. One error check is included to illustrate file pointer logic. This design also illustrates file pointers, multiple overlapped structures, and file updating with 64-bit file positions.

The total number of records in the file is specified on the command line; a large number will create a very large or even huge file as the record size is about 300 bytes. Some simple experiments will quickly show that large files should be sparse; otherwise, the entire file must be allocated and initialized on the disk, which can consume considerable time and disk space. While not shown in the listing for Program 3–1, the program contains optional code to create a sparse file; this code will not function properly on some systems, such as Windows XP Home.

The book's Web site provides three related programs: `tail.c` is another example of random file access; `getn.c` is a simpler version of `RecordAccess` that can only read records; and `atouMT` (included with the programs for Chapter 14 on the Web site, although not in the text) also illustrates direct file access.

Program 3–1 `RecordAccess`

```
/* Chapter 3. RecordAccess. */
/* Usage: RecordAccess FileName [nrec]
   If nrec is omitted, FileName must already exist.
   If nrec is supplied, create FileName (destroying an existing file).
   If the number of records is large, a sparse file is recommended. */

/* This program illustrates:
   1. Random file access.
   2. LARGE_INTEGER arithmetic and using the 64-bit file positions.
   3. Record update in place.
   4. File initialization to 0 (requires an NTFS file system).
*/

#include "EvryThng.h"
#define STRING_SIZE 256
typedef struct _RECORD { /* File record structure */
    DWORD         ReferenceCount;  /* 0 means an empty record. */
    SYSTEMTIME    RecordCreationTime;
    SYSTEMTIME    RecordLastReferenceTime;
    SYSTEMTIME    RecordUpdateTime;
    TCHAR         DataString[STRING_SIZE];
} RECORD;
typedef struct _HEADER { /* File header descriptor */
    DWORD       NumRecords;
    DWORD       NumNonEmptyRecords;
} HEADER;

int _tmain (int argc, LPTSTR argv [])
{
    HANDLE hFile;
    LARGE_INTEGER CurPtr;
    DWORD FPos, OpenOption, nXfer, RecNo;
    RECORD Record;
    TCHAR String[STRING_SIZE], Command, Extra;
    OVERLAPPED ov = {0, 0, 0, 0, NULL}, ovZero = {0, 0, 0, 0, NULL};
    HEADER Header = {0, 0};
    SYSTEMTIME CurrentTime;
    BOOLEAN HeaderChange, RecordChange;
```

```
OpenOption = (argc == 2) ? OPEN_EXISTING : CREATE_ALWAYS;
hFile = CreateFile (argv [1], GENERIC_READ | GENERIC_WRITE,
    0, NULL, OpenOption, FILE_ATTRIBUTE_NORMAL, NULL);

if (argc >= 3)  { /* Write the header and presize the new file) */
    Header.NumRecords = atoi(argv[2]);
    WriteFile(hFile, &Header, sizeof (Header), &nXfer, &ovZero);
    CurPtr.QuadPart = sizeof(RECORD)*atoi(argv[2])+sizeof(HEADER);
    FPos =         SetFilePointer (hFile, CurPtr.LowPart,
                                &CurPtr.HighPart, FILE_BEGIN);
    if (FPos == 0xFFFFFFFF && GetLastError () != NO_ERROR)
        ReportError (_T ("Set Pointer error."), 4, TRUE);
    SetEndOfFile(hFile);
}

/* Read file header: find number of records & nonempty records. */
ReadFile(hFile, &Header, sizeof (HEADER), &nXfer, &ovZero);
/* Prompt the user to read or write a numbered record. */
while (TRUE) {
    HeaderChange = FALSE; RecordChange = FALSE;
    _tprintf (_T("Enter r(ead)/w(rite)/d(elete)/q Record#\n"));
    _tscanf (_T ("%c" "%d" "%c"), &Command, &RecNo, &Extra );
    if (Command == 'q') break;
    CurPtr.QuadPart = RecNo * sizeof(RECORD) + sizeof(HEADER);
    ov.Offset = CurPtr.LowPart;
    ov.OffsetHigh = CurPtr.HighPart;
    ReadFile (hFile, &Record, sizeof (RECORD), &nXfer, &ov);
    GetSystemTime (&CurrentTime); /* To update record time fields */
    Record.RecordLastRefernceTime = CurrentTime;
    if (Command == 'r' || Command == 'd') { /* Report contents. */
        if (Record.ReferenceCount == 0) {
            _tprintf (_T("Record Number %d is empty.\n"), RecNo);
            continue;
        } else {
            _tprintf (_T("Record Number %d. Reference Count: %d \n"),
                RecNo, Record.ReferenceCount);
            _tprintf (_T("Data: %s\n"), Record.DataString);
            /* Exercise: Display times. See next example. */
            RecordChange = TRUE;
        }
        if (Command == 'd') { /* Delete the record. */
            Record.ReferenceCount = 0;
            Header.NumNonEmptyRecords--;
            HeaderChange = TRUE;
            RecordChange = TRUE;
        }
    } else if (Command == 'w') { /* Write the record. First time? */
        _tprintf (_T("Enter new data string for the record.\n"));
        _getts (String);
        if (Record.ReferenceCount == 0) {
```

```
            Record.RecordCreationTime = CurrentTime;
            Header.NumNonEmptyRecords++;
            HeaderChange = TRUE;
        }
        Record.RecordUpdateTime = CurrentTime;
        Record.ReferenceCount++;
        _tcsncpy (Record.DataString, String, STRING_SIZE-1);
        RecordChange = TRUE;
    } else {
        _tprintf (_T("Command must be r, w, or d. Try again.\n"));
    }
    /* Update record in place if any contents have changed. */
    if (RecordChange)
        WriteFile (hFile, &Record, sizeof (RECORD), &nXfer, &ov);
    /* Update the number of nonempty records if required. */
    if (HeaderChange)
        WriteFile(hFile, &Header, sizeof (Header), &nXfer, &ovZero);
}

_tprintf (_T("Computed number of nonempty records is: %d\n"),
        Header.NumNonEmptyRecords);

CloseHandle (hFile);
return 0;
}
```

File Attributes and Directory Processing

It is possible to search a directory for files and other directories that satisfy a specified name pattern and, at the same time, obtain file attributes. Searches require a *search handle* obtained by the FindFirstFile function. Obtain specific files with FindNextFile, and terminate the search with FindClose.

```
HANDLE FindFirstFile (
    LPCTSTR lpFileName,
    LPWIN32_FIND_DATA lpffd)
```

Return: A search handle. INVALID_HANDLE_VALUE indicates failure.

`FindFirstFile` examines both subdirectory and file names, looking for a name match. The returned `HANDLE` is used in subsequent searches.

Parameters

`lpFileName` points to a directory or pathname that can contain wildcard characters (`?` and `*`). Search for a single specific file by omitting wildcard characters.

`lpffd` points to a `WIN32_FIND_DATA` structure that contains information about the first file or directory to satisfy the search criteria, if any are found.

The `WIN32_FIND_DATA` structure is defined as follows:

```
typedef struct_WIN32_FIND_DATA {
    DWORD dwFileAttributes;
    FILETIME ftCreationTime;
    FILETIME ftLastAccessTime;
    FILETIME ftLastWriteTime;
    DWORD nFileSizeHigh;
    DWORD nFileSizeLow;
    DWORD dwReserved0;
    DWORD dwReserved1;
    TCHAR cFileName [MAX_PATH];
    TCHAR cAlternateFileName [14];
} WIN32_FIND_DATA;
```

`dwFileAttributes` can be tested for the values described with `CreateFile` along with some additional values, such as `FILE_ATTRIBUTE_SPARSE_FILE` and `FILE_ATTRIBUTE_ENCRYTPED`, which are not set by `CreateFile`. The three file times (creation, last access, and last write) are described in an upcoming section. The file size fields, giving the current file length, are self-explanatory. `cFileName` is not the pathname; it is the file name by itself. `cAlternateFileName` is the DOS 8.3 (including the period) version of the file name; this information is rarely used and is appropriate only to determine how a file would be named on a FAT16 file system.

Frequently, the requirement is to scan a directory for files that satisfy a name pattern containing `?` and `*` wildcard characters. To do this, use the search handle obtained from `FindFirstFile`, which retains information about the search name, and call `FindNextFile`.

```
BOOL FindNextFile (
    HANDLE hFindFile,
    LPWIN32_FIND_DATA lpffd)
```

`FindNextFile` will return `FALSE` in case of invalid arguments or if no more matching files can be found, in which case `GetLastError` will return `ERROR_NO_MORE_FILES`.

When the search is complete, close the search handle. Do not use `CloseHandle`. This is a rare exception to the rule that `CloseHandle` is for all handles—closing a search handle will cause an exception. Instead, use the following:

```
BOOL FindClose (HANDLE hFindFile)
```

The function `GetFileInformationByHandle` obtains the same information for a specific file, specified by an open handle. It also returns a field, `nNumberOf-Links`, which indicates the number of hard links set by `CreateHardLink`.

This method of wildcard expansion is necessary even in programs executed from the MS-DOS prompt because the DOS shell does not expand wildcards.

Pathnames

You can obtain a file's full pathname using `GetFullPathName`. `GetShortPath-Name` returns the name in DOS 8.3 format, assuming that the volume supports short names.

NT 5.1 introduced `SetFileShortName`, which allows you to change the existing short name of a file or directory. This can be convenient because the existing short names are often difficult to interpret.

Other Methods of Obtaining File and Directory Attributes

The `FindFirstFile` and `FindNextFile` functions can obtain the following file attribute information: attribute flags, three time stamps, and file size. There are several other related functions, including one to set attributes, and they can deal directly with the open file handle rather than scan a directory or use a file name. Three such functions, `GetFileSize`, `GetFileSizeEx`, and `SetEndOfFile`, were described previously in this chapter.

Distinct functions are used to obtain the other attributes. For example, to obtain the time stamps of an open file, use the `GetFileTime` function.

```
BOOL GetFileTime (
    HANDLE hFile,
    LPFILETIME lpftCreation,
    LPFILETIME lpftLastAccess,
    LPFILETIME lpftLastWrite)
```

The file times here and in the `WIN32_FIND_DATA` structure are 64-bit unsigned integers giving elapsed 100-nanosecond units (10^7 units per second) from a base time (January 1, 1601), expressed as Universal Coordinated Time (UTC).[3] There are several convenient functions for dealing with times.

- `FileTimeToSystemTime` (not described here; see the Windows references or Program 3–2) breaks the file time into individual units ranging from years down to seconds and milliseconds. These units are suitable, for example, when displaying or printing times.

- `SystemTimeToFileTime` reverses the process, converting time expressed in these individual units to a file time.

- `CompareFileTime` determines whether one file time is less than (−1), equal to (0), or greater than (+1) another.

- Change the time stamps with `SetFileTime`; times that are not to be changed are set to 0 in the function call. NTFS supports all three file times, but the FAT gives an accurate result only for the last access time.

- `FileTimeToLocalFileTime` and `LocalFileTimeToFileTime` convert between UTC and the local time.

`GetFileType`, not described in detail here, distinguishes among disk files, character files (actually, devices such as printers and consoles), and pipes (see Chapter 11). The file, again, is specified with a handle.

The function `GetFileAttributes` uses the file or directory name, and it returns just the `dwFileAttributes` information.

---

[3] Do not, however, expect to get 100-nanosecond precision; precision will vary depending on hardware characteristics.

> DWORD GetFileAttributes (LPCTSTR lpFileName)
>
> Return: The file attributes, or 0xFFFFFFFF in case of failure.

The attributes can be tested for appropriate combinations of several mask values. Some attributes, such as the temporary file attribute, are originally set with CreateFile. The attribute values include the following:

- FILE_ATTRIBUTE_DIRECTORY

- FILE_ATTRIBUTE_NORMAL

- FILE_ATTRIBUTE_READONLY

- FILE_ATTRIBUTE_TEMPORARY

The function SetFileAttributes changes these attributes in a named file.

---

opendir, readdir, and closedir in UNIX correspond to the three Find functions. The function stat obtains file size and times, in addition to owning user and group information that relates to UNIX security. fstat and lstat are variations. These functions can also obtain type information. utime sets file times in UNIX. There is no UNIX equivalent to the temporary file attribute.

Temporary File Names

The next function creates names for temporary files. The name can be in any specified directory and must be unique.

GetTempFileName gives a unique file name, with the .tmp suffix, in a specified directory and optionally creates the file. This function is used extensively in later examples (Program 6–1, Program 7–1, and elsewhere).

```
UINT GetTempFileName (
   LPCTSTR lpPathName,
   LPCTSTR lpPrefixString,
   UINT uUnique,
   LPTSTR lpTempFileName)
```

Return: A unique numeric value used to create the file name. This will be uUnique if uUnique is nonzero. On failure, the return value is zero.

Parameters

lpPathName is the directory for the temporary file. "." is a typical value specifying the current directory. Alternatively, use GetTempPath, a Windows function not described here, to give the name of a directory dedicated to temporary files.

lpPrefixString is the prefix of the temporary name. Only 8-bit ASCII characters are allowed. uUnique is normally zero so that the function will generate a unique four-digit suffix and will create the file. If this value is nonzero, the file is not created; do that with CreateFile, possibly using FILE_FLAG_DELETE_ON_CLOSE.

lpTempFileName points to the buffer that receives the temporary file name. The buffer's byte length should be at least the same value as MAX_PATH. The resulting pathname is a concatenation of the path, the prefix, the four-digit hex number, and the .tmp suffix.

Mount Points

NT 5.0 allows one file system to be mounted at a mount point within another. Managing mount points is generally an administrative function, but they can also be managed programmatically.

SetVolumeMountPoint mounts a drive (the second argument) at the point specified by the first argument. For example:

```
SetVolumeMountPoint ("C:\\mycd\\", "D:\\");
```

puts the D: drive (often the CD drive on a personal system) under the mycd directory (the mount point) on the C: drive. Note how the pathnames all end with a backslash. The path C:\mycd\memos\book.doc then corresponds to D:\memos\book.doc.

You can mount multiple file systems at a single mount point. Use `Delete-MountPoint` to reverse the process.

`GetVolumePathName` returns the root mount point of an absolute or relative path or file name. `GetVolumeNameForVolumeMountPoint`, in turn, gives the volume name, such as `C:\`, corresponding to a mount point.

Example: Listing File Attributes

It is now time to illustrate the file and directory management functions. Program 3–2 shows a limited version of the UNIX `ls` directory listing command, which can show file modification times and the file size, although this version gives only the low order of the file size.

The program scans the directory for files that satisfy the search pattern. For each file located, the program shows the file name and, if the `-l` option is specified, the file attributes. This program illustrates many, but not all, Windows directory management functions.

The bulk of Program 3–2 is concerned with directory traversal. Notice that each directory is traversed twice—once to process files and again to process subdirectories—in order to support the `-R` recursive option.

Program 3–2, as listed here, will properly carry out a command with a relative pathname such as:

```
lsW -R include\*.h
```

It will not work properly, however, with an absolute pathname such as:

```
lsW -R C:\Projects\ls\Debug\*.obj
```

because the program, as listed, depends on setting the directory relative to the current directory. The complete solution (on the Web site) analyzes pathnames and will also carry out the second command.

Program 3–2   `lsW`: File Listing and Directory Traversal
_____

```
/* Chapter 3. lsW file list command */
/* lsW [options] [files] */

#include "EvryThng.h"

BOOL TraverseDirectory (LPCTSTR, DWORD, LPBOOL);
DWORD FileType (LPWIN32_FIND_DATA);
BOOL ProcessItem (LPWIN32_FIND_DATA, DWORD, LPBOOL);
```

```
int _tmain (int argc, LPTSTR argv [])
{
    BOOL Flags [MAX_OPTIONS], ok = TRUE;
    TCHAR PathName [MAX_PATH + 1], CurrPath [MAX_PATH + 1];
    LPTSTR pSlash, pFileName;
    int i, FileIndex;

    FileIndex = Options (
            argc, argv, _T ("Rl"), &Flags [0], &Flags [1], NULL);

    /* "Parse" the search pattern into "parent" and file name. */
    GetCurrentDirectory (MAX_PATH, CurrPath); /* Save current path. */
    if (argc < FileIndex + 1) /* No path specified. Current dir. */
        ok = TraverseDirectory (_T ("*"), MAX_OPTIONS, Flags);
    else for (i = FileIndex; i < argc; i++) {
        /* Process all paths on the command line. */
        ok = TraverseDirectory (pFileName, MAX_OPTIONS, Flags) && ok;
        SetCurrentDirectory (CurrPath);    /* Restore directory. */
    }
    return ok ? 0 : 1;
}

static BOOL TraverseDirectory (LPCTSTR PathName, DWORD NumFlags,
        LPBOOL Flags)

/* Traverse a directory; perform ProcessItem for every match. */
/* PathName: Relative or absolute pathname to traverse. */
{
    HANDLE SearchHandle;
    WIN32_FIND_DATA FindData;
    BOOL Recursive = Flags [0];
    DWORD FType, iPass;
    TCHAR CurrPath [MAX_PATH + 1];

    GetCurrentDirectory (MAX_PATH, CurrPath);

    for (iPass = 1; iPass <= 2; iPass++) {
        /* Pass 1: List files. */
        /* Pass 2: Traverse directories (if -R specified). */
        SearchHandle = FindFirstFile (PathName, &FindData);
        do {
            FType = FileType (&FindData); /* File or directory? */
            if (iPass == 1) /* List name and attributes. */
                ProcessItem (&FindData, MAX_OPTIONS, Flags);
            if (FType == TYPE_DIR && iPass == 2 && Recursive) {
                /* Process a subdirectory. */
                _tprintf (_T ("\n%s\\%s:"), CurrPath,
                        FindData.cFileName);
                /* Prepare to traverse a directory. */
```

```
                SetCurrentDirectory (FindData.cFileName);
                TraverseDirectory (_T ("*"), NumFlags, Flags);
                /* Recursive call. */
                SetCurrentDirectory (_T (".."));
            }
        } while (FindNextFile (SearchHandle, &FindData));
        FindClose (SearchHandle);
    }
    return TRUE;
}

static BOOL ProcessItem (LPWIN32_FIND_DATA pFileData,
            DWORD NumFlags, LPBOOL Flags)
/* List file or directory attributes. */
{
    const TCHAR FileTypeChar [] = {' ', 'd'};
    DWORD FType = FileType (pFileData);
    BOOL Long = Flags [1];
    SYSTEMTIME LastWrite;

    if (FType != TYPE_FILE && FType != TYPE_DIR) return FALSE;

    _tprintf (_T ("\n"));
    if (Long) { /* Was "-1" option used on the command line? */
        _tprintf (_T ("%c"), FileTypeChar [FType - 1]);
        _tprintf (_T ("%10d"), pFileData->nFileSizeLow);
        FileTimeToSystemTime (&(pFileData->ftLastWriteTime),
            &LastWrite);
        _tprintf (_T (" %02d/%02d/%04d %02d:%02d:%02d"),
            LastWrite.wMonth, LastWrite.wDay,
            LastWrite.wYear, LastWrite.wHour,
            LastWrite.wMinute, LastWrite.wSecond);
    }
    _tprintf (_T (" %s"), pFileData->cFileName);
    return TRUE;
}

static DWORD FileType (LPWIN32_FIND_DATA pFileData)
/* Types supported - TYPE_FILE: file; TYPE_DIR: directory;
   TYPE_DOT:  . or .. directory */
{
    BOOL IsDir;
    DWORD FType;
    FType = TYPE_FILE;
    IsDir = (pFileData->dwFileAttributes &
            FILE_ATTRIBUTE_DIRECTORY) != 0;
    if (IsDir)
        if (lstrcmp (pFileData->cFileName, _T (".")) == 0
                || lstrcmp (pFileData->cFileName, _T ("..")) == 0)
            FType = TYPE_DOT;
```

```
        else FType = TYPE_DIR;
    return FType;
}
```

Example: Setting File Times

Program 3–3 implements the UNIX touch command, which changes file access and modifies times to the current value of the system time. Exercise 3–11 enhances touch so that the new file time is a command line option, as with the actual UNIX command.

Program 3–3   touch: Setting File Times

```
/* Chapter 3. touch command. */
/* touch [options] files */
#include "EvryThng.h"

int _tmain (int argc, LPTSTR argv [])
{
    SYSTEMTIME SysTime;
    FILETIME NewFileTime;
    LPFILETIME pAccessTime = NULL, pModifyTime = NULL;
    HANDLE hFile;
    BOOL Flags [MAX_OPTIONS], SetAccessTime, SetModTime, CreateNew;
    DWORD CreateFlag;
    int i, FileIndex;

    FileIndex = Options (argc, argv, _T ("amc"),
            &Flags [0], &Flags [1], &Flags [2], NULL);
    SetAccessTime = !Flags [0];
    SetModTime = !Flags [1];
    CreateNew = !Flags [2];
    CreateFlag = CreateNew ? OPEN_ALWAYS : OPEN_EXISTING;
    for (i = FileIndex; i < argc; i++) {
        hFile = CreateFile (argv [i], GENERIC_READ | GENERIC_WRITE,
                0, NULL, CreateFlag, FILE_ATTRIBUTE_NORMAL, NULL);
        GetSystemTime (&SysTime);
        SystemTimeToFileTime (&SysTime, &NewFileTime);
        if (SetAccessTime) pAccessTime = &NewFileTime;
        if (SetModTime) pModifyTime = &NewFileTime;
        SetFileTime (hFile, NULL, pAccessTime, pModifyTime);
        CloseHandle (hFile);
    }
    return 0;
}
```

File Processing Strategies

An early decision in any Windows development or porting project is to select whether file processing should be done with the C library or with the Windows functions. This is not an either/or decision because the functions can be mixed with caution even when you're processing the same file.

The C library offers several distinct advantages, including the following.

- The code will be portable to non-Windows systems.

- Convenient line- and character-oriented functions that do not have direct Windows equivalents simplify string processing.

- C library functions are generally easier to use than Windows functions.

- The line and stream character-oriented functions can easily be changed to generic calls, although the portability advantage will be lost.

- The C library will operate in a multithreaded environment, as shown in Chapter 7.

Nonetheless, there are some limitations to the C library. Here are some examples.

- The C library cannot manage or traverse directories, and it cannot obtain or set most file attributes.

- The C library uses 32-bit file position in the `fseek` function, so, while it can read huge files sequentially, it is not possible to position anywhere in a huge file, as is required, for instance, by Program 3–1.

- Advanced features such as file security, memory-mapped files, file locking, asynchronous I/O, and interprocess communication are not available with the C library. Some of the advanced features provide performance benefits, as shown in Appendix C.

Another possibility is to port existing UNIX code using a compatibility library. Microsoft C provides a limited compatibility library with many, but not all, UNIX functions. The Microsoft UNIX library includes I/O functions, but most process management and other functions are omitted. Functions are named with an underscore prefix—for example, `_read`, `_write`, `_stat`, and so on.

Decisions regarding the use and mix of C library, compatibility libraries, and the Win32/64 API should be driven by project requirements. Many of the Windows advantages will be shown in the following chapters, and the performance figures in Appendix C are useful when performance is a factor.

File Locking

An important issue in any system with multiple processes is coordination and synchronization of access to shared objects, such as files.

Windows can lock files, in whole or in part, so that no other process (running program) can access the locked file region. File locks can be read-only (shared) or read-write (exclusive). Most important, the locks belong to the process. Any attempt to access part of a file (using ReadFile or WriteFile) in violation of an existing lock will fail because the locks are mandatory at the process level. Any attempt to obtain a conflicting lock will also fail even if the process already owns the lock. File locking is a limited form of synchronization between concurrent processes and threads; synchronization is covered in much more general terms starting in Chapter 8.

The most general function is LockFileEx. The less general function, Lock-File, can be used on Windows 9x.

LockFileEx is a member of the *extended* I/O class of functions, so the overlapped structure, used earlier to specify file position to ReadFile and WriteFile, is required to specify the 64-bit file position and range of the file region that is to be locked.

```
BOOL LockFileEx (
    HANDLE hFile,
    DWORD dwFlags,
    DWORD dwReserved,
    DWORD nNumberOfBytesToLockLow,
    DWORD nNumberOfBytesToLockHigh,
    LPOVERLAPPED lpOverlapped)
```

LockFileEx locks a byte range in an open file for either shared (multiple readers) or exclusive (one reader-writer) access.

Parameters

hFile is the handle of an open file. The handle must have GENERIC_READ or both GENERIC_READ and GENERIC_WRITE file access.

dwFlags determines the lock mode and whether to wait for the lock to become available.

LOCKFILE_EXCLUSIVE_LOCK, if set, indicates a request for an exclusive, read-write lock. Otherwise, it requests a shared (read-only) lock.

LOCKFILE_FAIL_IMMEDIATELY, if set, specifies that the function should return immediately with FALSE if the lock cannot be acquired. Otherwise, the call blocks until the lock becomes available.

dwReserved must be 0. The two parameters with the length of the byte range are self-explanatory.

lpOverlapped points to an OVERLAPPED data structure containing the start of the byte range. The overlapped structure contains three data members that must be set (the others are ignored); the first two determine the start location for the locked region.

- DWORD Offset (this is the correct name; not OffsetLow).

- DWORD OffsetHigh.

- HANDLE hEvent should be set to 0.

A file lock is removed using a corresponding UnlockFileEx call; all the same parameters are used except dwFlags.

```
BOOL UnlockFileEx (
    HANDLE hFile,
    DWORD dwReserved,
    DWORD nNumberOfBytesToLockLow,
    DWORD nNumberOfBytesToLockHigh,
    LPOVERLAPPED lpOverlapped)
```

You should consider several factors when using file locks.

- The unlock must use exactly the same range as a preceding lock. It is not possible, for example, to combine two previous lock ranges or unlock a portion of a locked range. An attempt to unlock a region that does not correspond exactly with an existing lock will fail; the function returns FALSE and the system error message indicates that the lock does not exist.

- Locks cannot overlap existing locked regions in a file if a conflict would result.

- It is possible to lock beyond the range of a file's length. This approach could be useful when a process or thread extends a file.

- Locks are not inherited by a newly created process.

Table 3–1 shows the lock logic when all *or* part of a range already has a lock. This logic applies even if the lock is owned by the same process that is making the new request.

Table 3–2 shows the logic when a process attempts a read or write operation on a file region with one or more locks, owned by a separate process, on all or part of the read-write region. A failed read or write may take the form of a partially completed operation if only a portion of the read or write record is locked.

Read and write operations are normally in the form of `ReadFile` and `Write-File` calls or their extended versions, `ReadFileEx` and `WriteFileEx`. Diagnosing a read or write failure requires calling `GetLastError`.

Accessing memory that is mapped to a file is another form of file I/O, as will be discussed in Chapter 5. Lock conflicts are not detected at the time of memory reference; rather, they are detected at the time that the `MapViewOfFile` function is called. This function makes a part of the file available to the process, so the lock must be checked at that time.

Table 3–1 Lock Request Logic

	Requested Lock Type	
Existing Lock	Shared Lock	Exclusive Lock
None	Granted	Granted
Shared lock (one or more)	Granted	Refused
Exclusive lock	Refused	Refused

Table 3–2 Locks and I/O Operation

	I/O Operation	
Existing Lock	Read	Write
None	Succeeds	Succeeds
Shared lock (one or more)	Succeeds. It is not necessary for the calling process to own a lock on the file region.	Fails
Exclusive lock	Succeeds if the calling process owns the lock. Fails otherwise.	Succeeds if the calling process owns the lock. Fails otherwise.

The `LockFile` function is a limited, special case and is a form of advisory locking. It can be used on Windows 9x, which does not support `LockFileEx`. Only exclusive access is available, and `LockFile` returns immediately. That is, `LockFile` does not block. Test the return value to determine whether you obtained the lock.

Releasing File Locks

Every successful `LockFileEx` call must be followed by a single matching call to `UnlockFileEx` (the same is true for `LockFile` and `UnlockFile`). If a program fails to release a lock or holds the lock longer than necessary, other programs may not be able to proceed, or, at the very least, their performance will be negatively impacted. Therefore, programs should be carefully designed and implemented so that locks are released as soon as possible, and logic that might cause the program to skip the unlock should be avoided.

Termination handlers (Chapter 4) are a useful way to ensure that the unlock is performed.

Lock Logic Consequences

Although the file lock logic shown in Tables 3–1 and 3–2 is natural, it has consequences that may be unexpected and cause unintended program defects. Here are some examples.

- Suppose that process A and process B periodically obtain shared locks on a file, and process C blocks when attempting to gain an exclusive lock on the same file after process A gets its shared lock. Process B may now gain its shared lock even though C is still blocked, and C will remain blocked even after A releases the lock. C will remain blocked until all processes release their shared locks even if they obtained them after C blocked. In this scenario, it is possible that C will be blocked forever even though all the other processes manage their shared locks properly.

- Assume that process A has a shared lock on the file and that process B attempts to read the file without obtaining a shared lock first. The read will still succeed even though the reading process does not own any lock on the file because the read operation does not conflict with the existing shared lock.

- These statements apply both to entire files and to regions.

- A read or write may be able to complete a portion of its request before encountering a conflicting lock. The read or write will return `FALSE`, and the byte transfer count will be less than the number requested.

Using File Locks

File locking examples are deferred until Chapter 6, which covers process management. Programs 4–2, 6–4, 6–5, and 6–6 use locks to ensure that only one process at a time can modify a file.

UNIX has *advisory* file locking; an attempt to obtain a lock may fail (the logic is the same as in Table 3–1), but the process can still perform the I/O. Therefore, UNIX can achieve locking between cooperating processes, but any other process can violate the protocol.

To obtain an advisory lock, use options to the `fcntl` function. The commands (the second parameter) are `F_SETLK`, `F_SETLKW` (to wait), and `F_GETLK`. An additional block data structure contains a lock type that is one of `F_RDLCK`, `F_WRLCK`, or `F_UNLCK` and the range.

Mandatory locking is also available in some UNIX systems using a file's `set-group-ID` and `group-execute`, both using `chmod`.

UNIX file locking behavior differs in many ways. For example, locks are inherited through an `exec` call.

The C library does not support locking, although Visual C++ does supply nonstandard extensions for locking.

The Registry

The registry is a centralized, hierarchical database for application and system configuration information. Access to the registry is through *registry keys*, which are analogous to file system directories. A key can contain other keys or name/value pairs, where the name/value pairs are analogous to file names and contents.

The user or administrator can view and edit the registry contents through the registry editor, which is accessed by the REGEDIT command. Alternatively, programs can manage the registry through the registry API functions described in this section.

Note: Registry programming is discussed here due to its similarity to file processing and its importance in some, but not all, applications. The example will be a straightforward modification of the `lsW` example. This section could, however, be a separate short chapter. *Therefore, readers who are not concerned with registry programming may wish to skip this section, possibly returning at a later time.*

The registry name/value pairs contain information such as the following:

- Operating system version number, build number, and registered user.

- Similar information for every properly installed application.

- Information about the computer's processor type, number of processors, system memory, and so on.

- User-specific information, such as the home directory and application preferences.

- Security information such as user account names.

- Installed services (Chapter 13).

- Mappings from file name extensions to executable programs. These mappings are used by the user interface shell when the user clicks on a file name icon. For example, the .doc extension might be mapped to Microsoft Word.

- Mappings from network addresses to host machine names.

UNIX systems store similar information in the /etc directory and files in the user's home directory. Windows 3.1 used the .INI files for a similar purpose. The registry centralizes all this information in a uniform way. In addition, the registry can be secured using the security features described in Chapter 15.

The registry management API is described here, but the detailed contents and meaning of the various registry entries are beyond the scope of this book. Nonetheless, Figure 3–1 shows a typical view from the registry editor and gives an idea of the registry structure and contents.

The specific information regarding the host machine's processor is on the right side. The bottom of the left side shows that numerous keys contain information about the software applications on the host system. Notice that every key must have a default value, which is listed before any of the other name/value pairs.

Registry implementation, including registry data storage and retrieval, is beyond the book's scope; see the reference information at the end of the chapter.

Registry Keys

Figure 3–1 shows the analogy between file system directories and registry keys. Each key can contain other keys or a sequence of name/value pairs. Whereas a file system is accessed through pathnames, the registry is accessed through keys. Several predefined keys serve as entry points into the registry.

1. HKEY_LOCAL_MACHINE stores physical information about the machine, along with information about installed software. Installed software information is generally created in subkeys of the form SOFTWARE*CompanyName*\ *ProductName**Version*.

2. HKEY_USERS defines user configuration information.

Figure 3-1   The Registry Editor

3. HKEY_CURRENT_CONFIG contains current settings, such as display resolution and fonts.

4. HKEY_CLASSES_ROOT contains subordinate entries to define mappings from file extension names to classes and to applications used by the shell to access objects with the specified extension. All the keys necessary for Microsoft's Component Object Model (COM) are also subordinate to this key.

5. HKEY_CURRENT_USER contains user-specific information, including environment variables, printers, and application preferences that apply to the current user.

Registry Management

Registry management functions can query and modify name/value pairs and create new subkeys and name/value pairs. Key handles of type HKEY are used both to specify a key and to obtain new keys.[4] Values are typed; there are several types to select from, such as strings, double words, and expandable strings whose parameters can be replaced with environment variables.

Key Management

The first function, `RegOpenKeyEx`, opens a subkey. Starting from one of the predefined reserved key handles, you can traverse the registry and obtain a handle to any subordinate key.

```
LONG RegOpenKeyEx (
    HKEY hKey,
    LPCTSTR lpSubKey,
    DWORD ulOptions,
    REGSAM samDesired,
    PHKEY phkResult)
```

Parameters

hKey identifies a currently open key or one of the predefined reserved key handle values. phkResult points to a variable of type HKEY that is to receive the handle of the newly opened key.

lpSubKey is the name of the subkey. The subkey name can be a path, such as `Microsoft\WindowsNT\CurrentVersion`. A NULL value causes a new, duplicate key for hKey to be opened. ulOptions must be 0.

samDesired is the access mask describing the security for the new key. Values include KEY_ALL_ACCESS, KEY_WRITE, KEY_QUERY_VALUE, and KEY_ENUMERATE_SUBKEYS.

The return value is normally ERROR_SUCCESS. Any other value indicates an error. Close an open key handle with `RegCloseKey`, which takes the handle as its single parameter.

Obtain the names of subkeys by specifying a key to `RegEnumKeyEx`.

A complementary pair of functions is used to obtain name/value pairs: `RegEnumValue` and `RegQueryValueEx`.[5] `RegSetValueEx` stores typed data in

---

[4] It would be more convenient and consistent if the HANDLE type were used for registry management. There are several other gratuitous exceptions to standard Windows practice.

[5] Notice that the Ex suffix should be used or omitted exactly as shown. When Ex is used, the function extends a function of the same name without the suffix.

the value field of an open registry key. This Key Management subsection and the upcoming Value Management subsection provide descriptions of these functions, followed by an example.

`RegEnumKeyEx` enumerates subkeys of an open registry key, much as `Find-FirstFile` and `FindNextFile` enumerate directory contents. This function retrieves the key name, class string, and time of last modification.

```
LONG RegEnumKeyEx (
    HKEY hKey,
    DWORD dwIndex,
    LPTSTR lpName,
    LPDWORD lpcbName,
    LPDWORD lpReserved,
    LPTSTR lpClass,
    LPDWORD lpcbClass
    PFILETIME lpftLastWriteTime)
```

`dwIndex` should be 0 on the first call and then should be incremented on each subsequent call. The key name and its size, along with the class string and its size, are returned in the normal way. The function returns `ERROR_SUCCESS` or an error value.

You can also create new keys using `RegCreateKeyEx`. Keys can be given security attributes in the same way as with directories and files (Chapter 15).

```
LONG RegCreateKeyEx (
    HKEY hKey,
    LPCTSTR lpSubKey,
    DWORD Reserved,
    LPTSTR lpClass,
    DWORD dwOptions,
    REGSAM samDesired,
    LPSECURITY_ATTRIBUTES lpSecurityAttributes,
    PHKEY phkResult,
    LPDWORD lpdwDisposition)
```

Parameters

lpSubKey is the name of the new subkey under the open key indicated by the handle hKey.

lpClass is the class, or object type, of the key describing the data represented by the key. The many possible values include REG_SZ (null-terminated string) and REG_DWORD (double word).

dwOptions is either 0 or one of the mutually exclusive values: REG_OPTION_VOLATILE or REG_OPTION_NON_VOLATILE. Nonvolatile registry information is stored in a file and preserved when the system restarts. Volatile registry keys are kept in memory and will not be restored.

samDesired is the same as for RegOpenKeyEx.

lpSecurityAttributes can be NULL or can point to a security attribute. The rights can be selected from the same values as those used with samDesired.

lpdwDisposition points to a DWORD that indicates whether the key already existed (REG_OPENED_EXISTING_KEY) or was created (REG_CREATED_NEW_KEY).

To delete a key, use RegDeleteKey. The two parameters are an open key handle and a subkey name.

Value Management

You can enumerate the values for a specified open key using RegEnumValue. Specify an Index, originally 0, which is incremented in subsequent calls. On return, you get the string with the value name as well as its size. You also get the value and its type.

```
LONG RegEnumValue (
    HKEY hKey,
    DWORD dwIndex,
    LPTSTR lpValueName,
    LPDWORD lpcbValueName,
    LPDWORD lpReserved,
    LPDWORD lpType,
    LPBYTE lpData,
    LPDWORD lpcbData)
```

The actual value is returned in the buffer indicated by lpData. The size of the result can be found from lpcbData.

The data type, pointed to by lpType, has numerous possibilities, including REG_BINARY, REG_DWORD, REG_SZ (a string), and REG_EXPAND_SZ (an expandable string with parameters replaced by environment variables). See the on-line help for a list of all the value types.

Test the function's return value to determine whether you have enumerated all the keys. The value will be ERROR_SUCCESS if you have found a valid key.

RegQueryValueEx is similar except that you specify a value name rather than an index. If you know the value names, you can use this function. If you do not know the names, you can scan with RegEnumValueEx.

Set a value within an open key using RegSetValueEx, supplying the value name, value type, and actual value data.

```
LONG RegSetValueEx (
    HKEY hKey,
    LPCTSTR lpValueName,
    DWORD Reserved,
    DWORD dwType,
    CONST BYTE * lpData,
    CONST cbData)
```

Finally, delete named values using the function RegDeleteValue.

Example: Listing Registry Keys and Contents

Program 3–4, lsReg, is a modification of Program 3–2 (lsW, the file and directory listing program); it processes registry keys and name/value pairs rather than directories and files.

Program 3–4 lsReg: Listing Registry Keys and Contents

```
/* Chapter 3. lsReg: Registry list command. Adapted from Prog. 3-2. */
/* lsReg [options] SubKey */

#include "EvryThng.h"

BOOL TraverseRegistry (HKEY, LPTSTR, LPTSTR, LPBOOL);
BOOL DisplayPair (LPTSTR, DWORD, LPBYTE, DWORD, LPBOOL);
BOOL DisplaySubKey (LPTSTR, LPTSTR, PFILETIME, LPBOOL);

int _tmain (int argc, LPTSTR argv [])
{
    BOOL Flags [2], ok = TRUE;
```

```
    TCHAR KeyName [MAX_PATH + 1];
    LPTSTR pScan;
    DWORD i, KeyIndex;
    HKEY hKey, hNextKey;

    /* Tables of predefined key names and keys. */
    LPTSTR PreDefKeyNames [] = {
        _T ("HKEY_LOCAL_MACHINE"), _T ("HKEY_CLASSES_ROOT"),
        _T ("HKEY_CURRENT_USER"), _T ("HKEY_CURRENT_CONFIG"), NULL };
    HKEY PreDefKeys [] = {
        HKEY_LOCAL_MACHINE, HKEY_CLASSES_ROOT,
        HKEY_CURRENT_USER, HKEY_CURRENT_CONFIG };

    KeyIndex = Options (
            argc, argv, _T ("Rl"), &Flags [0], &Flags [1], NULL);

    /* "Parse" the search pattern into "key" and "subkey". */
    /* Build the key. */
    pScan = argv [KeyIndex];
    for (i = 0; *pScan != _T ('\\') && *pScan != _T ('\0');
            pScan++, i++) KeyName [i] = *pScan;
    KeyName [i] = _T ('\0');
    if (*pScan == _T ('\\')) pScan++;

    /* Translate predefined key name to an HKEY. */
    for (i = 0; PreDefKeyNames [i] != NULL &&
        _tcscmp (PreDefKeyNames [i], KeyName) != 0; i++);
    hKey = PreDefKeys [i];
    RegOpenKeyEx (hKey, pScan, 0, KEY_READ, &hNextKey);
    hKey = hNextKey;

    ok = TraverseRegistry (hKey, argv [KeyIndex], NULL, Flags);
    return ok ? 0 : 1;
}

BOOL TraverseRegistry (HKEY hKey, LPTSTR FullKeyName, LPTSTR SubKey,
        LPBOOL Flags)

/* Traverse registry key and subkeys if the -R option is set. */
{
    HKEY hSubK;
    BOOL Recursive = Flags [0];
    LONG Result;
    DWORD ValType, Index, NumSubKs, SubKNameLen, ValNameLen, ValLen;
    DWORD MaxSubKLen, NumVals, MaxValNameLen, MaxValLen;
    FILETIME LastWriteTime;
    LPTSTR SubKName, ValName;
    LPBYTE Val;
    TCHAR FullSubKName [MAX_PATH + 1];
```

```
    /* Open up the key handle. */
    RegOpenKeyEx (hKey, SubKey, 0, KEY_READ, &hSubK);

    /* Find max size info regarding the key and allocate storage. */
    RegQueryInfoKey (hSubK, NULL, NULL, NULL, &NumSubKs,
            &MaxSubKLen, NULL, &NumVals, &MaxValNameLen,
            &MaxValLen, NULL, &LastWriteTime);
    SubKName = malloc (MaxSubKLen+1); /* Size w/o null. */
    ValName = malloc (MaxValNameLen+1); /* Allow for null. */
    Val = malloc (MaxValLen); /* Size in bytes. */

    /* First pass for name/value pairs. */
    for (Index = 0; Index < NumVals; Index++) {
        ValNameLen = MaxValNameLen + 1; /* Set each time! */
        ValLen = MaxValLen + 1;
        RegEnumValue (hSubK, Index, ValName,
                &ValNameLen, NULL, &ValType, Val, &ValLen);
        DisplayPair (ValName, ValType, Val, ValLen, Flags);
    }

    /* Second pass for subkeys. */
    for (Index = 0; Index < NumSubKs; Index++) {
        SubKNameLen = MaxSubKLen + 1;
        RegEnumKeyEx (hSubK, Index, SubKName, &SubKNameLen,
                NULL, NULL, NULL, &LastWriteTime);
        DisplaySubKey (FullKName, SubKName, &LastWriteTime, Flags);
        if (Recursive) {

            _stprintf (FullSubKName, _T ("%s\\%s"), FullKName,
                    SubKName);
            TraverseRegistry (hSubK, FullSubKName, SubKName, Flags);
        }
    }

    _tprintf (_T ("\n"));
    free (SubKName); free (ValName); free (Val);
    RegCloseKey (hSubK);
    return TRUE;
}

BOOL DisplayPair (LPTSTR ValueName, DWORD ValueType,
        LPBYTE Value, DWORD ValueLen, LPBOOL Flags)
/* Function to display name/value pairs. */
{
    LPBYTE pV = Value;
    DWORD i;

    _tprintf (_T ("\nValue: %s = "), ValueName);
    switch (ValueType) {
    case REG_FULL_RESOURCE_DESCRIPTOR: /* 9: hardware description. */
```

```
        case REG_BINARY: /* 3: Binary data in any form. */
            for (i = 0; i < ValueLen; i++, pV++)
                _tprintf (_T (" %x"), *pV);
            break;

        case REG_DWORD: /* 4: A 32-bit number. */
            _tprintf (_T ("%x"), (DWORD)*Value);
            break;

        case REG_MULTI_SZ: /* 7: Array of null-terminated strings. */

        case REG_SZ: /* 1: A null-terminated string. */
            _tprintf (_T ("%s"), (LPTSTR) Value);
            break;
        /* ... Several other types ... */
        }
        return TRUE;
}

BOOL DisplaySubKey (LPTSTR KeyName, LPTSTR SubKeyName,
        PFILETIME pLastWrite, LPBOOL Flags)
{
    BOOL Long = Flags [1];
    SYSTEMTIME SysLastWrite;

    _tprintf (_T ("\nSubkey: %s"), KeyName);
    if (_tcslen (SubKeyName) > 0)
        _tprintf (_T ("\\%s "), SubKeyName);
    if (Long) {
        FileTimeToSystemTime (pLastWrite, &SysLastWrite);
        _tprintf (_T ("%02d/%02d/%04d %02d:%02d:%02d"),
                SysLastWrite.wMonth, SysLastWrite.wDay,
                SysLastWrite.wYear, SysLastWrite.wHour,
                SysLastWrite.wMinute, SysLastWrite.wSecond);
    }
    return TRUE;
}
```

Summary

Chapters 2 and 3 have described all the important basic functions for dealing with files, directories, and console I/O. Numerous examples show how to use these functions in building typical applications. The registry is managed in much the same way as the file system, as shown by the final example.

Later chapters will deal with advanced I/O, such as asynchronous operations and memory mapping. It is now possible to duplicate nearly any common UNIX or C library file processing.

Appendix B contains several tables showing the Windows, UNIX, and C library functions, noting how they correspond and pointing out some of the significant differences among them.

Looking Ahead

Chapter 4, Exception Handling, simplifies error and exception handling and extends the `ReportError` function to handle arbitrary exceptions.

Additional Reading

See Peter D. Hipson's *Expert Guide to Windows NT 4 Registry* for information on registry programming as well as registry usage.

Exercises

3–1. Use the `GetDiskFreeSpace` and `GetDiskFreeSpaceEx` functions to determine how the different Windows systems allocate file space sparsely. For instance, create a new file, set the file pointer to a large value, set the file size, and investigate the free space using `GetDiskFreeSpace`. The same Windows function can also be used to determine how the disk is configured into sectors and clusters. Determine whether the newly allocated file space is initialized. `FreeSpace.c`, provided on the book's Web site, is the solution. Compare the results for Windows NT and even 9x. It is also interesting to investigate how to make a file be sparse.

3–2. What happens if you attempt to set a file's length to a size larger than the disk? Does Windows fail gracefully?

3–3. Modify the `tail.c` program provided on the Web site so that it does not use `SetFilePointer`; use overlapped structures.

3–4. Examine the "number of links" field obtained using the function `GetFileInformationByHandle`. Is its value always 1? Are the answers different for the NTFS and FAT file systems? Do the link counts appear to count hard links and links from parent directories and subdirectories, as they do in UNIX? Does Windows open the directory as a file to get a handle before using this function? What about the shortcuts supported by the user interface?

3–5. Program 3–2 checks for "." and ".." to detect the names of the current and parent directories. What happens if there are actual files with these names? Can files have these names?

3–6. Does Program 3–2 list local times or UCTs? If necessary, modify the program to give the results in local time.

3–7. Enhance Program 3–2 so that it also lists the "." and ".." (current and parent) directories (the complete program is on the Web site). Also, add options to display the file creation and last access times along with the last write time.

3–8. Create a file deletion command, `rm`, by modifying the `ProcessItem` function in Program 3–2. A solution is on the Web site.

3–9. Enhance the file copy command, `cp`, from Chapter 2 so that it will copy files to a target directory. Further extensions allow for recursive copying (`-r` option) and for preserving the modification time of the copied files (`-p` option). Implementing the recursive copy option will require that you create new directories.

3–10. Write an `mv` command, similar to the UNIX command of the same name, that will move a complete directory. One significant consideration is whether the target is on a different drive from that of the source file or directory. If it is, copy the file(s); otherwise, use `MoveFile` or `MoveFileEx`.

3–11. Enhance Program 3–3 (`touch`) so that the new file time is specified on the command line. The UNIX command allows the time stamp to appear (optionally) after the normal options and before the file names. The format for the time is `MMddhhmm [yy]`, where the uppercase `MM` is the month and `mm` is for minutes. A two-digit year is not sufficient, so require a four-digit year.

3–12. Program 3–1 is written to work with large NTFS file systems. If you have sufficient free disk space, test this program with a very large file (length greater than 4GB). Verify that the 64-bit arithmetic is correct. It is not recommended that you perform this exercise on a network drive without permission from the network administrator. And don't forget to delete the test file on completion.

3–13. Write a program that locks a specified file and holds the lock for a long period of time (you may find the `Sleep` function useful). While the lock is held, try to access the file (use a text file) with an editor. What happens? Is the file properly locked? Alternatively, write a program that will prompt the user to specify a lock on a test file. Two instances of the program can be run in separate windows to verify that file locking works as described. `TestLock.c` on the Web site is a solution to this exercise.

3–14. Investigate the Windows file time representation in `FILETIME`. It uses 64 bits to count the elapsed number of 100-nanosecond units from January 1, 1601. When will the time expire? When will the UNIX file time representation expire?

3–15. Write an interactive utility that will prompt the user for a registry key name and a value name. Display the current value and prompt the user for a new value.

3–16. This chapter, along with most other chapters, describes the most important functions. There are often other functions that may be useful. The on-line help pages for each function provide links to related functions. Examine several, such as `FindFirstFileEx`, `ReplaceFile`, `SearchPath`, and `WriteFileGather`. Some of these functions are not available in all NT5 versions.

CHAPTER

4 | Exception Handling

Windows Structured Exception Handling (SEH) is the principal focus of this chapter, which also describes console control handlers and vectored exception handling.

SEH provides a robust mechanism that allows applications to respond to unexpected events, such as addressing exceptions, arithmetic faults, and system errors. SEH also allows a program to exit from anywhere in a code block and automatically perform programmer-specified processing and error recovery. SEH ensures that the program will be able to free resources and perform other cleanup processing before the block, thread, or process terminates either under program control or because of an unexpected exception. Furthermore, SEH can be added easily to existing code, often simplifying program logic.

SEH will prove to be useful in the examples and also will allow extension of the `ReportError` error-processing function introduced in Chapter 2. SEH is usually confined to C programs. C++, C#, and other languages have very similar mechanisms, however, and these mechanisms build on the SEH facilities presented here.

Console control handlers, also described in this chapter, allow a program to detect external signals such as a `Ctrl-c` from the console or the user logging off or shutting down the system. These signals also provide a limited form of process-to-process signaling.

The final topic is vectored exception handling, which requires Windows XP or 2003 Server. This feature allows the user to specify functions to be executed directly when an exception occurs, and the functions are executed before SEH is invoked.

Exceptions and Their Handlers

Without some form of exception handling, an unintended program exception, such as dereferencing a `NULL` pointer or division by zero, will terminate a program immediately. This could be a problem, for example, if the program has created a temporary file that should be deleted before program termination. SEH allows specification of a code block, or *exception handler*, that can delete the temporary file when an exception occurs.

SEH is supported through a combination of Windows functions, language support provided by the compiler, and run-time support. The exact language support may vary; the examples here were all developed for Microsoft C.

Try and Except Blocks

Start by determining which code blocks to monitor and provide them with exception handlers, as described next. It is possible to monitor an entire function or to have separate exception handlers for different code blocks and functions.

A code block is a good candidate for an exception handler in situations that include the following.

- Detectable errors, including system call errors, might occur, and you need to recover from the error rather than terminate the program.

- Pointers are used extensively, so there is a possibility of dereferencing pointers that have not been properly initialized.

- There is extensive array manipulation, because it is possible for array indices to go out of bounds.

- The code performs floating-point arithmetic, and there is concern with zero divides, imprecise results, and overflows.

- The code calls a function that might generate an exception, either intentionally or because the function has not been well tested.

In the examples in this chapter and throughout the book, once you have decided to monitor a block, create the try and except blocks as follows:

```
__try {
    /* Block of monitored code */
}
__except (filter_expression) {
    /* Exception handling block */
}
```

Notice that __try and __except are keywords recognized by the compiler.

The try block is part of normal application code. If an exception occurs in the block, the OS transfers control to the exception handler, which is the code in the block associated with the __except clause. The actions that follow are determined by the value of the *filter_expression*.

Notice that the exception might occur within a block embedded in the try block, in which case the run-time support "unwinds" the stack to find the exception handler and then gives control to the handler. The same thing happens when an exception occurs within a function called within a try block.

Figure 4–1 shows how an exception handler is located on the stack when an exception occurs. Once the exception handler block completes, control passes to the next statement after the exception block unless there is some other control flow statement in the handler.

Filter Expressions and Their Values

The *filter_expression* in the __except clause is evaluated immediately after the exception occurs. The expression is usually a literal constant, a call to a *filter function*, or a conditional expression. In all cases, the expression should return one of three values.

1. EXCEPTION_EXECUTE_HANDLER—The system executes the except block as shown in Figure 4–1 (see Program 4–1). This is the normal case.

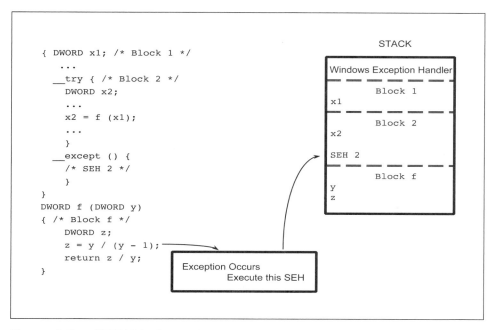

Figure 4-1   SEH, Blocks, and Functions

2. EXCEPTION_CONTINUE_SEARCH—The system ignores the exception handler and searches for an exception handler in the enclosing block, continuing until it finds a handler.

3. EXCEPTION_CONTINUE_EXECUTION—The system immediately returns control to the point at which the exception occurred. It is not possible to continue after some exceptions, and another exception is generated immediately if the program attempts to do so.

Here is a simple example using an exception handler to delete a temporary file if an exception occurs in the loop body. Notice that the __try clause can be applied to any block, including the block associated with a while, if, or other flow control statement. In this example, the temporary file is deleted and the handle is closed, in the case of any exception, and then the loop iteration continues.

```
GetTempFileName (TempFile, ...);
while (...) __try {
    hFile = CreateFile (TempFile, ..., OPEN_ALWAYS, ...);
    SetFilePointer (hFile, 0, NULL, FILE_END);
    ...
    WriteFile (hFile, ...);
    i = *p; /* An addressing exception could occur. */
    ...
    CloseHandle (hFile);
}
__except (EXCEPTION_EXECUTE_HANDLER) {
    CloseHandle (hFile);
    DeleteFile (TempFile);
    /* The loop will now execute the next iteration .*/
}
/* Control passes here after normal loop termination.
   The file handle is always closed and the temp file
   will not exist if an exception occurred. */
```

The logic of this code fragment is as follows.

- Each loop iteration appends new data to the end of the temporary file.

- If an exception occurs in any loop iteration, all data accumulated in the temporary file is deleted, and the next iteration, if any, starts to accumulate data in the temporary file again.

- If an exception occurs on the last iteration, the file will not exist. In any case, the file will contain all data generated since the last exception.

- The example shows just one location where an exception could occur, although the exception could occur anywhere within the loop body.

- The file handle is assured of being closed when exiting the loop or starting a new loop iteration.

Exception Codes

The except block or the filter expression can determine the exact exception using this function:

```
DWORD GetExceptionCode (VOID)
```

The exception code must be obtained immediately after an exception. Therefore, the filter function itself cannot call GetExceptionCode (the compiler enforces this restriction). A common usage is to invoke it in the filter expression, as in the following example, where the exception code is the argument to a user-supplied filter function.

```
__except (MyFilter (GetExceptionCode ())) {
}
```

In this situation, the filter function determines and returns the filter expression value, which must be one of the three values enumerated earlier. The function can use the exception code to determine the function value; for example, the filter may decide to pass floating-point exceptions to an outer handler (by returning EXCEPTION_CONTINUE_SEARCH) and to handle a memory access violation in the current handler (by returning EXCEPTION_EXECUTE_HANDLER).

A large number of possible exception code values can be returned by GetExceptionCode, and the codes are in several categories.

- Program violations such as the following:

  - EXCEPTION_ACCESS_VIOLATION—An attempt to read or write a virtual address for which the process does not have access.

  - EXCEPTION_DATATYPE_MISALIGNMENT—Many processors insist, for example, that DWORDs be aligned on four-byte boundaries.

- — EXCEPTION_NONCONTINUABLE_EXECUTION—The filter expression was EXCEPTION_CONTINUE_EXECUTION, but it is not possible to continue after the exception that occurred.

- Exceptions raised by the memory allocation functions—HeapAlloc and HeapCreate—if they use the HEAP_GENERATE_EXCEPTIONS flag (see Chapter 5). The value will be either STATUS_NO_MEMORY or EXCEPTION_ACCESS_VIOLATION.

- A user-defined exception code generated by the RaiseException function, which is explained in the User-Generated Exceptions subsection.

- A large variety of arithmetic (especially floating-point) codes such as EXCEPTION_INT_DIVIDE_BY_ZERO and EXCEPTION_FLT_OVERFLOW.

- Exceptions used by debuggers, such as EXCEPTION_BREAKPOINT and EXCEPTION_SINGLE_STEP.

The GetExceptionInformation function is an alternative function, callable only from within the filter expression, which returns additional information, some of which is processor-specific.

```
LPEXCEPTION_POINTERS GetExceptionInformation (VOID)
```

The EXCEPTION_POINTERS structure contains both processor-specific and processor-independent information organized into two other structures.

```
typedef struct _EXCEPTION_POINTERS {
    PEXCEPTION_RECORD ExceptionRecord;
    PCONTEXT ContextRecord;
} EXCEPTION_POINTERS;
```

EXCEPTION_RECORD contains a member for the ExceptionCode, with the same set of values as returned by GetExceptionCode. The ExceptionFlags member of the EXCEPTION_RECORD is either 0 or EXCEPTION_NONCONTINUABLE, which allows the filter function to determine that it should not attempt to continue execution. Other data members include a virtual memory address, ExceptionAddress, and a parameter array, ExceptionInformation. In the case of `EXCEPTION_ACCESS_VIOLATION`, the first element indicates whether the violation was a memory write (1) or read (0). The second element is the virtual memory address.

`ContextRecord`, the second `EXCEPTION_POINTERS` member, contains processor-specific information. There are different structures for each type of processor, and the structure can be found in `<winnt.h>`.

Summary: Exception Handling Sequence

Figure 4–2 shows the sequence of events that takes place when an exception occurs. The code is shown on the left side, and the circled numbers on the right show the steps carried out by the language run-time support. The steps are as follows.

1. The exception occurs, in this case a division by zero.

2. Control transfers to the exception handler, where the filter expression is evaluated. `GetExceptionCode` is called first, and its return value is the argument to the function `Filter`.

```
_try {
        ...
        i = j / 0;
        ...
}
_except (Filter (GetExceptionCode ())) {
        ...
}
        ...
DWORD Filter (DWORD ExCode)
{
        switch (ExCode) {
        ...
        case EXCEPTION_INT_DIVIDE_BY_ZERO:
        ...
        return EXCEPTION_EXECUTE_HANDLER;
        case ...

        }
}
```

Figure 4–2   Exception Handling Sequence

3. The filter function bases its actions on the exception code value.

4. The exception code is EXCEPTION_INT_DIVIDE_BY_ZERO in this case.

5. The filter function determines that the exception handler should be executed, so the return value is EXCEPTION_EXECUTE_HANDLER.

6. The exception handler, which is the code associated with the __except clause, executes.

7. Control passes out of the try-except block.

Floating-Point Exceptions

The exception codes include seven distinct codes for floating-point exceptions. These exceptions are disabled initially and will not occur without first setting the processor-independent floating-point mask with the _controlfp function. There are specific exceptions for underflow, overflow, division by zero, inexact results, and so on, as shown in a later code fragment. Turn the mask bit *off* to enable the particular exception.

```
DWORD _controlfp (DWORD new, DWORD mask)
```

The actual value of the floating-point mask is determined by its current value (current_mask) and the two arguments as follows:

```
(current_mask & ~mask) | (new & mask)
```

The function sets the bits specified by new that are enabled by mask. All bits *not* in mask are unaltered. The floating-point mask also controls precision, rounding, and infinity values, so it is important not to alter these settings when you're enabling floating-point exceptions.

The return value will be the actual setting. Thus, if both argument values are 0, the return value is the current mask setting, which can be used later to restore the mask. On the other hand, if mask is 0xFFFFFFFF, then the register is set to new, so that, for example, an old value can be restored.

Normally, to enable the floating-point exceptions, use the floating-point exception mask value, MCW_EM, as shown in the following example. Notice also that, when a floating-point exception is processed, the exception must be cleared using the _clearfp function.

```
#include <float.h>
DWORD FPOld, FPNew; /* Old and new mask values. */
    ...
FPOld = _controlfp (0, 0); /* Saved old mask. */
/* Specify six exceptions to be enabled. */
    FPNew = FPOld & ~(EM_OVERFLOW | EM_UNDERFLOW
    | EM_INEXACT | EM_ZERODIVIDE | EM_DENORMAL | EM_INVALID);
/* Set new control mask. MCW_EM combines the six
    exceptions in the previous statement. */
_controlfp (FPNew, MCW_EM);
while (...) __try { /* Perform FP calculations. */
    ... /* An FP exception could occur here. */
}
__except (EXCEPTION_EXECUTE_HANDLER) {
    ... /* Process the FP exception. */
    _clearfp (); /* Clear the exception. */
    _controlfp (FPOld, 0xFFFFFFFF); /* Restore mask. */
}
```

This example enables all possible floating-point exceptions except for the floating-point stack overflow, EXCEPTION_FLT_STACK_CHECK. Alternatively, enable specific exceptions by using only selected exception masks, such as EM_OVERFLOW. Program 4–3 uses similar code in the context of a larger example.

Errors and Exceptions

An error can be thought of as a situation that could occur occasionally in known locations. System call errors, for example, should be detected and reported immediately by logic in the code. Thus, programmers normally include an explicit test to see, for instance, whether a file read operation has failed. The ReportError function was developed in Chapter 2 to diagnose and respond to errors.

An exception, on the other hand, could occur nearly anywhere, and it is not possible or practical to test for an exception. Division by zero and memory access violations are examples.

Nonetheless, the distinction is sometimes blurred. Windows will, optionally, generate exceptions during memory allocation using the HeapAlloc and HeapCreate functions if memory is insufficient. This is described in Chapter 5. Programs can also raise their own exceptions with programmer-defined exception codes using the RaiseException function, as described next.

Exception handlers provide a convenient mechanism for exiting from inner blocks or functions under program control without resorting to a goto or longjmp to transfer control. This capability is particularly important if the block has accessed resources, such as open files, memory, or synchronization objects, because the handler can release them. It is also possible to continue program execution after the exception handler, rather than terminate the program. Additionally, a program can restore system state, such as the floating-point mask, on exiting from a block. Many examples use handlers in this way.

User-Generated Exceptions

It is possible to raise an exception at any point during program execution using the `RaiseException` function. In this way, your program can detect an error and treat it as an exception.

```
VOID RaiseException (
    DWORD dwExceptionCode,
    DWORD dwExceptionFlags,
    DWORD cArguments,
    CONST DWORD *lpArguments)
```

Parameters

`dwExceptionCode` is the user-defined code. Do not use bit 28, which is reserved for the system. The error code is encoded in bits 27–0 (all except the most significant hex digit). Bit 29 should be set to indicate a "customer" (not Microsoft) exception. Bits 31–30 encode the severity as follows, where the resulting lead exception code hex digit is shown with bit 29 set.

- 0—Success (lead exception code hex digit is 2).

- 1—Informational (lead exception code hex digit is 6).

- 2—Warning (lead exception code hex digit is A).

- 3—Error (lead exception code hex digit is E).

`dwExceptionFlags` is normally set to 0, but setting the value to `EXCEPTION_NONCONTINUABLE` indicates that the filter expression should not generate `EXCEPTION_CONTINUE_EXECUTION`; doing so will cause an immediate `EXCEPTION_NONCONTINUABLE_EXCEPTION` exception.

`lpArguments`, if not `NULL`, points to an array of size `cArguments` (the third parameter) containing 32-bit values to be passed to the filter expression. There is a maximum number, EXCEPTION_MAXIMUM_PARAMETERS, which is currently defined to be 15. This structure should be accessed using GetException-Information.

Note that it is not possible to raise an exception in another process. Under very limited circumstances, however, console control handlers, described at the end of this chapter and in Chapter 6, can be used for this purpose.

Example: Treating Errors as Exceptions

Previous examples use ReportError to process system call and other errors. The function terminates the process when the programmer indicates that the error is fatal. This approach, however, prevents an orderly shutdown, and it also prevents program continuation after recovering from an error. For example, the program may have created temporary files that should be deleted, or the program may simply proceed to do other work after abandoning the failed task. ReportError has other limitations, including the following.

- A fatal error shuts down the entire process when only a single thread (Chapter 7) should terminate.

- You may wish to continue program execution rather than terminate the process.

- Synchronization resources (Chapter 8), such as mutexes, will not be released in many circumstances.

Open handles will be closed by a terminating process (but not by a terminating thread), but it is necessary to address the other deficiencies.

The solution is to write a new function, ReportException. This function invokes ReportError (developed in Chapter 2) with a nonfatal code in order to generate the error message. Next, on a fatal error, it will raise an exception. The system will use an exception handler from the calling try block, so the exception may not actually be fatal if the handler allows the program to recover. Essentially, ReportException augments normal defensive programming techniques, previously limited to ReportError. Once an error is detected, the exception handler allows the program to recover and continue after the error. Program 4–2 illustrates this capability.

Program 4–1 shows the function. It is in the same source module as Report-Error, so the definitions and include files are omitted.

Program 4-1   `ReportException`: Exception Reporting Function

```
/* Extension of ReportError to generate a user-exception
   code rather than terminating the process. */

VOID ReportException (LPCTSTR UserMessage, DWORD ExceptionCode)
          /* Report as a nonfatal error. */
{
   ReportError (UserMessage, 0, TRUE);
          /* If fatal, raise an exception. */
   if (ExceptionCode != 0)
      RaiseException (
        (0x0FFFFFFF & ExceptionCode) | 0xE0000000, 0, 0, NULL);
   return;
}
```

`ReportException` is used in several subsequent examples.

The UNIX signal model is significantly different from SEH. Signals can be missed or ignored, and the flow is different. Nonetheless, there are points of comparison.

UNIX signal handling is largely supported through the C library, which is also available in a limited implementation under Windows. In many cases, Windows programs can use console control handlers, which are described near the end of this chapter, in place of signals.

Some signals correspond to Windows exceptions.

Here is the limited signal-to-exception correspondence:

- `SIGILL`—`EXCEPTION_PRIV_INSTRUCTION`

- `SIGSEGV`—`EXCEPTION_ACCESS_VIOLATION`

- `SIGFPE`—Seven distinct floating-point exceptions, such as `EXCEPTION_FLT_DIVIDE_BY_ZERO`

- `SIGUSR1` and `SIGUSR2`—User-defined exceptions

The C library `raise` function corresponds to `RaiseException`.

Windows will not generate `SIGILL`, `SIGSEGV`, or `SIGTERM`, although `raise` can generate one of them. Windows does not support `SIGINT`.

The UNIX `kill` function (`kill` is not in the Standard C library), which can send a signal to another process, is comparable to the Windows function `Generate-ConsoleCtrlEvent` (Chapter 6). In the limited case of `SIGKILL`, Windows has `TerminateProcess` and `TerminateThread`, allowing one process (or thread) to "kill" another, although these functions should be used with care (see Chapters 6 and 7).

Termination Handlers

A termination handler serves much the same purpose as an exception handler, but it is executed when a thread leaves a block as a result of normal program flow as well as when an exception occurs. On the other hand, a termination handler cannot diagnose an exception.

Construct a termination handler using the __finally keyword in a try-finally statement. The structure is the same as for a try-except statement, but there is no filter expression. Termination handlers, like exception handlers, are a convenient way to close handles, release resources, restore masks, and otherwise restore the process to a known state when leaving a block. For example, a program may execute return statements in the middle of a block, and the termination handler can perform the cleanup work. In this way, there is no need to include the cleanup code in the code block itself, nor is there a need for a goto statement to reach the cleanup code.

```
__try {
    /* Code block. */
}
__finally {
    /* Termination handler (finally block). */
}
```

Leaving the Try Block

The termination handler is executed whenever the control flow leaves the try block for any of the following reasons:

- Reaching the end of the try block and "falling through" to the termination handler

- Execution of one of the following statements in such a way as to leave the block:

    return

    break

    goto[1]

---

[1] It may be a matter of taste, either individual or organizational, but many programmers never use the goto statement and try to avoid break, except with the switch statement and sometimes in loops, and with continue. Reasonable people continue to differ on this subject. The termination and exception handlers can perform many of the tasks that you might want to perform with a goto to a labeled statement.

```
longjmp
continue
__leave²
```

- An exception

Abnormal Termination

Termination for any reason other than reaching the end of the try block and falling through or performing a __leave statement is considered an abnormal termination. The effect of __leave is to transfer to the end of the __try block and fall through, which is more efficient than a goto because there is no stack unwind required. Within the termination handler, use this function to determine how the try block terminated.

```
BOOL AbnormalTermination (VOID)
```

The return value will be TRUE for an abnormal termination or FALSE for a normal termination.

Note: The termination would be abnormal even if, for example, a return statement were the last statement in the try block.

Executing and Leaving the Termination Handler

The termination handler, or __finally block, is executed in the context of the block or function that it monitors. Control can pass from the end of the termination handler to the next statement. Alternatively, the termination handler can execute a flow control statement (return, break, continue, goto, longjmp, or __leave). Leaving the handler because of an exception is another possibility.

Combining Finally and Except Blocks

A single try block must have a single finally or except block; it cannot have both. Therefore, the following code would cause a compile error.

---

[2] This statement is specific to the Microsoft C compiler and is an efficient way to leave a try-finally block without an abnormal termination.

```
__try {
    /* Block of monitored code. */
}
__except (filter_expression) {
    /* Except block. */
}
__finally {
    /* Do not do this! It will not compile. */
}
```

It is possible, however, to embed one block within another, a technique that is frequently useful. The following code is valid and ensures that the temporary file is deleted if the loop exits under program control or because of an exception. This technique is also useful to ensure that file locks are released, as will be shown in Program 4–2. There is also an inner try-except block where some floating-point processing is performed.

```
__try { /* Outer try-except block. */
    while (...) __try { /* Inner try-finally block. */
        hFile = CreateFile (TempFile, ...);
        if (...) __try { /* Inner try-except block. */
        /* Enable FP exceptions. Perform computations. */
        ...
        }
        __except (EXCEPTION_EXECUTE_HANDLER) {
            ... /* Process FP exception. */ _clearfp ();
        }
        ... /* Non-FP processing. /*
    }
    __finally { /* End of while loop. */
    /* Executed on EVERY loop iteration. */
        CloseHandle (hFile); DeleteFile (TempFile);
    }
}
__except (filter-expression) {
    /* Exception handler. */
}
```

Global and Local Unwinds

Exceptions and abnormal terminations will cause a *global stack unwind* to search for a handler, as shown earlier in Figure 4–1.

For example, suppose an exception occurs in the monitored block of the example at the end of the preceding section before the floating-point exceptions are enabled. The termination handler will be executed first, followed by the exception handler. There might be numerous termination handlers on the stack before the exception handler is located.

Recall that the stack structure is dynamic, as shown in Figure 4–1, and that it contains, among other things, the exception and termination handlers. The actual contents at any time depend on:

- The *static* structure of the program's blocks

- The *dynamic* structure of the program as reflected in the sequence of open function calls

Termination Handlers: Process and Thread Termination

Termination handlers do not execute if a process or thread terminates, whether the process or thread terminates itself by using `ExitProcess` or `ExitThread`, or whether the termination is external, caused by a call to `TerminateProcess` or `TerminateThread` from elsewhere. Therefore, a process or thread should not execute one of these functions inside a try-except or try-finally block.

Notice also that the C library `exit` function or a return from a `main` function will exit the process.

SEH and C++ Exception Handling

C++ exception handling uses the keywords `catch` and `throw` and is implemented using SEH. Nonetheless, C++ exception handling and SEH are distinct. They should be mixed with care because the user-written and C++-generated exception handlers may interfere with expected operation. For example, an __except handler may be on the stack and catch a C++ exception so that the C++ handler will never receive the exception. The converse is also possible, with a C++ handler catching, for example, an SEH exception generated with `RaiseException`. The Microsoft documentation recommends that Windows exception handlers not be used in C++ programs at all but instead that C++ exception handling be used exclusively.

Furthermore, a Windows exception or termination handler will not call destructors to destroy C++ object instances.

Example: Using Termination Handlers to Improve Program Quality

Termination and exception handlers allow you to make your program more robust by both simplifying recovery from errors and exceptions and helping to ensure that resources and file locks are freed at critical junctures.

Program 4–2, toupper, illustrates these points, using ideas from the preceding code fragments. toupper processes multiple files, as specified on the command line, rewriting them so that all letters are in uppercase. Converted files are named by prefixing UC_ to the original file name, and the program "specification" states that an existing file should not be overridden. File conversion is performed in memory, so a large buffer (sufficient for the entire file) is allocated for each file. Furthermore, both the input and output files are locked to ensure that no other process can modify either file during processing and that the new output file is an accurate transformation of the input file. Thus, there are multiple possible failure points for each file that is processed, but the program must defend against all such errors and then recover and attempt to process all the remaining files named on the command line. Program 4–2 achieves this and ensures that the files are unlocked in all cases without resorting to the elaborate control flow methods that would be necessary without SEH. More extensive comments are included in the code from the book's Web site.

Program 4–2   toupper: File Processing with Error Recovery

```
/* Chapter 4. toupper command. */
/* Convert one or more files, changing all letters to uppercase.
   The output file will be the same name as the input file, except
   a UC_ prefix will be attached to the file name. */

#include "EvryThng.h"

int _tmain (DWORD argc, LPTSTR argv [])
{
    HANDLE hIn = INVALID_HANDLE_VALUE, hOut = INVALID_HANDLE_VALUE;
    DWORD FileSize, nXfer, iFile, j;
    CHAR OutFileName [256] = "", *pBuffer = NULL;
    OVERLAPPED ov == {0, 0, 0, 0, NULL}; /* Used for file locks. */

    if (argc <= 1)
        ReportError (_T ("Usage: toupper files"), 1, FALSE);
                /* Process all files on the command line. */
    for (iFile = 1; iFile < argc; iFile++) __try { /* Excptn block. */
        /* All file handles are invalid, pBuffer == NULL, and
           OutFileName is empty. This is ensured by the handlers. */
        _stprintf (OutFileName, "UC_%s", argv [iFile]);
```

```
__try { /* Inner try-finally block. */
    /* An error at any step will raise an exception, */
    /* and the next file will be processed after cleanup. */
    /* Amount of cleanup depends on where the error occurs. */
    /* Create the output file (fail if file exists). */
    hIn = CreateFile (argv [iFile], GENERIC_READ, 0,
            NULL, OPEN_EXISTING, 0, NULL);
    if (hIn == INVALID_HANDLE_VALUE)
            ReportException (argv [iFile], 1);
    FileSize = GetFileSize (hIn, NULL);
    hOut = CreateFile (OutFileName,
            GENERIC_READ | GENERIC_WRITE, 0, NULL,
            CREATE_NEW, 0, NULL);
    if (hOut == INVALID_HANDLE_VALUE)
            ReportException (OutFileName, 1);
    /* Allocate memory for the file contents. */
    pBuffer = malloc (FileSize);
    if (pBuffer == NULL)
        ReportException (_T ("Memory allocation error"), 1);
    /* Lock both files to ensure integrity of the copy. */
    if (!LockFileEx (hIn, LOCKFILE_FAIL_IMMEDIATELY, 0,
            FileSize, 0, &ov)
        ReportException (_T ("Input file lock error"), 1);
    if (!LockFileEx (hOut,
            LOCKFILE_EXCLUSIVE_LOCK | LOCKFILE_FAIL_IMMEDIATELY,
            0, FileSize, 0, &ov)
        ReportException (_T ("Output file lock error"), 1);

    /* Read data, convert, and write to the output file. */
    /* Free resources on completion or error; */
    /* process next file. */
    if (!ReadFile (hIn, pBuffer, FileSize, &nXfer, NULL))
        ReportException (_T ("ReadFile error"), 1);
    for (j = 0; j < FileSize; j++) /* Convert data. */
        if (isalpha (pBuffer [j]))
            pBuffer [j] = toupper (pBuffer [j]);
    if (!WriteFile (hOut, pBuffer, FileSize, &nXfer, NULL))
        ReportException (_T ("WriteFile error"), 1);

} __finally { /* Locks are released, file handles closed, */
    /* memory freed, and handles and pointer reinitialized. */
    if (pBuffer != NULL) free (pBuffer); pBuffer = NULL;
    if (hIn != INVALID_HANDLE_VALUE) {
        UnlockFileEx (hIn, 0, FileSize, 0, &ov);
        CloseHandle (hIn);
        hIn = INVALID_HANDLE_VALUE;
    }
    if (hOut != INVALID_HANDLE_VALUE) {
        UnlockFileEx (hOut, 0, FileSize, 0, &ov);
        CloseHandle (hOut);
```

```
                hOut = INVALID_HANDLE_VALUE;
            }
            _tcscpy (OutFileName, _T (""));
        }
    }   /* End of main file processing loop and try block. */
        /* This exception handler applies to the loop body. */

    __except (EXCEPTION_EXECUTE_HANDLER) {
        _tprintf (_T ("Error processing file %s\n"), argv [iFile]);
        DeleteFile (OutFileName);
    }
    _tprintf (_T ("All files converted, except as noted above\n"));
    return 0;
}
```

Example: Using a Filter Function

Program 4–3 is a skeleton program that illustrates exception and termination handling with a filter function. This example prompts the user to specify the exception type and then proceeds to generate an exception. The filter function disposes of the different exception types in various ways; the selections here are arbitrary and are intended simply to illustrate the possibilities. In particular, the program diagnoses memory access violations, giving the virtual address of the reference.

The __finally block restores the state of the floating-point mask. Restoring state, as done here, is clearly not important when the process is about to terminate, but it is important later when a thread is terminated. In general, a process should still restore system resources by, for example, deleting temporary files and releasing synchronization resources (Chapter 8) and file locks (Chapters 3 and 6). The filter function is shown in Program 4–4.

This example does not illustrate memory allocation exceptions; they will be used extensively starting in Chapter 5.

Program 4–3   Excption: Processing Exceptions and Termination

```
#include "EvryThng.h"
#include <float.h>

DWORD Filter (LPEXCEPTION_POINTERS, LPDWORD);
double x = 1.0, y = 0.0;

int _tmain (int argc, LPTSTR argv [])
{
    DWORD ECatgry, i = 0, ix, iy = 0;
```

```
LPDWORD pNull = NULL;
BOOL Done = FALSE;
DWORD FPOld, FPNew;
FPOld = _controlfp (0, 0); /* Save old control mask. */
                /* Enable floating-point exceptions. */
FPNew = FPOld & ~(EM_OVERFLOW | EM_UNDERFLOW | EM_INEXACT
        | EM_ZERODIVIDE | EM_DENORMAL | EM_INVALID);
_controlfp (FPNew, MCW_EM);

while (!Done) _try { /* Try-finally. */
    _tprintf (_T ("Enter exception type: "));
    _tprintf (_T
        (" 1: Mem, 2: Int, 3: Flt 4: User 5: __leave "));
    _tscanf (_T ("%d"), &i);
    __try { /* Try-except block. */
        switch (i) {
        case 1: /* Memory reference. */
            ix = *pNull; *pNull = 5; break;
        case 2: /* Integer arithmetic. */
            ix = ix / iy; break;
        case 3: /* Floating-point exception. */
            x = x / y;
            _tprintf (_T ("x = %20e\n"), x); break;
        case 4: /* User-generated exception. */
            ReportException (_T ("User exception"), 1); break;
        case 5: /* Use the _leave statement to terminate. */
            __leave;
        default: Done = TRUE;
        }
    } /* End of inner __try. */

    __except (Filter (GetExceptionInformation (), &ECatgry))
    {
        switch (ECatgry) {
            case 0:
                _tprintf (_T ("Unknown Exception\n")); break;
            case 1:
                _tprintf (_T ("Memory Ref Exception\n")); continue;
            case 2:
                _tprintf (_T ("Integer Exception\n")); break;
            case 3:
                _tprintf (_T ("Floating-Point Exception\n"));
                _clearfp (); break;
            case 10:
                _tprintf (_T ("User Exception\n")); break;
            default:
                _tprintf ( _T ("Unknown Exception\n")); break;
        } /* End of switch statement. */

        _tprintf (_T ("End of handler\n"));
```

```
    } /* End of try-except block. */
} /* End of While loop -- the termination handler is below. */

__finally { /* This is part of the while loop. */
    _tprintf (_T ("Abnormal Termination?: %d\n"),
        AbnormalTermination ());
}
_controlfp (FPOld, 0xFFFFFFFF); /* Restore old FP mask.*/
return 0;
}
```

Program 4–4 shows the filter function used in Program 4–3. This function simply checks and categorizes the various possible exception code values. The code on the book's Web site checks every possible value; here the function tests only for a few that are relevant to the test program.

Program 4–4 The Filter Function

```
static DWORD Filter (LPEXCEPTION_POINTERS pExP, LPDWORD ECatgry)
/* Categorize the exception and decide action. */
{
    DWORD ExCode, ReadWrite, VirtAddr;
    ExCode = pExP->ExceptionRecord->ExceptionCode;
    _tprintf (_T ("Filter. ExCode: %x\n"), ExCode);
    if ((0x20000000 & ExCode) != 0) { /* User exception. */
        *ECatgry = 10;
        return EXCEPTION_EXECUTE_HANDLER;
    }

    switch (ExCode) {
        case EXCEPTION_ACCESS_VIOLATION:
            ReadWrite = /* Was it a read or a write? */
                    pExP->ExceptionRecord->ExceptionInformation [0];
            VirtAddr = /* Virtual address of the violation. */
                    pExP->ExceptionRecord->ExceptionInformation [1];
            _tprintf (
            _T ("Access Violation. Read/Write: %d. Address: %x\n"),
                    ReadWrite, VirtAddr);
            *ECatgry = 1;
            return EXCEPTION_EXECUTE_HANDLER;
        case EXCEPTION_INT_DIVIDE_BY_ZERO:
        case EXCEPTION_INT_OVERFLOW:
            *ECatgry = 2;
            return EXCEPTION_EXECUTE_HANDLER;
        case EXCEPTION_FLT_DIVIDE_BY_ZERO:
```

```
         case EXCEPTION_FLT_OVERFLOW:
            _tprintf (_T ("Flt Exception - large result.\n"));
            *ECatgry = 3;
            _clearfp ();
            return (DWORD) EXCEPTION_EXECUTE_HANDLER;

         default:
            *ECatgry = 0;
            return EXCEPTION_CONTINUE_SEARCH;
   }
}
```

Console Control Handlers

Exception handlers can respond to a variety of events, but they do not detect situations such as the user logging off or entering a Ctrl-c from the keyboard to stop a program. Console control handlers are required to detect such events.

The function SetConsoleCtrlHandler allows one or more specified functions to be executed on receipt of a Ctrl-c, Ctrl-break, or one of three other console-related signals. The GenerateConsoleCtrlEvent function, described in Chapter 6, also generates these signals, and the signals can be sent to other processes that are sharing the same console. The handlers are user-specified Boolean functions that take a DWORD argument identifying the actual signal.

Multiple handlers can be associated with a signal, and handlers can be removed as well as added. Here is the function used to add or delete a handler.

```
BOOL SetConsoleCtrlHandler (
    PHANDLER_ROUTINE HandlerRoutine,
    BOOL Add)
```

The handler routine is added if the Add flag is TRUE; otherwise, it is deleted from the list of console control routines. Notice that the actual signal is not specified. The handler must test to see which signal was received.

The actual handler routine returns a Boolean value and takes a single DWORD parameter that identifies the actual signal. The handler name in the definition is a placeholder; the programmer specifies the name.

Here are some other considerations when using console control handlers.

- If the *HandlerRoutine* parameter is NULL and Add is TRUE, Ctrl-c signals will be ignored.

- The ENABLE_PROCESSED_INPUT flag on SetConsoleMode (Chapter 2) will cause Ctrl-c to be treated as keyboard input rather than as a signal.

- The handler routine actually executes as an *independent thread* (see Chapter 7) within the process. The normal program will continue to operate, as shown in the next example.

- Raising an exception in the handler *will not* cause an exception in the thread that was interrupted because exceptions apply to threads, not to an entire process. If you wish to communicate with the interrupted thread, use a variable, as in the next example, or a synchronization method (Chapter 8).

There is one other important distinction between exceptions and signals. A signal applies to the entire process, whereas an exception applies only to the thread executing the code where the exception occurs.

```
BOOL HandlerRoutine (DWORD dwCtrlType)
```

dwCtrlType identifies the actual signal (or *event*) and can take on one of the following five values.

1. CTRL_C_EVENT indicates that the Ctrl-c sequence was entered from the keyboard.

2. CTRL_CLOSE_EVENT indicates that the console window is being closed.

3. CTRL_BREAK_EVENT indicates the Ctrl-break signal.

4. CTRL_LOGOFF_EVENT indicates that the user is logging off.

5. CTRL_SHUTDOWN_EVENT indicates that the system is shutting down.

The signal handler can perform cleanup operations just as an exception or termination handler would. The signal handler should return TRUE to indicate that the function handled the signal. If the signal handler returns FALSE, the next handler function in the list is executed. The signal handlers are executed in the reverse order from the way they were set, so that the most recently set handler is executed first and the system handler is executed last.

Example: A Console Control Handler

Program 4–5 loops forever, calling the self-explanatory `Beep` function every 5 seconds. The user can terminate the program with a `Ctrl-c` or by closing the console. The handler routine will put out a message, wait 10 seconds, and, it would appear, return `TRUE`, terminating the program. The main program, however, actually detects the `Exit` flag and stops the process. This illustrates the concurrent operation of the handler routine; note that the timing of the signal determines the extent of the signal handler's output. Examples in later chapters also use console control handlers.

Note the use of `WINAPI`; this macro is used for user functions passed as arguments to Windows functions to assure the proper calling conventions. It is defined in the Microsoft C header file `WTYPES.H`.

Program 4–5   `Ctrlc`: Signal Handling Program

```
/* Chapter 4. Ctrlc.c */
/* Catch console events. */

#include "EvryThng.h"

static BOOL WINAPI Handler (DWORD CtrlEvent); /* See WTYPES.H. */
volatile static BOOL Exit = FALSE;

int _tmain (int argc, LPTSTR argv [])

/* Beep periodically until signaled to stop. */
{
    /* Add an event handler. */
    if (!SetConsoleCtrlHandler (Handler, TRUE))
        ReportError (_T ("Error setting event handler."), 1, TRUE);

    while (!Exit) {
        Sleep (5000); /* Beep every 5 seconds. */
        Beep (1000 /* Frequency. */, 250 /* Duration. */);
    }
    _tprintf (_T ("Stopping the program as requested.\n"));
    return 0;
}

BOOL WINAPI Handler (DWORD CtrlEvent)
{
    Exit = TRUE;

    switch (CntrlEvent) {
        /* Timing determines if you see the second handler message. */
        case CTRL_C_EVENT:
```

```
            _tprintf (_T ("Ctrl-c received. Leaving in 10 sec.\n"));
            Sleep (4000); /* Decrease this to get a different effect. */
            _tprintf (_T ("Leaving handler in 6 seconds.\n"));
            Sleep (6000); /* Also try decreasing this time. */
            return TRUE; /* TRUE indicates signal was handled. */
        case CTRL_CLOSE_EVENT:
            _tprintf (_T ("Leaving the handler in 10 seconds.\n"));
            Sleep (4000);
            _tprintf (_T ("Leaving handler in 6 seconds.\n"));
            Sleep (6000); /* Also try decreasing this time. */
            return TRUE; /* Try returning FALSE. Any difference? */
        default:
            _tprintf (_T ("Event: %d. Leaving in 10 seconds.\n"),
                CntrlEvent);
            Sleep (4000);
            _tprintf (_T ("Leaving handler in 6 seconds.\n"));
            Sleep (6000);
            return TRUE;
    }
}
```

Vectored Exception Handling

Exception handling functions can be directly associated with exceptions, just as console control handlers can be associated with console control events. When an exception occurs, the *vectored exception handlers* are called first, before the system unwinds the stack to look for structured exception handlers. No keywords, such as __try and __catch, are required. This feature is only available on Windows XP and 2003 Server.

Vectored exception handling (VEH) management is similar to console control handler management, although the details are different. Add, or register, a handler using AddVectoredExceptionHandler.

```
PVOID AddVectoredExceptionHandler (
    ULONG FirstHandler,
    PVECTORED_EXCEPTION_HANDLER VectoredHandler)
```

Handlers can be chained, so the FirstHandler parameter specifies that the handler should either be the first one called when the exception occurs (nonzero value) or the last one called (zero value). Subsequent AddVectoredException-Handler calls can update the order. For example, if two handlers are added, both with a zero `FirstHandler` value, the handlers will be called in the order in which they were added.

`RemoveVectoredExceptionHandler` returns a non-`NULL` value if it succeeds, and it requires a single parameter, the handler address.

The successful return value is a pointer to the exception handler, that is, *VectoredHandler*. A `NULL` return value indicates failure.

VectoredHandler is a pointer to the handler function, which is of the form:

```
LONG WINAPI VectoredHandler (PEXCEPTION_POINTERS
    ExceptionInfo)
```

`PEXCEPTION_POINTERS` is the address of an `EXCEPTION_POINTERS` struc-ture with processor-specific and general information. This is the same structure returned by `GetExceptionInformation` and used in Program 4–4.

A VEH handler function should be fast, and it should never access a synchronization object, such as a mutex (see Chapter 8). In most cases, the VEH simply accesses the exception structure, performs some minimal processing (such as setting a flag), and returns. There are two possible return values, both of which are familiar from the SEH discussion.

1. `EXCEPTION_CONTINUE_EXECUTION`—No more handlers are executed, SEH is not performed, and control is returned to the point where the exception occurred. As with SEH, this may not always be possible.

2. `EXCEPTION_CONTINUE_SEARCH`—The next VEH handler, if any, is executed. If there are no additional handlers, the stack is unwound to search for SEH handlers.

Exercise 4–9 asks you to add VEH to Programs 4–3 and 4–4.

Summary

Windows SEH provides a robust mechanism for C programs to respond to and recover from exceptions and errors. Exception handling is efficient and can result in more understandable, maintainable, and safer code, making it an essential aid to defensive programming and higher-quality programs. Similar concepts are implemented in most languages and OSs, although Windows' solution allows you to analyze the exact cause of an exception.

Console control handlers can respond to external events that do not generate exceptions. VEH is a newer feature that allows functions to be executed before SEH processing occurs. VEH is similar to conventional interrupt handling.

Looking Ahead

ReportException and exception and termination handlers are used as convenient in subsequent examples. Chapter 5 covers memory management, and, in the process, SEH is used to detect memory allocation errors.

Exercises

4–1. Extend Program 4–2 so that every call to ReportException contains sufficient information so that the exception handler can report precisely what error occurred and also delete the output file if its contents are not meaningful.

4–2. Extend Program 4–3 by generating memory access violations, such as array index out of bounds and arithmetic faults and other types of floating-point exceptions not illustrated in Program 4–3.

4–3. Augment Program 4–3 so as to print the actual value of the floating-point mask after enabling the exceptions. Are all the exceptions actually enabled? Explain the results.

4–4. What values do you actually get after a floating-point exception, such as division by zero? Can you set the result in the filter function as Program 4–3 attempts to do?

4–5. What happens in Program 4–3 if you do not clear the floating-point exception? Explain the results. *Hint*: Request an additional exception after the floating-point exception.

4–6. Extend Program 4–5 so that the handler routine raises an exception rather than returning. Explain the results.

4–7. Extend Program 4–5 so that it can handle shutdown and log-off signals.

4–8. Confirm through experiment that Program 4–5's handler routine executes concurrently with the main program.

4–9. Enhance Programs 4–3 and 4–4. Specifically, handle floating-point and arithmetic exceptions before invoking SEH.

CHAPTER

5 | Memory Management, Memory-Mapped Files, and DLLs

Most programs require some form of dynamic memory management. This need arises whenever it is necessary to create data structures whose size cannot be determined statically when the program is built. Search trees, symbol tables, and linked lists are common examples of dynamic data structures.

Windows provides flexible mechanisms for managing a program's dynamic memory. Windows also provides memory-mapped files to associate a process's address space directly with a file, allowing the OS to manage all data movement between the file and memory so that the programmer never needs to deal with `ReadFile`, `WriteFile`, `SetFilePointer`, or the other file I/O functions. With memory-mapped files, the program can maintain dynamic data structures conveniently in permanent files, and memory-based algorithms can process file data. What is more, memory mapping can significantly speed up sequential file processing, and it provides a mechanism for memory sharing between processes.

Dynamic link libraries (DLLs) are an essential special case of file mapping and shared memory in which files (primarily read-only code files) are mapped into the process address space for execution.

This chapter describes the Windows memory management and file mapping functions, illustrates their use with several examples, and describes both implicitly and explicitly linked DLLs.

Win32 and Win64 Memory Management Architecture

Win32 (the Win32/64distinction is important here) is an API for the Windows 32-bit OS family. The "32-bitness" manifests itself in memory addresses, and pointers (LPCTSTR, LPDWORD, and so on) are 4-byte (32-bit) objects. The Win64 API provides a much larger virtual address space and 64-bit pointers and is a natural evolution of Win32. Nonetheless, some care is required to ensure portability to Win64. The discussion here refers to Win32; Chapter 16 discusses Win64 migration strategies and information sources.

Every Win32 process, then, has its own private virtual address space of 4GB (2^{32} bytes). The Win64 address space is, of course, much larger. Win32 makes at least half of this (2–3GB; 3GB must be enabled at boot time) available to a process. The remainder of the virtual address space is allocated to shared data and code, system code, drivers, and so on.

The details of these memory allocations, although interesting, are not discussed here; the abstractions provided by the Win32 API are used by application programs. From the programmer's perspective, the OS provides a large address space for code, data, and other resources. This chapter concentrates on exploiting Windows memory management without being concerned with OS implementation. Nonetheless, a very short overview follows.

Memory Management Overview

The OS manages all the details of mapping virtual to physical memory and the mechanics of page swapping, demand paging, and the like. This subject is discussed thoroughly in OS texts and also in *Inside Windows 2000* (Solomon and Russinovich). Here's a brief summary.

- The system has a relatively small amount of physical memory; 128MB is the practical minimum for all but Windows XP, and much larger physical memories are typical.[1]

- Every process—and there may be several user and system processes—has its own virtual address space, which may be much larger than the physical memory available. For example, the virtual address space of a 1GB process is eight times larger than 128MB of physical memory, and there may be many such processes.

- The OS maps virtual addresses to physical addresses.

---

[1] Memory prices continue to decline, and "typical" memory sizes keep increasing, so it is difficult to define typical memory size. At the time of writing, inexpensive systems contain 128–256MB, which is sufficient but not optimal for Windows XP. Windows 2003 systems generally contain much more memory.

- Most virtual pages will not be in physical memory, so the OS responds to *page faults* (references to pages not in memory) and loads the data from disk, either from the system swap file or from a normal file. Page faults, while transparent to the programmer, have an impact on performance, and programs should be designed to minimize faults; again, many OS texts treat this important subject, which is beyond the scope of this book.

Figure 5–1 shows the Windows memory management API layered on the Virtual Memory Manager. The Virtual Memory Windows API (`VirtualAlloc`, `VirtualFree`, `VirtualLock`, `VirtualUnlock`, and so on) deals with whole pages. The Windows Heap API manages memory in user-defined units.

The layout of the virtual memory address space is not shown because it is not directly relevant to the API, the Windows 9x and NT layouts are different, and the layout may change in the future. The Microsoft documentation provides this information.

Nonetheless, many programmers want to know more about their environment. To start to explore the memory structure, invoke the following.

```
VOID GetSystemInfo (LPSYSTEM_INFO lpSystemInfo)
```

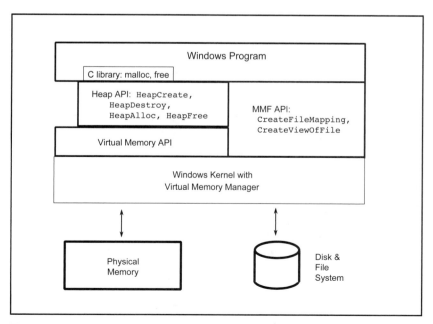

Figure 5-1   Windows Memory Management Architecture

The parameter is the address of a `PSYSTEM_INFO` structure containing information on the system's page size and the application's physical memory address.

Heaps

Windows maintains pools of memory in *heaps*. A process can contain several heaps, and you allocate memory from these heaps.

One heap is often sufficient, but there are good reasons, explained below, for multiple heaps. If a single heap is sufficient, just use the C library memory management functions (`malloc`, `free`, `calloc`, `realloc`).

Heaps are Windows objects; therefore, they have handles. The heap handle is necessary when you're allocating memory. Each process has its own default heap, which is used by `malloc`, and the next function obtains its handle.

```
HANDLE GetProcessHeap (VOID)

Return: The handle for the process's heap; NULL on failure.
```

Notice that `NULL` is the return value to indicate failure rather than `INVALID_HANDLE_VALUE`, which is returned by `CreateFile`.

A program can also create distinct heaps. It is convenient at times to have separate heaps for allocation of separate data structures. The benefits of separate heaps include the following.

- **Fairness**. No single thread can obtain more memory than is allocated to its heap. In particular, a memory leak defect, caused by a program neglecting to free data elements that are no longer needed, will affect only one thread of a process.[2]

- **Multithreaded performance**. By giving each thread its own heap, contention between threads is reduced, which can substantially improve performance. See Chapter 9.

- **Allocation efficiency**. Allocation of fixed-size data elements within a small heap can be more efficient than allocating elements of many different sizes in a single large heap. Fragmentation is also reduced. Furthermore, giving each thread a unique heap simplifies synchronization, resulting in additional efficiencies.

---

[2] Chapter 7 introduces threads.

- **Deallocation efficiency.** An entire heap and all the data structures it contains can be freed with a single function call. This call will also free any leaked memory allocations in the heap.

- **Locality of reference efficiency.** Maintaining a data structure in a small heap ensures that the elements will be confined to a relatively small number of pages, potentially reducing page faults as the data structure elements are processed.

The value of these advantages varies depending on the application, and many programmers use only the process heap and the C library. Such a choice, however, prevents the program from exploiting the exception generating capability of the Windows memory management functions (described along with the functions). In any case, the next two functions create and destroy heaps.[3]

The initial heap size, which can be zero and is always rounded up to a multiple of the page size, determines how much physical storage (in a *paging file*) is *committed* to the heap (that is, the required space is allocated from the heap) initially, rather than on demand as memory is allocated from the heap. As a program exceeds the initial size, additional pages are committed automatically up to the maximum size. Because the paging file is a limited resource, deferring commitment is a good practice unless it is known ahead of time how large the heap will become. dwMaximumSize, if nonzero, determines the heap's maximum size as it expands dynamically. The process heap will also grow dynamically.

```
HANDLE HeapCreate (
    DWORD flOptions,
    SIZE_T dwInitialSize,
    SIZE_T dwMaximumSize)

Return: A heap handle, or NULL on failure.
```

The two size fields are of type SIZE_T rather than DWORD. SIZE_T is defined to be either a 32-bit or 64-bit unsigned integer, depending on compiler flags (_WIN32 and _WIN64). SIZE_T was introduced to allow for Win64 migration (see Chapter 16) and can span the entire range of a 32- or 64-bit pointer. SSIZE_T is the signed version.

---

[3] In general, create objects of type X with the CreateX system call. HeapCreate is an exception to this rule.

flOptions is a combination of two flags.

- HEAP_GENERATE_EXCEPTIONS—With this option, failed allocations generate an exception to be processed by SEH (see Chapter 4). HeapCreate itself will not cause an exception; rather, functions such as HeapAlloc, which will be explained shortly, cause an exception on failure if this flag is set.
- HEAP_NO_SERIALIZE—Set this flag under certain circumstances to get a small performance improvement, as discussed later.

There are several other important points regarding dwMaximumSize.

- If dwMaximumSize is nonzero, the virtual address space is allocated accordingly, even though it may not be committed in its entirety. This is the maximum size of the heap, which is said to be *nongrowable*. This option limits a heap's size, perhaps to gain the fairness advantage cited previously.
- If, on the other hand, dwMaximumSize is 0, then the heap is *growable* beyond the initial size. The limit is determined by the available virtual address space not currently allocated to other heaps and swap file space.

Note that heaps do not have security attributes because they are not accessible outside the process. File mapping objects, described later in the chapter, can be secured (Chapter 15) as they allow memory sharing between processes.

To destroy an entire heap, use HeapDestroy. This is another exception to the general rule that CloseHandle is the function for removing unwanted handles.

```
BOOL HeapDestroy (HANDLE hHeap)
```

hHeap should specify a heap generated by HeapCreate. Be careful not to destroy the process's heap (the one obtained from GetProcessHeap). Destroying a heap frees the virtual memory space and physical storage in the paging file. Naturally, well-designed programs should destroy heaps that are no longer needed.

Destroying a heap is also a quick way to free data structures without traversing them to delete one element at a time, although C++ object instances will not be destroyed inasmuch as their destructors are not called. Heap destruction has three benefits.

1. There is no need to write the data structure traversal code.

2. There is no need to deallocate each individual element.

3. The system does not spend time maintaining the heap since all data structure elements are deallocated with a single call.

The C library uses only a single heap. There is, therefore, nothing similar to Windows' heap handles.

The UNIX sbrk function can increase a process's address space, but it is not a general-purpose memory manager.

UNIX does not generate signals when memory allocation fails; the programmer must explicitly test the returned pointer.

Managing Heap Memory

Obtain memory blocks from a heap by specifying the heap's handle, the block size, and several flags.

```
LPVOID HeapAlloc (
    HANDLE hHeap,
    DWORD dwFlags,
    SIZE_T dwBytes)
```

Return: A pointer to the allocated memory block, or NULL on failure (unless exception generation is specified).

Parameters

hHeap is the handle of the heap in which the memory block is to be allocated. This handle should come from either GetProcessHeap or HeapCreate.

dwFlags is a combination of three flags.

- HEAP_GENERATE_EXCEPTIONS and HEAP_NO_SERIALIZE—These flags have the same meaning as for HeapCreate. The first flag is ignored if it was set with the heap's HeapCreate function and enables exceptions for the specific HeapAlloc call, even if HEAP_GENERATE_EXCEPTIONS was not specified by HeapCreate. The second should not be used when allocating within the process heap.

- HEAP_ZERO_MEMORY—This flag specifies that the allocated memory will be initialized to 0; otherwise, the memory contents are not specified.

dwBytes is the size of the block of memory to allocate. For nongrowable heaps, this is limited to 0x7FFF8 (approximately 0.5MB).

Note: Once HeapAlloc returns a pointer, use the pointer in the normal way; there is no need to make reference to its heap. Notice, too, that the LPVOID data type represents either a 32-bit or 64-bit pointer.

Deallocating memory from a heap is simple.

```
BOOL HeapFree (
    HANDLE hHeap,
    DWORD dwFlags,
    LPVOID lpMem)
```

dwFlags should be 0 or HEAP_NO_SERIALIZE. lpMem should be a value returned by HeapAlloc or HeapReAlloc (described next), and, of course, hHeap should be the heap from which lpMem was allocated.

Memory blocks can be reallocated to change their size.

```
LPVOID HeapReAlloc (
    HANDLE hHeap,
    DWORD dwFlags,
    LPVOID lpMem,
    SIZE_T dwBytes)
```

Return: A pointer to the reallocated block. Failure returns NULL or causes an exception.

Parameters

The first parameter, hHeap, is the same heap used with the HeapAlloc call that returned the lpMem value (the third parameter). dwFlags specifies some essential control options.

- HEAP_GENERATE_EXCEPTIONS and HEAP_NO_SERIALIZE—These flags are the same as described for HeapAlloc.

- HEAP_ZERO_MEMORY—Only newly allocated memory (when dwBytes is larger than the original block) is initialized. The original block contents are not modified.

- HEAP_REALLOC_IN_PLACE_ONLY—This flag specifies that the block cannot be moved. When you're increasing a block's size, the new memory must be allocated at the address immediately after the existing block.

lpMem specifies the existing block in hHeap to be reallocated.

dwBytes is the new block size, which can be larger or smaller than the existing size.

Normally, the returned pointer is the same as lpMem. If, on the other hand, a block is moved (permit this by omitting the HEAP_REALLOC_IN_PLACE_ONLY flag), the returned value will be different. Be careful to update any references to the block. The data in the block is unchanged, regardless of whether or not it is moved; however, some data will be lost if the block size is reduced.

Determine the size of an allocated block by calling HeapSize (this function should have been named BlockSize because it does not obtain the size of the heap) with the heap handle and block pointer.

```
DWORD HeapSize (
    HANDLE hHeap,
    DWORD dwFlags,
    LPCVOID lpMem)
```

Return: The size of the block, or zero on failure.

The HEAP_NO_SERIALIZE Flag

The functions HeapCreate, HeapAlloc, and HeapReAlloc can specify the HEAP_NO_SERIALIZE flag. There can be a small performance gain with this flag because the functions do not provide mutual exclusion to threads accessing the heap. Some simple tests that do nothing except allocate memory blocks measured a performance improvement of about 16 percent. This flag is safe in a few situations, such as the following.

- The program does not use threads (Chapter 7), or, more accurately, the process (Chapter 6) has only a single thread. All examples in this chapter use the flag.

- Each thread has its own heap or set of heaps, and no other thread accesses the heap.

- The program has its own mutual exclusion mechanism (Chapter 8) to prevent concurrent access to a heap by several threads using `HeapAlloc` and `HeapReAlloc`. `HeapLock` and `HeapUnlock` are also available for this purpose.

The `HEAP_GENERATE_EXCEPTIONS` Flag

Forcing exceptions in the case of memory allocation failure avoids the need for annoying error tests after each allocation. Furthermore, the exception or termination handler can clean up memory that did get allocated. This technique is used in some examples.

Two exception codes are possible.

1. `STATUS_NO_MEMORY` indicates that the system could not create a block of the requested size. Causes can include fragmented memory, a nongrowable heap that has reached its limit, or even exhaustion of all memory with growable heaps.

2. `STATUS_ACCESS_VIOLATION` indicates that the specified heap has been corrupted. For example, a program may have written memory beyond the bounds of an allocated block.

Other Heap Functions

`HeapCompact` attempts to consolidate, or *defragment*, adjacent free blocks in a heap. `HeapValidate` attempts to detect heap corruption. `HeapWalk` enumerates the blocks in a heap, and `GetProcessHeaps` obtains all the heap handles that are valid in a process.

`HeapLock` and `HeapUnlock` allow a thread to serialize heap access, as described in Chapter 8.

Note that these functions do not work under Windows 9x or CE. Also, some obsolete functions, such as `GlobalAlloc` and `LocalAlloc`, were used for compatibility with 16-bit systems. These functions are mentioned simply as a reminder that many functions continue to be supported even though they are no longer relevant.

Summary: Heap Management

The normal process for using heaps is straightforward.

1. Get a heap handle with either `CreateHeap` or `GetProcessHeap`.

2. Allocate blocks within the heap using `HeapAlloc`.

3. Optionally, free some or all of the individual blocks with `HeapFree`.

4. Destroy the heap and close the handle with `HeapDestroy`.

This process is illustrated in both Figure 5–2 and Program 5–1.

Normally, programmers use the C library `<stdlib.h>` memory management functions and can continue to do so if separate heaps or exception generation are not needed. `malloc` is then equivalent to `HeapAlloc` using the process heap, re-`alloc` to `HeapReAlloc`, and `free` to `HeapFree`. `calloc` allocates and initializes objects, and `HeapAlloc` can easily emulate this behavior. There is no C library equivalent to `HeapSize`.

Example: Sorting Files with a Binary Search Tree

A search tree is a common dynamic data structure requiring memory management. Search trees are a convenient way to maintain collections of records, and they have the additional advantage of allowing efficient sequential traversal.

Program 5–1 implements a sort (`sortBT`, a limited version of the UNIX `sort` command) by creating a binary search tree using two heaps. The keys go into the *node heap*, which represents the search tree. Each node contains left and right pointers, a key, and a pointer to the data record in the *data heap*. The complete record, a line of text from the input file, goes into the data heap. Notice that the node heap consists of fixed-size blocks, whereas the data heap contains strings with different lengths. Finally, the sorted file is output by traversing the tree.

This example arbitrarily uses the first 8 bytes of a string as the key rather than using the complete string. Two other sort implementations in this chapter (Programs 5–4 and 5–5) sort keyed files, and Appendix C compares their performance.

Figure 5–2 shows the sequence of operations for creating heaps and allocating blocks. The program code on the right is *pseudocode* in that only the essential function calls and arguments are shown. The virtual address space on the left shows the three heaps along with some allocated blocks in each. The figure differs slightly from the program in that the root of the tree is allocated in the process heap in the figure but not in Program 5–1.

Note: The actual locations of the heaps and the blocks within the heaps depend on the Windows implementation and on the process's history of previous memory use, including heap expansion beyond the original size. Furthermore, a growable heap may not occupy contiguous address space after it grows beyond the originally committed size. The best programming practice is to make no assumptions; just use the memory management functions as specified.

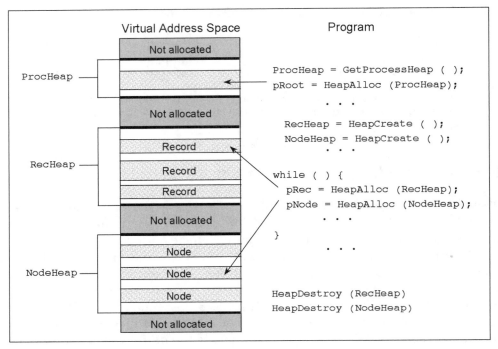

Figure 5-2   Memory Management in Multiple Heaps

Program 5–1 illustrates some techniques that simplify the program and would not be possible with the C library alone or with the process heap.

- The node elements are of fixed size and go in a heap of their own, whereas the varying-length data elements are in a separate heap.

- The program prepares to sort the next file by destroying the two heaps rather than freeing individual elements.

- Allocation errors are processed as exceptions so that it is not necessary to test for NULL pointers.

An implementation such as Program 5–1 is limited to smaller files when using Windows because the complete file and a copy of the keys must reside in virtual memory. The absolute upper limit of the file length is determined by the available virtual address space (3GB at most); the practical limit is less. With Win64, there is no such practical limit.

Program 5–1 calls several tree management functions: FillTree, Insert-Tree, Scan, and KeyCompare. They are shown in Program 5–2.

This program uses heap exceptions. An alternative would be to eliminate use of the HEAP_GENERATE_EXCEPTIONS flag and test directly for memory allocation errors.

Program 5–1   sortBT: Sorting with a Binary Search Tree

```
/* Chapter 5. sortBT command. Binary Tree version. */
#include "EvryThng.h"
#define KEY_SIZE 8
typedef struct _TreeNode {/* Tree node structure definition. */
    struct _TreeNode *Left, *Right;
    TCHAR Key [KEY_SIZE];
    LPTSTR pData;
} TREENODE, *LPTNODE, **LPPTNODE;
#define NODE_SIZE sizeof (TREENODE)
#define NODE_HEAP_ISIZE 0x8000
#define DATA_HEAP_ISIZE 0x8000
#define MAX_DATA_LEN 0x1000
#define TKEY_SIZE KEY_SIZE * sizeof (TCHAR)

LPTNODE FillTree (HANDLE, HANDLE, HANDLE);
BOOL Scan (LPTNODE);
int KeyCompare (LPCTSTR, LPCTSTR); iFile;

BOOL InsertTree (LPPTNODE, LPTNODE);

int _tmain (int argc, LPTSTR argv [])
{
    HANDLE hIn, hNode = NULL, hData = NULL;
    LPTNODE pRoot;
    CHAR ErrorMessage[256];
    int iFirstFile = Options (argc, argv, _T ("n"), &NoPrint, NULL);
                /* Process all files on the command line. */
    for (iFile = iFirstFile; iFile < argc; iFile++) __try {
                /* Open the input file. */
        hIn = CreateFile (argv [iFile], GENERIC_READ, 0, NULL,
            OPEN_EXISTING, 0, NULL);
        if (hIn == INVALID_HANDLE_VALUE)
            RaiseException (0, 0, 0, NULL);
        __try { /* Allocate the two heaps. */
            hNode = HeapCreate (
                HEAP_GENERATE_EXCEPTIONS | HEAP_NO_SERIALIZE,
                NODE_HEAP_ISIZE, 0);
            hData = HeapCreate (
                HEAP_GENERATE_EXCEPTIONS | HEAP_NO_SERIALIZE,
                DATA_HEAP_ISIZE, 0);
```

```
                /* Process the input file, creating the tree. */
        pRoot = FillTree (hIn, hNode, hData);
                /* Display the tree in Key order. */
        _tprintf (_T ("Sorted file: %s\n"), argv [iFile]);
        Scan (pRoot);
    } __finally { /* Heaps and file handles are always closed. */
        /* Destroy the two heaps and data structures. */

        if (hNode != NULL) HeapDestroy (hNode);
        if (hNode != NULL) HeapDestroy (hData);
        hNode = NULL; hData = NULL;
        if (hIn != INVALID_HANDLE_VALUE) CloseHandle (hIn);
    }
} /* End of main file processing loop and try block. */

__except (EXCEPTION_EXECUTE_HANDLER) {
    _stprintf (ErrorMessage, _T ("\n%s %s"),
        _T ("sortBT error on file:"), argv [iFile]);
    ReportError (ErrorMessage, 0, TRUE);
}
return 0;
}
```

Program 5–2 shows the functions that actually implement the search tree algorithms. `FillTree`, the first function, allocates memory in the two heaps. `KeyCompare`, the second function, is used in several other programs in this chapter. Notice that these functions are called by Program 5–1 and use the completion and exception handlers in that program. Thus, a memory allocation error would be handled by the main program, and the program would continue to process the next file.

Program 5–2   `FillTree` and Other Tree Management Functions

```
LPTNODE FillTree (HANDLE hIn, HANDLE hNode, HANDLE hData)

/* Fill the tree with records from the input file.
   Use the calling program's exception handler. */
{
    LPTNODE pRoot = NULL, pNode;
    DWORD nRead, i;
    BOOL AtCR;
    TCHAR DataHold [MAX_DATA_LEN];
    LPTSTR pString;

    while (TRUE) {
        /* Allocate and initialize a new tree node. */
        pNode = HeapAlloc (hNode, HEAP_ZERO_MEMORY, NODE_SIZE);
```

```c
        /* Read the key from the next file record. */
        if (!ReadFile (hIn, pNode->Key, TKEY_SIZE,
               &nRead, NULL) || nRead != TKEY_SIZE)
            return pRoot;

        AtCR = FALSE; /* Read data until end of line. */
        for (i = 0; i < MAX_DATA_LEN; i++) {
            ReadFile (hIn, &DataHold [i], TSIZE, &nRead, NULL);
            if (AtCR && DataHold [i] == LF) break;
            AtCR = (DataHold [i] == CR);
        }
        DataHold [i - 1] = '\0';

        /* Combine Key and Data -- Insert in tree. */
        pString = HeapAlloc (hData, HEAP_ZERO_MEMORY,
               (SIZE_T)(KEY_SIZE + _tcslen (DataHold) + 1) * TSIZE);
        memcpy (pString, pNode->Key, TKEY_SIZE);
        pString [KEY_SIZE] = '\0';
        _tcscat (pString, DataHold);
        pNode->pData = pString;
        InsertTree (&pRoot, pNode);
    } /* End of while (TRUE) loop. */
    return NULL; /* Failure */
}

BOOL InsertTree (LPPTNODE ppRoot, LPTNODE pNode)
/* Add a single node, with data, to the tree. */
{
    if (*ppRoot == NULL) {
        *ppRoot = pNode;
        return TRUE;
    }
    /* Note the recursive calls to InsertTree. */
    if (KeyCompare (pNode->Key, (*ppRoot)->Key) < 0)
        InsertTree (&((*ppRoot)->Left), pNode);
    else
        InsertTree (&((*ppRoot)->Right), pNode);
}

static int KeyCompare (LPCTSTR pKey1, LPCTSTR pKey2)

/* Compare two records of generic characters. */
{
    return _tcsncmp (pKey1, pKey2, KEY_SIZE);
}

static BOOL Scan (LPTNODE pNode)

/* Recursively scan and print the contents of a binary tree. */
```

```
{
    if (pNode == NULL) return TRUE;
    Scan (pNode->Left);
    _tprintf (_T ("%s\n"), pNode->pData);
    Scan (pNode->Right);
    return TRUE;
}
```

Note: This search tree implementation is clearly not the most efficient because the tree may become unbalanced. Implementing a balanced search tree would be worthwhile but would not change the program's memory management.

Memory-Mapped Files

Dynamic memory in heaps must be physically allocated in a paging file. The OS's memory management controls page movement between physical memory and the paging file and also maps the process's virtual address space to the paging file. When the process terminates, the physical space in the file is deallocated.

Windows' memory-mapped file functionality can also map virtual memory space directly to normal files. This has several advantages.

- There is no need to perform direct file I/O (reads and writes).

- The data structures created in memory will be saved in the file for later use by the same or other programs. Be careful about pointer usage, as Program 5–5 illustrates.

- Convenient and efficient in-memory algorithms (sorts, search trees, string processing, and so on) can process file data even though the file may be much larger than available physical memory. The performance will still be influenced by paging behavior if the file is large.

- File processing performance can be significantly improved in some cases.

- There is no need to manage buffers and the file data they contain. The OS does this hard work and does it efficiently and reliably.

- Multiple processes (Chapter 6) can share memory by mapping their virtual address spaces to the same file or to the paging file (interprocess memory sharing is the principal reason for mapping to the paging file).

- There is no need to consume paging file space.

The OS itself uses memory mapping to implement DLLs and to load and execute executable (.EXE) files. DLLs are described at the end of this chapter.

File Mapping Objects

The first step is to create a *file mapping object*, which has a handle, on an open file and then map the process's address space to all or part of the file. File mapping objects can be given names so that they are accessible to other processes for shared memory. Also, the mapping object has protection and security attributes and a size.

```
HANDLE CreateFileMapping (
    HANDLE hFile,
    LPSECURITY_ATTRIBUTES lpsa,
    DWORD dwProtect,
    DWORD dwMaximumSizeHigh,
    DWORD dwMaximumSizeLow,
    LPCTSTR lpMapName)

Return: A file mapping handle, or NULL on failure.
```

Parameters

hFile is the handle of an open file with protection flags compatible with dwProtect. The value (HANDLE) 0xFFFFFFFF (equivalently, INVALID_HANDLE_VALUE) refers to the paging file, and you can use this value for interprocess memory sharing without creating a separate file.

LPSECURITY_ATTRIBUTES allows the mapping object to be secured.

dwProtect specifies the mapped file access with the following flags. Additional flags are allowed for specialized purposes. For example, the SEC_IMAGE flag specifies an executable image; see the on-line documentation for more information.

- PAGE_READONLY means that the program can only read the pages in the mapped region; it can neither write nor execute them. hFile must have GENERIC_READ access.

- PAGE_READWRITE gives full access to the object if hFile has both GENERIC_READ and GENERIC_WRITE access.

- PAGE_WRITECOPY means that when mapped memory is changed, a private (to the process) copy is written to the paging file and not to the original file. A debugger might use this flag when setting breakpoints in shared code.

dwMaximumSizeHigh and dwMaximumSizeLow specify the size of the mapping object. If it is 0, the current file size is used; be sure to specify a size when using the paging file. If the file is expected to grow, use a size equal to the expected file size, and, if necessary, the file size will be set to that size immediately. Do not map to a file region beyond this specified size; the mapping object cannot grow.

lpMapName names the mapping object, allowing other processes to share the object; the name is case-sensitive. Use NULL if you are not sharing memory.

An error is indicated by a return value of NULL (not INVALID_HANDLE_VALUE).

Obtain a file mapping handle by specifying an existing mapping object name. The name comes from a previous call to CreateFileMapping. Two processes can share memory by sharing a file mapping. The first process creates the named mapping, and subsequent processes open this mapping with the name. The open will fail if the named object does not exist.

```
HANDLE OpenFileMapping (
    DWORD dwDesiredAccess,
    BOOL bInheritHandle,
    LPCTSTR lpMapName)

Return: A file mapping handle, or NULL on failure.
```

dwDesiredAccess uses the same set of flags as dwProtect in CreateFileMapping. lpMapName is the name created by a CreateFileMapping call. Handle inheritance (bInheritHandle) is a subject for Chapter 6.

The CloseHandle function, as expected, destroys mapping handles.

Mapping Process Address Space to Mapping Objects

The next step is to allocate virtual memory space and map it to a file through the mapping object. From the programmer's perspective, this allocation is similar to HeapAlloc, although it is much coarser, with larger allocation units. A pointer to the allocated block (or file *view*) is returned; the difference lies in the fact that the allocated block is mapped to the user-specified file rather than the paging file. The file mapping object plays the same role played by the heap when `HeapAlloc` is used.

```
LPVOID MapViewOfFile (
    HANDLE hMapObject,
    DWORD dwAccess,
    DWORD dwOffsetHigh,
    DWORD dwOffsetLow,
    SIZE_T cbMap)
```

Return: The starting address of the block (file view), or `NULL` on failure.

Parameters

`hMapObject` identifies a file mapping object obtained from either `Create-FileMapping` or `OpenFileMapping`.

`dwAccess` must be compatible with the mapping object's access. The three possible flag values are `FILE_MAP_WRITE`, `FILE_MAP_READ`, and `FILE_MAP_ALL_ACCESS`. (This is the bit-wise "or" of the previous two flags.)

`dwOffsetHigh` and `dwOffsetLow` specify the starting location of the mapped file region. The start address must be a multiple of 64K. Use a zero offset to map from the beginning of the file.

`cbMap` is the size, in bytes, of the mapped region. Zero indicates the entire file at the time of the `MapViewOfFile` call.

`MapViewOfFileEx` is similar except that you must specify the starting memory address. This address might, for instance, be the address of an array in the program's data space. Windows fails if the process has already mapped the requested space.

Just as it is necessary to release memory allocated in a heap with `HeapFree`, it is necessary to release file views.

```
BOOL UnmapViewOfFile (LPVOID lpBaseAddress)
```

Figure 5–3 shows the relationship between process address space and a mapped file.

```
                                                  Program

File
                                         fH = CreateFile ( );
                                         mH = CreateFileMapping (fH);
                                               . . .

                                         while ( ) {
                                           pRecA = MapViewOfFile (mH);
                                           pRecB = MapViewOfFile (mH);
                                           pRecB -> Data = pRecA -> Data;
                                               . . .
Process                                  UnmapViewOfFile (pRecA);
Address                                  UnmapViewOfFile (pRecB);
Space                                    }
                                         CloseHandle (mH);
                                         CloseHandle (fH);
```

Figure 5–3   Process Address Space Mapped to a File

FlushViewOfFile forces the system to write "dirty" (changed) pages to disk. Normally, a process accessing a file through mapping and another process accessing it through conventional file I/O will not have coherent views of the file. Performing the file I/O without buffering will not help because the mapped memory will not be written to the file immediately.

Therefore, it is not a good idea to access a mapped file with ReadFile and WriteFile; coherency is not ensured. On the other hand, processes that share a file through shared memory will have a coherent view of the file. If one process changes a mapped memory location, the other process will obtain that new value when it accesses the corresponding area of the file in its mapped memory. This mechanism is illustrated in Figure 5–4, and coherency works because both processes' virtual addresses, although distinct, are in the same physical memory locations. The obvious synchronization issues are addressed in Chapters 8–10.[4]

UNIX, at the SVR4 and 4.3+BSD releases, supports the mmap function, which is similar to MapViewOfFile. The parameters specify the same information except that there is no mapping object.

munmap is the UnmapViewOfFile equivalent.

---

[4] Statements regarding coherency of mapped views do not apply to networked files. The files must be local.

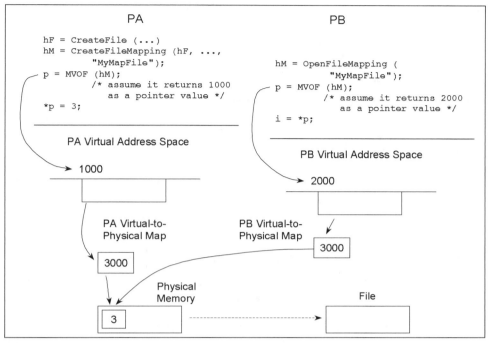

Figure 5–4 Shared Memory

There are no equivalents to the `CreateFileMapping` and `OpenFileMapping` functions. Any normal file can be mapped directly. UNIX does not use mapped files to share memory; rather, it has explicit API functions for memory sharing. The UNIX functions are `shmget`, `shmctl`, `shmat`, and `shmdt`.

File Mapping Limitations

File mapping, as mentioned previously, is a powerful and useful feature. The disparity between Windows' 64-bit file system and 32-bit addressing limits these benefits; Win64 does not have these limitations.

The principal problem is that if the file is large (greater than 2–3GB in this case), it is not possible to map the entire file into virtual memory space. Furthermore, the entire 3GB will not be available because virtual address space will be allocated for other purposes and available contiguous blocks will be much smaller than the theoretical maximum. Win64 will largely remove this limitation.

When you're dealing with large files that cannot be mapped to one view, create code that carefully maps and unmaps file regions as they are needed. This technique can be as complex as managing memory buffers, although it is not necessary to perform the explicit reads and writes.

File mapping has two other notable limitations.

- A file mapping cannot be expanded. You need to know the maximum size when creating the file mapping, and it may be difficult or impossible to determine this size.

- There is no way to allocate memory within a mapped memory region without creating your own memory management functions. It would be convenient if there were a way to specify a file mapping and a pointer returned by `MapViewOfFile` and obtain a heap handle.

Summary: File Mapping

Here is the standard sequence required by file mapping.

1. Open the file. Be certain that it has `GENERIC_READ` access.

2. If the file is new, set its length either with `CreateFileMapping` (step 3 below) or by using `SetFilePointer` followed by `SetEndOfFile`.

3. Map the file with `CreateFileMapping` or `OpenFileMapping`.

4. Create one or more views with `MapViewOfFile`.

5. Access the file through memory references. If necessary, change the mapped regions with `UnmapViewOfFile` and `MapViewOfFile`.

6. On completion, perform, in order, `UnmapViewOfFile`, `CloseHandle` for the mapping handle, and `CloseHandle` for the file handle.

Example: Sequential File Processing with Mapped Files

The `atou` program (Program 2–4) illustrates sequential file processing by converting ASCII files to Unicode, doubling the file length. This is an ideal application for memory-mapped files because the most natural way to convert the data is to process it one character at a time without being concerned with file I/O. Program 5–3 simply maps the input file and the output file—first computing the output file length by doubling the input file length—and converts the characters one at a time.

This example clearly illustrates the trade-off between the file mapping complexity required to initialize the program and the resulting processing simplicity. This complexity may not seem worthwhile given the simplicity of a simple file I/O implementation, but there is a significant performance advantage. Appendix C shows that the memory-mapped version can be considerably faster than the file access versions for NTFS files, so the complexity is worthwhile. The book's Web site contains additional performance studies; the highlights are summarized here.

- Memory-mapping performance improvements apply only to Windows NT and the NTFS.

- Compared with the best sequential file processing techniques, the performance improvements can be 3:1 or greater.

- The performance advantage disappears for larger files. In this example, as the input file size approaches about one-third of the physical memory size, normal sequential scanning is preferable. The mapping performance degrades at this point since the input file fills one-third of the memory and the output file, which is twice as long, fills the other two-thirds, forcing parts of the output files to be flushed to disk. Thus, on a 192MB system, mapping performance degenerates for input files longer than 60MB. Most file processing deals with smaller files and can take advantage of file mapping.

Program 5–3 shows only the function `Asc2UnMM`. The main program is the same as for Program 2–4.

Program 5–3 `Asc2UnMM`: File Conversion with Memory Mapping

```
/* Chapter 5. Asc2UnMM.c: Memory-mapped implementation. */

#include "EvryThng.h"
BOOL Asc2Un (LPCTSTR fIn, LPCTSTR fOut, BOOL bFailIfExists)
{
    HANDLE hIn, hOut, hInMap, hOutMap;
    LPSTR pIn, pInFile;
    LPWSTR pOut, pOutFile;
    DWORD FsLow, dwOut;

    /* Open and map both the input and output files. */
    hIn = CreateFile (fIn, GENERIC_READ, 0, NULL,
            OPEN_EXISTING, FILE_ATTRIBUTE_NORMAL, NULL);
    hInMap = CreateFileMapping (hIn, NULL, PAGE_READONLY,
                0, 0, NULL);
    pInFile = MapViewOfFile (hInMap, FILE_MAP_READ, 0, 0, 0);

    dwOut = bFailIfExists ? CREATE_NEW : CREATE_ALWAYS;
    hOut = CreateFile (fOut, GENERIC_READ | GENERIC_WRITE,
            0, NULL, dwOut, FILE_ATTRIBUTE_NORMAL, NULL);
    FsLow = GetFileSize (hIn, NULL); /* Set the map size. */
    hOutMap = CreateFileMapping (hOut, NULL, PAGE_READWRITE,
            0, 2 * FsLow, NULL);
    pOutFile = MapViewOfFile (hOutMap, FILE_MAP_WRITE, 0, 0,
```

```
                    (SIZE_T)(2 * FsLow));

    /* Convert the mapped file data from ASCII to Unicode. */
    pIn = pInFile;
    pOut = pOutFile;
    while (pIn < pInFile + FsLow)
    {
        *pOut = (WCHAR) *pIn;
        pIn++;
        pOut++;
    }

    UnmapViewOfFile (pOutFile); UnmapViewOfFile (pInFile);
    CloseHandle (hOutMap); CloseHandle (hInMap);
    CloseHandle (hIn); CloseHandle (hOut);
    return TRUE;
}
```

Example: Sorting a Memory-Mapped File

Another advantage of memory mapping is the ability to use convenient memory-based algorithms to process files. Sorting data in memory, for instance, is much easier than sorting records in a file.

Program 5–4 sorts a file with fixed-length records. This program, called sortFL, is similar to Program 5–1 in that it assumes an 8-byte sort key at the start of the record, but it is restricted to fixed records. Program 5–5 will rectify this shortcoming, but at the cost of increased complexity.

The sorting is performed by the <stdlib.h> C library function qsort. Notice that qsort requires a programmer-defined record comparison function, which is the same as the KeyCompare function in Program 5–2.

This program structure is straightforward. Simply create the file mapping on a temporary copy of the input file, create a single view of the file, and invoke qsort. There is no file I/O. Then the sorted file is sent to standard output using _tprintf, although a null character is appended to the file map.

Program 5–4   sortFL: Sorting a File with Memory Mapping

```
/* Chapter 5. sortFL. File sorting. Fixed-length records. */
/* Usage: sortFL file */

#include "EvryThng.h"
typedef struct _RECORD {
    TCHAR Key [KEY_SIZE];
    TCHAR Data [DATALEN];
```

```
} RECORD;

#define RECSIZE sizeof (RECORD)

int _tmain (int argc, LPTSTR argv [])
{
    HANDLE hFile = INVALID_HANDLE_VALUE, hMap = NULL;
    LPVOID pFile = NULL;
    DWORD FsLow, Result = 2;
    TCHAR TempFile [MAX_PATH];
    LPTSTR pTFile;

    /* Create the name for a temporary file to hold a copy of
       the file to be sorted. Sorting is done in the temp file. */

    /* Alternatively, retain the file as a permanent sorted version. */
    _stprintf (TempFile, _T ("%s%s"), argv [1], _T (".tmp"));
    CopyFile (argv [1], TempFile, TRUE);

    Result = 1; /* Temp file is new and should be deleted. */

    /* Map the temporary file and sort it in memory. */

    hFile = CreateFile (TempFile, GENERIC_READ | GENERIC_WRITE,
            0, NULL, OPEN_EXISTING, 0, NULL);
    FsLow = GetFileSize (hFile, NULL);
    hMap = CreateFileMapping (hFile, NULL, PAGE_READWRITE,
            0, FsLow + TSIZE, NULL);
    pFile = MapViewOfFile (hMap, FILE_MAP_ALL_ACCESS, 0,
            0 /* FsLow + TSIZE */, 0);

    qsort (pFile, FsLow / RECSIZE, RECSIZE, KeyCompare);
                        /* KeyCompare is as in Program 5-2. */

    /* Print the sorted file. */

    pTFile = (LPTSTR) pFile;
    pTFile [FsLow/TSIZE] = '\0';
    _tprintf (_T ("%s"), pFile);
    UnmapViewOfFile (pFile);
    CloseHandle (hMap);
    CloseHandle (hFile);
    DeleteFile (TempFile);
    return 0;
}
```

This implementation is straightforward, but there is an alternative that does not require mapping. Just allocate memory, read the complete file, sort it in memory, and write it. Such a solution, included on the book's Web site, would be as effective as Program 5–4 and is often faster, as shown in Appendix C.

Based Pointers

File maps are convenient, as the preceding examples demonstrate. Suppose, however, that the program creates a data structure with pointers in a mapped file and expects to access that file in the future. Pointers will all be relative to the virtual address returned from `MapViewOfFile`, and they will be meaningless when mapping the file the next time. The solution is to use based pointers, which are actually offsets relative to another pointer. The Microsoft C syntax, available in Visual C++ and some other systems, is:

```
type _based (base) declarator
```

Here are two examples.

```
LPTSTR pInFile = NULL;
DWORD _based (pInFile) *pSize;
TCHAR _based (pInFile) *pIn;
```

Notice that the syntax forces use of the *, a practice that is contrary to Windows convention.

Example: Using Based Pointers

Previous programs have shown how to sort files in various situations. The object, of course, is to illustrate different ways to manage memory, not to discuss sorting techniques. Program 5–1 uses a binary search tree that is destroyed after each sort, and Program 5–4 sorts an array of fixed-size records in mapped memory. Appendix C shows performance results for different implementations, including the next one in Program 5–5.

Suppose that it is necessary to maintain a permanent index file representing the sorted keys of the original file. The apparent solution is to map a file that contains the permanent index in a search tree or sorted key form to memory. Unfortunately, there is a major difficulty with this solution. All pointers in the tree, as stored in the file, are relative to the address returned by `MapViewOfFile`. The next time the program runs and maps the file, the pointers will be useless.

Program 5–5, together with Program 5–6, solves this problem, which is characteristic of any mapped data structure that uses pointers. The solution uses the _based keyword available with Microsoft C. An alternative is to map the file to an array and use indexing to access records in the mapped files.

The program is written as yet another version of the sort command, this time called sortMM. There are enough new features, however, to make it interesting.

- The records are of varying lengths.

- The program uses the first field as a key but detects its length.

- There are two file mappings. One mapping is for the original file, and the other is for the file containing the sorted keys. The second file is the *index file*, and each of its records contains a key and a pointer (base address) in the original file. qsort sorts the key file, much as in Program 5–4.

- The index file is saved and can be used later, and there is an option (-I) that bypasses the sort and uses an existing index file. The index file can also be used to perform a fast key file search by performing a binary search (using, perhaps, the C library bsearch function) on the index file.

Figure 5–5 shows the relationship of the index file to the file to be sorted. Program 5–5, sortMM, is the main program that sets up the file mapping, sorts the index file, and displays the results. It calls a function, CreateIndexFile, which is shown in Program 5–6.

Program 5–5   sortMM: Based Pointers in an Index File

```
/* Chapter 5. sortMM command.
   Memory Mapped sorting -- one file only. Options:
   -r Sort in reverse order.
   -I Use existing index file to produce sorted file. */

#include "EvryThng.h"
int KeyCompare (LPCTSTR , LPCTSTR);
DWORD CreateIndexFile (DWORD, LPCTSTR, LPTSTR);
DWORD KStart, KSize; /* Key start position & size (TCHAR). */
BOOL Revrs;
```

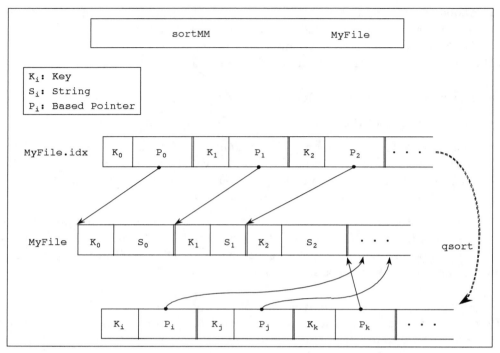

Figure 5–5   Sorting with a Memory-Mapped Index File

```
int _tmain (int argc, LPTSTR argv [])
{
    HANDLE hInFile, hInMap; /* Input file handles. */
    HANDLE hXFile, hXMap; /* Index file handles. */
    HANDLE hStdOut = GetStdHandle (STD_OUTPUT_HANDLE);
    BOOL IdxExists;
    DWORD FsIn, FsX, RSize, iKey, nWrite, *pSizes;
    LPTSTR pInFile = NULL;
    LPBYTE pXFile = NULL, pX;
    TCHAR _based (pInFile) *pIn;
    TCHAR IdxFlNam [MAX_PATH], ChNewLine = TNEWLINE;
    int FlIdx =
            Options (argc, argv, _T ("rI"), &Revrs, &IdxExists, NULL);

    /* Step 1: Open and map the input file. */
    hInFile = CreateFile (argv [FlIdx], GENERIC_READ | GENERIC_WRITE,
            0, NULL, OPEN_EXISTING, 0, NULL);
    hInMap = CreateFileMapping (hInFile, NULL,
            PAGE_READWRITE, 0, 0, NULL);
    pInFile = MapViewOfFile (hInMap, FILE_MAP_ALL_ACCESS, 0, 0, 0);
```

```
FsIn = GetFileSize (hInFile, NULL);

/* Steps 2 and 3: Create the index file name. */
_stprintf (IdxFlNam, _T ("%s%s"), argv [FlIdx], _T (".idx"));
if (!IdxExists)
    RSize = CreateIndexFile (FsIn, IdxFlNam, pInFile);

/* Step 4: Map the index file. */
hXFile = CreateFile (IdxFlNam, GENERIC_READ | GENERIC_WRITE,
        0, NULL, OPEN_EXISTING, 0, NULL);
hXMap = CreateFileMapping (hXFile, NULL, PAGE_READWRITE,
        0, 0, NULL);
pXFile = MapViewOfFile (hXMap, FILE_MAP_ALL_ACCESS, 0, 0, 0);
FsX = GetFileSize (hXFile, NULL);
pSizes = (LPDWORD) pXFile; /* Size fields in .idx file. */
KSize = *pSizes; /* Key size */
KStart = *(pSizes + 1); /* Start position of key in record. */
FsX -= 2 * sizeof (DWORD);

/* Step 5: Sort the index file with qsort. */
if (!IdxExists)
    qsort (pXFile + 2 * sizeof (DWORD), FsX / RSize,
            RSize, KeyCompare);

/* Step 6: Output the input file in sorted order. */
pX = pXFile + 2 * sizeof (DWORD) + RSize - sizeof (LPTSTR);
for (iKey = 0; iKey < FsX / RSize; iKey++) {
    WriteFile (hStdOut, &ChNewLine, TSIZE, &nWrite, NULL);
            /* The cast on pX is necessary! */
    pIn = (TCHAR _based (pInFile)*) *(LPDWORD) pX;
    while ((*pIn != CR || *(pIn + 1) != LF)
            && (DWORD) pIn < FsIn) {
        WriteFile (hStdOut, pIn, TSIZE, &nWrite, NULL);
        pIn++;
    }
    pX += RSize;
}
UnmapViewOfFile (pInFile);
CloseHandle (hInMap);
CloseHandle (hInFile);
UnmapViewOfFile (pXFile);
CloseHandle (hXMap);
CloseHandle (hXFile);
return 0;
}
```

Program 5–6 is the `CreateIndexFile` function, which creates the index file. It initially scans the input file to determine the key length from the first record.

Subsequently, it must scan the input file to find the bound of each varying-length record to set up the structure shown in Figure 5–5.

Program 5–6 sortMM: Creating the Index File

```
DWORD CreateIndexFile (DWORD FsIn, LPCTSTR IdxFlNam, LPTSTR pInFile)
{
   HANDLE hXFile;
   TCHAR _based (pInFile) *pInScan = 0;
   DWORD nWrite;

   /* Step 2a: Create an index file. Do not map it yet. */
   hXFile = CreateFile (IdxFlNam, GENERIC_READ | GENERIC_WRITE,
         FILE_SHARE_READ, NULL, CREATE_ALWAYS, 0, NULL);

   /* Step 2b: Get first key & determine key size/start.
      Skip white space and get key length. */
   KStart = (DWORD) pInScan;
   while (*pInScan != TSPACE && *pInScan != TAB)
      pInScan++; /* Find the first key field. */
   KSize = ((DWORD) pInScan - KStart) / TSIZE;

   /* Step 3: Scan the complete file, writing keys
      and record pointers to the key file. */
   WriteFile (hXFile, &KSize, sizeof (DWORD), &nWrite, NULL);
   WriteFile (hXFile, &KStart, sizeof (DWORD),&nWrite, NULL);
   pInScan = 0;
   while ((DWORD) pInScan < FsIn) {
      WriteFile (hXFile, pInScan + KStart, KSize * TSIZE,
            &nWrite, NULL);
      WriteFile (hXFile, &pInScan, sizeof (LPTSTR),
            &nWrite, NULL);
      while ((DWORD) pInScan < FsIn && ((*pInScan != CR)
            || (*(pInScan + 1) != LF))) {
         pInScan++; /* Skip to end of line. */
      }
      pInScan += 2; /* Skip past CR, LF. */
   }
   CloseHandle (hXFile);
                  /* Size of an individual record. */
   return KSize * TSIZE + sizeof (LPTSTR);
}
```

Dynamic Link Libraries

We have now seen that memory management and file mapping are important and useful techniques in a wide class of programs. The OS itself also uses memory management, and DLLs are the most visible and important use of file mapping. DLLs are used extensively by Windows applications. DLLs are also essential to higher-level technologies, such as COM, and many software components are provided as DLLs.

The first step is to consider the different methods of constructing libraries of commonly used functions.

Static and Dynamic Libraries

The most direct way to construct a program is to gather the source code of all the functions, compile them, and link everything into a single executable image. Common functions, such as `ReportError`, can be put into a library to simplify the build process. This technique was used with all the sample programs presented so far, although there were only a few functions, most of them for error reporting.

This monolithic, single-image model is simple, but it has several disadvantages.

- The executable image may be large, consuming disk space and physical memory at run time and requiring extra effort to manage and deliver to users.

- Each program update requires a rebuild of the complete program even if the changes are small or localized.

- Every program in the system that uses the functions will have a copy of the functions, possibly different versions, in its executable image. This arrangement increases disk space usage and, perhaps more important, physical memory usage when several such programs are running simultaneously.

- Distinct versions of the program, using different techniques, might be required to get the best performance in different environments. For example, the `Asc2Un` function is implemented differently in Program 2–4 (`atou`) and Program 5–3 (`Asc2UnMM`). The only method of executing different implementations is to decide which of the two versions to run based on environmental factors.

DLLs solve these and other problems quite neatly.

- Library functions are not linked at build time. Rather, they are linked at program load time (*implicit linking*) or at run time (*explicit linking*). As a result, the program image can be much smaller because it does not include the library functions.

- DLLs can be used to create *shared libraries*. Multiple programs share a single library in the form of a DLL, and only a single copy is loaded into memory. All programs map their process address space to the DLL code, although each thread will have its own copy of nonshared storage on the stack. For example, the ReportError function was used by nearly every example program; a single DLL implementation could be shared by all the programs.

- New versions or alternative implementations can be supported simply by supplying a new version of the DLL, and all programs that use the library can use the new version without modification.

- With explicit linking, a program can decide at run time which version of a library to use. The different libraries may be alternative implementations of the same function or may carry out totally different tasks, just as separate programs do. The library will run in the same process and thread as the calling program.

DLLs, sometimes in limited form, are used in nearly every OS. For example, UNIX uses the term "shared libraries" for the same concept. Windows uses DLLs to implement the OS interfaces, among other things. The entire Windows API is supported by a DLL that invokes the Windows kernel for additional services.

Multiple Windows processes can share DLL code, but the code, when called, runs as part of the calling process and thread. Therefore, the library will be able to use the resources of the calling process, such as file handles, and will use the calling thread's stack. DLLs should, therefore, be written to be thread-safe. (See Chapters 8, 9, and 10 for more information on thread safety and DLLs. Programs 12–4 and 12–5 illustrate techniques for creating thread-safe DLLs.) A DLL can also export variables as well as function entry points.

Implicit Linking

Implicit or *load-time* linking is the easier of the two techniques. The required steps, using Microsoft Visual C++, are as follows.

1. The functions in a new DLL are collected and built as a DLL, rather than, for example, a console application.

2. The build process constructs a .LIB library file, which is a *stub* for the actual code. This file should be placed in a common user library directory specified to the project.

3. The build process also constructs a `.DLL` file that contains the executable image. This file is typically placed in the same directory as the application that will use it, and the application loads the DLL during its initialization. The current working directory is the secondary location, and the OS will next look in the system directory, the Windows directory, and the path specified with the `PATH` environment variable.

4. Take care to export the function interfaces in the DLL source, as described next.

Exporting and Importing Interfaces

The most significant change required to put a function into a DLL is to declare it to be exportable (UNIX and some other systems do not require this explicit step). This is achieved either by using a `.DEF` file or, more simply, with Microsoft C, by using the `_declspec (dllexport)` storage modifier as follows:

```
_declspec (dllexport) DWORD MyFunction (...);
```

The build process will then create a `.DLL` file and a `.LIB` file. The `.LIB` file is the stub library that should be linked with the calling program to satisfy the external references and to create the actual links to the `.DLL` file at load time.

The calling or *client* program should declare that the function is to be imported by using the `_declspec (dllimport)` storage modifier. A standard technique is to write the include file by using a preprocessor variable created by appending the Microsoft Visual C++ project name, in uppercase letters, with `_EXPORTS`.

One further definition is required. If the calling (importing) client program is written in C++, `__cplusplus` is defined, and it is necessary to specify the C calling convention, using:

```
extern "C"
```

For example, if `MyFunction` is defined as part of a DLL build in project `MyLibrary`, the header file would contain:

```
#if defined(MYLIBRARY_EXPORTS)
#define LIBSPEC _declspec (dllexport)
#elif defined(__cplusplus)
#define LIBSPEC extern "C" _declspec (dllimport)
#else
#define LIBSPEC _declspec (dllimport)
#endif
LIBSPEC DWORD MyFunction (...);
```

Visual C++ automatically defines `MYLIBRARY_EXPORTS` when invoking the compiler within the `MyLibrary` DLL project. A client project that uses the DLL does not define `MYLIBRARY_EXPORTS`, so the function name is imported from the library.

When building the calling program, specify the `.LIB` file. When executing the calling program, ensure that the `.DLL` file is available to the calling program; this is frequently done by placing the `.DLL` file in the same directory as the executable. As mentioned previously, there is a set of DLL search rules that specify the order in which Windows searches for the specified `.DLL` file *as well as* for all other DLLs or executables that the specified file requires, stopping with the first instance located. The following *standard search order* is used for both explicit and implicit linking:

- The directory containing the loaded application.

- The current directory, if different from the executable image directory.

- The Windows system directory. You can determine this path with `GetSystemDirectory`; normally its value is `c:\WINDOWS\SYSTEM32`.

- The 16-bit Windows system directory, which does not exist on 9x systems. There is no function to obtain this path, and it is obsolete for our purposes.

- The Windows directory (`GetWindowsDirectory`).

- Directories specified by the `PATH` environment variable, in the order in which they occur.

Note that the standard order can be modified, as explained in the Explicit Linking section. For some additional detailed information on the search strategy, see http://msdn.microsoft.com/library/default.asp?url=/library/en-us/dllproc/base/loadlibrary.asp and the `SetDllDirectory` function, which was introduced with NT 5.1 (i.e., XP). `LoadLibraryEx`, described in the next section, also alters the search strategy.

The standard search strategy is illustrated by the Utilities project on the book's Web site, and the utility functions, such as `ReportError`, are used by nearly every example project.

It is also possible to export and import variables as well as function entry points, although this capability is not illustrated in the examples.

Explicit Linking

Explicit or *run-time* linking requires the program to request specifically that a DLL be loaded or freed. Next, the program obtains the address of the required entry point and uses that address as the pointer in the function call. The function is not declared in the calling program; rather, you declare a variable as a pointer to a function. Therefore, there is no need for a library at link time. The three required functions are LoadLibrary (or LoadLibraryEx), GetProcAddress, and FreeLibrary. *Note*: The function definitions show their 16-bit legacy through far pointers and different handle types.

The two functions to load a library are LoadLibrary and LoadLibraryEx.

```
HINSTANCE LoadLibrary (LPCTSTR lpLibFileName)
```

```
HINSTANCE LoadLibraryEx (
    LPCTSTR lpLibFileName,
    HANDLE hFile,
    DWORD dwFlags)
```

In both cases, the returned handle (HINSTANCE rather than HANDLE) will be NULL on failure. The .DLL suffix is not required on the file name. .EXE files can also be loaded with the LoadLibrary functions. Pathnames must use backslashes (\); forward slashes (/) will not work.

Since DLLs are shared, the system maintains a reference count to each DLL (incremented by the two load functions) so that the actual file does not need to be remapped. Even if the DLL file is found, LoadLibrary will fail if the DLL is implicitly linked to other DLLs that cannot be located.

LoadLibraryEx is similar to LoadLibrary but has several flags that are useful for specifying alternative search paths and loading the library as a data file. The hFile parameter is reserved for future use. dwFlags can specify alternate behavior with one of three values.

1. LOAD_WITH_ALTERED_SEARCH_PATH overrides the previously described standard search order, changing just the first step of the search strategy. The pathname specified as part of lpLibFileName is used rather than the directory from which the application was loaded.

2. LOAD_LIBRARY_AS_DATAFILE allows the file to be data only, and there is no preparation for execution, such as calling DllMain (see the DLL Entry Point section later in the chapter).

3. DONT_RESOLVE_DLL_REFERENCE means that DllMain is not called for process and thread initialization, and additional modules referenced within the DLL are not loaded.

When you're finished with a DLL instance, possibly to load a different version of the DLL, you free the library handle, thereby freeing the resources, including virtual address space, allocated to the library. The DLL will, however, remain loaded if the reference count indicates that other processes are still using it.

```
BOOL FreeLibrary (HINSTANCE hLibModule)
```

After loading a library and before freeing it, you can obtain the address of any entry point using GetProcAddress.

```
FARPROC GetProcAddress (
    HMODULE hModule,
    LPCSTR lpProcName)
```

hModule, despite the different type name (HINSTANCE is defined as HMODULE), is an instance produced by LoadLibrary or GetModuleHandle (see the next paragraph). lpProcName, which cannot be Unicode, is the entry point name. The return result is NULL in case of failure. FARPROC, like "long pointer," is an anachronism.

It is possible to obtain the file name associated with an hModule handle using GetModuleFileName. Conversely, given a file name (either a .DLL or .EXE file), GetModuleHandle will return the handle, if any, associated with this file if the current process has loaded it.

The next example shows how to use the entry point address to invoke a function.

Example: Explicitly Linking a File Conversion Function

Program 2–4 is an ASCII-to-Unicode file conversion program that calls the function Asc2Un (Program 2–5) to process the file using file I/O. Program 5–3 (Asc2UnMM) is an alternative function that uses memory mapping to perform exactly the same operation. The circumstances under which `Asc2UnMM` is faster were described earlier; essentially, the file system should be NTFS and the file should not be too large.

Program 5–7 reimplements the calling program so that it can decide which implementation to load at run time. It then loads the DLL and obtains the address of the `Asc2Un` entry point and calls the function. There is only one entry point in this case, but it would be equally easy to locate multiple entry points. The main program is as before, except that the DLL to use is a command line parameter. Exercise 5–9 suggests that the DLL is determined on the basis of system and file characteristics. Also notice how the `FARPROC` address is cast to the appropriate function type using the required, but complex, C syntax.

Program 5–7   `atouEL`: File Conversion with Explicit Linking

```
/* Chapter 5. atou Explicit Link version. */

#include "EvryThng.h"

int _tmain (int argc, LPTSTR argv [])
{
    /* Declare variable Asc2Un to be a function. */
    BOOL (*Asc2Un)(LPCTSTR, LPCTSTR, BOOL);
    DWORD LocFileIn, LocFileOut, LocDLL, DashI;
    HINSTANCE hDLL;
    FARPROC pA2U;

    LocFileIn = Options (argc, argv, _T ("i"), &DashI, NULL);
    LocFileOut = LocFileIn + 1;
    LocDLL = LocFileOut + 1;

    /* Test for existing file && DashI is omitted. */
    /* Load the ASCII-to-Unicode function. */

    hDLL = LoadLibrary (argv [LocDLL]);
    if (hDLL == NULL)
        ReportError (_T ("Failed loading DLL."), 1, TRUE);

    /* Get the entry point address. */

    pA2U = GetProcAddress (hDLL, "Asc2Un");
    if (pA2U == NULL)
        ReportError (_T ("Failed to find entry point."), 2, TRUE);

    /* Cast the pointer. A typedef could be used here. */

    Asc2Un = (BOOL (*)(LPCTSTR, LPCTSTR, BOOL)) pA2U;
```

```
        /* Call the function. */
        Asc2Un (argv [LocFileIn], argv [LocFileOut], FALSE);
        FreeLibrary (hDLL);
        return 0;
}
```

Building the `Asc2Un` DLLs

This program was tested with the two file conversion functions, which must be built as DLLs with different names but identical entry points. There is only one entry point in this case. The only significant change in the source code is the addition of a storage modifier, `_declspec (dllexport)`, to export the function.

The DLL Entry Point

Optionally, you can specify an entry point for every DLL you create, and this entry point is normally invoked automatically every time a process attaches or detaches the DLL. `LoadLibraryEx`, however, allows you to prevent entry point execution. For implicitly linked (load-time) DLLs, process attachment and detachment occur when the process starts and terminates. In the case of explicitly linked DLLs, `LoadLibrary`, `LoadLibraryEx`, and `FreeLibrary` cause the attachment and detachment calls.

The entry point is also invoked when new threads (Chapter 7) are created or terminated by the process.

The DLL entry point, `DllMain`, is introduced here but will not be fully exploited until Chapter 12 (Program 12–4), where it provides a convenient way for threads to manage resources and so-called Thread Local Storage (TLS) in a thread-safe DLL.

```
    BOOL DllMain (
        HINSTANCE hDll,
        DWORD Reason,
        LPVOID Reserved)
```

The `hDll` value corresponds to the instance obtained from `LoadLibrary`. `Reserved`, if `NULL`, indicates that the process attachment was caused by `LoadLibrary`; otherwise, it was caused by implicit load-time linking. Likewise, `FreeLibrary` gives a `NULL` value for process detachment.

Reason will have one of four values: `DLL_PROCESS_ATTACH`, `DLL_THREAD_ATTACH`, `DLL_THREAD_DETACH`, and `DLL_PROCESS_DETACH`. DLL entry point functions are normally written as `switch` statements and return `TRUE` to indicate correct operation.

The system serializes calls to `DllMain` so that only one thread at a time can execute it (threads are thoroughly discussed starting in Chapter 7). This serialization is essential because `DllMain` must perform initializations that must be completed without interruption. As a consequence, however, it is recommended that there not be any blocking calls, such as I/O or wait functions (see Chapter 8) within the entry point, because they would prevent other threads from entering. `LoadLibrary` and `LoadLibraryEx`, in particular, should never be called from a DLL entry point as that would create additional DLL entry point calls.

`DisableThreadLibraryCalls` will disable thread attachment/detachment calls for a specified DLL instance. Disabling the thread calls can be helpful when threads do not require any unique resources during initialization.

DLL Version Management

A common problem with DLLs concerns difficulties that occur as a library is upgraded with new symbols and features are added. A major DLL advantage is that multiple applications can share a single implementation. This power, however, leads to compatibility complications, such as the following.

- New functions may be added, invalidating the offsets that implicitly linked applications assume when they link with a `.LIB` file. Explicit linking avoids this problem.

- A new version may change behavior, causing problems to existing applications that have not been updated.

- Applications that depend on new DLL functionality sometimes link with older DLL versions.

DLL version compatibility problems, popularly referred to as "DLL hell," can be irreconcilable if only one version of the DLL is to be maintained in a single directory. However, it is not necessarily simple to provide distinct version-specific directories for different versions. There are several solutions.

- Use the DLL version number as part of the `.DLL` and `.LIB` file names, usually as a suffix. For example, `Utility_3_0.DLL` and `Utility_3_0.LIB` are used on the examples on the book's Web site and with all the projects to correspond with the book version number. By using either explicit or implicit linking, applications can then determine their version requirements and access files with distinct names. This solution is commonly used with UNIX applications.

- Microsoft introduced the concept of side-by-side DLLs or assemblies and components. This solution requires adding a manifest, written in XML, to the application so as to define the DLL requirements. This topic is beyond the book's scope, but additional information can be found on the Microsoft developer Web site.

- The .NET Framework provides additional support for side-by-side execution.

The first approach, including the version number as part of the file name, is used in the example projects. To provide additional support so that applications can determine the DLL information, `DllGetVersion` is implemented in all the DLLs; many Microsoft DLLs also provide this callback function as a standard method to obtain version information dynamically. The function takes the following form:

```
HRESULT CALLBACK DllGetVersion(
        DLLVERSIONINFO *pdvi

)
```

Information about the DLL is returned in the `DLLVERSIONINFO` structure, which contains `DWORD` fields for `cbSize` (the structure size), `dwMajorVersion`, `dwMinorVersion`, `dwBuildNumber`, and `dwPlatformID`. The last field, `dwPlatformID`, can be set to `DLLVER_PLATFORM_NT` if the DLL cannot run on Windows 9x or to `DLLVER_PLATFORM_WINDOWS` if there are no restrictions. The `cbSize` field should be set to `sizeof(DLLVERSIONINFO)`. The normal return value is `NOERROR`. `Utility_3_0` implements `DllGetVersion`.

Summary

Windows memory management includes the following features.

- Logic can be simplified by allowing the Windows heap management and exception handlers to detect and process allocation errors.

- Multiple independent heaps provide several advantages over allocation from a single heap.

- Memory-mapped files, available with UNIX but not with the C library, allow files to be processed in memory, as illustrated by several examples. File mapping is independent of heap management, and it can simplify many programming tasks. Appendix C shows the performance advantage of using memory-mapped files.

- DLLs are an essential special case of mapped files, and DLLs can be loaded either explicitly or implicitly. DLLs used by numerous applications should provide version information.

Looking Ahead

This completes coverage of what can be achieved within a single process. The next step is to learn how to manage concurrent processing, first with processes (Chapter 6) and then with threads (Chapter 7). Subsequent chapters will show how to synchronize and communicate between concurrent processing activities.

Additional Reading

Memory Mapping, Virtual Memory, and Page Faults

David Solomon and Mark Russinovich, in *Inside Windows 2000*, describe the important concepts, and most OS texts provide good in-depth discussion.

Data Structures and Algorithms

Search trees and sort algorithms are explained in numerous texts, including the books by Thomas A. Standish and Robert Sedgewick.

Using Explicit Linking

DLLs and explicit linking are fundamental to the operation of COM, which is widely used in Windows software development. Chapter 1 of Don Box's *Essential COM* shows the importance of `LoadLibrary` and `GetProcAddress`.

Exercises

5–1. Design and carry out experiments to evaluate the performance gains from the HEAP_NO_SERIALIZE flag with HeapCreate and HeapAlloc. How are the gains affected by the heap size and by the block size? Are there differences under different Windows versions? The book's Web site contains a program, HeapNoSr.c, to help you get started on this exercise and the next one.

5–2. Modify the test in the preceding exercise to determine whether malloc generates exceptions or returns a null pointer when there is no memory. Is this the correct behavior? Also compare malloc performance with the results from the preceding exercise.

5–3. Windows versions differ significantly in terms of the overhead memory in a heap, especially when using obsolete Windows 9x versions. Design and carry out an experiment to measure how many fixed-size blocks each system will give in a single heap. Using SEH to detect when all blocks have been allocated makes the program easier. A test program, clear.c, on the Web site will show this behavior if the explicit OS test in the code is ignored. This program, incidentally, is used in some of the timing tests to assure that data from a previous test run is not still in memory.

5–4. Modify sortFL (Program 5–4) to create sortHP, which allocates a memory buffer large enough to hold the file, and read the file into that buffer. There is no memory mapping. Compare the performance of the two programs.

5–5. Program 5–5 exploits the _based pointers that are specific to Microsoft C. If you have a compiler that does not support this feature (or simply for the exercise), reimplement Program 5–5 with a macro, arrays, or some other mechanism to generate the based pointer values.

5–6. Write a search program that will find a record with a specified key in a file that has been indexed by Program 5–5. The C library bsearch function would be convenient here.

5–7. Implement the tail program from Chapter 3 with memory mapping.

5–8. Put the `ReportError`, `PrintStrings`, `PrintMsg`, and `ConsolePrompt` utility functions into a DLL and rebuild some of the earlier programs. Do the same with `Options` and `GetArgs`, the command line option and argument processing functions. It is important that both the utility DLL and the calling program also use the C library in DLL form. Within Visual C++ and Visual Studio 6.0, for instance, select, from the title bar, Project ... Settings ... C/C++ tab ... Category (Code Generation) ... Use Run-Time Library (Multithreaded DLL). Note that DLLs must, in general, be multithreaded because they will be used by threads from several processes. See the `Utilities_3_0` project on the Web site for a solution.

5–9. Modify Program 5–7 so that the decision as to which DLL to use is based on the file size and system configuration. The `.LIB` file is not required, so figure out how to suppress `.LIB` file generation. Use `GetVolumeInformation` to determine the file system type.

5–10. Create additional DLLs for the conversion function in the previous exercise, each version using a different file processing technique, and extend the calling program to decide when to use each version.

6 | Process Management

A process contains its own independent virtual address space with both code and data, protected from other processes. Each process, in turn, contains one or more independently executing *threads*. A thread running within a process can create new threads, create new independent processes, and manage communication and synchronization between the objects.

By creating and managing processes, applications can have multiple, concurrent tasks processing files, performing computations, or communicating with other networked systems. It is even possible to exploit multiple processors to speed processing.

This chapter explains the basics of process management and also introduces the basic synchronization operations that will be used throughout the rest of the book.

Windows Processes and Threads

Every process contains one or more threads, and the Windows thread is the basic executable unit. Threads are scheduled on the basis of the usual factors: availability of resources such as CPUs and physical memory, priority, fairness, and so on. Windows has supported symmetric multiprocessing (SMP) since NT4, so threads can be allocated to separate processors within a system.

From the programmer's perspective, each Windows process includes resources such as the following components:

- One or more threads.

- A virtual address space that is distinct from other processes' address spaces, except where memory is explicitly shared. Note that shared memory-mapped files share physical memory, but the sharing processes will use different virtual addresses to access the mapped file.

- One or more code segments, including code in DLLs.

- One or more data segments containing global variables.

- Environment strings with environment variable information, such as the current search path.

- The process heap.

- Resources such as open handles and other heaps.

Each thread in a process shares code, global variables, environment strings, and resources. Each thread is independently scheduled, and a thread has the following elements:

- A stack for procedure calls, interrupts, exception handlers, and automatic storage.

- Thread Local Storage (TLS)—arrays of pointers giving each thread the ability to allocate storage to create its own unique data environment.

- An argument on the stack, from the creating thread, which is usually unique for each thread.

- A context structure, maintained by the kernel, with machine register values.

Figure 6–1 shows a process with several threads. This figure is schematic and does not indicate actual memory addresses, nor is it drawn to scale.

This chapter shows how to work with processes consisting of a single thread. Chapter 7 shows how to use multiple threads.

Note: Figure 6–1 is a high-level overview from the programmer's perspective. There are numerous technical and implementation details, and interested readers can find out more in *Inside Windows 2000* (Solomon and Russinovich).

A UNIX process is comparable to a Windows process with a single thread.

Threads, in the form of POSIX Pthreads, are a recent addition to UNIX implementations and are now nearly universally used. Stevens (1992) does not discuss threads; everything is done with processes.

Needless to say, vendors and others have provided various thread implementations for many years; they are not a new concept. Pthreads is, however, the most widely used standard, and proprietary implementations are obsolete.

Figure 6-1   A Process and Its Threads

Process Creation

The fundamental Windows process management function is `CreateProcess`, which creates a process with a single thread. It is necessary to specify the name of an executable program file as part of the `CreateProcess` call.

It is common to speak of *parent* and *child* processes, but these relationships are not actually maintained by Windows. It is simply convenient to refer to the process that creates a child process as the parent.

`CreateProcess` has ten parameters to support its flexibility and power. Initially, it is simple to use default values. Just as with `CreateFile`, it is appropriate to explain all the `CreateProcess` parameters. Related functions then become easier to understand.

Note first that the function does not return a `HANDLE`; rather, two separate handles, one each for the process and the thread, are returned in a structure specified in the call. `CreateProcess` creates a new process with a *primary* thread. The example programs are always very careful to close both of these handles when they are no longer needed in order to avoid resource leaks; a common defect is to neglect to close the thread handle. Closing a thread handle, for instance, does not terminate the thread; the `CloseHandle` function only deletes the reference to the thread within the process that called `CreateProcess`.

```
BOOL CreateProcess (
    LPCTSTR lpApplicationName,
    LPTSTR lpCommandLine,
    LPSECURITY_ATTRIBUTES lpsaProcess,
    LPSECURITY_ATTRIBUTES lpsaThread,
    BOOL bInheritHandles,
    DWORD dwCreationFlags,
    LPVOID lpEnvironment,
    LPCTSTR lpCurDir,
    LPSTARTUPINFO lpStartupInfo,
    LPPROCESS_INFORMATION lpProcInfo)
```

Return: TRUE only if the process and thread are successfully created.

Parameters

Some parameters require extensive explanations in the following sections, and many are illustrated in the program examples.

lpApplicationName and lpCommandLine (this is an LPTSTR and not an LPCTSTR) together specify the executable program and the command line arguments, as explained in the next section.

lpsaProcess and lpsaThread point to the process and thread security attribute structures. NULL values imply default security and will be used until Chapter 15, which covers Windows security.

bInheritHandles indicates whether the new process inherits copies of the calling process's inheritable open handles (files, mappings, and so on). Inherited handles have the same attributes as the originals and are discussed in detail in a later section.

dwCreationFlags combines several flags, including the following.

- CREATE_SUSPENDED indicates that the primary thread is in a suspended state and will run only when ResumeThread is called.

- DETACHED_PROCESS and CREATE_NEW_CONSOLE are mutually exclusive; don't set both. The first flag creates a process without a console, and the second flag gives the new process a console of its own. If neither flag is set, the process inherits the parent's console.

- CREATE_NEW_PROCESS_GROUP specifies that the new process is the root of a new process group. All processes in a group receive a console control signal (Ctrl-c or Ctrl-break) if they all share the same console. Console control handlers were described in Chapter 4 and illustrated in Program 4–5. These process groups have similarities to UNIX process groups and are described later in this chapter.

Several of the flags control the priority of the new process's threads. The possible values are explained in more detail at the end of Chapter 7. For now, just use the parent's priority (specify nothing) or NORMAL_PRIORITY_CLASS.

lpEnvironment points to an environment block for the new process. If NULL, the process uses the parent's environment. The environment block contains name and value strings, such as the search path.

lpCurDir specifies the drive and directory for the new process. If NULL, the parent's working directory is used.

lpStartupInfo specifies the main window appearance and standard device handles for the new process. Use the parent's information, which is obtained from GetStartupInfo. Alternatively, zero out the associated STARTUPINFO structure before calling CreateProcess. To specify the standard input, output, and error handles, set the standard handler fields (hStdInput, hStdOutput, and hStdError) in the STARTUPINFO structure. For this to be effective, also set another STARTUPINFO member, dwFlags, to STARTF_USESTDHANDLES, and set all the handles that the child process will require. Be certain that the handles are inheritable and that the CreateProcess bInheritHandles flag is set. The Inheritable Handles subsection gives more information and an example.

lpProcInfo specifies the structure for containing the returned process, thread handles, and identification. The PROCESS_INFORMATION structure is as follows:

```
typedef struct PROCESS_INFORMATION {
    HANDLE hProcess;
    HANDLE hThread;
    DWORD dwProcessId;
    DWORD dwThreadId;
} PROCESS_INFORMATION;
```

Why do processes and threads need handles in addition to IDs? The ID is unique to the object for its entire lifetime and in all processes, whereas a given process may have several handles, each having distinct attributes, such as security access. For this reason, some process management functions require IDs, and others require handles. Furthermore, process handles are required for the general-purpose, handle-based functions. Examples include the wait functions discussed later in this chapter, which allow waiting on handles for several different object types, including processes. Just as with file handles, process and thread handles should be closed when no longer required.

Note: The new process obtains environment, working directory, and other information from the `CreateProcess` call. Once this call is complete, any changes in the parent will not be reflected in the child process. For example, the parent might change its working directory after the `CreateProcess` call, but the child process working directory will not be affected, unless the child changes its own working directory. The two processes are entirely independent.

The UNIX and Windows process models are considerably different. First, Windows has no equivalent to the UNIX `fork` function, which makes a copy of the parent, including the parent's data space, heap, and stack. `fork` is difficult to emulate exactly in Windows, and, while this may seem to be a limitation, `fork` is also difficult to use in a multithreaded UNIX system because there are numerous problems with creating an exact replica of a multithreaded system with exact copies of all threads and synchronization objects, especially on an SMP system. Therefore, `fork`, by itself, is not really appropriate in any multithreaded system.

`CreateProcess` is, however, similar to the common UNIX sequence of successive calls to `fork` and `execl` (or one of five other `exec` functions). In contrast to Windows, the search directories in UNIX are determined entirely by the PATH environment variable.

As previously mentioned, Windows does not maintain parent-child relationships among processes. Thus, a child process will continue to run after the creating parent process terminates. Furthermore, there are no process groups in Windows. There is, however, a limited form of process group that specifies all the processes to receive a console control event.

Windows processes are identified both by handles and by process IDs, whereas UNIX has no process handles.

Specifying the Executable Image and the Command Line

Either `lpApplicationName` or `lpCommandLine` specifies the executable image name. The rules are as follows.

- `lpApplicationName`, if not NULL, is the name of the executable. Quotation marks can be used if the image name contains spaces. More detailed rules are described below.

- Otherwise, the executable is the first token in `lpCommandLine`.

Usually, only `lpCommandLine` is specified, with `lpApplicationName` being NULL. Nonetheless, there are detailed rules for `lpApplicationName`.

- If `lpApplicationName` is not NULL, it specifies the executable module. Specify the full path and file name, or use a partial name and the current drive and directory will be used; there is no additional searching. Include the file extension, such as `.EXE` or `.BAT`, in the name.

- If the `lpApplicationName` string is NULL, the first white-space-delimited token in `lpCommandLine` is the program name. If the name does not contain a full directory path, the search sequence is as follows:

  1. The directory of the current process's image

  2. The current directory

  3. The Windows system directory, which can be retrieved with `GetSystem-Directory`

  4. The Windows directory, which is retrievable with `GetWindowsDirectory`

  5. The directories as specified in the environment variable `PATH`

The new process can obtain the command line using the usual `argv` mechanism, or it can invoke `GetCommandLine` to obtain the command line as a single string.

Notice that the command line is not a constant string. This is consistent with the fact that the `argv` parameters to the main program are not constant. A program could modify its arguments, although it is advisable to make any changes in a copy of the argument string.

The new process is not required to be built with the same UNICODE definition as that of the parent process. All combinations are possible. Using `_tmain` as discussed in Chapter 2 is helpful in developing code for either UNICODE or ASCII operation.

Inheritable Handles

Frequently, a child process requires access to an object referenced by a handle in the parent; if this handle is inheritable, the child can receive a copy of the parent's open handle. The standard input and output handles are frequently shared with the child in this way. To make a handle inheritable so that a child receives and can use a copy requires several steps.

The `bInheritHandles` flag on the `CreateProcess` call determines whether the child process will inherit copies of the inheritable handles of open files, processes, and so on. The flag can be regarded as a master switch applying to all handles.

It is also necessary to make an individual handle inheritable; it is not done by default. To create an inheritable handle, use a SECURITY_ATTRIBUTES structure at creation time or duplicate an existing handle.

The SECURITY_ATTRIBUTES structure has a flag, bInheritHandle, that should be set to TRUE. Also, recall that nLength should be set to sizeof (SECURITY_ATTRIBUTES).

The following code segment shows how an inheritable file or other handle is typically created. In this example, the security descriptor within the security attributes structure is NULL; Chapter 15 shows how to include a security descriptor.

```
HANDLE h1, h2, h3;
SECURITY_ATTRIBUTES sa =
    {sizeof(SECURITY_ATTRIBUTES), NULL, TRUE };
...
h1 = CreateFile (..., &sa, ... ); /* Inheritable. */
h2 = CreateFile (..., NULL, ... ); /* Not inheritable. */
h3 = CreateFile (..., &sa, ...);
    /* Inheritable. sa can be reused. */
```

A child process still needs to know the value of an inheritable handle, so the parent needs to communicate handle values to the child using an interprocess communication (IPC) mechanism or by assigning the handle to standard I/O in the STARTUPINFO structure, as is done in the first example of this chapter (Program 6–1) and in several additional examples throughout the book. This is generally the preferred technique because it allows I/O redirection in a standard way and no changes are needed in the child program.

Alternatively, nonfile handles and handles that are not used to redirect standard I/O can be converted to text and placed in a command line or in an environment variable. This approach is valid if the handle is inheritable because both parent and child processes identify the handle with the same handle value. Exercise 6–2 suggests how to demonstrate this, and a solution is presented on the book's Web site.

The inherited handles are distinct copies. Therefore, a parent and child might be accessing the same file using different file pointers. Furthermore, each of the two processes can and should close its own handle.

Figure 6–2 shows how two processes can have distinct handle tables with two distinct handles associated with the same file or other object. Process 1 is the parent, and Process 2 is the child. The handles will have identical values in both

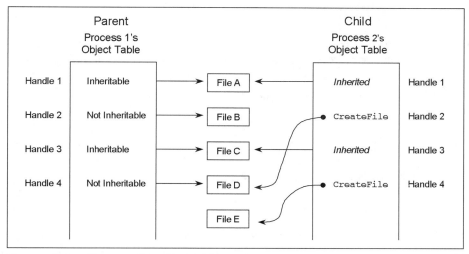

Figure 6-2 Process Handle Tables

processes if the child's handle has been inherited, as is the case with Handles 1 and 3.

On the other hand, the handle values may be distinct. For example, there are two handles for File D, where Process 2 obtained a handle by calling `CreateFile` rather than by inheritance. Finally, as is the case with Files B and E, one process may have a handle to an object while the other does not. This would be the case when the child process creates the handle or when a handle is duplicated from one process to another, as described in the upcoming Duplicating Handles section.

Process Handle Counts

A common programming error is to neglect to close handles when they are no longer needed; this can result in resource leakage, which in turn can degrade performance, cause program failures, and even impact other processes. NT 5.1 added a new function that allows you to determine how many handles any process has open. In this way, you can monitor your own process or other processes.

Here is the function definition, which is self-explanatory:

```
BOOL GetProcessHandleCount (
    HANDLE hProcess,
    PDWORD pdwHandleCount)
```

Process Identities

A process can obtain the identity and handle of a new child process from the PROCESS_INFORMATION structure. Closing the child handle does not, of course, destroy the child process; it destroys only the parent's access to the child. A pair of functions is used to obtain current process identification.

```
HANDLE GetCurrentProcess (VOID)

DWORD GetCurrentProcessId (VOID)
```

GetCurrentProcess actually returns a *pseudohandle* and is not inheritable. This value can be used whenever a process needs its own handle. You create a real process handle from a process ID, including the one returned by GetCurrent-ProcessId, by using the OpenProcess function. As is the case with all sharable objects, the open call will fail if you do not have sufficient security rights.

```
HANDLE OpenProcess (
    DWORD dwDesiredAccess,
    BOOL bInheritHandle,
    DWORD dwProcessId)

Return: A process handle, or NULL on failure.
```

Parameters

dwDesiredAccess determines the handle's access to the process. Some of the values are as follows.

- SYNCHRONIZE—This flag enables processes to wait for the process to terminate using the wait functions described later in this chapter.

- PROCESS_ALL_ACCESS—All the access flags are set.

- PROCESS_TERMINATE—It is possible to terminate the process with the TerminateProcess function.

- PROCESS_QUERY_INFORMATION—The handle can be used by GetExit-CodeProcess and GetPriorityClass to obtain process information.

bInheritHandle specifies whether the new handle is inheritable. dwProcessId is the identifier of the process requiring a handle.

Finally, a running process can determine the full pathname of the executable used to run it with GetModuleFileName or GetModuleFileNameEx, using a NULL value for the hModule parameter. A call from within a DLL will return the DLL's file name, not that of the .EXE file that uses the DLL.

Duplicating Handles

The parent and child processes may require different access to an object identified by a handle that the child inherits. A process may also need a real, inheritable process handle—rather than the pseudohandle produced by GetCurrent-Process—for use by a child process. To address this issue, the parent process can create a duplicate handle with the desired access and inheritability. Here is the function to duplicate handles:

```
BOOL DuplicateHandle (
    HANDLE hSourceProcessHandle,
    HANDLE hSourceHandle,
    HANDLE hTargetProcessHandle,
    LPHANDLE lphTargetHandle,
    DWORD dwDesiredAccess,
    BOOL bInheritHandle,
    DWORD dwOptions)
```

Upon completion, lphTargetHandle points to a copy of the original handle, hSourceHandle. hSourceHandle is a handle in the process indicated by hSourceProcessHandle and must have PROCESS_DUP_HANDLE access; DuplicateHandle will fail if the source handle does not exist in the source process. The new handle, which is pointed to by lphTargetHandle, is valid in the target process, hTargetProcessHandle. Note that three processes are involved, including the calling process. Frequently, these target and source processes are the calling process, and the handle is obtained from GetCurrentProcess. Also notice that it is possible to create a handle in another process; if you do this, you then need a mechanism for informing the other process of the new handle's identity.

DuplicateHandle can be used for any handle type.

If dwDesiredAccess is not overridden by DUPLICATE_SAME_ACCESS in dwOptions, it has many possible values (see the MSDN library on-line help).

dwOptions is any combination of two flags.

- DUPLICATE_CLOSE_SOURCE causes the source handle to be closed.
- DUPLICATE_SAME_ACCESS causes dwDesiredAccess to be ignored.

Reminder: The Windows kernel maintains a reference count for all objects; this count represents the number of distinct handles referring to the object. This count is not available to the application program, however. An object cannot be destroyed until the last handle is closed and the reference count becomes zero. Inherited and duplicate handles are both distinct from the original handles and are represented in the reference count. Program 6–1, later in the chapter, uses inheritable handles. On the other hand, a handle passed from one process to another through some form of IPC is not a distinct handle, so if one process closes the handle, the handle cannot be used by any other process. This technique is rarely used, but Exercise 6–2 uses IPC to send the value of the inherited handle to another process.

Next, it is necessary to learn how to determine whether a process has terminated.

Exiting and Terminating a Process

After a process is complete, the process, or more accurately, a thread running in the process, can call ExitProcess with an exit code.

```
VOID ExitProcess (UINT uExitCode)
```

This function does not return. Rather, the calling process and all its threads terminate. Termination handlers are ignored, but there will be detach calls to DllMain (see Chapter 5). The exit code is associated with the process. A return from the main program, with a return value, will have the same effect as calling ExitProcess with the return value as the exit code.

Another process can use GetExitCodeProcess to determine the exit code.

```
BOOL GetExitCodeProcess (
    HANDLE hProcess,
    LPDWORD lpExitCode)
```

The process identified by hProcess must have PROCESS_QUERY_INFOR-MATION access (see OpenProcess, discussed earlier). lpExitCode points to the DWORD that receives the value. One possible value is STILL_ACTIVE, meaning that the process has not terminated.

Finally, one process can terminate another process if the handle has PROCESS_TERMINATE access. The terminating function also specifies the exit code.

```
BOOL TerminateProcess (
    HANDLE hProcess,
    UINT uExitCode)
```

Caution: Before exiting from a process, be certain to free all resources that might be shared with other processes. In particular, the synchronization resources of Chapter 8 (mutexes, semaphores, and events) must be handled carefully. SEH (Chapter 4) can be helpful in this regard, and the ExitProcess call can be in the handler. However, __finally and __except handlers are *not* executed when ExitProcess is called, so it is not a good idea to exit from inside a program. TerminateProcess is especially risky because the terminated process will not have an opportunity to execute its SEH or DLL DllMain functions. Console control handlers (Chapter 4 and later in this chapter) are a limited alternative, allowing one process to send a signal to another process, which can then shut itself down cleanly.

Program 6–3 shows a technique whereby processes cooperate. One process sends a shutdown request to a second process, which proceeds to perform an orderly shutdown.

UNIX processes have a process ID, or pid, comparable to the Windows process ID. getpid is similar to GetCurrentProcessId, but there are no Windows equivalents to getppid and getgpid because Windows has no process parents or groups.

Conversely, UNIX does not have process handles, so it has no functions comparable to GetCurrentProcess or OpenProcess.

UNIX allows open file descriptors to be used after an exec if the file descriptor does not have the close-on-exec flag set. This applies only to file descriptors, which are then comparable to inheritable file handles.

UNIX exit, actually in the C library, is similar to ExitProcess; to terminate another process, signal it with SIGKILL.

Waiting for a Process to Terminate

The simplest, and most limited, method of synchronizing with another process is to wait for that process to complete. The general-purpose Windows wait functions introduced here have several interesting features.

- The functions can wait for many different types of objects; process handles are just the first use of the wait functions.

- The functions can wait for a single process, the first of several specified processes, or all processes in a group to complete.

- There is an optional time-out period.

The two general-purpose wait functions wait for synchronization objects to become *signaled*. The system sets a process handle, for example, to the signaled state when the process terminates or is terminated. The wait functions, which will get lots of future use, are as follows:

```
DWORD WaitForSingleObject (
   HANDLE hObject,
   DWORD dwMilliseconds)
```

```
DWORD WaitForMultipleObjects (
   DWORD nCount,
   CONST HANDLE *lpHandles,
   BOOL fWaitAll,
   DWORD dwMilliseconds)
```

Return: The cause of the wait completion, or 0XFFFFFFFF for an error (use GetLastError for more information).

Specify either a single process handle (hObject) or an array of distinct object handles in the array referenced by lpHandles. nCount, the size of the array, should not exceed MAXIMUM_WAIT_OBJECTS (defined as 64 in WINNT.H).

dwMilliseconds is the time-out period in milliseconds. A value of 0 means that the function returns immediately after testing the state of the specified objects, thus allowing a program to poll for process termination. Use `INFINITE` for no time-out to wait until a process terminates.

`fWaitAll`, a parameter of the second function, specifies (if `TRUE`) that it is necessary to wait for all processes, rather than only one, to terminate.

The possible successful return values for this function are as follows.

- `WAIT_OBJECT_0` means that the handle is signaled in the case of `WaitForSingleObject` or all `nCount` objects are simultaneously signaled in the special case of `WaitForMultipleObjects` with `fWaitAll` set to `TRUE`.

- `WAIT_OBJECT_0+n`, where $0 \leq n < nCount$. Subtract `WAIT_OBJECT_0` from the return value to determine which process terminated when waiting for any of a group of processes to terminate. If several handles are signaled, the returned value is the smallest possible value. `WAIT_ABANDONED_0` is a possible base value when using mutex handles; see Chapter 8.

- `WAIT_TIMEOUT` indicates that the time-out period elapsed before the wait could be satisfied by signaled handle(s).

- `WAIT_FAILED` indicates that the call failed; for example, the handle may not have `SYNCHRONIZE` access.

- `WAIT_ABANDONED_0` is not possible with processes. This value is discussed in Chapter 8 along with mutex handles.

Determine the exit code of a process using `GetExitCodeProcess`, as described in the preceding section.

Environment Blocks and Strings

Figure 6–1 includes the process environment block. The environment block contains a sequence of strings of the form

```
Name = Value
```

Each environment string, being a string, is `NULL`-terminated, and the entire block of strings is itself `NULL`-terminated. `PATH` is one example of a commonly used environment variable.

To pass the parent's environment to a child process, set `lpEnvironment` to `NULL` in the `CreateProcess` call. Any process, in turn, can interrogate or modify its environment variables or add new environment variables to the block.

The two functions used to get and set variables are as follows:

```
DWORD GetEnvironmentVariable (
    LPCTSTR lpName,
    LPTSTR lpValue,
    DWORD cchValue)

BOOL SetEnvironmentVariable (
    LPCTSTR lpName,
    LPCTSTR lpValue)
```

`lpName` is the variable name. On setting a value, the variable is added to the block if it does not exist and if the value is not `NULL`. If, on the other hand, the value is `NULL`, the variable is removed from the block. The "=" character cannot appear in a value string.

`GetEnvironmentVariable` returns the length of the value string, or 0 on failure. If the `lpValue` buffer is not long enough, as indicated by `cchValue`, then the return value is the number of characters actually required to hold the complete string. Recall that `GetCurrentDirectory` (Chapter 2) uses a similar mechanism.

Process Security

Normally, `CreateProcess` gives `PROCESS_ALL_ACCESS` rights. There are, however, several specific rights, including `PROCESS_QUERY_INFORMATION`, `CREATE_PROCESS`, `PROCESS_TERMINATE`, `PROCESS_SET_INFORMATION`, `DUPLICATE_HANDLE`, and `CREATE_THREAD`. In particular, it can be useful to limit `PROCESS_TERMINATE` rights to the parent process given the frequently mentioned dangers of terminating a running process. Chapter 15 describes security attributes for processes and other objects.

UNIX waits for process termination using `wait` and `waitpid`, but there are no time-outs even though `waitpid` can poll (there is a nonblocking option). These functions wait only for child processes, and there is no equivalent to the multiple wait on a collection of processes, although it is possible to wait for all processes in a process group. One slight difference is that the exit code is returned with `wait` and `waitpid`, so there is no need for a separate function equivalent to `GetExitCodeProcess`.

UNIX also supports environment strings similar to those in Windows. `getenv` (in the C library) has the same functionality as `GetEnvironmentVariable` except that the programmer must be sure to have a sufficiently large buffer. putenv, setenv, and unsetenv (not in the C library) are different ways to add, change, and remove variables and their values, with functionality equivalent to SetEnvironmentVariable.

Example: Parallel Pattern Searching

Now is the time to put Windows processes to the test. This example, grepMP, creates processes to search for patterns in files, one process per search file. The pattern search program is modeled after the UNIX grep utility, although the technique would apply to any program that uses standard output. The search program should be regarded as a black box and is simply an executable program to be controlled by a parent process.

The command line to the program is of the form

```
grepMP pattern F1 F2 ... FN
```

The program, Program 6–1, performs the following processing:

- Each input file, F1 to FN, is searched using a separate process running the same executable. The program creates a command line of the form grep *pattern* FK.

- The handle of the temporary file, specified to be inheritable, is assigned to the hStdOutput field of the new process's start-up information structure.

- Using WaitForMultipleObjects, the program waits for all search processes to complete.

- As soon as all searches are complete, the results (temporary files) are displayed in order, one at a time. A process to execute the cat utility (Program 2–3) outputs the temporary file.

- WaitForMultipleObjects is limited to MAXIMUM_WAIT_OBJECTS (64) handles, so it is called multiple times.

- The program uses the grep process exit code to determine whether a specific process detected the pattern.

Figure 6–3 shows the processing performed by Program 6–1.

Figure 6-3   File Searching Using Multiple Processes

Program 6-1   grepMP: Parallel Searching

```
/* Chapter 6. grepMP. */
/* Multiple process version of grep command. */

#include "EvryThng.h"
int _tmain (DWORD argc, LPTSTR argv [])
/* Create a separate process to search each file on the
   command line. Each process is given a temporary file,
   in the current directory, to receive the results. */
{
    HANDLE hTempFile;
    SECURITY_ATTRIBUTES StdOutSA = /* SA for inheritable handle. */
         {sizeof (SECURITY_ATTRIBUTES), NULL, TRUE};
    TCHAR CommandLine [MAX_PATH + 100];
    STARTUPINFO StartUpSearch, StartUp;
    PROCESS_INFORMATION ProcessInfo;
    DWORD iProc, ExCode;
    HANDLE *hProc; /* Pointer to an array of proc handles. */
    typedef struct {TCHAR TempFile [MAX_PATH];} PROCFILE;
    PROCFILE *ProcFile; /* Pointer to array of temp file names. */
```

```
GetStartupInfo (&StartUpSearch);
GetStartupInfo (&StartUp);
ProcFile = malloc ((argc - 2) * sizeof (PROCFILE));
hProc = malloc ((argc - 2) * sizeof (HANDLE));

/* Create a separate "grep" process for each file. */
for (iProc = 0; iProc < argc - 2; iProc++) {
    _stprintf (CommandLine, _T ("%s%s %s"),
        _T ("grep "), argv [1], argv [iProc + 2]);
    GetTempFileName (_T ("."), _T ("gtm"), 0,
        ProcFile [iProc].TempFile); /* For search results. */
    hTempFile = /* This handle is inheritable */
        CreateFile (ProcFile [iProc].TempFile,
            GENERIC_WRITE,
            FILE_SHARE_READ | FILE_SHARE_WRITE, &StdOutSA,
            CREATE_ALWAYS, FILE_ATTRIBUTE_NORMAL, NULL);
    StartUpSearch.dwFlags = STARTF_USESTDHANDLES;
    StartUpSearch.hStdOutput = hTempFile;
    StartUpSearch.hStdError = hTempFile;
    StartUpSearch.hStdInput = GetStdHandle (STD_INPUT_HANDLE);

    /* Create a process to execute the command line. */
    CreateProcess (NULL, CommandLine, NULL, NULL,
            TRUE, 0, NULL, NULL, &StartUpSearch, &ProcessInfo);
    /* Close unwanted handles. */
    CloseHandle (hTempFile); CloseHandle (ProcessInfo.hThread);
    hProc [iProc] = ProcessInfo.hProcess;
}

/* Processes are all running. Wait for them to complete. */
for (iProc = 0; iProc < argc - 2; iProc += MAXIMUM_WAIT_OBJECTS)
    WaitForMultipleObjects ( /* Allows a large # of processes */
            min (MAXIMUM_WAIT_OBJECTS, argc - 2 - iProc),
            &hProc [iProc], TRUE, INFINITE);
/* Result files sent to std output using "cat." */
for (iProc = 0; iProc < argc - 2; iProc++) {
    if (GetExitCodeProcess(hProc [iProc], &ExCode) && ExCode==0) {
        /* Pattern was detected -- List results. */
        if (argc > 3) _tprintf (_T ("%s:\n"), argv [iProc + 2]);
        fflush (stdout); /* Multiple processes use stdout. */
        _stprintf (CommandLine, _T ("%s%s"),
                _T ("cat "), ProcFile [iProc].TempFile);
        CreateProcess (NULL, CommandLine, NULL, NULL,
                TRUE, 0, NULL, NULL, &StartUp, &ProcessInfo);
        WaitForSingleObject (ProcessInfo.hProcess, INFINITE);
        CloseHandle (ProcessInfo.hProcess);
        CloseHandle (ProcessInfo.hThread);
    }
```

```
        CloseHandle (hProc [iProc]);
        DeleteFile (ProcFile [iProc].TempFile);
    }
    free (ProcFile);
    free (hProc);
    return 0;
}
```

Processes in a Multiprocessor Environment

In Program 6–1, the processes and their primary (and only) threads run almost totally independently of one another. The only dependence is created at the end of the parent process as it waits for all the processes to complete so that the output files can be processed sequentially. Therefore, the Windows scheduler can and will run the process threads concurrently on the separate processors of an SMP system. This can result in substantial performance improvement when performance is measured as elapsed time to execute the program, and no explicit actions are required to get the performance improvement.

Appendix C shows some typical results. The performance improvement is not linear in terms of the number of processors due to overhead costs and the need to output the results sequentially. Nonetheless, the improvements are worthwhile and result automatically as a consequence of the program design, which delegates independent computational tasks to independent processes.

It is possible, however, to constrain the processes to specific processors if you wish to be sure that other processors are free to be allocated to other critical tasks. This can be accomplished using the processor affinity mask (see Chapter 9) in a job object. Job objects are described in a later section.

Finally, it is possible to create independent threads within a process, and these threads will also be scheduled on separate SMP processors. Chapter 7 describes threads and performance issues related to their use.

Process Execution Times

You can determine the amount of time that a process requires (elapsed, kernel, and user times) using the GetProcessTimes function, which is not available on Windows 9x.

```
BOOL GetProcessTimes (
    HANDLE hProcess,
    LPFILETIME lpCreationTime,
    LPFILETIME lpExitTime,
    LPFILETIME lpKernelTime,
    LPFILETIME lpUserTime)
```

The process handle can refer to a process that is still running or to one that has terminated. Elapsed time can be computed by subtracting the creation time from the exit time, as shown in the next example. The FILETIME type is a 64-bit item; create a union with a LARGE_INTEGER to perform the subtraction. The lsW example in Chapter 3 showed how to convert and display file times.

GetThreadTimes is similar and requires a thread handle for a parameter. Chapter 7 covers thread management.

Example: Process Execution Times

The next example (Program 6–2) is a command called timep (time print) that is similar to the UNIX time command (time is supported by the command prompt, so a different name is required). Elapsed, kernel, and system times can be printed, although only elapsed time is available on Windows 9x.

One use for this command is to compare the execution times and efficiencies of the various file copy and ASCII to Unicode functions implemented in previous chapters.

This program uses GetCommandLine, a Windows function that returns the complete command line as a single string rather than individual argv strings.

The program also uses a utility function, SkipArg, to scan the command line and skip past the executable name. The SkipArg listing is in Appendix A.

Program 6–2 uses the GetVersionEx function to determine the OS version. With Windows 9x and CE, only the elapsed time is available. The code for these systems is shown to illustrate that a program can, in some cases, be made to operate, at least partially, on a range of Windows versions.

Program 6–2   timep: Process Times

```
/* Chapter 6. timep. */

#include "EvryThng.h"
int _tmain (int argc, LPTSTR argv [])
{
```

```
STARTUPINFO StartUp;
PROCESS_INFORMATION ProcInfo;
union { /* Structure required for file time arithmetic. */
    LONGLONG li;
    FILETIME ft;
} CreateTime, ExitTime, ElapsedTime;
FILETIME KernelTime, UserTime;
SYSTEMTIME ElTiSys, KeTiSys, UsTiSys, StartTimeSys, ExitTimeSys;
LPTSTR targv = SkipArg (GetCommandLine ());
OSVERSIONINFO OSVer;
BOOL IsNT;
HANDLE hProc;

OSVer.dwOSVersionInfoSize = sizeof(OSVERSIONINFO);
GetVersionEx (&OSVer);
IsNT = (OSVer.dwPlatformId == VER_PLATFORM_WIN32_NT);
/* NT (all versions) returns VER_PLATFORM_WIN32_NT. */
GetStartupInfo (&StartUp);
GetSystemTime (&StartTimeSys);

/* Execute the command line; wait for process to complete. */
CreateProcess (NULL, targv, NULL, NULL, TRUE,
        NORMAL_PRIORITY_CLASS, NULL, NULL, &StartUp, &ProcInfo);

/* Assure that we have all REQUIRED access to the process. */
DuplicateHandle (GetCurrentProcess (), ProcInfo.hProcess,
        GetCurrentProcess (), &hProc,
        PROCESS_QUERY_INFORMATION | SYNCHRONIZE, FALSE, 0);
WaitForSingleObject (hProc, INFINITE);
GetSystemTime (&ExitTimeSys);

if (IsNT) { /* W NT. Elapsed, Kernel, & User times. */
    GetProcessTimes (hProc, &CreateTime.ft,
        &ExitTime.ft, &KernelTime, &UserTime);
    ElapsedTime.li = ExitTime.li - CreateTime.li;
    FileTimeToSystemTime (&ElapsedTime.ft, &ElTiSys);
    FileTimeToSystemTime (&KernelTime, &KeTiSys);
    FileTimeToSystemTime (&UserTime, &UsTiSys);
    _tprintf (_T ("Real Time: %02d:%02d:%02d:%03d\n"),
        ElTiSys.wHour, ElTiSys.wMinute, ElTiSys.wSecond,
        ElTiSys.wMilliseconds);
    _tprintf (_T ("User Time: %02d:%02d:%02d:%03d\n"),
        UsTiSys.wHour, UsTiSys.wMinute, UsTiSys.wSecond,
        UsTiSys.wMilliseconds);
    _tprintf (_T ("Sys Time: %02d:%02d:%02d:%03d\n"),
        KeTiSys.wHour, KeTiSys.wMinute, KeTiSys.wSecond,
        KeTiSys.wMilliseconds);
} else {
    /* Windows 9x and CE. Elapsed time only. */
    ...
```

```
    }
    CloseHandle (ProcInfo.hThread); CloseHandle (ProcInfo.hProcess);
    CloseHandle (hProc);
    return 0;
}
```

Using the `timep` Command

`timep` can now be used to compare the various ASCII to Unicode file copy and sorting utilities such as `atou` (Program 2-4) and `sortMM` (Program 5–5). Appendix C summarizes and briefly analyzes some results.

Notice that measuring a program such as `grepMP` (Program 6–1) gives kernel and user times only for the parent process. Job objects, described near the end of this chapter, allow you to collect information on a group of processes. Appendix C shows that, on an SMP system, performance can improve as the separate processes, or more accurately, threads, run on different processors. There can also be performance gains if the files are on different physical drives.

Generating Console Control Events

Terminating a process can cause problems because the terminated process cannot clean up. SEH does not help because there is no general method for one process to cause an exception in another.[1] Console control events, however, allow one process to send a console control signal, or event, to another process in certain limited circumstances. Program 4–5 illustrated how a process can set up a handler to catch such a signal, and the handler could generate an exception. In that example, the user generated a signal from the user interface.

It is possible, then, for a process to generate a signal event in another specified process or set of processes. Recall the `CreateProcess` creation flag value, `CREATE_NEW_PROCESS_GROUP`. If this flag is set, the new process ID identifies a group of processes, and the new process is the *root* of the group. All new processes created by the parent are in this new group until another `CreateProcess` call uses the `CREATE_NEW_PROCESS_GROUP` flag. The grouped processes are similar to UNIX process groups.

One process can generate a `CTRL_C_EVENT` or `CTRL_BREAK_EVENT` in a specified process group, identifying the group with the root process ID. The target processes must have the same console as that of the process generating the event. In

---

[1] Chapter 10 shows an indirect way for one thread to cause an exception in another thread, and the same technique can be used between threads in different processes.

particular, the calling process cannot be created with its own console (using the CREATE_NEW_CONSOLE or DETACHED_PROCESS flag).

```
BOOL GenerateConsoleCtrlEvent (
    DWORD dwCtrlEvent,
    DWORD dwProcessGroup)
```

The first parameter, then, must be one of either CTRL_C_EVENT or CTRL_BREAK_EVENT. The second parameter identifies the process group.

Example: Simple Job Management

UNIX shells provide commands to execute processes in the background and to obtain their current status. This section develops a simple "job shell" with a similar set of commands. The commands are as follows.

- jobbg uses the remaining part of the command line as the command line for a new process, or *job*, but the jobbg command returns immediately rather than waiting for the new process to complete. The new process is optionally given its own console, or is *detached*, so that it has no console at all. This approach is similar to running a UNIX command with the & option at the end.

- jobs lists the current active jobs, giving the job numbers and process IDs. This is similar to the UNIX command of the same name.

- kill terminates a job. This implementation uses the TerminateProcess function, which, as previously stated, does not provide a clean shutdown. There is also an option to send a console control signal.

It is straightforward to create additional commands for suspending existing jobs or moving them to the foreground.

Because the shell, which maintains the job list, may terminate, the shell employs a user-specific shared file to contain the process IDs, the command, and related information. In this way, the shell can restart and the job list will still be intact. Furthermore, several shells can run concurrently. An exercise places this information in the registry, rather than in a temporary file.

Concurrency issues will arise. Several processes, running from separate command prompts, might perform job control simultaneously. The job management functions use file locking (Chapter 3) on the job list file so that a user can invoke job management from separate shells or processes.

The full program on the book's Web site has a number of additional features, not shown in the listings, such as the ability to take command input from a file. JobShell will be the basis for a more general "service shell" in Chapter 13 (Program 13–3). Windows NT services are background processes, usually servers, that can be controlled with start, stop, pause, and other commands.

Creating a Background Job

Program 6–3 is the job shell that prompts the user for one of three commands and then carries out the command. This program uses a collection of job management functions, which are shown in Programs 6–4, 6–5, and 6–6.

Program 6–3   JobShell: Create, List, and Kill Background Jobs

```
/* Chapter 6. */
/* JobShell.c -- job management commands:
   jobbg -- Run a job in the background.
   jobs -- List all background jobs.
   kill -- Terminate a specified job of job family.
         There is an option to generate a console control signal. */

#include "EvryThng.h"
#include "JobMgt.h"

int _tmain (int argc, LPTSTR argv [])
{
    BOOL Exit = FALSE;
    TCHAR Command [MAX_COMMAND_LINE + 10], *pc;
    DWORD i, LocArgc; /* Local argc. */
    TCHAR argstr [MAX_ARG] [MAX_COMMAND_LINE];
    LPTSTR pArgs [MAX_ARG];

    for (i = 0; i < MAX_ARG; i++) pArgs [i] = argstr [i];
    /* Prompt user, read command, and execute it. */
    _tprintf (_T ("Windows Job Management\n"));
    while (!Exit) {
        _tprintf (_T ("%s"), _T ("JM$"));
        _fgetts (Command, MAX_COMMAND_LINE, stdin);
        pc = strchr (Command, '\n');
        *pc = '\0';
        /* Parse the input to obtain command line for new job. */
        GetArgs (Command, &LocArgc, pArgs); /* See Appendix A. */
        CharLower (argstr [0]);
```

```
        if (_tcscmp (argstr [0], _T ("jobbg")) == 0) {
            Jobbg (LocArgc, pArgs, Command);
        }
        else if (_tcscmp (argstr [0], _T ("jobs")) == 0) {
            Jobs (LocArgc, pArgs, Command);
        }
        else if (_tcscmp (argstr [0], _T ("kill")) == 0) {
            Kill (LocArgc, pArgs, Command);
        }
        else if (_tcscmp (argstr [0], _T ("quit")) == 0) {
            Exit = TRUE;
        }
        else _tprintf (_T ("Illegal command. Try again\n"));
    }
    return 0;
}

/* jobbg [options] command-line [Options are mutually exclusive]
        -c: Give the new process a console.
        -d: The new process is detached, with no console.
        If neither is set, the process shares console with jobbg. */
int Jobbg (int argc, LPTSTR argv [], LPTSTR Command)
{
    DWORD fCreate;
    LONG JobNo;
    BOOL Flags [2];
    STARTUPINFO StartUp;
    PROCESS_INFORMATION ProcessInfo;
    LPTSTR targv = SkipArg (Command);

    GetStartupInfo (&StartUp);
    Options (argc, argv, _T ("cd"), &Flags [0], &Flags [1], NULL);
        /* Skip over the option field as well, if it exists. */
    if (argv [1] [0] == '-') targv = SkipArg (targv);

    fCreate = Flags [0] ? CREATE_NEW_CONSOLE :
            Flags [1] ? DETACHED_PROCESS : 0;

        /* Create job/thread suspended. Resume once job entered. */
    CreateProcess (NULL, targv, NULL, NULL, TRUE,
            fCreate | CREATE_SUSPENDED | CREATE_NEW_PROCESS_GROUP,
            NULL, NULL, &StartUp, &ProcessInfo);
        /* Create a job number and enter the process ID and handle
            into the job "data base." */

    JobNo = GetJobNumber (&ProcessInfo, targv); /* See "JobMgt.h" */
    if (JobNo >= 0)
        ResumeThread (ProcessInfo.hThread);
    else {
        TerminateProcess (ProcessInfo.hProcess, 3);
```

```
        CloseHandle (ProcessInfo.hProcess);
        ReportError (_T ("Error: No room in job list."), 0, FALSE);
        return 5;
    }
    CloseHandle (ProcessInfo.hThread);
    CloseHandle (ProcessInfo.hProcess);
    _tprintf (_T (" [%d] %d\n"), JobNo, ProcessInfo.dwProcessId);
    return 0;
}

/* jobs: List all running or stopped jobs. */
int Jobs (int argc, LPTSTR argv [], LPTSTR Command)
{
    if (!DisplayJobs ()) return 1; /* See job mgmt functions. */
    return 0;
}

/* kill [options] JobNumber
   -b Generate a Ctrl-Break
   -c Generate a Ctrl-C
      Otherwise, terminate the process. */
int Kill (int argc, LPTSTR argv [], LPTSTR Command)
{
    DWORD ProcessId, JobNumber, iJobNo;
    HANDLE hProcess;
    BOOL CntrlC, CntrlB, Killed;

    iJobNo =
        Options (argc, argv, _T ("bc"), &CntrlB, &CntrlC, NULL);

    /* Find the process ID associated with this job. */
    JobNumber = _ttoi (argv [iJobNo]);
    ProcessId = FindProcessId (JobNumber); /* See job mgmt. */
    hProcess = OpenProcess (PROCESS_ALL_ACCESS, FALSE, ProcessId);
    if (hProcess == NULL) { /* Process ID may not be in use. */
        ReportError (_T ("Process already terminated.\n"), 0, FALSE);
        return 2;
    }
    if (CntrlB)
        GenerateConsoleCtrlEvent (CTRL_BREAK_EVENT, ProcessId);
    else if (CntrlC)
        GenerateConsoleCtrlEvent (CTRL_C_EVENT, ProcessId);
    else
        TerminateProcess (hProcess, JM_EXIT_CODE);
    WaitForSingleObject (hProcess, 5000);
    CloseHandle (hProcess);
    _tprintf (_T ("Job [%d] terminated or timed out\n"), JobNumber);
    return 0;
}
```

Notice how the `jobbg` command creates the process in the suspended state and then calls the job management function, `GetJobNumber` (Program 6–4), to get a new job number and to register the job and its associated process. If the job cannot be registered for any reason, the job's process is terminated immediately. Normally, the job number is generated correctly, and the primary thread is resumed and allowed to run.

Getting a Job Number

The next three programs show three individual job management functions. These functions are all included in a single source file, `JobMgt.c`.

The first, Program 6–4, shows the `GetJobNumber` function. Notice the use of file locking with a completion handler to unlock the file. This technique protects against exceptions and inadvertent transfers around the unlock call. Such a transfer might be inserted accidentally during code maintenance even if the original program is correct. Also notice how the record past the end of the file is locked in the event that the file needs to be expanded with a new record.

Program 6–4   `JobMgt`: Creating New Job Information

```
/* Job management utility function. */

#include "EvryThng.h"
#include "JobMgt.h" /* Listed in Appendix A. */
void GetJobMgtFileName (LPTSTR);
LONG GetJobNumber (PROCESS_INFORMATION *pProcessInfo,
        LPCTSTR Command)

/* Create a job number for the new process, and enter
   the new process information into the job database. */
{
    HANDLE hJobData, hProcess;
    JM_JOB JobRecord;
    DWORD JobNumber = 0, nXfer, ExitCode, FsLow, FsHigh;
    TCHAR JobMgtFileName [MAX_PATH];
    OVERLAPPED RegionStart;

    if (!GetJobMgtFileName (JobMgtFileName)) return -1;
                /* Produces "\tmp\UserName.JobMgt" */
    hJobData = CreateFile (JobMgtFileName,
            GENERIC_READ | GENERIC_WRITE,
            FILE_SHARE_READ | FILE_SHARE_WRITE,
            NULL, OPEN_ALWAYS, FILE_ATTRIBUTE_NORMAL, NULL);
    if (hJobData == INVALID_HANDLE_VALUE) return -1;
```

```
    /* Lock the entire file plus one possible new
       record for exclusive access. */

    RegionStart.Offset = 0;
    RegionStart.OffsetHigh = 0;
    RegionStart.hEvent = (HANDLE)0;
    FsLow = GetFileSize (hJobData, &FsHigh);
    LockFileEx (hJobData, LOCKFILE_EXCLUSIVE_LOCK,
            0, FsLow + SJM_JOB, 0, &RegionStart);

    __try {
        /* Read records to find empty slot. */
        while (ReadFile (hJobData, &JobRecord, SJM_JOB, &nXfer, NULL)
                && (nXfer > 0)) {
            if (JobRecord.ProcessId == 0) break;
            hProcess = OpenProcess(PROCESS_ALL_ACCESS,
                    FALSE, JobRecord.ProcessId);
            if (hProcess == NULL) break;
            if (GetExitCodeProcess (hProcess, &ExitCode)
                    && (ExitCode != STILL_ACTIVE)) break;
            JobNumber++;
        }

        /* Either an empty slot has been found, or we are at end
           of file and need to create a new one. */

        if (nXfer != 0) /* Not at end of file. Back up. */
            SetFilePointer (hJobData, -(LONG)SJM_JOB,
                    NULL, FILE_CURRENT);
        JobRecord.ProcessId = pProcessInfo->dwProcessId;
        _tcsnccpy (JobRecord.CommandLine, Command, MAX_PATH);
        WriteFile (hJobData, &JobRecord, SJM_JOB, &nXfer, NULL);
    } /* End try. */

    __finally {
        UnlockFileEx (hJobData, 0, FsLow + SJM_JOB, 0,
                &RegionStart);
        CloseHandle (hJobData);
    }
    return JobNumber + 1;
}
```

Listing Background Jobs

Program 6–5 shows the DisplayJobs job management function.

Program 6–5   JobMgt: Displaying Active Jobs

```
BOOL DisplayJobs (void)

/* Scan the job database file, reporting job status. */
{
    HANDLE hJobData, hProcess;
    JM_JOB JobRecord;
    DWORD JobNumber = 0, nXfer, ExitCode, FsLow, FsHigh;
    TCHAR JobMgtFileName [MAX_PATH];
    OVERLAPPED RegionStart;

    GetJobMgtFileName (JobMgtFileName);
    hJobData = CreateFile (JobMgtFileName,
            GENERIC_READ | GENERIC_WRITE,
            FILE_SHARE_READ | FILE_SHARE_WRITE,
            NULL, OPEN_EXISTING, FILE_ATTRIBUTE_NORMAL, NULL);

    RegionStart.Offset = 0;
    RegionStart.OffsetHigh = 0;
    RegionStart.hEvent = (HANDLE)0;
    FsLow = GetFileSize (hJobData, &FsHigh);
    LockFileEx (hJobData, LOCKFILE_EXCLUSIVE_LOCK,
            0, FsLow, FsHigh, &RegionStart);

    __try {
    while (ReadFile (hJobData, &JobRecord, SJM_JOB, &nXfer, NULL)
        && (nXfer > 0)){
      JobNumber++;
      if (JobRecord.ProcessId == 0)
        continue;
      hProcess = OpenProcess (PROCESS_ALL_ACCESS, FALSE,
          JobRecord.ProcessId);
      if (hProcess != NULL)
        GetExitCodeProcess (hProcess, &ExitCode);
      _tprintf (_T (" [%d] "), JobNumber);
      if (hProcess == NULL)
        _tprintf (_T (" Done"));
      else if (ExitCode != STILL_ACTIVE)
        _tprintf (_T ("+ Done"));
      else _tprintf (_T (" "));
      _tprintf (_T (" %s\n"), JobRecord.CommandLine);

      /* Remove processes that are no longer in system. */

      if (hProcess == NULL) { /* Back up one record. */
        SetFilePointer (hJobData, -(LONG)nXfer,
              NULL, FILE_CURRENT);
        JobRecord.ProcessId = 0;
```

```
            WriteFile (hJobData, &JobRecord, SJM_JOB, &nXfer, NULL);
        }
    } /* End of while. */
    } /* End of __try. */

    __finally {
        UnlockFileEx (hJobData, 0, FsLow, FsHigh, &RegionStart);
        CloseHandle (hJobData);
    }

    return TRUE;
}
```

Finding a Job in the Job List File

Program 6–6 shows the final job management function, `FindProcessId`, which obtains the process ID of a specified job number. The process ID, in turn, can be used by the calling program to obtain a handle and other process status information.

Program 6–6   `JobMgt`: Getting the Process ID from a Job Number

```
DWORD FindProcessId (DWORD JobNumber)

/* Obtain the process ID of the specified job number. */
{
    HANDLE hJobData;
    JM_JOB JobRecord;
    DWORD nXfer;
    TCHAR JobMgtFileName [MAX_PATH];
    OVERLAPPED RegionStart;

    /* Open the job management file. */
    GetJobMgtFileName (JobMgtFileName);

    hJobData = CreateFile (JobMgtFileName, GENERIC_READ,
            FILE_SHARE_READ | FILE_SHARE_WRITE,
            NULL, OPEN_EXISTING, FILE_ATTRIBUTE_NORMAL, NULL);
    if (hJobData == INVALID_HANDLE_VALUE) return 0;

    /* Position to the entry for the specified job number.
     * The full program assures that JobNumber is in range. */

    SetFilePointer (hJobData, SJM_JOB * (JobNumber - 1),
            NULL, FILE_BEGIN);

    /* Lock and read the record. */
```

```
    RegionStart.Offset = SJM_JOB * (JobNumber - 1);
    RegionStart.OffsetHigh = 0; /* Assume a "short" file. */
    RegionStart.hEvent = (HANDLE)0;
    LockFileEx (hJobData, 0, 0, SJM_JOB, 0, &RegionStart);
    ReadFile (hJobData, &JobRecord, SJM_JOB, &nXfer, NULL);
    UnlockFileEx (hJobData, 0, SJM_JOB, 0, &RegionStart);
    CloseHandle (hJobData);
    return JobRecord.ProcessId;
}
```

Job Objects

Processes can be collected together into *job objects* where the processes can be controlled as a group, resource limits can be specified for all the job object member processes, and accounting information can be maintained. Job objects were introduced with Windows 2000 and are supported in all NT5 systems.

The first step is to create an empty job object with `CreateJobObject`, which takes two arguments, a name and security attributes, and returns a job object handle. There is also an `OpenJobObject` function to use with a named object. `CloseHandle` destroys the job object.

`AssignProcessToJobObject` simply adds a process specified by a process handle to a job object; there are just two parameters. A process cannot be a member of more than one job, so `AssignProcessToJobObject` fails if the process associated with the handle is already a member of some job. A process that is added to a job inherits all the limits associated with the job and adds its accounting information to the job, such as the processor time used.

By default, a new child process created with `CreateProcess` will also belong to the job unless the `CREATE_BREAKAWAY_FROM_JOB` flag is specified in the `dwCreationFlags` argument to `CreateProcess`. In the default case, `AssignProcessToJobObject` will fail if you attempt to assign the child process to a job.

Finally, you can specify control limits on the processes in a job using `SetInformationJobObject`.

```
BOOL SetInformationJobObject (
    HANDLE hJob,
    JOBOBJECTINFOCLASS JobObjectInformationClass,
    LPVOID lpJobObjectInformation,
    DWORD cbJobObjectInformationLength)
```

- `hJob` is a handle for an existing job object.

- `JobObjectInformationClass` specifies the information class for the limits you wish to set. There are five values; `JobObjectBasicLimitInformation` is one value and is used to specify information such as the total and per-process time limits, working set size limits,[2] limits on the number of active processes, priority, and processor affinity (the processors of an SMP system that can be used by threads in the job processes).

- `lpJobObjectInformation` points to the actual information required by the preceding parameter. There is a different structure for each class.

- `JOBOBJECT_BASIC_ACCOUNTING_INFORMATION` allows you to get the total time (user, kernel, and elapsed) of the processes in a job.

- The last parameter is the length of the preceding structure.

`QueryJobInformationObject` obtains the current limits. Other information classes impose limits on the user interface, I/O completion ports (see Chapter 14), security, and job termination.

Summary

Windows provides a straightforward mechanism for managing processes and synchronizing their execution. Examples have shown how to manage the parallel execution of multiple processes and how to obtain information about execution times. Windows does not maintain a parent-child relationship among processes, so the programmer must manage this information if it is required.

Looking Ahead

Threads, which are independent units of execution within a process, are described in the next chapter. Thread management is similar in some ways to process management, and there are exit codes, termination, and waiting on thread handles. To illustrate this similarity, `grepMP` (Program 6–1) will be reimplemented with threads in the first example program of Chapter 7.

Chapter 8 will then introduce synchronization, which can be used to coordinate operation between threads in the same or different processes.

---

[2] The working set is the set of virtual address space pages that the OS determines must be loaded in memory before any thread in the process is ready to run. This subject is covered in most OS texts.

Exercises

6–1. Extend Program 6–1 (grepMP) so that it accepts command line options and not just the pattern.

6–2. Rather than pass the temporary file name to the child process in Program 6–1, convert the inheritable file handle to a DWORD (a HANDLE requires 4 bytes) and then to a character string. Pass this string to the child process on the command line. The child process, in turn, must convert the character string back to a handle value to use for output. The catHA.c and grepHA.c programs on the book's Web site illustrate this technique.

6–3. Program 6–1 waits for all processes to complete before listing the results. It is impossible to determine the order in which the processes actually complete within the current program. Modify the program so that it can also determine the termination order. *Hint*: Modify the call to WaitForMultipleObjects so that it returns after each individual process terminates. An alternative would be to sort by the process termination times.

6–4. The temporary files in Program 6–1 must be deleted explicitly. Can you use FILE_FLAG_DELETE_ON_CLOSE when creating the temporary files so that deletion is not required?

6–5. Determine any grepMP performance advantages (compared with sequential execution) when you have an SMP system or when the files are on separate or network drives. Appendix C presents some partial results.

6–6. Can you find a way, perhaps using job objects, to collect the user and kernel time required by grepMP? It may be necessary to modify grepMP to use job objects.

6–7. Enhance the DisplayJobs function (Program 6–5) so that it reports the exit code of any completed job. Also, give the times (elapsed, kernel, and user) used so far by all jobs.

6–8. The job management functions have a defect that is difficult to fix. Suppose that a job is killed and the executive reuses its process ID before the process ID is removed from the job management file. There could be an `OpenProcess` on the process ID that now refers to a totally different process. The fix requires creating a helper process that holds duplicated handles for every created process so that the ID will not be reused. Another technique would be to include the process start time in the job management file. This time should be the same as the process start time of the process obtained from the process ID. *Note*: Process IDs will be reused quickly. UNIX, however, increments a counter to get a new process ID, and IDs will repeat only after the 32-bit counter wraps around. Therefore, Windows programs cannot assume that IDs will not, for all practical purposes, be reused.

6–9. Modify `JobShell` so that job information is maintained in the registry rather than in a temporary file.

6–10. Extend `JobShell` so that the processes are associated with a job object. Impose time and other limits on the jobs, allowing the user to enter some of these limits.

6–11. Enhance `JobShell` so that the `jobs` command will include a count of the number of handles that each job is using. *Hint*: Use `GetProcessHandle-Count`, which requires NT 5.1.

6–12. Build project `Version` (on the Web site), which uses `version.c`. Run the program on as many different Windows versions as you can access, including Windows 9x and NT 4.0 systems if possible. What are the major and minor version numbers for those systems, and what other information is available?

7 | Threads and Scheduling

The thread is Windows' basic unit of execution, and a process can contain multiple, independent threads sharing the process's address space and other resources. Chapter 6 limited processes to a single thread, but there are many situations in which multiple threads are desirable. This chapter describes and illustrates Windows thread management. The example programs use threads to simplify program design and to enhance performance. Chapter 8 continues with a description of synchronization objects and the impact, positive and negative, of threads on performance, and Chapter 9 examines performance tuning and trade-off issues. Chapter 10 describes advanced synchronization programming methods and models that greatly simplify the design and development of reliable multithreaded programs. The techniques will then be used in the remaining chapters.

This chapter ends with a very brief discussion of fibers, which allow you to create separate tasks within a thread. *Fibers are rarely used, and many readers will wish to skip the topic.*

Thread Overview

A *thread* is an independent unit of execution within a process. The multithreaded programming challenge requires organization and coordination of thread execution to simplify programs and to take advantage of the inherent parallelism of the host computer.

Traditionally, programs execute as a single thread of execution. While several processes can execute concurrently, as in the Chapter 6 examples, and even interact through mechanisms such as shared memory or pipes (Chapter 11), single-threaded processes have several disadvantages.

- It is expensive and time consuming for the OS to switch running processes, and, in cases such as the multiprocess search (grepMP, Program 6–1), the processes are all executing the same program. Threads allow concurrent file processing within a single process, reducing overall system overhead.

- Except in the case of shared memory, processes are not tightly coupled to one another, and it is difficult to share resources, such as open files.

- It is difficult and inefficient for single-threaded processes to manage several concurrent and interacting tasks, such as waiting for and processing user input, waiting for file or network input, and performing computation.

- I/O-bound programs, such as the ASCII to Unicode conversion program in Chapter 2 (atou, Program 2–4) are confined to a simple read-modify-write model. When you're processing sequential files, it can be more efficient to initiate as many read operations as possible. Windows NT also allows asynchronous overlapped I/O (Chapter 14), but threads can achieve the same effect with less programming effort.

- The Windows executive will schedule independent threads on separate processors of an SMP system, frequently improving performance.

This chapter discusses Windows threads and how to manage them. The examples illustrate thread usage with parallel file searching and a multithreaded sort. These two examples contrast I/O- and compute-intensive concurrent activities performed with threads. This chapter also presents an overview of Windows process and thread scheduling.

Perspectives and Issues

This chapter and those that follow take the point of view that not only do threads make certain programs simpler to design and implement but, with attention to a few basic rules and programming models, threaded programs also can improve performance and be reliable, easy to understand, and maintainable. Thread management functions are very similar to the process management functions so that, as just one example, there is a GetThreadExitCode function that is comparable to GetProcessExitCode.

This point of view is not universally accepted. Many writers and software developers mention thread risks and issues and prefer to use multiple processes when concurrency is required. Issues and concerns include the following.

- Threads share storage and other resources within a process, so one thread can accidentally modify another thread's data.

- In certain circumstances, concurrency can drastically degrade, rather than improve, performance.

- Threads share storage and other resources within a process, and this can lead to defects such as race conditions and deadlocks.

Some of the issues are real but can be avoided with careful design and programming, and many of the issues are inherent to concurrency, whether using threads within a process, multiple processes, or special-purpose techniques, such as Windows asynchronous I/O.

Thread Basics

Figure 6–1 in the previous chapter shows how threads exist in a process environment. Figure 7–1 illustrates threads by showing a multithreaded server that can process simultaneous requests from multiple networked clients; a distinct thread is dedicated to each client. This model will be implemented in Chapter 11.

Threads within a process share the same data and code, so it is essential that threads also have their own unique storage. Windows satisfies this requirement in several ways.

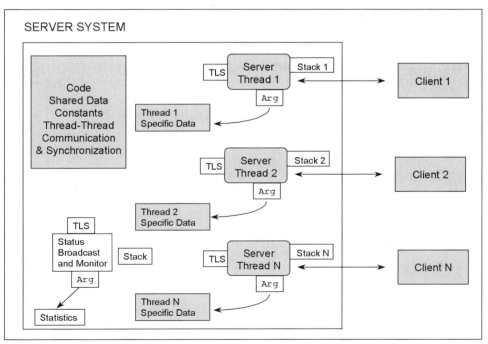

Figure 7–1   Threads in a Server Environment

- Each thread has its own stack for use in function calls and other processing.

- The calling process can pass an argument (`Arg` in Figure 7–1), usually a pointer, to a thread at creation time. This argument is actually on the thread's stack.

- Each thread can allocate its own Thread Local Storage (TLS) indexes and read and set TLS values. TLS, described later, provides small data arrays to threads, and a thread can access only its own TLS array. Among other advantages, TLS assures that threads will not modify one another's data.

The thread argument—or, alternatively, TLS—can be used to point to an arbitrary data structure. In Figure 7–1's server example, this structure might contain the current request and the thread's response to that request as well as other working storage.

Windows exploits SMP systems by allowing different threads, even from the same process, to run concurrently on separate processors. This capability, if used properly, can enhance performance, but without sufficient care and a good strategy to exploit multiple processors, execution on an SMP system can actually be slower than on a single-processor system, as we'll see in the next two chapters.

Thread Management

It should come as no surprise that threads, like any other Windows object, have handles and that there is a `CreateThread` system call to create an executable thread in the calling process's address space. As with processes, we will sometimes speak of "parent" and "child" threads, although the OS does not make any such distinction. `CreateThread` has several unique requirements.

- Specify the thread's start address within the process's code.

- Specify the stack size, and the stack space is allocated from the process's virtual address space. The default stack size is the parent's virtual memory stack size (normally 1MB). One page is initially committed to the stack (see Chapter 5). New stack pages are committed as required until the stack reaches its maximum size and cannot grow anymore.

- Specify a pointer to an argument for the thread. The argument can be nearly anything and is interpreted by the thread itself.

- `CreateThread` returns a thread's ID value and its handle. A `NULL` handle value indicates a failure.

```
HANDLE CreateThread (
    LPSECURITY_ATTRIBUTES lpsa,
    DWORD dwStackSize,
    LPTHREAD_START_ROUTINE lpStartAddr,
    LPVOID lpThreadParm,
    DWORD dwCreationFlags,
    LPDWORD lpThreadId)
```

Parameters

lpsa is the familiar security attributes structure.

dwStackSize is the byte size of the new thread's stack. Use 0 to default to the primary thread's stack size.

lpStartAddr points to the function (within the calling process) to be executed. This function accepts a single pointer argument and returns a 32-bit DWORD exit code. The thread can interpret the argument as a DWORD or a pointer. The thread function signature, then, is as follows:

```
DWORD WINAPI ThreadFunc (LPVOID)
```

lpThreadParm is the pointer passed as the thread argument and is interpreted by the thread, normally as a pointer to an argument structure.

dwCreationFlags, if 0, means that the thread is ready to run immediately. If dwCreationFlags is CREATE_SUSPENDED, the new thread will be in the suspended state, requiring a ResumeThread function call to move the thread to the ready state.

lpThreadId points to a DWORD that receives the new thread's identifier. The pointer can also be NULL, indicating that no thread ID will be returned; Windows 9x and NT Version 3.51 did not allow NULL for this parameter.

All threads in a process can terminate themselves using the ExitThread function. A common alternative, however, is for a thread to terminate itself by returning from the thread function using the exit code as the return value. The thread's stack is deallocated on termination. If the thread was created within a DLL, then the associated DllMain (Chapter 4) will be called with DLL_THREAD_DETACH as the "reason."

```
VOID ExitThread (DWORD dwExitCode)
```

When the last thread in a process terminates, the process itself terminates.

One thread can terminate another thread with the `TerminateThread` function, but the thread's resources will not be deallocated, completion handlers will not be executed, and attached DLLs will not be notified. It is best if the thread terminates itself; `TerminateThread` usage is strongly discouraged. `TerminateThread` has the same disadvantages as those of `TerminateProcess`.

A terminated thread (again, a thread normally should terminate itself) will continue to exist until the last handle to it is closed using `CloseHandle`. Any other thread, perhaps one waiting for some other thread to terminate, can retrieve the exit code.

```
BOOL GetExitCodeThread (
    HANDLE hThread,
    LPDWORD lpExitCode)
```

`lpExitCode` will contain the thread's exit code. If the thread is still running, the value is `STILL_ACTIVE`.

Thread Identity

You can obtain thread IDs and handles using functions that are similar to those used with processes.

- `GetCurrentThread` returns a noninheritable pseudohandle to the calling thread.

- `GetCurrentThreadId` obtains the thread ID, rather than the handle.

- `GetThreadId` obtains a thread's ID from its handle; this function requires Windows 2003.

- `OpenThread` creates a thread handle from a thread ID. `OpenProcess` was very useful in `JobShell` (Program 6–3), and `OpenThread` can be used in a similar fashion.

Additional Thread Management Functions

While the thread management functions discussed above are sufficient in most cases, including the examples in this book, two additional functions were introduced in XP and Windows 2003. Brief descriptions follow.

1. `GetProcessIdOfThread`, which requires Windows 2003, finds the process ID of a thread from the thread's handle. You could use this function in a program that manages or interacts with threads in other processes. If necessary, use `OpenProcess` to obtain a process handle.

2. `GetThreadIOPendingFlag` determines whether the thread, identified by its handle, has any outstanding I/O requests. For example, the thread might be blocked on a `ReadFile` operation. The result is the status at the time that the function is executed; the actual status could change at any time if the target thread completes or initiates an operation. This function requires NT 5.1 and is therefore available only in XP and Windows 2003.

Suspending and Resuming Threads

Every thread has a *suspend count*, and a thread can execute only if this count is 0. One thread can increment or decrement the suspend count of another thread using `SuspendThread` and `ResumeThread`. Recall that a thread can be created in the suspended state with a count of 1.

```
DWORD ResumeThread (HANDLE hThread)

DWORD SuspendThread (HANDLE hThread)
```

Both functions, if successful, return the previous suspend count. `0xFFFFFFFF` indicates failure.

Waiting for Threads to Terminate

One thread can wait for another thread to terminate in the same way that threads wait for process termination, as discussed in Chapter 6. Use a wait function (`WaitForSingleObject` or `WaitForMultipleObjects`) using thread handles instead of process handles. Note that the handles in the array passed to `WaitForMultipleObjects` do not all need to be of the same type; for example, thread, process, and other handle types can be mixed in a single call.

`WaitForMultipleObjects` can wait for only `MAXIMUM_WAIT_OBJECTS` (64) handles at one time, but you can perform a series of waits if you have a large number of threads. Program 6–1 already illustrated this technique; the programs in this book will perform single waits, but the full solution is on the book's Web site.

The wait function waits for the object, indicated by the handle, to become *signaled*. In the case of threads, `ExitThread` and `TerminateThread` set the object to the signaled state, releasing all other threads waiting on the object, including threads that might wait in the future after the thread terminates. Once a thread handle is signaled it never becomes nonsignaled. The same is true of process handles but not of handles to some other objects, such as mutexes and events (described in the next chapter).

Note that multiple threads can wait on the same object. Similarly, the `ExitProcess` function sets the process state and the states of all its threads to signaled.

Remote Threads

The `CreateRemoteThread` function allows creation of a thread in another process. Compared with `CreateThread`, there is an additional parameter for the process handle, and the function addresses must be in the target process's address space. `CreateRemoteThread` is one of several interesting, and potentially dangerous, ways for one process to affect another directly, and it might be useful in writing, for example, a debugger.

`CreateRemoteThread` has one very interesting application. Rather than calling `TerminateProcess`, a controlling process can create a thread in a different process, and that thread can shut down the process in an orderly fashion. Chapter 10, however, shows a much safer method for one thread to cancel another, using asynchronous procedure calls.

Threads are a well-established concept in many OSs, and historically, many UNIX vendors and users have provided their own proprietary implementations. Some thread libraries have been implemented outside the kernel. POSIX Pthreads are now the standard. Pthreads are included as part of commercial UNIX and Linux implementations and are sometimes considered to be a part of UNIX. The system calls are distinguished from normal UNIX system calls by the `pthread_` prefix name. Pthreads are also supported on some proprietary non-UNIX systems such as OpenVMS.

`pthread_create` is the equivalent of `CreateThread`, and `pthread_exit` is the equivalent of `ExitThread`. One thread waits for another to exit with `pthread_join`. Pthreads provide the very useful `pthread_cancel` function, which, unlike `TerminateThread`, ensures that completion handlers and cancellation handlers are executed. Thread cancellation would be a welcome addition to Windows, but Chapter 10 will show a method to achieve the same effect.

Using the C Library in Threads

Most code requires the C library, even if it is just to manipulate strings. Historically, the C library was written to operate in single-threaded processes, so many functions use global storage to store intermediate results. Such libraries are not *thread-safe* because two separate threads might, for example, be simultaneously accessing the library and modifying the library's global storage. Proper design of threaded code will be discussed again in Chapter 8, which describes Windows synchronization.

The function `strtok` illustrates why some C library functions were not written to be thread-safe. `strtok`, which scans a string to find the next occurrence of a token, maintains *persistent state* between successive calls to the function, and this state is in static storage, shared by all the threads calling the function.

Microsoft C solves such problems by supplying a thread-safe C library implementation named `LIBCMT.LIB`. There is more. Do not use `CreateThread`; rather, use a special C function, `_beginthreadex`, to start a thread and create thread-specific working storage for `LIBCMT.LIB`. Use `_endthreadex` in place of `ExitThread` to terminate a thread.

Note: There is a `_beginthread` function, intended to be simpler to use, *but it should be avoided*. First, `_beginthread` does not have security attributes or flags and does not return a thread ID. More importantly, it actually closes the thread handle it creates, and the returned thread handle may be invalid by the time the parent thread stores it. Also avoid `_endthread`; it does not allow for a return value.

The `_beginthreadex` arguments are exactly the same as for the Windows functions, but without the Windows type definitions; therefore, it is necessary to cast the `_beginthreadex` return value to a `HANDLE` to avoid warning messages. Be certain to define `_MT` before any include files; this definition is included in `Envirmnt.h` for the sample programs. That is all there is to it. In summary, when you're using the Visual C++ development environment, be sure to do the following:

- Link with `LIBCMT.LIB` and override the default library.

- Include `#define _MT` in all source files that use the C library.

- Include `<process.h>` for the `_beginthreadex` and `_endthreadex` definitions.

- Create threads with `_beginthreadex`; do not use `CreateThread`.

- Terminate threads with `_endthreadex` or simply use a `return` statement at the end of the thread routine.

Appendix A gives instructions on how to build threaded applications. In particular, it is possible, and recommended, to specify the library and the _MT setting directly from the development environment.

All examples will operate this way, and the programs will never use CreateThread directly, even if the thread functions do not use the C library.

Thread-Safe Libraries

User-developed libraries must be carefully designed to avoid thread safety issues, especially when persistent state is involved. An example in Chapter 12 (Program 12–4), where a DLL maintains state in a parameter, shows one strategy.

Another Chapter 12 example (Program 12–5) demonstrates an alternative approach that exploits the DllMain function and TLS, which is described later in this chapter.

Example: Multithreaded Pattern Searching

Program 6–1, grepMP, used processes to search multiple files simultaneously. Program 7–1, grepMT, includes the grep pattern searching source code so that threads can perform the searching within a single process. The pattern searching code relies on the C library for file I/O. The main control program is similar to the process implementation.

This example also shows that asynchronous I/O can be achieved with threads without using the explicit methods described in Chapter 14. In this example, the program is managing concurrent I/O to multiple files, and the main thread, or any other thread, can perform additional processing before waiting for I/O completion. In the author's opinion, threads are a much simpler method of achieving asynchronous I/O, and Chapter 14 compares the methods, allowing readers to form their own opinions. We will see, however, that asynchronous I/O, combined with I/O completion ports, is useful and often necessary when the number of threads is large.

grepMT, for the purposes of illustration, differs in another way from grepMP. Here, WaitForMultipleObjects waits for a *single* thread to terminate rather than waiting for all the threads. The appropriate output is displayed before waiting for another thread to complete. The completion order will, in most cases, vary from one run to the next. It is easy to modify the program to display the results in the order of the command line arguments; just imitate grepMP.

Finally, notice that there is a limit of 64 threads due to the value of MAXIMUM_WAIT_OBJECTS, which limits the number of handles in the WaitFor-MultipleObjects call. If more threads are required, create the appropriate logic to loop on either WaitForSingleObject or WaitForMultipleObjects.

Caution: `grepMT` performs asynchronous I/O in the sense that separate threads are concurrently, and synchronously, reading different files with read operations that block until the read is complete. You can also concurrently read from the same file if you have distinct handles on the file (typically, one per thread). These handles should be generated by `CreateFile` rather than `DuplicateHandle`. Chapter 14 describes asynchronous I/O, with and without user threads, and an example on the book's Web site (`atouMT`, described in Chapter 14) has several threads performing I/O to the same file.

Program 7–1 `grepMT`: Multithreaded Pattern Searching

```
/* Chapter 7. grepMT. */
/* Parallel grep -- multiple thread version. */

#include "EvryThng.h"
typedef struct { /* grep thread's data structure. */
    int argc;
    TCHAR targv [4] [MAX_PATH];
} GREP_THREAD_ARG;
typedef GREP_THREAD_ARG *PGR_ARGS;
static DWORD WINAPI ThGrep (PGR_ARGS pArgs);

int _tmain (int argc, LPTSTR argv [])
{
    GREP_THREAD_ARG * gArg;
    HANDLE * tHandle;
    DWORD ThdIdxP, ThId, ExitCode;
    TCHAR CmdLine [MAX_COMMAND_LINE];
    int iThrd, ThdCnt;
    STARTUPINFO StartUp;
    PROCESS_INFORMATION ProcessInfo;

    GetStartupInfo (&StartUp);
    /* Boss thread: create separate "grep" thread for each file. */
    tHandle = malloc ((argc - 2) * sizeof (HANDLE));
    gArg = malloc ((argc - 2) * sizeof (GREP_THREAD_ARG));

    for (iThrd = 0; iThrd < argc - 2; iThrd++) {
        _tcscpy (gArg [iThrd].targv [1], argv [1]); /* Pattern. */
        _tcscpy (gArg [iThrd].targv [2], argv [iThrd + 2]);
        GetTempFileName /* Temp file name. */
                (".", "Gre", 0, gArg [iThrd].targv [3]);
        gArg [iThrd].argc = 4;

        /* Create a worker thread to execute the command line. */
        tHandle [iThrd] = (HANDLE)_beginthreadex (
                NULL, 0, ThGrep, &gArg [iThrd], 0, &ThId);
    }
```

```
    /* Redirect std output for file listing process. */
    StartUp.dwFlags = STARTF_USESTDHANDLES;
    StartUp.hStdOutput = GetStdHandle (STD_OUTPUT_HANDLE);

    /* Worker threads are all running. Wait for them to complete. */
    ThdCnt = argc - 2;
    while (ThdCnt > 0) {
        ThdIdxP = WaitForMultipleObjects (
                ThdCnt, tHandle, FALSE, INFINITE);
        iThrd = (int) ThdIdxP - (int) WAIT_OBJECT_0;
        GetExitCodeThread (tHandle [iThrd], &ExitCode);
        CloseHandle (tHandle [iThrd]);
        if (ExitCode == 0) { /* Pattern found. */
            if (argc > 3) {
            /* Print file name if more than one. */
                _tprintf (_T ("\n**Search results - file: %s\n"),
                        gArg [iThrd].targv [2]);
                fflush (stdout);
            }
            /* Use the "cat" program to list the result files. */
            _stprintf (CmdLine, _T ("%s%s"), _T ("cat "),
                    gArg [iThrd].targv [3]);
            CreateProcess (NULL, CmdLine, NULL, NULL,
                    TRUE, 0, NULL, NULL, &StartUp, &ProcessInfo);
            WaitForSingleObject (ProcessInfo.hProcess, INFINITE);
            CloseHandle (ProcessInfo.hProcess);
            CloseHandle (ProcessInfo.hThread);
        }
        DeleteFile (gArg [iThrd].targv [3]);

        /* Adjust thread and file name arrays. */
        tHandle [iThrd] = tHandle [ThdCnt - 1];
        _tcscpy (gArg [iThrd].targv [3], gArg [ThdCnt - 1].targv [3]);
        _tcscpy (gArg [iThrd].targv [2], gArg [ThdCnt - 1].targv [2]);
        ThdCnt--;
    }
}

/* The form of the grep thread function code is:
static DWORD WINAPI ThGrep (PGR_ARGS pArgs)
{
} */
```

Performance Impact

grepMP and grepMT are comparable in terms of program structure and complexity, but grepMT has the expected advantage of better performance; it is more efficient for the kernel to switch between threads than between processes. Appendix C shows that the theoretical advantage is real, especially when the files are on different disk drives. Both implementations exploit SMP systems, giving a considerable improvement in the elapsed time; threads, whether in the same process or in different processes, run in parallel on the different processors. The measured user time actually exceeds the elapsed time because the user time is the total for all the processors.

There is a common misconception, however, that this sort of parallelism using either grepMP or grepMT only yields performance improvements on SMP systems. You can also gain performance when there are multiple disk drives or some other parallelism in the storage system. In such cases, multiple I/O operations to different files will run concurrently.

The Boss/Worker and Other Threading Models

grepMT illustrates the "boss/worker" threading model, and Figure 6–3 illustrates the relationship if "thread" is substituted for "process." The boss thread (the main thread in this case) assigns tasks for the worker threads to perform. Each worker thread is given a file to search, and the worker threads pass their results to the boss thread in a temporary file.

There are numerous variations, such as the *work crew model* where the workers cooperate on a single task, each performing a small piece. The next example uses a work crew (see Figure 7–2). The workers might even divide up the work themselves without direction from the boss. Nearly every management arrangement used by humans can be employed by multithreaded programs.

The two other major models are the *client/server model* (illustrated in Figure 7–1 and developed in Chapter 11) and the *pipeline model*, where work moves from one thread to the next (see Chapter 10 and Figure 10–1 for an example of a multistage pipeline).

There are many advantages to using these models when designing a multithreaded system, including the following.

- Most multithreaded programming problems can be solved using one of the standard models, expediting design, development, and debugging.

- Not only does using a well-understood and tested model avoid many of the mistakes that are so easy to make in a multithreaded program, but the model also helps you obtain the best performance.

- The models correspond naturally to the structures of most programming problems.

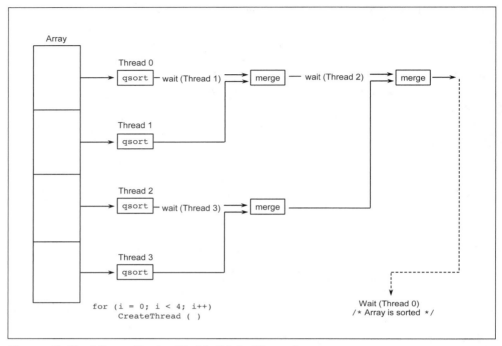

Figure 7-2   Merge-Sort with Multiple Threads

- Programmers who maintain the program will be able to understand it much more easily if documentation describes the program in terms that everyone understands.

- Troubleshooting an unfamiliar program is much easier if you analyze it in terms of models. Frequently, an underlying problem is found when the program is seen to violate the basic principles of one of the models.

- Many common defects, such as race conditions and deadlocks, are also described by simple models, as are effective methods of using the synchronization objects described in Chapters 9 and 10.

These classical thread models are used in many OSs. The Component Object Model (COM), widely used in Windows systems, uses different terminology, and, while COM is outside the scope of this book, the COM models are mentioned at the end of Chapter 11 and compared with program examples in this book.

Example: Merge-Sort—Divide and Conquer to Exploit SMP

This example shows how to use threads to get significant performance gains, especially on an SMP system. The basic idea is to divide the problem into component tasks, give each task to a separate thread, and then combine the results to get the complete solution. The Windows executive will automatically assign the threads to separate processors, so the tasks will be performed in parallel, reducing elapsed time.

This strategy, often called the *divide and conquer strategy* or the *work crew model*, is useful both for performance and as an algorithm design method. The implementation of grepMT, Program 7–1, could be considered one example; it creates a thread for each file or pattern matching task. Appendix C shows that there are performance gains on SMP systems because the executive can schedule the threads on different processors.

Next, consider another example in which a single task, sorting a file, is divided into subtasks delegated to separate threads.

Merge-sort, in which the array to be sorted is divided into smaller arrays, is a classic divide and conquer algorithm. Each small array is sorted individually, and the individual sorted arrays are merged in pairs to yield larger sorted arrays. The pairwise merging continues until completion. Generally, merge-sort starts with arrays of size 1, which need no sorting. This example starts with larger arrays so that there is one array for each processor. Figure 7–2 is a sketch of the algorithm.

Program 7–2 shows the details of the implementation. The user specifies the number of tasks on the command line. Appendix C shows the timing results. Exercise 7–9 suggests that sortMT use GetSystemInfo to find the number of processors and then create one thread per processor.

Notice that the program runs efficiently on single-processor systems with sufficient memory and gains a significant performance improvement on SMP systems. *Caution*: The algorithm as shown will work only if the number of records in the sort file is divisible by the number of threads and if the number of threads is a power of 2. Exercise 7–8 removes these limitations.

Note: In understanding this program, it is important to concentrate on the thread management logic separately from the logic that determines which portion of the array a thread is to sort. Notice too that the C library qsort function is used, so there is no need to be concerned with developing an efficient sort function.

Program 7–2 sortMT: Merge-Sort with Multiple Threads

```
/* Chapter 7. SortMT.
   File sorting with multiple threads (a work crew).
   sortMT [options] nt file */
```

```c
#include "EvryThng.h"
#define DATALEN 56 /* Key: 8 bytes; Data: 56 bytes. */
#define KEYLEN 8
typedef struct _RECORD {
     CHAR Key [KEYLEN]; TCHAR Data [DATALEN];
} RECORD;
#define RECSIZE sizeof (RECORD)
typedef RECORD * LPRECORD;

typedef struct _THREADARG {        /* Thread argument */
   DWORD iTh;                      /* Thread number: 0, 1, 2, ... */
   LPRECORD LowRec;                /* Low record */
   LPRECORD HighRec;               /* High record */
} THREADARG, *PTHREADARG;

static int KeyCompare (LPCTSTR, LPCTSTR);
static DWORD WINAPI ThSort (PTHREADARG pThArg);
static DWORD nRec; /* Total number of records to be sorted. */
static HANDLE * ThreadHandle;

int _tmain (int argc, LPTSTR argv [])
{
   HANDLE hFile;
   LPRECORD pRecords = NULL;
   DWORD FsLow, nRead, LowRecNo, nRecTh, NPr, ThId, iTh;
   BOOL NoPrint;
   int iFF, iNP;
   PTHREADARG ThArg;
   LPTSTR StringEnd;

   iNP = Options (argc, argv, _T ("n"), &NoPrint, NULL);
   iFF = iNP + 1;
   NPr = _ttoi (argv [iNP]); /* Number of threads. */
   hFile = CreateFile (argv [iFF], GENERIC_READ | GENERIC_WRITE,
         0, NULL, OPEN_EXISTING, 0, NULL);
   FsLow = GetFileSize (hFile, NULL);
   nRec = FsLow / RECSIZE; /* Total number of records. */
   nRecTh = nRec / NPr; /* Records per thread. */

   /* Allocate thread args and handle array
      and space for the file. Read the complete file. */

   ThArg = malloc (NPr * sizeof (THREADARG)); /* Thread args. */
   ThreadHandle = malloc (NPr * sizeof (HANDLE));
   pRecords = malloc (FsLow + sizeof (TCHAR));
   ReadFile (hFile, pRecords, FsLow, &nRead, NULL);
   CloseHandle (hFile);
```

```
        LowRecNo = 0; /* Create the sorting threads. */
        for (iTh = 0; iTh < NPr; iTh++) {
            ThArg [iTh].iTh = iTh;
            ThArg [iTh].LowRec = pRecords + LowRecNo;
            ThArg [iTh].HighRec = pRecords + (LowRecNo + nRecTh);
            LowRecNo += nRecTh;
            ThreadHandle [iTh] = (HANDLE) _beginthreadex (NULL, 0,
                    ThSort, &ThArg [iTh], CREATE_SUSPENDED, &ThId);
        }

        for (iTh = 0; iTh < NPr; iTh++) /* Run all sort threads. */
            ResumeThread (ThreadHandle [iTh]);
        WaitForSingleObject (ThreadHandle [0], INFINITE);
        for (iTh = 0; iTh < NPr; iTh++) CloseHandle (ThreadHandle [iTh]);

        StringEnd = (LPTSTR) pRecords + FsLow;
        *StringEnd = '\0';
        if (!NoPrint) printf ("\n%s", (LPCTSTR) pRecords);
        free (pRecords);
        free (ThArg);
        free (ThreadHandle);
        return 0;
}   /* End of _tmain. */

static VOID MergeArrays (LPRECORD, LPRECORD);
DWORD WINAPI ThSort (PTHREADARG pThArg)
{
    DWORD GrpSize = 2, RecsInGrp, MyNumber, TwoToI = 1;
    LPRECORD First;

    MyNumber = pThArg->iTh;
    First = pThArg->LowRec;
    RecsInGrp = pThArg->HighRec - First;
    qsort (First, RecsInGrp, RECSIZE, KeyCompare);
    while ((MyNumber % GrpSize) == 0 && RecsInGrp < nRec) {
                    /* Merge with the adjacent sorted array. */
        WaitForSingleObject (
                ThreadHandle [MyNumber + TwoToI], INFINITE);
        MergeArrays (First, First + RecsInGrp);
        RecsInGrp *= 2;
        GrpSize *= 2;
        TwoToI *= 2;
    }
    _endthreadex (0);
    return 0; /* Suppress a warning message. */
}

static VOID MergeArrays (LPRECORD p1, LPRECORD p2)
{
```

```
    DWORD iRec = 0, nRecs, i1 = 0, i2 = 0;
    LPRECORD pDest, p1Hold, pDestHold;

    nRecs = p2 - p1;
    pDest = pDestHold = malloc (2 * nRecs * RECSIZE);
    p1Hold = p1;
    while (i1 < nRecs && i2 < nRecs) {
        if (KeyCompare ((LPCTSTR) p1, (LPCTSTR) p2) <= 0) {
            memcpy (pDest, p1, RECSIZE);
            i1++; p1++; pDest++;
        }

        else {
            memcpy (pDest, p2, RECSIZE);
            i2++; p2++; pDest++;
        }
    }

    if (i1 >= nRecs) memcpy (pDest, p2, RECSIZE * (nRecs - i2));
    else memcpy (pDest, p1, RECSIZE * (nRecs - i1));

    memcpy (p1Hold, pDestHold, 2 * nRecs * RECSIZE);
    free (pDestHold);
    return;
}
```

Performance

Appendix C includes the results of sorting large files of 64-byte records using one, two, and four threads. SMP systems give significantly better results. Divide and conquer is more than just a strategy for algorithm design; it can also be the key to exploiting threads and SMP. The single-processor results can vary. On a system with limited memory (that is, insufficient physical memory to hold the entire file, in addition to the OS and other active processes), the use of multiple threads increases the sort time because the threads contend for available physical memory. On the other hand, multiple threads can improve performance with a single processor when there is sufficient memory. The results are also heavily dependent on the initial data arrangement, as discussed in Appendix C.

Thread Local Storage

Threads may need to allocate and manage their own storage independently of and protected from other threads in the same process. One technique is to have the creating thread call CreateThread (or _beginthreadex) with lpvThreadParm pointing to a data structure that is unique for each thread. The thread can then allocate additional data structures and access them through `lpvThreadParm`. Program 7–1 used this technique.

Windows also provides TLS, which gives each thread its own array of pointers. Figure 7–3 shows this TLS arrangement.

Initially, no TLS indexes (rows) are allocated, but new rows can be allocated and deallocated at any time, with a maximum of `TLS_MINIMUM_AVAILABLE` (at least 64) indexes for any process. The number of columns can change as new threads are created and old ones terminate.

The first issue is TLS index management. The primary thread is a logical place to do this, but any thread can manage thread indexes.

`TlsAlloc` returns the allocated index (≥ 0), with –1 (`0xFFFFFFFF`) if no index is available.

```
DWORD TlsAlloc (VOID)

BOOL TlsFree (DWORD dwIndex)
```

An individual thread can get and set its values (void pointers) from its slot using a TLS index.

The programmer must ensure that the TLS index parameter is valid—that is, that it has been allocated with `TlsAlloc` and has not been freed.

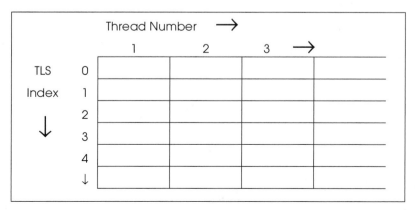

Figure 7–3   Thread Local Storage within a Process

```
LPVOID TlsGetValue (DWORD dwTlsIndex)

BOOL TlsSetValue (DWORD dwTlsIndex,
    LPVOID lpTlsValue)
```

TLS provides a convenient mechanism for storage that is global within a thread but unavailable to other threads. Normal global storage is shared by all threads. Although no thread can access another thread's TLS, any thread can call `TlsFree` and destroy an index for all threads, so `TlsFree` should be used carefully. TLS is frequently used by DLLs as a replacement for global storage in a library; each thread, in effect, has its own global storage. TLS also provides a convenient way for a calling program to communicate with a DLL function, and this is the most common use of TLS. An example in Chapter 12 (Program 12–4) exploits TLS to build a thread-safe DLL; DLL thread and process attach/detach calls (Chapter 5) are another important element in the solution.

Process and Thread Priority and Scheduling

The Windows kernel always runs the highest-priority thread that is ready for execution. A thread is not ready if it is waiting, suspended, or blocked for some reason.

Threads receive priority relative to their process priority classes. Four process priority classes are set initially by `CreateProcess`, as described in Chapter 6, and each has a *base priority*.

- `IDLE_PRIORITY_CLASS`, base priority 4
- `NORMAL_PRIORITY_CLASS`, base priority 9 or 7
- `HIGH_PRIORITY_CLASS`, base priority 13
- `REALTIME_PRIORITY_CLASS`, base priority 24

The two extreme classes are rarely used, and the normal class can be used most of the time. Windows NT (all versions) is not a real-time OS, but CE is, and `REALTIME_PRIORITY_CLASS` should be used with care so as not to prevent other processes from running. The normal base priority is 9 if the window has the focus for keyboard input; otherwise, the priority is 7.

A process can change or determine its own priority or that of another process, security permitting.

```
BOOL SetPriorityClass (HANDLE hProcess,
    DWORD dwPriority)

DWORD GetPriorityClass (HANDLE hProcess)
```

Thread priorities are set relative to the process base priority, and, at thread creation time, the priority is set to that of the process. The thread priorities are in a range of ±2 from the process's base. The symbolic names of the resulting five thread priorities are as follows:

- THREAD_PRIORITY_LOWEST

- THREAD_PRIORITY_BELOW_NORMAL

- THREAD_PRIORITY_NORMAL

- THREAD_PRIORITY_ABOVE_NORMAL

- THREAD_PRIORITY_HIGHEST

Use these values to set and read a thread's relative priority. Note the use of signed integers rather than DWORDs.

```
BOOL SetThreadPriority (HANDLE hThread,
    int nPriority)

int GetThreadPriority (HANDLE hThread)
```

There are actually two additional thread priority values. They are absolute rather than relative and are used only in special cases.

- THREAD_PRIORITY_IDLE is a value of 1 (or 16 for real-time processes).

- THREAD_PRIORITY_TIME_CRITICAL is 15 (or 31 for real-time processes).

Thread priorities change automatically with process priority. In addition, the OS may adjust thread priorities dynamically on the basis of thread behavior. You can enable and disable this feature with the SetThreadPriorityBoost function.

Thread and Process Priority Cautions

High thread priorities and process priority classes should be used with caution. Real-time priorities should definitely be avoided for normal user processes; real-time priorities should be used only if the application is truly real-time. Among other dangers, user threads may preempt threads in the executive.

Furthermore, everything that we say in the following chapters about the correctness of threaded programs assumes, without comment, that thread scheduling is *fair*. Fairness ensures that all threads will, eventually, run. Without fairness, a low-priority thread could hold resources required by a high-priority thread. *Thread starvation* and *priority inversion* are terms used to describe the defects that occur when scheduling is not fair.

Thread States

Figure 7–4, which is taken from Custer's *Inside Windows NT*, page 210 (also see Solomon and Russinovich's updated version of this book), shows how the executive manages threads and shows the possible thread states. This figure also shows the effect of program actions. Such state diagrams are common to all multitasking OSs and help clarify how a thread is scheduled for execution and how a thread moves from one state to another.

Here is a quick summary of the fundamentals. See Solomon and Russinovich or an OS text for more information.

- A thread is in the *running* state when it is actually running on a processor. More than one thread can be in the running state on an SMP system.

- The executive places a running thread in the *wait* state when the thread performs a wait on a nonsignaled handle, such as a thread or process handle, or on a synchronization object handle, as described in Chapter 8. I/O operations will also wait for completion of a disk or other data transfer, and numerous other functions can cause waiting. It is common to say that a thread is *blocked*, or *sleeping*, when in the wait state.

- A thread is *ready* if it could be running. The executive's scheduler could put it in the running state at any time. The scheduler will run the highest-priority ready thread when a processor becomes available, and it will run the one that has been in the ready state for the longest time if several threads have the same high priority. The thread moves through the *standby* state.

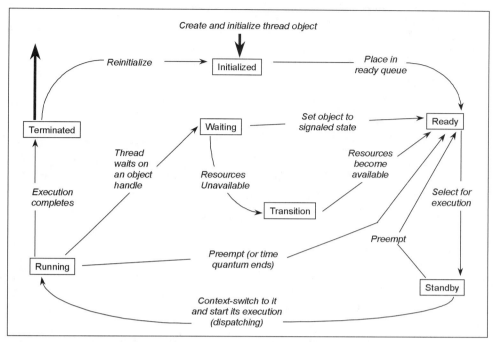

Figure 7–4 Thread States and Transitions
(From *Inside Windows NT*, Copyright © 1993, by Helen Custer. Copyright Microsoft Press. Reproduced by permission of Microsoft Press. All rights reserved.)

- Normally, as described above, the scheduler will place a ready thread on any available processor. The programmer can specify a thread's *processor affinity* (see Chapter 9) by giving the processors on which a thread is to be run. In this way, the programmer can allocate processors to threads. The appropriate functions are `SetProcessorAffinityMask` and `GetProcessorAffinityMask`. `SetThreadIdealProcessor` can be used to specify a preferred processor that the scheduler will use whenever possible.

- The executive will move a running thread to the ready state if the thread's time slice expires without the thread waiting. Executing `Sleep(0)` will also move a thread from the running state to the ready state.

- The executive will place a waiting thread in the ready state as soon as the appropriate handles are signaled, although the thread actually goes through an intermediate *transition* state. It is common to say that the thread *wakes up*.

- There is no way for a program to determine the state of another thread (of course, a thread, if it is running, must be in the running state, so it would be meaningless for a thread to find its own state). Even if there were, the state might change before the inquiring thread would be able to act on the information.

- A thread, regardless of its state, can be *suspended*, and a ready thread will not be run if it is suspended. If a running thread is suspended, either by itself or by a thread on a different processor, it is placed in the ready state.

- A thread is in the *terminated* state after it terminates and remains there as long as there are any open handles on the thread. This arrangement allows other threads to interrogate the thread's state and exit code.

Pitfalls and Common Mistakes

There are several factors to keep in mind as you develop threaded programs; lack of attention to a few basic principles can result in serious defects, and it is best to avoid the problems in the first place rather than try to find them during testing or debugging.

The essential factor is that the threads execute asynchronously. There is no sequencing unless you create it explicitly. This asynchronous behavior is what makes threads so useful, but, without proper care, serious difficulties can occur.

Here are a few guidelines; there will be more in later chapters.

- Make no assumptions about the order in which the parent and child threads execute. It is possible for a child thread to run to completion before the parent returns from `CreateThread`, or, conversely, the child thread may not run at all for a considerable period of time. On an SMP system, the parent and one or more children may even run concurrently.

- Ensure that all initialization required by the child is complete before the `CreateThread` call, or else use thread suspension or some other technique. Failure by the parent to initialize data required by the child is a common cause of "race conditions" wherein the parent "races" the child to initialize data before the child needs it. `sortMT` illustrates this principle.

- Be certain that each distinct child has its own data structure passed through the thread function's parameter. Do not assume that one child thread will complete before another (this is another form of race condition).

- Any thread, at any time, can be preempted, and any thread, at any time, may resume execution.

- Do not use thread priority as a substitute for explicit synchronization.

- Do not use reasoning such as "that will hardly ever happen" as an argument that a program is correct. If it can happen, it will, possibly at a very embarrassing moment.

- Even more so than with single-threaded programs, testing is necessary, but not sufficient, to ensure program correctness. It is common for a program to pass extensive tests despite code defects. There is no substitute for careful design, implementation, and code inspection.

- Threaded program behavior varies widely with processor speed, number of processors, OS version, and more. Testing on a variety of systems can isolate numerous defects, but the preceding precaution still applies.

- Be certain that threads have a sufficiently large stack, although the default 1MB will suffice in nearly all cases.

- Threads should be used only as appropriate. Thus, if there are activities that are naturally concurrent, each such activity can be represented by a thread. If, on the other hand, the activities are naturally sequential, threads only add complexity and performance overhead.

- Fortunately, correct programs are frequently the simplest and have the most elegant designs. Complexity should be avoided wherever possible.

Timed Waits

The final function, `Sleep`, allows a thread to give up the processor and move from the running to the wait state for a specified period of time. A thread can, for example, perform a task periodically by sleeping after carrying out the task. Once the time period is over, the scheduler moves the thread back to the ready state. A program in Chapter 11 (Program 11–4) uses this technique.

```
VOID Sleep (DWORD dwMilliseconds)
```

The time period is in milliseconds and can even be INFINITE, in which case the thread will never resume. A value of 0 will cause the thread to relinquish the remainder of the time slice; the kernel moves the thread from the running state to the ready state, as shown in Figure 7–4.

The function SwitchToThread provides another way for a thread to yield its processor to another ready thread, if there is one.

The UNIX sleep function is similar to Sleep, but time periods are measured in seconds. To obtain millisecond resolution, use the select or poll functions with no file descriptors.

Fibers

Note: Fibers are of specialized interest. See the comment after the first bulleted item below to determine if you want to skip this section.

A *fiber*, as the name implies, is a piece of a thread. More precisely, a fiber is a unit of execution within a thread that can be scheduled by the application rather than by the kernel. A thread can create numerous fibers, and the fibers themselves determine which of the thread's fibers will execute next. The fibers have independent stacks but otherwise run entirely in the context of the thread, having access, for example, to the thread's TLS and any mutexes[1] owned by the thread. Furthermore, fiber management occurs entirely in user space outside the kernel. Fibers can be thought of as lightweight threads, although there are numerous differences.

Fibers can be used for several purposes.

- Most importantly, many applications, especially some written for UNIX using proprietary thread implementations, now generally obsolete, are written to schedule their own threads. Fibers make it easier to port such applications to Windows. *Most readers will not have such requirements and may want to skip this section.*

- A thread does not need to block waiting for a file lock, mutex, named pipe input, or other resource. Rather, one fiber can poll the resource and, if the resource is not available, switch control to another specific fiber.

- Fibers operate within a thread and have access to thread and process resources. Unlike threads, fibers are not preemptively scheduled. The Windows executive, in fact, is not aware of fibers; fibers are managed within the fiber DLL entirely within user space.

- Fibers allow you to implement *co-routines*, whereby an application switches among several interrelated tasks. Threads do not allow this. The programmer has no direct control over which thread will be executed next.

---

[1] A mutex, as explained in the next chapter, is a synchronization object that threads can own.

- Major software vendors have used fibers and claim performance advantages. For example, Oracle Database 10g has an optional "fiber mode" (see http://download.oracle.com/owsf_2003/40171_colello.ppt; this presentation also describes the threading model).

Six functions make up the fiber API. They are used in the following sequence and as shown in Figure 7–5.

1. A thread must first enable fiber operation by calling `ConvertThreadToFiber`. The thread then consists of a single fiber, which can be considered the *primary* fiber. This call provides a pointer to fiber data, which can be used in much the same way that the thread argument was used to create unique data for a thread.

2. Primary or other fibers create additional fibers using `CreateFiber`. Each fiber has a start address, a stack size, and a parameter. Each new fiber is identified by an address rather than by a handle.

3. An individual fiber can obtain its data, as received from `CreateFiber`, by calling `GetFiberData`.

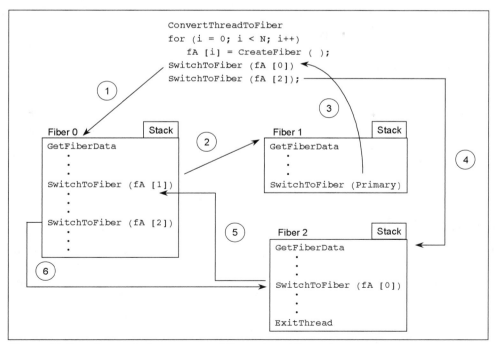

Figure 7–5   Control Flow among Fibers in a Thread

4. Similarly, a fiber can obtain its identity with `GetCurrentFiber`.

5. A running fiber yields control to another fiber by calling `SwitchToFiber`, indicating the address of the other fiber. Fibers must explicitly indicate the next fiber that is to run within the thread.

6. The `DeleteFiber` function deletes an existing fiber and all its associated data.

7. New functions, such as `ConvertFiberToThread` (which releases resources created by `ConvertThreadToFiber`), have been added to XP (NT 5.1), along with fiber local storage.

Figure 7–5 shows fibers in a thread. This example shows two ways in which fibers schedule each other.

- *Master-slave* **scheduling**. One fiber, the primary fiber in this case, decides which fiber to run, and that fiber always yields control to the master fiber. Fiber 1 in Figure 7–5 behaves in this way.

- *Peer-to-peer* **scheduling**. A fiber determines the next fiber to run. The determination can be based on policies such as round-robin scheduling, priority scheduling based on a priority scheme, and so on. Co-routines would be implemented with peer-to-peer scheduling. In Figure 7–5, Fibers 0 and 2 switch control in this way.

Summary

Windows supports threads that are independently scheduled but share the same process address space and resources. Threads give the programmer an opportunity to simplify program design and to exploit parallelism in the application to improve performance. Threads can even yield performance benefits on single-processor systems.

Looking Ahead

Chapter 8 describes and compares the Windows synchronization objects, and Chapters 9 and 10 continue with more advanced synchronization topics and extended examples. Chapter 11 implements the threaded server shown in Figure 7–1.

Additional Reading

Windows

Multithreading Applications in Win32, by Jim Beveridge and Robert Wiener, is an entire book devoted to Win32 threads. *Multithreaded Programming with Win32,* by Thuan Pham and Pankaj Garg, and *Win32 Multithreaded Programming,* by Aaron Cohen et al., are two additional choices. Many of these books have not been updated for Windows 2000, XP, and 2003, however.

UNIX and Pthreads

Stevens (1992) does not cover threads in UNIX, but *Programming with POSIX Threads,* by David Butenhof, is recommended. This book provides numerous guidelines for threaded program design and implementation. The information applies to Windows as well as to Pthreads, and many of the examples can be easily ported to Windows. There is also good coverage of the boss/worker, client/server, and pipeline threading models, and Butenhof's presentation is the basis for the model descriptions in this chapter.

Exercises

7–1. Implement a set of functions that will suspend and resume threads but also allow you to obtain a thread's suspend count.

7–2. Compare the performance of the parallel search programs, one using threads (Program 7–1, `grepMT`) and the other using processes (Program 6–1, `grepMP`). Compare the results with those in Appendix C.

7–3. Perform additional performance studies with `grepMT` where the files are on different disk drives or are networked files. Also determine the performance gain, if any, on SMP systems.

7–4. Modify `grepMT`, Program 7–1, so that it puts out the results in the same order as that of the files on the command line. Does this affect the performance measurements in any way?

7–5. Further enhance `grepMT`, Program 7–1, so that it prints the time required by each worker thread. `GetThreadTimes` will be required, and this function is similar to `GetProcessTimes`, which was used in Chapter 6. This enhancement will work only on Windows NT4 and later.

7–6. The book's Web site includes a multithreaded word count program, wcMT.c, that has a structure similar to that of grepMT.c. A defective version, wcMTx.c, is also included. Without referring to the correct solution, analyze and fix the defects in wcMTx.c, including any syntax errors. Also, create test cases that illustrate these defects and carry out performance experiments similar to those suggested for grepMT. There is also a single-threaded version, wcST.c, that can be used to determine whether threads give performance advantages over sequential processing.

7–7. The Web site includes grepMTx.c, which is defective because it violates basic rules for thread safety. Describe the failure symptoms, identify the errors, and fix them.

7–8. sortMT requires that the number of records in the array to be sorted be divisible by the number of threads and that the number of threads be a power of 2. Remove these restrictions.

7–9. Enhance sortMT so that if the number of threads specified on the command line is zero, the program will determine the number of processors on the host system using GetSystemInfo. Set the number of threads to different multiples (1, 2, 4, and so on) of the number of processors and determine the effect on performance.

7–10. Modify sortMT so that the worker threads are not suspended when they are created. What failure symptoms, if any, does the program demonstrate as a result of the race condition defect?

7–11. sortMT reads the entire file in the primary thread before creating the sorting threads. Modify the program so that each thread reads the portion of the file that it requires.

7–12. Modify one of the two programs in this chapter (grepMT or sortMT) so that some or all of the thread-specific information is passed through TLS rather than through a data structure.

7–13. Is there any performance benefit if you give some of the threads in sortMT higher priority than others? For example, it might be beneficial to give the threads that only sort and do not merge, such as Thread 3 in Figure 7–2, a higher priority. Explain the results.

7–14. sortMT creates all the threads in a suspended state so as to avoid a race condition. Modify the program so that it creates the threads in reverse order and in a running state. Are there any remaining race conditions? Compare performance with the original version.

7–15. Quicksort, the algorithm generally used by the C library `qsort` function, is usually fast, but it can be slow in certain cases. Most texts on algorithms show a version that is fastest when the array is reverse sorted and slowest when it is already sorted. The Microsoft C library implementation is different. Determine from the library code which sequences will produce the best and worst behavior, and study `sortMT`'s performance in these extreme cases. What is the effect of increasing or decreasing the number of threads? *Note*: The C library source code can be installed in the `CRT` directory under your Visual Studio installation. Look for `qsort.c`. Alternatively, you can find it on the installation CD.

7–16. The Web site contains a defective `sortMTx.c` program. Demonstrate the defects with test cases and then explain and fix the defects without reference to the correct solutions. *Caution*: The defective version may have syntax errors as well as errors in the thread logic.

7–17. Read "Waiting for More than 64 Objects" by Jason Clark in the October 1997 *Windows Developer's Journal*. Apply that solution to `grepMT`. Older journal issues can be difficult to find, so an on-line search with your favorite search engine should locate several items. I used the search phrase "wait for multiple objects more than 64," although other searches may be more effective.

8 Thread Synchronization

Threads can simplify program design and implementation and also improve performance, but thread usage requires care to ensure that shared resources are protected against simultaneous modification and that threads run only when requested or required. This chapter shows how to use Windows' synchronization objects—CRITICAL_SECTIONs, mutexes, semaphores, and events—to solve these problems and describes some of the problems, such as deadlocks and race conditions, that can occur when the synchronization objects are not used properly. Synchronization objects can be used to synchronize threads in the same process or in separate processes.

The examples illustrate the synchronization objects and discuss the performance impacts, both positive and negative, of different synchronization methods. The following chapters then show how to use synchronization to solve additional programming problems, improve performance, avoid pitfalls, and use more advanced features.

Thread synchronization is a fundamental and interesting topic, and it is essential in nearly all threaded applications. *Nonetheless, readers who are primarily interested in interprocess communication, network programming, and building threaded servers can skip to Chapter 11 and return to Chapters 8 through 10 for background material as required.*

The Need for Thread Synchronization

Chapter 7 showed how to create and manage worker threads, where each worker thread accessed its own resources. In the Chapter 7 examples, each thread processes a separate file or a separate area of storage, yet simple synchronization during thread creation and termination is still required. For example, the grepMT worker threads all run independently of one another, but the boss thread must wait for the workers to complete before reporting the results generated by the worker threads. Notice that the boss shares memory with the workers, but the program design assures that the boss will not access the memory until the worker terminates.

`sortMT` is slightly more complicated because the workers need to synchronize by waiting for adjacent workers to complete, and the worker threads are not allowed to start until the boss thread has created all the workers. As with `grepMT`, synchronization is achieved by waiting for one or more threads to terminate.

In many cases, however, it is necessary for two or more threads to coordinate execution throughout each thread's lifetime. For instance, several threads may access the same variable or set of variables, and this raises the issue of mutual exclusion. In other cases, a thread cannot proceed until another thread reaches a designated point. How can the programmer assume that two or more threads do not, for example, simultaneously modify the same global storage, such as the performance statistics? Furthermore, how can the programmer ensure that a thread does not attempt to remove an element from a queue before there are any elements in the queue?

Several examples illustrate situations that can prevent code from being thread-safe. (Code is thread-safe if several threads can execute the code simultaneously without any undesirable results.) Thread safety is discussed later in this chapter and the following chapters.

Figure 8–1 shows what can happen when two unsynchronized threads share a resource such as a memory location. Both threads increment variable N, but, because of the particular sequence in which the threads might execute, the final value of N is 5, whereas the correct value is 6. Notice that the particular result shown here is neither repeatable nor predictable; a different thread execution sequence could yield the correct results. Execution on an SMP system can aggravate this problem.

Critical Code Sections

Incrementing N with a single statement such as N++ is no better because the compiler will generate a sequence of one or more machine-level instructions that are not necessarily executed *atomically* as a single unit.

The core problem is that there is a *critical section* of code (the code that increments N in this example) such that, once a thread starts to execute the critical section, no other thread can be allowed to enter until the first thread exits from the code section. This critical section problem can be considered a type of race condition because the first thread "races" to complete the critical section before any other thread starts to execute the critical code section. Thus, we need to synchronize thread execution in order to ensure that only one thread at a time executes the critical section.

Defective Solutions to the Critical Section Problem

Similarly unpredictable results will occur with a code sequence that attempts to protect the increment with a polled flag.

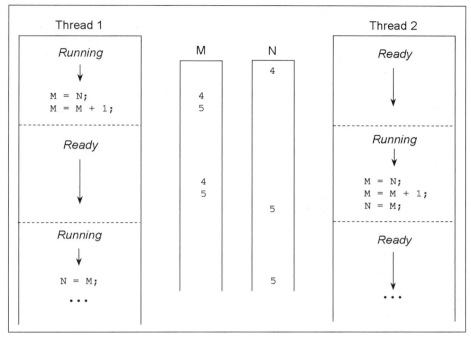

Figure 8–1   Unsynchronized Threads Sharing Memory

```
while (Flag) Sleep (1000);
Flag = TRUE;
N++;
Flag = FALSE;
```

Even in this case, the thread could be preempted between the time Flag is tested and the time Flag is set to TRUE; the first two statements form a critical code section that is not properly protected from concurrent access by two or more threads.

Another attempted solution to the critical section synchronization problem might be to give each thread its own copy of the variable N, as follows:

```
DWORD WINAPI ThFunc (TH_ARGS pArgs);
{   volatile DWORD N;
    ... N++; ...
}
```

This approach is no better, however, because each thread has its own copy of the variable on its stack, where it may have been required to have N represent, for example, the total number of threads in operation. Such a solution is necessary, however, in the case in which each thread needs its own distinct copy of the variable. This technique occurs frequently in the examples.

Notice that such problems are not limited to threads within a single process. They can also occur if two processes share mapped memory or modify the same file.

volatile Storage

Yet another latent defect exists even after we solve the synchronization problem. An optimizing compiler might leave the value of N in a register rather than storing it back in N. An attempt to solve this problem by resetting compiler optimization switches would impact performance throughout the code. The correct solution is to use the ANSI C volatile storage qualifier, which ensures that the variable will be stored in memory after modification and will always be fetched from memory before use. The volatile quantifier informs the compiler that the variable can change value at any time.

Interlocked Functions

If all we need is to increment, decrement, or exchange variables, as in this simple initial example, then the *interlocked* functions will suffice. The interlocked functions are simpler and faster than any of the alternatives and will not block the thread. The two members of the interlocked function family that are important here are InterlockedIncrement and InterlockedDecrement. They apply to 32-bit signed integers. These functions are of limited utility, but they should be used wherever possible.

The task of incrementing N in Figure 8–1 could be implemented with a single line:

```
InterlockedIncrement (&N);
```

N is a signed long integer, and the function returns its new value, although another thread could modify N's value before the thread that called InterlockedIncrement can use the returned value.

Be careful, however, not to call this function twice in succession if, for example, you need to increment the variable by 2. The thread might be preempted between the two calls. Instead, use the InterlockedExchangeAdd function described near the end of the chapter.

Local and Global Storage

Another requirement for correct thread code is that global storage not be used for local purposes. For example, the ThFunc function example presented earlier would be necessary and appropriate if each thread required its own separate copy of N. N might hold temporary results or retain the argument. If, however, N were placed in global storage, all processes would share a single copy of N, resulting in incorrect behavior no matter how well your program synchronized access. Here is an example of such incorrect usage. N should be a local variable, allocated on the thread function's stack.

```
DWORD N;
DWORD WINAPI ThFunc (TH_ARGS pArgs);
{
    . . .
    N = 2 * pArgs->Count; ...
}
```

Summary: Thread-Safe Code

Before we proceed to the synchronization objects, here are five initial guidelines to help ensure that the code will run correctly in a threaded environment.

1. Variables that are local to the thread should not be static and should be on the thread's stack or in a data structure or TLS that only the individual thread can access directly.

2. If a function is called by several threads and a thread-specific state value, such as a counter, is to persist from one function call to the next, store the state value in TLS or in a data structure dedicated to that thread, such as the data structure passed to the thread when it is created. Do not store the persistent value on the stack. Programs 12–4 and 12–5 show the required techniques when building thread-safe DLLs.

3. Avoid race conditions such as the one that would occur in Program 7–2 (sortMT) if the threads were not created in a suspended state. If some condition is assumed to hold at a specific point in the program, wait on a synchronization object to ensure that, for example, a handle references an existing thread.

4. Threads should not, in general, change the process environment because that would affect all threads. Thus, a thread should not set the standard input or output handles or change environment variables. An exception would be the primary thread, which might make such changes before creating other threads.

5. Variables shared by all threads should be static or in global storage, declared `volatile`, and protected with the synchronization mechanisms that will be described next.

The next section discusses the synchronization objects. With that discussion, there will be enough to develop a simple producer/consumer example.

Thread Synchronization Objects

Two mechanisms discussed so far allow processes and threads to synchronize with one another.

1. A thread running in a process can wait for another process to terminate, using `ExitProcess`, by waiting on the process handle using `WaitForSingle-Object` or `WaitForMultipleObjects`. A thread can wait for another thread to terminate (`ExitThread` or `return`) in the same way.

2. File locks are specifically for synchronizing file access.

Windows provides four other objects designed for thread and process synchronization. Three of these objects—mutexes, semaphores, and events—are kernel objects that have handles. Events are also used for other purposes, such as asynchronous I/O (Chapter 14).

The fourth object, the `CRITICAL_SECTION`, is discussed first. Because of their simplicity and performance advantages, `CRITICAL_SECTION`s are the preferred mechanism when they are adequate for a program's requirements. There are some performance issues, however, which are described in Chapter 9.

Caution: There are risks inherent to the use of synchronization objects if they are not used properly. These risks, such as deadlocks, are described in this and subsequent chapters, along with techniques for developing reliable code. First, however, we'll show some synchronization examples in realistic situations.

Two other synchronization objects, waitable timers and I/O completion ports, are deferred until Chapter 14. Both these objects require the Windows asynchronous I/O techniques described in that chapter.

The `CRITICAL_SECTION` Object

A critical section, as described earlier, is a section of code that only one thread can execute at a time; more than one thread executing the critical section concurrently can result in unpredictable and incorrect results.

Windows provides the CRITICAL_SECTION object as a simple mechanism for implementing and enforcing the critical section concept.

CRITICAL_SECTION (CS) objects are initialized and deleted but do not have handles and are not shared by other processes. A variable should be declared to be of type CRITICAL_SECTION. Threads enter and leave a CS, and only one thread at a time can be in a specific CS. A thread can, however, enter and leave a specific CS at several places in the program.

To initialize and delete a CRITICAL_SECTION variable and its resources, use InitializeCriticalSection and DeleteCriticalSection, respectively.

```
VOID InitializeCriticalSection (
   LPCRITICAL_SECTION lpCriticalSection)
```

```
VOID DeleteCriticalSection (
   LPCRITICAL_SECTION lpCriticalSection)
```

EnterCriticalSection blocks a thread if another thread is in the section. The waiting thread unblocks when another thread executes LeaveCritical-Section. We say that a thread *owns* the CS once it returns from EnterCritical-Section, and LeaveCriticalSection relinquishes ownership. *Always be certain to relinquish a CS; failure to do so will cause other threads to wait forever, even if the owning thread terminates.*

We will often say that a CS is *locked* or *unlocked*, and entering a CS is the same as locking the CS.

```
VOID EnterCriticalSection (
   LPCRITICAL_SECTION lpCriticalSection)

VOID LeaveCriticalSection (
   LPCRITICAL_SECTION lpCriticalSection)
```

If a thread already owns the CS, it can enter again without blocking; that is, CRITICAL_SECTIONs are *recursive*. A count is maintained so that the thread must leave as many times as it enters in order to unlock the CS for other threads. This capability can be useful in implementing recursive functions and making shared library functions thread-safe.

Leaving a CS that a thread does not own can produce unpredictable results, including thread blockage.

There is no time-out from `EnterCriticalSection`; a thread will block forever if the owning thread never leaves the CS. You can, however, test or poll to see whether another thread owns a CS using `TryEnterCriticalSection`.

```
BOOL TryEnterCriticalSection (
    LPCRITICAL_SECTION lpCriticalSection)
```

A `TRUE` return value from `TryEnterCriticalSection` indicates that the calling thread now owns the CS, and a `FALSE` return indicates that some other thread already owns the CS.

`CRITICAL_SECTION`s have the advantage of not being kernel objects and are maintained in user space. This usually, but not always, provides performance improvements. We will discuss the performance benefit once kernel synchronization objects have been introduced.

Adjusting the Spin Count

Normally, if a thread finds that a CS is already owned when executing `Enter-CriticalSection`, it enters the kernel and blocks until the `CRITICAL_SECTION` is released, which is time consuming. On SMP systems, however, you can require that the thread try again before blocking as the owning thread may be running on a separate processor and could release the CS at any time. This can be useful for performance when there is high contention among threads for a single `CRITICAL_SECTION`. Performance implications are discussed later in this chapter and the next.

The two functions to adjust spin count are `SetCriticalSectionSpin-Count`, which allows you to adjust the count dynamically, and `Initialize-CriticalSectionAndSpinCount`, which is a substitute for `InitializeCriticalSection`. Spin count tuning is a topic in Chapter 9.

A CRITICAL_SECTION for Protecting Shared Variables

Using CRITICAL_SECTIONs is simple, and one common use is to allow threads to access global shared variables. For example, consider a threaded server (as in Figure 7–1) in which there might be a need to maintain usage statistics such as:

- The total number of requests received

- The total number of responses sent

- The number of requests currently being processed by server threads

Because the count variables are global to the process, two threads must not modify the counts simultaneously. CRITICAL_SECTION objects provide one means of ensuring this, as shown by the code sequence below and in Figure 8–2. Program 8–1, much simpler than the server system, illustrates this CRITICAL_SECTION usage.

CSs can be used to solve problems such as the one shown in Figure 8–1, in which two threads increment the same variable. The following code segment will do more than increment the variable because simple incrementing is possible with the interlocked functions. Notice the use of volatile so that an optimizing compiler will not leave the current variable value in a register rather than store it back into the variable. This example also uses an intermediate variable; this unnecessary inefficiency more clearly illustrates how the problem in Figure 8–1 is solved.

```
CRITICAL_SECTION cs1;
volatile DWORD N = 0, M;
/* N is a global variable, shared by all threads. */
InitializeCriticalSection (&cs1);
   ...
EnterCriticalSection (&cs1);
if (N < N_MAX) { M = N; M += 1; N = M; }
LeaveCriticalSection (&cs1);
   ...
DeleteCriticalSection (&cs1);
```

Figure 8–2 shows one possible execution sequence for the Figure 8–1 example and illustrates how CSs can solve synchronization problems.

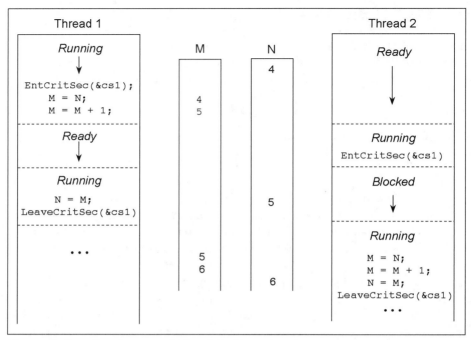

Figure 8–2   Synchronized Threads Sharing Memory

Example: A Simple Producer/Consumer System

Program 8–1 shows how CS objects can be useful. The program also shows how to build protected data structures for storing object state and introduces the concept of an *invariant*, which is a property of an object's state that is guaranteed (by the proper program implementation) to be true outside a critical code section. Here is a description of the problem.

- There are two threads, a *producer* and a *consumer*, that act entirely asynchronously.

- The producer periodically creates messages containing a table of numbers, such as current stock prices, periodically updating the table.

- The consumer, on request from the user, displays the current data. The requirement is that the displayed data must be the *most recent complete set of data, but no data should be displayed twice.*

- Do not display data while the producer is updating it, and do not display old data. Note that many produced messages are never used and are "lost." This example is a special case of the pipeline model in which data moves from one thread to the next.

- As an integrity check, the producer also computes a simple checksum[1] of the data in the table, and the consumer validates the checksum to ensure that the data has not been corrupted in transmission from one thread to the next. If the consumer accesses the table while it is still being updated, the table will be invalid; the CS ensures that this does not happen. The message block invariant is that the checksum is correct for the current message contents.

- The two threads also maintain statistics on the total number of messages produced, consumed, and lost.

Program 8-1   `simplePC`: A Simple Producer and Consumer

```
/* Chapter 8. simplePC.c */
/* Maintain two threads, a producer and a consumer. */
/* The producer periodically creates checksummed data buffers, */
/* or "message blocks," that the consumer displays when prompted. */

#include "EvryThng.h"
#include <time.h>
#define DATA_SIZE 256

typedef struct msg_block_tag { /* Message block. */
    volatile DWORD f_ready, f_stop; /* Msg ready and stop flags. */
    volatile DWORD sequence; /* Message block sequence number. */
    volatile DWORD nCons, nLost;
    time_t timestamp;
    CRITICAL_SECTION mguard; /* Guard message block structure. */
    DWORD checksum; /* Message contents checksum. */
    DWORD data [DATA_SIZE]; /* Message contents. */
} MSG_BLOCK;

/* Single message block, ready to fill with a new message. */
MSG_BLOCK mblock = { 0, 0, 0, 0, 0 };

DWORD WINAPI produce (void *);
DWORD WINAPI consume (void *);
void MessageFill (MSG_BLOCK *);
void MessageDisplay (MSG_BLOCK *);
```

[1] This checksum, an "exclusive or" of the message bits, is for illustration only. Much more sophisticated message digest techniques are available and should be used in a production application.

```
DWORD _tmain (DWORD argc, LPTSTR argv [])
{
    DWORD Status, ThId;
    HANDLE produce_h, consume_h;

    /* Initialize the message block CRITICAL SECTION. */
    InitializeCriticalSection (&mblock.mguard);

    /* Create the two threads. */
    produce_h =
        (HANDLE)_beginthreadex (NULL, 0, produce, NULL, 0, &ThId);
    consume_h =
        (HANDLE)_beginthreadex (NULL, 0, consume, NULL, 0, &ThId);

    /* Wait for the producer and consumer to complete. */
    WaitForSingleObject (consume_h, INFINITE);
    WaitForSingleObject (produce_h, INFINITE);
    DeleteCriticalSection (&mblock.mguard);

    _tprintf (_T ("Producer and consumer threads terminated\n"));
    _tprintf (_T ("Produced: %d, Consumed: %d, Known Lost: %d\n"),
            mblock.sequence, mblock.nCons, mblock.nLost);
    return 0;
}

DWORD WINAPI produce (void *arg)
/* Producer thread -- create new messages at random intervals. */
{
    srand ((DWORD) time (NULL)); /* Seed the random # generator. */
    while (!mblock.f_stop) {
        /* Random delay. */
        Sleep (rand () / 100);
        /* Get the buffer, fill it. */
        EnterCriticalSection (&mblock.mguard);
        __try {
            if (!mblock.f_stop) {
                mblock.f_ready = 0;
                MessageFill (&mblock);
                mblock.f_ready = 1;
                mblock.sequence++;
            }
        }
        __finally { LeaveCriticalSection (&mblock.mguard); }
    }
    return 0;
}

DWORD WINAPI consume (void *arg)
{
    DWORD ShutDown = 0;
```

```
    CHAR command, extra;
    /* Consume the NEXT message when prompted by the user. */
    while (!ShutDown) { /* Only thread accessing stdin, stdout. */
        _tprintf (_T ("\n**Enter 'c' for consume; 's' to stop: "));
        _tscanf ("%c%c", &command, &extra);
        if (command == 's') {
            EnterCriticalSection (&mblock.mguard);
            ShutDown = mblock.f_stop = 1;
            LeaveCriticalSection (&mblock.mguard);
        } else if (command == 'c') { /* Get new buffer to consume. */
            EnterCriticalSection (&mblock.mguard);
            __try {
                if (mblock.f_ready == 0)
                    _tprintf (_T ("No new messages. Try again.\n"));
                else {
                    MessageDisplay (&mblock);
                    mblock.nCons++;
                    mblock.nLost = mblock.sequence - mblock.nCons;
                    mblock.f_ready = 0; /* No new messages. */
                }
            }
            __finally { LeaveCriticalSection (&mblock.mguard); }
        } else {
            _tprintf (_T ("Illegal command. Try again.\n"));
        }
    }
    return 0;
}

void MessageFill (MSG_BLOCK *mblock)
{
    /* Fill the message buffer, including checksum and timestamp. */

    DWORD i;

    mblock->checksum = 0;
    for (i = 0; i < DATA_SIZE; i++) {
        mblock->data [i] = rand ();
        mblock->checksum ^= mblock->data [i];
    }
    mblock->timestamp = time (NULL);
    return;
}
void MessageDisplay (MSG_BLOCK *mblock)
{
    /* Display message buffer, timestamp, and validate checksum. */
    DWORD i, tcheck = 0;
    for (i = 0; i < DATA_SIZE; i++)
    tcheck ^= mblock->data [i];
    _tprintf (_T ("\nMessage number %d generated at: %s"),
```

```
        mblock->sequence, _tctime (&(mblock->timestamp)));
_tprintf (_T ("First and last entries: %x %x\n"),
        mblock->data [0], mblock->data [DATA_SIZE - 1]);
if (tcheck == mblock->checksum)
    _tprintf (_T ("GOOD ->Checksum was validated.\n"));
else
    _tprintf (_T ("BAD ->Checksum failed. Message corrupted.\n"));
return;
}
```

Comments on the Simple Producer/Consumer Example

This example illustrates several points and programming conventions that will be important throughout this and the following chapters.

* The CRITICAL_SECTION object is a part of the object (the message block) that it protects.

* Every access to the message block is performed in a critical code section.

* The variables that are accessed by the different threads are volatile.

* Termination handlers are used to ensure that the CS is released. This technique, while not essential, helps to ensure that later code modifications do not inadvertently skip the LeaveCriticalSection call. Also, the termination handler is limited to C and should not be used with C++.

* The MessageFill and MessageDisplay functions are called only within critical code sections, and both functions use local, rather than global, storage for their computations. Incidentally, these two functions will be used in subsequent examples but will not be listed again.

* The producer does not have a useful way to tell the consumer that there is a new message, so the consumer simply has to wait until the ready flag, indicating a new message, is set. Event kernel objects will give us a way to eliminate this inefficiency.

* One of the invariant properties that this program ensures is that the message block checksum is always correct, *outside* the critical code sections. Another invariant property is:

```
0 <= nLost + nCons <= sequence
```

There will be more about this important concept later.

- The producer thread only knows that it should stop by examining a flag in the message block, where the flag is set by the consumer. Because one thread cannot send any sort of signal to another and `TerminateThread` has undesirable side effects, this technique is the simplest way to stop another thread. Of course, the threads must cooperate for this method to be effective. This solution requires, however, that the thread must not be blocked so that it can test the flag; Chapter 10 shows how to cancel a blocked thread.

The `CRITICAL_SECTION` object is a powerful synchronization mechanism, yet it does not provide all the functionality needed. The inability to signal another thread was noted earlier, and there is also no time-out capability. The Windows kernel synchronization objects address these limitations and more.

Mutexes

A *mutex* ("mutual exclusion") object provides functionality beyond that of `CRITICAL_SECTION`s. Because mutexes can be named and have handles, they can also be used for interprocess synchronization between threads in separate processes. For example, two processes that share memory by means of memory-mapped files can use mutexes to synchronize access to the shared memory.

Mutex objects are similar to CSs, but, in addition to being process-sharable, mutexes allow time-out values and become signaled when *abandoned* by a terminating process.[2] A thread gains mutex ownership (or *locks* the mutex) by waiting on the mutex handle (`WaitForSingleObject` or `WaitForMultipleObjects`), and it releases ownership with `ReleaseMutex`.

As always, threads should be careful to release resources they own as soon as possible. A thread can acquire a specific mutex several times; the thread will not block if it already has ownership. Ultimately, it must release the mutex the same number of times. This recursive ownership feature, also available with CSs, can be useful for restricting access to a recursive function or in an application that implements nested transactions.

Windows functions are `CreateMutex`, `ReleaseMutex`, and `OpenMutex`.

---

[2] As a rule of thumb, use a `CRITICAL_SECTION` if the limitations are acceptable, and use mutexes when you have more than one process or need some other mutex capability. Also, CSs are generally, but not always, faster. This topic is discussed in detail in Chapter 9.

```
HANDLE CreateMutex (
    LPSECURITY_ATTRIBUTES lpsa,
    BOOL bInitialOwner,
    LPCTSTR lpMutexName)
```

The `bInitialOwner` flag, if `TRUE`, gives the calling thread immediate owner-ship of the new mutex. This atomic operation prevents a different thread from gaining mutex ownership before the creating thread does. This flag is overridden if the mutex already exists, as determined by the name.

`lpMutexName` indicates the mutex name; unlike files, mutex names are case-sensitive. The mutexes are unnamed if the parameter is `NULL`. Events, mutexes, semaphores, file mapping, and other kernel objects used in this book all share the same name space, which is distinct from the file system name space. Therefore, all synchronization objects should have distinct names. These names are limited to 260 characters.

A `NULL` return `HANDLE` value indicates failure.

`OpenMutex` is for opening an existing named mutex. This function is not discussed further but is used in some examples. It allows threads in different processes to synchronize just as if the threads were in the same process. The `Create` in one process must precede the `Open` in another. Semaphores and events also have `Create` and `Open` functions, as do file mappings (Chapter 5). The assumption always is that one process, such as a server, first performs the `Create` call to create the named object, and other processes perform the `Open` call, failing if the named object has not already been created. Alternatively, all processes can use the `Create` call with the same name if the order is not important.

`ReleaseMutex` frees a mutex that the calling thread owns. It fails if the thread does not own the mutex.

```
BOOL ReleaseMutex (HANDLE hMutex)
```

The POSIX Pthreads specification supports mutexes. The four basic functions are as follows:

- `pthread_mutex_init`
- `pthread_mutex_destroy`

- · `pthread_mutex_lock`

- · `pthread_mutex_unlock`

`pthread_mutex_lock` will block and is therefore equivalent to `WaitFor-SingleObject` when used with a mutex handle. `pthread_mutex_trylock` is a nonblocking, polling version that corresponds to `WaitForSingleObject` with a zero time-out value. Pthreads do not provide for a time-out, nor is there anything similar to Windows' `CRITICAL_SECTION`.

Abandoned Mutexes

If a thread terminates without releasing a mutex that it owns, the mutex becomes abandoned and the handle is in the signaled state. `WaitForSingleObject` will return `WAIT_ABANDONED_0`, and `WaitForMultipleObjects` will use `WAIT_ABANDONED_0` as the base value to indicate that the signaled handle(s) represents abandoned mutex(es).

The fact that abandoned mutex handles are signaled is a useful feature not available with CSs. If an abandoned mutex is detected, there is a possibility of a defect in the thread code because threads should be programmed to release their resources before terminating. It is also possible that the thread was terminated by some other thread.

Mutexes, `CRITICAL_SECTIONS`, and Deadlocks

Although CSs and mutexes can solve problems such as the one in Figure 8–1, you must use them carefully to avoid *deadlocks*, in which two threads become blocked waiting for a resource owned by the other thread.

Deadlocks are one of the most common and insidious defects in synchronization, and they frequently occur when two or more mutexes must be locked at the same time. Consider the following problem.

- There are two linked lists, List A and List B, each containing identical structures and maintained by worker threads.

- For one class of list element, correct operation depends on the fact that a given element, X, is either in both lists or in neither. The invariant, stated informally, is: "X is either in both lists or in neither."

- In other situations, an element is allowed to be in one list but not in the other. *Motivation*: The lists might be employees in Departments A and B, where some employees are allowed to be in both departments.

- Therefore, distinct mutexes (or `CRITICAL_SECTIONS`) are required for both lists, but both mutexes must be locked when adding or deleting a shared element.

Using a single mutex would degrade performance, prohibiting concurrent independent updates to the two lists, because the mutex would be "too large."

Here is a possible implementation of the worker thread functions for adding and deleting shared list elements.

```
static struct {
    /* Invariant: List is a valid list. */
    HANDLE guard; /* Mutex handle. */
    struct ListStuff;
}  ListA, ListB;
...
DWORD WINAPI AddSharedElement (void *arg)
/* Add a shared element to lists A and B. */
{ /* Invariant: New element is in both or neither list. */
    WaitForSingleObject (ListA.guard, INFINITE);
    WaitForSingleObject (ListB.guard, INFINITE);
    /* Add the element to both lists ... */
    ReleaseMutex (ListB.guard);
    ReleaseMutex (ListA.guard);
    return 0;
}
DWORD WINAPI DeleteSharedElement (void *arg)
/* Delete a shared element to lists A and B. */
{
    WaitForSingleObject (ListB.guard, INFINITE);
    WaitForSingleObject (ListA.guard, INFINITE);
    /* Delete the element from both lists ... */
    ReleaseMutex (ListB.guard);
    ReleaseMutex (ListA.guard);
    return 0;
}
```

The code looks correct by all the previous guidelines. However, a preemption of the AddSharedElement thread immediately after it locks List A and immediately before it tries to lock List B will deadlock if the DeleteSharedElement thread starts before the add thread resumes. Each thread owns a mutex the other requires, and neither thread can proceed to the ReleaseMutex call that would unblock the other thread.

Notice that deadlocks are really another form of race condition, as one thread races to acquire all its mutexes before the other thread starts to do so.

One way to avoid deadlock is the "try and back off" strategy, whereby a thread calls `WaitForSingleObject` with a finite time-out value and, when detecting an owned mutex, "backs off" by yielding the processor or sleeping for a brief time before trying again. Designing for deadlock-free systems is even better and more efficient, as described next.

A far simpler method, covered in nearly all OS texts, is to specify a "mutex hierarchy" such that all threads are programmed to assure that they acquire the mutexes in exactly the same order and release them in the opposite order. This hierarchical sequence might be arbitrary or could be natural from the structure of the problem, but, whatever the hierarchy, it must be observed by all threads. In this example, all that is needed is for the delete function to wait for List A and List B in order, and the threads will never deadlock as long as this hierarchical sequence is observed everywhere by all threads.

Another good way to reduce deadlock potential is to put the two mutex handles in an array and use `WaitForMultipleObjects` with the `fWaitAll` flag set to `TRUE` so that a thread acquires either both or neither of the mutexes in an atomic operation. This technique is not possible with `CRITICAL_SECTION`s.

Review: Mutexes vs. `CRITICAL_SECTIONS`

As stated several times, mutexes and `CRITICAL_SECTION`s are very similar and solve the same set of problems. In particular, both objects can be owned by a single thread, and other threads attempting to gain ownership will block until the object is released. Mutexes do provide greater flexibility, but with a performance penalty. In summary, the differences are as follows.

- Mutexes, when abandoned by a terminated thread, are signaled so that other threads are not blocked forever.

- Mutex waits can time out, whereas you can only poll a CS.

- Mutexes can be named and are sharable by threads in different processes.

- You can use `WaitForMultipleObjects` with mutexes, which is both a programming convenience and a way to avoid deadlocks if used properly.

- The thread that creates a mutex can specify immediate ownership. With a CS, several threads could race to acquire the CS.

- CSs are usually, but not always, considerably faster than mutexes. There will be more on this in Chapter 9.

Heap Synchronization

A pair of functions for NT—HeapLock and HeapUnlock—is used to synchronize heap access (Chapter 5). The heap handle is the only argument. These functions are helpful when the HEAP_NO_SERIALIZE flag is used or when it is necessary for a thread to have exclusive access to a heap.

Semaphores

Semaphores, the second of the three kernel synchronization objects, maintain a count, and the semaphore object is signaled when the count is greater than 0. The semaphore object is unsignaled when the count is 0.

Threads or processes wait in the normal way, using one of the wait functions. When a waiting thread is released, the semaphore's count is decremented by 1.

The semaphore functions are CreateSemaphore, OpenSemaphore, and ReleaseSemaphore, which can increment the count by 1 or more. These functions are similar to their mutex counterparts.

```
HANDLE CreateSemaphore (
    LPSECURITY_ATTRIBUTES lpsa,
    LONG lSemInitial,
    LONG lSemMax,
    LPCTSTR lpSemName)
```

lSemMax, which must be 1 or greater, is the maximum value for the semaphore. lSemInitial, with 0 ≤ lSemInitial ≤ lSemMax, is the initial value, and the semaphore value is never allowed to go outside this range. A NULL return value indicates failure.

It is possible to decrease the count only by 1 with any given wait operation, but a semaphore release can increment its count by any value up to the maximum.

```
BOOL ReleaseSemaphore (
    HANDLE hSemaphore,
    LONG cReleaseCount,
    LPLONG lpPreviousCount)
```

Notice that you can find the count preceding the release, but the pointer can be NULL if this value is not needed.

The release count must be greater than 0, but if it would cause the semaphore count to exceed the maximum, the call will fail, returning FALSE, and the count will remain unchanged. Use the previous count value with caution as the semaphore count can also be changed by other threads. Also, you cannot determine whether the count is at its maximum as there is no legal release count. An example in the Web site code demonstrates using the previous count.

While it is tempting to think of a semaphore as a special case of a mutex with a maximum value of 1, this would be misleading because there is no ownership of a semaphore. Any thread can release a semaphore, not just the one that performed the wait. Likewise, since there is no ownership, there is no concept of an abandoned semaphore.

Using Semaphores

The classic semaphore application regards the semaphore count as representing the number of available resources, such as the number of messages waiting in a queue. The semaphore maximum then represents the maximum queue size. Thus, a producer would place a message in the buffer and call ReleaseSemaphore, usually with a release count of 1. Consumer threads would wait on the semaphore, consuming a message and decrementing the semaphore count.

Another important use is described in the discussion following Program 9–1, where a semaphore can be used to limit the number of worker threads actually running at any one time, thereby decreasing contention between threads and, in some cases, improving performance. Chapter 9 discusses this technique, using a semaphore throttle.

The potential race condition in sortMT (Program 7–2) illustrates another use of a semaphore to control the exact number of threads to wake up. All the threads could be created without being suspended. All of them would immediately wait on a semaphore initialized to 0. The boss thread, rather than resuming the threads, would simply call ReleaseSemaphore with a count of 4 (or whatever the number of threads is), and the four threads could then proceed.

While semaphores can be convenient, they are redundant in the sense that mutexes and events (described in the next major section), used together, are more powerful than semaphores. See Chapter 10 for more information.

A Semaphore Limitation

There is still an important limitation with the Windows semaphore implementation. How can a thread request that the count be decremented by 2? The thread can wait twice in succession, as shown below, but this would not be an atomic operation because the thread could be preempted between waits. A deadlock could result, as described next.

```
/* hsem is a semaphore handle.
The maximum semaphore count is 2. */
   . . .
/* Decrement the semaphore by 2. */
WaitForSingleObject (hSem, INFINITE);
WaitForSingleObject (hSem, INFINITE);
   . . .
/* Release two semaphore counts. */
ReleaseSemaphore (hSem, 2, &PrevCount);
```

To see how a deadlock is possible in this situation, suppose that the maximum and original semaphore counts are set to 2 and that the first of two threads completes the first wait and is then preempted. A second thread could then complete the first wait, reducing the count to 0. Both threads will block forever because neither will be able to get past the second wait. This simple deadlock situation is typical.

A possible correct solution, shown in the following code fragment, is to protect the waits with a mutex or CRITICAL_SECTION.

```
/* Decrement the semaphore by 2. */
EnterCriticalSection (&csSem);
WaitForSingleObject (hSem, INFINITE);
WaitForSingleObject (hSem, INFINITE);
LeaveCriticalSection (&csSem);
   . . .
ReleaseSemaphore (hSem, 2, &PrevCount);
```

Even this implementation, in general form, is limited. Suppose, for example, that the semaphore has two remaining units, and that Thread A needs three units and Thread B needs just two. If Thread A arrives first, it will complete two waits and block on the third while owning the mutex. Thread B, which only needs the two remaining units, will still be blocked.

Another proposed solution would be to use WaitForMultipleObjects with the same semaphore handle used several times in the handle array. This suggestion fails for two reasons. First, WaitForMultipleObjects will return an error if it detects two handles for the same objects. What is more, the handles would all be signaled, even if the semaphore count were only 1, which would defeat the purpose.

Exercise 10–11 provides a complete solution to this multiple-wait problem.

The Windows semaphore design would be more convenient if we could perform an atomic multiple-wait operation.

Events

Events are the final kernel synchronization object. Events are used to signal other threads that some event, such as a message being available, has occurred.

The important additional capability offered by events is that multiple threads can be released from a wait simultaneously when a single event is signaled. Events are classified as manual-reset and auto-reset, and this event property is set by the `CreateEvent` call.

- A manual-reset event can signal several threads waiting on the event simultaneously and can be reset.

- An auto-reset event signals a single thread waiting on the event, and the event is reset automatically.

Events use five new functions: `CreateEvent`, `OpenEvent`, `SetEvent`, `ResetEvent`, and `PulseEvent`.

```
HANDLE CreateEvent (
    LPSECURITY_ATTRIBUTES lpsa,
    BOOL bManualReset,
    BOOL bInitialState,
    LPTCSTR lpEventName)
```

Specify a manual-reset event by setting `bManualReset` to TRUE. Similarly, the event is initially set to signaled if `bInitialState` is TRUE. You open a named event, possibly from another process, with `OpenEvent`.

The following three functions are used for controlling events:

```
BOOL SetEvent (HANDLE hEvent)

BOOL ResetEvent (HANDLE hEvent)

BOOL PulseEvent (HANDLE hEvent)
```

A thread can signal an event using `SetEvent`. If the event is auto-reset, a single waiting thread, possibly one of many, is released, and the event automatically returns to the nonsignaled state. If no threads are waiting on the event, the event remains in the signaled state until a thread waits on it, and the thread is immediately released. Notice that a semaphore with a maximum count of 1 would have the same effect.

If, on the other hand, the event is manual-reset, it remains signaled until a thread calls `ResetEvent` for that event. During this time, all waiting threads are released, and it is possible that other threads will wait, and be released, before the reset.

`PulseEvent` releases all threads currently waiting on a manual-reset event, but the event is then automatically reset. In the case of an auto-reset event, `PulseEvent` releases a single waiting thread, if any.

Note: While many writers and even some Microsoft documentation (see the remarks in the MSDN `PulseEvent` entry) advise readers to avoid `PulseEvent`, I find it not only useful but essential, as discussed with extensive examples in the next two chapters.

Notice that `ResetEvent` is useful only after a manual-reset event is signaled with `SetEvent`. Be careful when using `WaitForMultipleObjects` to wait for *all* events to become signaled. A waiting thread will be released only when all events are simultaneously in the signaled state, and some signaled events might be reset before the thread is released.

Exercise 8–5 suggests how to modify `sortMT`, Program 7–2, to exploit events.

Pthreads' *condition variables* are somewhat comparable to events, but they are used in conjunction with a mutex. This usage is actually very useful and will be described in Chapter 10. `pthread_cond_init` and `pthread_cond_destroy` create and destroy condition variables. `pthread_cond_wait` and `pthread_cond_timedwait` are the waiting functions. `pthread_cond_signal` signals one waiting thread, as when pulsing a Windows auto-reset event. `pthread_cond_broadcast` signals all waiting threads and is therefore similar to `PulseEvent` applied to a manual-reset event. There is no exact equivalent of `PulseEvent` or of `ResetEvent` used with manual-reset events.

Review: The Four Event Usage Models

The combination of auto- and manual-reset events with `SetEvent` and `PulseEvent` gives four distinct ways to use events. Each combination is unique and each is useful, or even necessary, in some situations, and each model combination will be used in an example or exercise, either in this chapter or the next.

Warning: Events, if not used properly, can cause race conditions, deadlocks, and other subtle and difficult-to-diagnose errors. Chapter 10 describes techniques that are almost always required if you are using events in any but the simplest situations.

Table 8–1 describes the four situations.

Table 8-1   Summary of Event Behavior

	Auto-Reset Event	Manual-Reset Event
`SetEvent`	Exactly one thread is released. If none is currently waiting on the event, the first thread to wait on it in the future will be released immediately. The event is automatically reset.	All currently waiting threads are released. The event remains signaled until reset by some thread.
`PulseEvent`	Exactly one thread is released, but only if a thread is currently waiting on the event.	All currently waiting threads, if any, are released, and the event is then reset to nonsignaled.

An auto-reset event can be thought of as a door with a spring that slams the door shut, whereas a manual-reset event does not have a spring and will remain open. Using this metaphor, `PulseEvent` opens the door and immediately shuts it after one (auto-reset) or all (manual-reset) waiting threads go through the door. `SetEvent` opens the door and releases it.

Example: A Producer/Consumer System

This example extends Program 8–1 so that the consumer can wait until there is an available message. This eliminates the problem that requires the consumer to try again if a new message is not available. The resulting program, Program 8–2, is called `eventPC`.

Notice that the solution uses a mutex rather than a `CRITICAL_SECTION`; there is no reason for this other than to illustrate mutex usage. The use of an auto-reset event and `SetEvent` in the producer are, however, essential for correct operation to ensure that just one thread is released.

Also notice how the mutex and event are both associated with the message block data structure. The mutex enforces the critical code section for accessing the data structure object, and the event is used to signal the fact that there is a new message. Generalizing, the mutex ensures the object's invariants, and the event signals that the object is in a specified state. This basic technique is used extensively in later chapters.

Program 8–2   `eventPC`: A Signaling Producer and Consumer

```
/* Chapter 8. eventPC.c */
/* Maintain two threads, a producer and a consumer. */
```

```
/* The producer periodically creates checksummed data buffers, */
/* or "message blocks," signaling the consumer that a message */
/* is ready. The consumer displays when prompted. */

#include "EvryThng.h"
#include <time.h>
#define DATA_SIZE 256

typedef struct msg_block_tag { /* Message block. */
    volatile DWORD f_ready, f_stop;
        /* Ready state flag, stop flag. */
    volatile DWORD sequence; /* Message block sequence number. */
    volatile DWORD nCons, nLost;
    time_t timestamp;
    HANDLE mguard; /* Mutex to guard the message block structure. */
    HANDLE mready; /* "Message ready" event. */
    DWORD checksum; /* Message contents checksum. */
    DWORD data [DATA_SIZE]; /* Message contents. */
} MSG_BLOCK;

/* ... */

DWORD _tmain (DWORD argc, LPTSTR argv [])
{
    DWORD Status, ThId;
    HANDLE produce_h, consume_h;

    /* Initialize the message block mutex and event (auto-reset). */
    mblock.mguard = CreateMutex (NULL, FALSE, NULL);
    mblock.mready = CreateEvent (NULL, FALSE, FALSE, NULL);

    /* Create producer and consumer; wait until they terminate. */
    /* ... As in Program 9-1 ... */
    CloseHandle (mblock.mguard);
    CloseHandle (mblock.mready);

    _tprintf (_T ("Producer and consumer threads terminated\n"));
    _tprintf (_T ("Produced: %d, Consumed: %d, Known Lost: %d\n"),
            mblock.sequence, mblock.nCons, mblock.nLost);
    return 0;
}

DWORD WINAPI produce (void *arg)
/* Producer thread -- create new messages at random intervals. */
{
    srand ((DWORD)time(NULL)); /* Seed the random # generator. */
    while (!mblock.f_stop) {
        /* Random delay. */
        Sleep (rand () / 10); /* Wait a long period for next message. */
```

```
        /* Get the buffer, fill it. */
        WaitForSingleObject (mblock.mguard, INFINITE);
        __try {
            if (!mblock.f_stop) {
                mblock.f_ready = 0;
                MessageFill (&mblock);
                mblock.f_ready = 1;
                mblock.sequence++;
                SetEvent(mblock.mready); /* Signal "message ready." */
            }
        }
        __finally { ReleaseMutex (mblock.mguard); }
    }
    return 0;
}

DWORD WINAPI consume (void *arg)
{
    DWORD ShutDown = 0;
    CHAR command, extra;
    /* Consume the NEXT message when prompted by the user. */
    while (!ShutDown) { /* Only thread accessing stdin, stdout. */
        _tprintf (_T ("\n**Enter 'c' for consume; 's' to stop: "));
        _tscanf ("%c%c", &command, &extra);
        if (command == 's') {
            WaitForSingleObject (mblock.mguard, INFINITE);
            ShutDown = mblock.f_stop = 1;
            ReleaseMutex (mblock.mguard);
        } else if (command == 'c') { /* Get new buffer to consume. */
            WaitForSingleObject (mblock.mready, INFINITE);
            WaitForSingleObject (mblock.mguard, INFINITE);
            __try {
                if (!mblock.f_ready) _leave;
                /* Wait for the event indicating a message is ready. */
                MessageDisplay (&mblock);
                mblock.nCons++;
                mblock.nLost = mblock.sequence - mblock.nCons;
                mblock.f_ready = 0; /* No new messages are ready. */
            }
            __finally { ReleaseMutex (mblock.mguard); }
        } else {
            _tprintf (_T ("Illegal command. Try again.\n"));
        }
    }
    return 0;
}
```

Note: There is a possibility that the consumer, having received the message ready event, will not actually process the current message if the producer generates yet another message before the consumer acquires the mutex. This behavior could cause a consumer to process a single message twice if it were not for the test at the start of the consumer's __try block. This and similar issues will be addressed in Chapter 10.

Review: Windows Synchronization Objects

Table 8–2 reviews and compares the essential features of the Windows synchronization objects.

Table 8-2 Comparison of Windows Synchronization Objects

	CRITICAL_SECTION	Mutex	Semaphore	Event
Named, Securable Synchronization Object	No	Yes	Yes	Yes
Accessible from Multiple Processes	No	Yes	Yes	Yes
Synchronization	Enter	Wait	Wait	Wait
Release	Leave	Release or abandoned	Any thread can release.	Set, pulse
Ownership	One thread at a time. The owning thread can enter multiple times without blocking.	One thread at a time. The owning thread can wait multiple times without blocking.	N/A. Many threads at a time, up to the maximum count.	N/A. Any thread can set or pulse an event.
Effect of Release	One waiting thread can enter.	One waiting thread can gain ownership after last release.	Multiple threads can proceed, depending on release count.	One or several waiting threads will proceed after a set or pulse.

Message and Object Waiting

The function `MsgWaitForMultipleObjects` is similar to `WaitForMultiple-Objects`. Use this function to allow a thread to process user interface events, such as mouse clicks, while waiting on synchronization objects.

More Mutex and CRITICAL_SECTION Guidelines

We are now familiar with all the Windows synchronization objects and have explored their utility in the examples. Mutexes and CSs were the first objects described and, because events will be used extensively in the next chapter, it is worthwhile to conclude this chapter with some guidelines for using mutexes and CSs to help ensure program correctness, maintainability, and performance.

Nearly everything is stated in terms of mutexes; the statements also apply to CSs unless noted otherwise.

- If there is no time-out associated with `WaitForSingleObject` on a mutex handle, the calling thread could block forever. It is the programmer's responsibility to ensure that an owned (or locked) mutex is eventually unlocked.

- If a thread terminates, or is terminated, before it leaves (unlocks) a CS, the CS remains locked. Mutexes have the very useful abandonment property.

- If `WaitForSingleObject` times out waiting for a mutex, do not access the resources that the mutex is designed to protect.

- There may be multiple threads waiting on a given locked mutex. When the mutex is unlocked, *exactly one* of the waiting threads is given mutex ownership and moved to the ready state by the OS scheduler based on priority and scheduling policy. Do not assume that any particular thread will have priority; as always, program so that your application will operate correctly regardless of which waiting thread gains mutex ownership and resumes execution. The same comment applies to threads waiting on an event; do not assume that a specific thread will be the one released when the event is signaled or that threads will be unblocked in any specific order.

- A code critical section is everything between the points where the thread gains and relinquishes mutex ownership. A single mutex can be used to define several critical sections. If properly implemented, at most one thread can execute a mutex's critical section at any time.

- *Mutex granularity* affects performance and is an important consideration. *Each critical section should be just as long as necessary, and no longer, and a mutex should be owned just as long as necessary, and no longer.* Large critical sections, held for a long period of time, defeat concurrency and can impact performance.

- Associate the mutex directly with the resource it is designed to protect, possibly in a data structure. (Programs 8–1 and 8–2 use this technique.)

- Document the invariant as precisely as possible, in words or even as a logical, or Boolean, expression. The invariant is a property of the protected resource that you guarantee holds outside the critical code section. An invariant might be of the form: "the element is in both or neither list," "the checksum on the data buffer is valid," "the linked list is valid," or "0 <= nLost + nCons <= sequence." A precisely formulated invariant can be used with the ASSERT macro when debugging a program, although the ASSERT statement should be in its own critical code section.

- Ensure that each critical section has exactly one entrance, where the thread locks the mutex, and exactly one exit, where the thread unlocks the mutex. Avoid complex conditional code and avoid premature exits, such as break, return, and goto statements, from within the critical section. Termination handlers are useful for protecting against such problems.

- If the critical section code becomes too lengthy (longer than one page, perhaps), but all the logic is required, consider putting the code in a function so that the synchronization can be easily comprehended. For example, the code to delete a node from a balanced search tree while the tree is locked might best be put in a function.

More Interlocked Functions

InterlockedIncrement and InterlockedDecrement have already been shown to be useful when all you need to do is perform very simple operations on thread-shared variables. Several other functions allow you to perform atomic operations to compare and exchange variable pairs.

Interlocked functions are as useful as they are efficient; they are implemented in user space with a few machine instructions.

InterlockedExchange stores one variable into another, as follows:

```
LONG InterlockedExchange (
    LPLONG Target,
    LONG Value)
```

The function returns the current value of `*Target` and sets `*Target` to `Value`.

`InterlockedExchangeAdd` adds the second value to the first.

```
LONG InterlockedExchangeAdd (
    PLONG Addend,
    LONG Increment)
```

Increment is added to `*Addend`, and the original value of `*Addend` is returned. This function allows you to increment a variable by 2 (or more) atomically, which is not possible with successive calls to `InterlockedIncrement`.

The final function, `InterlockedCompareExchange`, is similar to `InterlockedExchange` except that the exchange is done only if a comparison is satisfied.

```
PVOID InterlockedCompareExchange (
    PVOID *Destination,
    PVOID Exchange,
    PVOID Comparand)
```

This function atomically performs the following (the use of `PVOID` types for the last two parameters is confusing):

```
Temp = *Destination;
if (*Destination == Comparand) *Destination = Exchange;
return Temp;
```

One use of this function is as a lock to implement a code critical section. `*Destination` is the *lock variable*, with 1 indicating unlocked and 0 indicating locked. `Exchange` is 0 and `Comparand` is 1. A calling thread knows that it owns the critical section if the function returns 1. Otherwise, it should sleep or "spin"— that is, execute a meaningless loop that consumes time for a short period and then try again. This spinning is essentially what `EnterCriticalSection` does when waiting for a `CRITICAL_SECTION` that has a nonzero spin count; see Chapter 9 for more information.

Memory Management Performance Considerations

Program 9–1, in the next chapter, illustrates the potential performance impact when multiple threads contend for a shared resource. A similar effect will be seen if threads perform memory management using `malloc` and `free` from the multithreaded Standard C library because these functions use a `CRITICAL_SECTION` to synchronize access to a heap data structure (you can confirm this by examining the C library source code). Here are two possible methods of improving performance.

- Each thread that performs memory management can create a `HANDLE` to its own heap using `HeapCreate` (Chapter 5). Memory allocation is then performed using `HeapAlloc` and `HeapFree` rather than using `malloc` and `free`.

- A run-time environment variable, `__MSVCRT_HEAP_SELECT`, can be set to `__GLOBAL_HEAP_SELECTED`. This will cause `malloc` and `free` to use Windows memory management, which uses spin locks rather than CSs and can be more efficient. This method was developed by Gerbert Orasche in a May 2000 *Windows Developer's Journal* article, "Configuring VC++ Multithreaded Memory Management," and the article shows some favorable performance results.

Summary

Windows supports a complete set of synchronization operations that allows threads and processes to be implemented safely. Synchronization introduces a host of program design and development issues that must be considered carefully, to ensure both program correctness and good performance.

Looking Ahead

Chapter 9 concentrates on multithreaded and synchronization performance issues. The first topic is the performance impact of SMP systems; in some cases, resource contention can dramatically reduce performance, and several strategies are provided to assure robust or even improved performance on SMP systems. Trade-offs between mutexes and `CRITICAL_SECTION`s, followed by `CRITICAL_SECTION` tuning with spin counts, are treated next. The chapter concludes with guidelines summarizing the performance-enhancing techniques, as well as performance pitfalls.

Additional Reading

Windows

Synchronization issues are independent of the OS, and many OS texts discuss the issue at length and within a more general framework.

Other books on Windows synchronization have already been mentioned. When dealing with more general Windows books, however, exercise caution because some are misleading when it comes to threads and synchronization, and most have not been updated to reflect the NT5 features used here. One very popular and well-reviewed book, for instance, while consuming a large number of pages of prose, never mentions the need for `volatile` storage, does not explain the four event combinations adequately, and recommends the deadlock-prone multiple semaphore wait solution (discussed in the section on semaphores) as a technique for obtaining more than one semaphore unit.

David Butenhof's *Programming with POSIX Threads* is recommended for in-depth thread and synchronization understanding, even for the Windows programmer. The discussions and descriptions generally apply equally well to Windows, and porting the example programs can be a good exercise.

Exercises

8–1. The book's Web site contains a defective version of `simplePC.c` (Program 8–1) called `simplePCx.c`. Test this program and describe the defect symptoms, if any. Fix the program without reference to the correct solution.

8–2. Modify `simplePC.c` so that the time period between new messages is increased. (*Suggestion*: Eliminate the division in the `sleep` call.) Ensure that the logic that determines whether there is a new message is correct. Also experiment with the defective version, `simplePCx.c`.

8–3. Reimplement `simplePC.c` with a mutex.

8–4. Reimplement `sortMT.c` (Program 7–2) using a semaphore, rather than thread suspension, to synchronize worker thread start-up.

8–5. Reimplement `sortMT.c` (Program 7–2) using an event rather than thread suspension to synchronize worker thread start-up. The recommended solution uses `SetEvent` and a manual-reset event. Other combinations would not be assured of correct operation. Explain.

8–6. Experiment with Program 8–2 by using different combinations of auto- and manual-reset events and `SetEvent` and `PulseEvent` (the current solution uses `SetEvent` and an auto-reset event). Are the alternate implementations and the original implementation correct, given the definition of the program's intended functionality? (See the note after Program 8–2.) Explain the results and explain how the alternate functionality might be useful. Can you make any of the alternate implementations work by changing the program logic?

8–7. Create a worker thread pool but control the rate of worker thread operation so that only one thread is allowed to run in any 1-second interval. Modify the program so that two threads can run in the interval but the overall rate of thread operation is limited to one per second. *Hint*: The worker threads should wait on an event (what type of event?), and a controlling thread should signal the event (`SetEvent` or `PulseEvent`?) every second.

8–8. *Advanced exercise*: `CRITICAL_SECTION`s are intended to be used by threads within the same process. What happens if you create a CS in shared, memory-mapped storage? Can both processes use the CS? You can perform this experiment by modifying so that the producer and consumer run in different processes.

9 | Synchronization Performance Impact and Guidelines

The last chapter introduced synchronization operations and demonstrated their usage in some relatively simple examples. The next chapter provides more complex but realistic and useful examples and describes a general synchronization model that solves many practical problems and enhances program reliability. This short chapter is concerned with the impact that synchronization can have on application performance and techniques to minimize the impact.

While thread synchronization is essential, there are some significant performance pitfalls, and we describe some of the major performance issues, both on single-processor and multiple-processor (SMP) systems. There are also trade-offs among alternative solutions. For example, CRITICAL_SECTIONs (CSs) and mutexes are nearly identical and solve the same fundamental problem. CSs are generally, but not always, the most efficient locking mechanism. CSs are also not as convenient to use as mutexes, as Chapter 10 demonstrates. In other cases, interlocked operations are sufficient, and it may even be possible to avoid synchronization altogether with careful design and implementation.

CS–mutex trade-offs are discussed first, along with SMP implications. CS spin counts, semaphore throttles, and processor affinity are other topics. The chapter ends with a set of performance guidelines.

Note: NT 5.0 made some significant performance improvements. Some of the issues identified here were much more severe with earlier NT versions and 9x.

Synchronization Performance Impact

Synchronization can and will impact the performance of your program, and you need to be especially careful when running on SMP systems. This may seem counterintuitive, as we might expect that SMP would generally improve performance and certainly never slow down a program. However, it turns out that internal implementation mechanisms and processor contention for memory access can produce unexpected effects, including dramatic performance degradation.

CRITICAL_SECTION–Mutex Trade-offs

The first step is to assess the performance impact of synchronization and compare CRITICAL_SECTIONs to mutexes. Program 9–1 shows statsMX.c, which uses a mutex to synchronize access to a thread-specific data structure. statsCS.c, not shown but included on the book's Web site, does exactly the same thing using a CRITICAL_SECTION, and statsIN.c uses interlocked functions. Finally, statsNS.c, also not shown, uses no synchronization at all; it turns out, in this example, that synchronization is not required because each worker accesses its own unique storage. See the cautionary note after the bulleted list following the program. The actual programs allow any number of worker threads, although, for simplicity, Program 9–1 as listed can support only 64.

This set of examples not only illustrates the relative performance impact of three types of synchronization but also shows the following concepts.

- Synchronization can sometimes be avoided with careful program design.

- The interlocked functions can be used in simple situations, such as incrementing a shared variable.

- CSs are measurably faster than mutexes in most situations.

- A common technique is to specify the thread argument data structure so that it contains state data to be maintained by the thread along with a pointer to a mutex or other synchronization object.

Program 9–1 statsMX: Maintaining Thread Statistics

```
/* Chapter 9. statsMX.c */
/* Simple boss/worker system, where each worker reports */
/* its work output back to the boss for display. */
/* MUTEX VERSION. */

#include "EvryThng.h"
```

```
#define DELAY_COUNT 20

/* Usage: statsMX nthread ntasks */
/* Start up nthread worker threads, each assigned to perform */
/* "ntasks" work units. Each thread reports its progress */
/* in its own unshared slot in a work-performed array. */

DWORD WINAPI worker (void *);

typedef struct _THARG {
    int thread_number;
    HANDLE *phMutex;
    unsigned int tasks_to_complete;
    unsigned int *tasks_complete;
} THARG;

int _tmain (DWORD argc, LPTSTR argv [])
{
    INT tstatus, nthread, ithread;
    HANDLE *worker_t, hMutex;
    unsigned int * task_count, tasks_per_thread;
    THARG * thread_arg;

    /* Create the mutex. */
    hMutex = CreateMutex (NULL, FALSE, NULL);

    nthread = _ttoi (argv [1]);
    tasks_per_thread = _ttoi (argv [2]);
    worker_t = malloc (nthread * sizeof (HANDLE));
    task_count = calloc (nthread, sizeof (unsigned int));
    thread_arg = calloc (nthread, sizeof (THARG));

    for (ithread = 0; ithread < nthread; ithread++) {
        /* Fill in the thread arg. */
        thread_arg [ithread].thread_number = ithread;
        thread_arg [ithread].tasks_to_complete = tasks_per_thread;
        thread_arg [ithread].tasks_complete = &task_count [ithread];
        thread_arg [ithread].phMutex = &hMutex;
        worker_t [ithread] = (HANDLE)_beginthreadex (NULL, 0, worker,
                &thread_arg [ithread], 0, &ThId);
    }

    /* Wait for the threads to complete. */
    WaitForMultipleObjects (nthread, worker_t, TRUE, INFINITE);
    free (worker_t);
    printf ("Worker threads have terminated\n");
    for (ithread = 0; ithread < nthread; ithread++) {
        _tprintf (_T ("Tasks completed by thread %5d: %6d\n"),
            ithread, task_count [ithread]);
    }
```

```
        return 0;
        free (task_count);
        free (thread_arg);
}

DWORD WINAPI worker (void *arg)
{
    THARG * thread_arg;
    int ithread;

    thread_arg = (THARG *) arg;
    ithread = thread_arg->thread_number;

    while (*thread_arg->tasks_complete <
            thread_arg->tasks_to_complete) {
        delay_cpu (DELAY_COUNT);
        WaitForSingleObject (*(thread_arg->phMutex), INFINITE);
        (*thread_arg->tasks_complete)++;
        ReleaseMutex (*(thread_arg->phMutex));
    }
    return 0;
}
```

You can use the `timep` program from Chapter 6 (Program 6–2) to examine the behavior of the different implementations. Tests performed on otherwise idle systems with 256,000 work units and 1, 2, 4, 8, 16, 32, 64, and 128 worker threads show the following results.

- For a small number of threads (4 or fewer), the NS (no synchronization), IN (interlocked functions), and CS (`CRITICAL_SECTION`) programs all require about the same amount of time. The CS version can be marginally (10–20 percent) slower, showing a typical synchronization slowdown. The MX (mutex) version, however, requires two to three times as long to execute.

- CS performance does not always scale with the number of threads on a single-processor system when the number of threads is 5 or more. Results vary from one NT5 system to another but appear to be consistent on a given system. On some systems, elapsed times double at each step using 1, 2, 4, ... threads, but in one case (Windows 2000, 1GHz, Pentium laptop) the times, in seconds, were 0.5, 1.0, 2.0, 4.0, 14.9, 16.0, 32.1, and 363.4; in another (Windows 2000, 50 MHz, Pentium desktop), they were 1.2, 2.3, 4.7, 9.3, 42.7, 101.3, 207.8, and 1212.5. The breaks usually occur after 4 or 8 threads, but performance is acceptable until 128 threads.

- MX performance is slower than CS on a single processor, with ratios varying from 2:1 to 10:1, depending on the system.

- *Performance on an SMP system can be very poor,* by a factor of 10:1 or even 100:1. Intuitively, we would expect better performance with multiple processors, but the internal implementation means that the processors are contending for locks and memory access, which explains why the MX and CS results are nearly equivalent. Tuning the CS spin count can help, as described in a later section.

- A semaphore can be used to limit the number of ready worker threads without changing the basic programming model. This technique is the subject of a later section in this chapter.

Cautionary note: The `task_count` array deliberately uses 32-bit integers to allow for a large task count and to avoid the potential for "word tearing" or a "cache line conflict" on SMP systems. Two separate processors, running adjacent worker threads, could concurrently modify adjacent task counts, making the modification in their caches (32 bits on Intel x86 systems). Only one cache, however, would actually be written back to memory, producing invalid results. Prevention requires that each thread's working storage be properly separated and aligned according to cache size. In this example, the task count could be grouped with the thread argument, and there is no good reason not to use a 32-bit count. Exercise 9–6 explores this subject.

A Model Program for Performance Experimentation

The book's Web site includes a project, `TimedMutualExclusion`, that can be used to experiment with different boss/worker models and application program characteristics. Program features, controlled from the command line, include the following.

- The use of either a CS or a mutex lock.

- The depth, or *recursion*, count.

- The lock holding time, or *delay*, which models the amount of work done in the critical code section.

- The number of worker threads, limited only by system resources.

- The number of *sleep points* where a worker yields the processor, using `Sleep(0)`, while owning the lock. Sleep points model a worker thread that waits for I/O or an event, while the delay models CPU activity.

- The number of active threads, as explained in the later section on semaphore throttles.

The delay and sleep point parameters significantly affect performance because they affect the amount of time that a worker holds a lock, preventing other workers from running.

The program listing contains extensive comments explaining how to run the program and set the parameters. Exercise 9–1 suggests some experiments to perform on as wide a variety of systems as you can access. A variation, `Timed-MutualExclusionSC`, supports spin counts, as explained in the next section.

Note: `TimedMutualExclusion` is a *simple* model that captures many worker thread features. It can often be tuned to represent a real application, and if the model shows performance problems, the application is at risk for similar problems. On the other hand, good performance in the model does not necessarily indicate good performance in the real application, even though the model may assist you in application performance tuning.

Tuning SMP Performance with CS Spin Counts

`CRITICAL_SECTION` locking (enter) and unlocking (leave) are efficient because CS testing is performed in user space without making the kernel system call required by a mutex. Unlocking is performed entirely in user space, whereas `ReleaseMutex` requires a system call. CSs operate as follows.

- A thread executing `EnterCriticalSection` (ECS) tests the CS's lock bit. If the bit is off (unlocked), then ECS sets it atomically as part of the test and proceeds without ever waiting. Thus, locking an unlocked CS is extremely efficient, normally taking just one or two machine instructions. The owning thread identity is maintained in the CS data structure, as is a recursion count.

- If the CS is locked, ECS enters a tight loop on an SMP system, repetitively testing the lock bit without yielding the processor (of course, the thread could be preempted). The CS spin count determines the number of times ECS repeats the loop before giving up. A single-processor system gives up immediately; spin counts are useful only on an SMP system.

- Once ECS gives up testing the lock bit (immediately on a single-processor system), ECS enters the kernel and the thread goes into a wait state, using a semaphore wait. Hence, CS locking is efficient only when contention is low or when the spin count gives another processor time to unlock the CS.

- `LeaveCriticalSection` is implemented by turning off the lock bit, after checking that the thread actually owns the CS. The kernel must also be notified if there are any waiting threads, using `ReleaseSemaphore`.

Consequently, CSs are efficient on single-processor systems if the CS is likely to be unlocked, as shown by the CS version of Program 9–1. The SMP advantage comes from the fact that the CS can be unlocked by a thread running on a different processor while the waiting thread spins.

The next steps are to show how to set spin counts and how to tune an application by determining the best spin count value. Again, spin counts are useful only on SMP systems; they are ignored on single-processor systems.

Setting the Spin Count

CS spin counts can be set at CS initialization or dynamically. In the first case, replace `InitializeCriticalSection` with `InitializeCriticalSectionAndSpinCount`, where a count parameter is added. There is no way to read a CS's spin count, however.

```
VOID InitializeCriticalSectionAndSpinCount (
    LPCRITICAL_SECTION lpCriticalSection,
    DWORD dwCount)
```

You can change a spin count at any time.

```
VOID SetCriticalSectionSpinCount (
    LPCRITICAL_SECTION lpCriticalSection,
    DWORD dwCount)
```

The Microsoft documentation mentions that 4,000 is a good spin count for heap management. The best value is, however, application specific, so spin counts should be adjusted with the application running in a realistic SMP environment. The best values will vary according to the number of processors, the nature of the application, and so on.

`TimedMutualExclusionSC` is on the book's Web site. It is a variation of the familiar `TimedMutualExclusion` program, and it includes a spin count argument on the command line. You can run it on your host processor to find a good value for this particular test program on your SMP systems, as suggested in Exercise 9–2.

Semaphore "Throttles" to Reduce Thread Contention

A large number of threads contending for a single resource, such as a mutex or CS, can degrade performance on both single- and multiple-processor systems. Frequently, the negative performance impact can be minimized by spin counts, careful use of the right synchronization objects, or restructuring of your program to increase lock granularity and locking times.

If all those techniques fail, it might seem as if there is no recourse but to reduce the number of threads, but this could force a single thread to multiplex operations that naturally should be performed by individual threads. Semaphores, however, give a natural way to retain a simple threading model while still minimizing the number of active, contending threads. The solution is simple conceptually and can be added to an existing application program, such as the TimedMutualExclusion example, very quickly. The solution, called a *semaphore throttle*, in a boss/worker system uses the following techniques.

- The boss thread creates a semaphore with a small maximum value, such as 4, which represents the maximum number of active threads, possibly the number of processors, compatible with good performance. Set the initial count to the maximum value as well. This number can be a parameter and tuned to the best value after experimentation, just as spin lock counts can be tuned. Another possible value is the number of processors, which can be obtained at run time (see the next section).

- Each worker thread waits on the semaphore before entering its critical code section. The semaphore wait can immediately precede the mutex or CS wait.

- The worker thread should then release the semaphore (release count of 1) immediately after leaving the critical code section.

- If the semaphore maximum is 1, the mutex is redundant. This is often the best SMP solution.

- Overall CS or mutex contention is reduced as the thread execution is serialized with only a few threads waiting on the mutex or CS.

The semaphore count simply represents the number of threads that can be active at any one time, limiting the number of threads contending for the mutex, CS, or other resource. The boss thread can even throttle the workers and dynamically tune the application by waiting on the semaphore to reduce the count if the boss determines that there is too much contention, and it can release semaphore units to allow more workers to run. Note, however, that the maximum semaphore count is set at create time and cannot be changed.

The following code fragment illustrates a modified worker loop with two semaphore operations.

```
while (TRUE) { // Worker loop
    WaitForSingleObject (hThrottleSem, INFINITE);
    WaitForSingleObject (hMutex, INFINITE);
    ... Critical code section ...
    ReleaseMutex (hMutex);
    ReleaseSemaphore (hThrottleSem, 1, NULL);
} // End of worker loop
```

There is one more variation. If a worker is considered to be "expensive" in some sense, it can be made to wait for several semaphore units. As noted in the previous chapter, however, two successive waits can create a deadlock. An exercise in the next chapter (Exercise 10–11) shows how to build an atomic multiple-wait compound semaphore object.

`TimedMutualExclusion`, the familiar example, adds a sixth parameter that is the initial throttle semaphore count for the number of active threads. You can experiment with this count as suggested in one of the exercises. Figure 9–1 shows the time required for six worker threads synchronizing with a single CS, with 1, 2, ..., 6 active threads. In all cases, the amount of work is the same, but the elapsed time rises sharply with more than 4 active threads.

These times were originally obtained on an older, slower system. On a much faster Windows 2000 586 (Pentium) system, the corresponding time values for 1–6 threads, in seconds, are 0.8, 0.8, 2.3, 21.2, 28.4, and 29.0, and these results can be reproduced consistently. In this case, performance started to degrade with only 3 active threads. *However*, on a random collection of similar systems, the times were approximately constant, regardless of the number of active threads. After some experimentation, it appears that the following conclusions hold.

- NT5 made substantial improvements over NT4, where results such as Figure 9–1 were seen consistently.

- Foreground and background operation, determined by whether or not the application window is in focus, can have some impact, as does the amount of other activity on the system.

- Mutexes are generally slower than CSs, but elapsed time is fairly constant on NT5, regardless of the number of active threads.

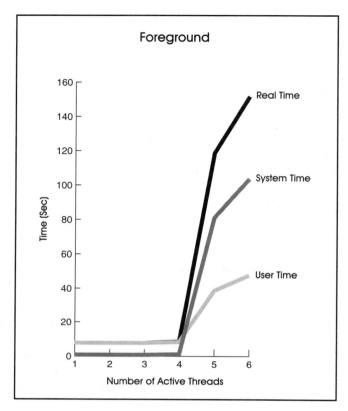

Figure 9-1   Thread Performance with a Semaphore Throttle

- SMP systems benefit from a throttle with a count of 1. The semaphore then makes the mutex redundant. For example, on a two-processor, 1.8GHz Xeon system, the CS timings for 1, 2, and 4 active threads were 1.8, 33.0, and 31.9. The corresponding mutex timings were 34.0, 66.5, and 65.0.

Summary: A semaphore throttle can maintain good performance for both foreground and background operation, even on a busy system. On an SMP system, they can be essential, where the active thread count should be 1. Semaphore waiting appears to be much more efficient than mutex waiting.

Processor Affinity

All the preceding discussion has assumed that all processors of an SMP system are available to all threads, with the kernel making scheduling decisions and allocating processors to threads. This approach is simple, natural, and consistent with SMP. It is possible, however, to assign threads to specific processors by setting processor affinity. Processor affinity can be used in several situations.

- A processor can be dedicated to a small set of one or more high-priority threads.

- Worker threads that contend for a single resource can be allocated to a single processor, avoiding the SMP performance issues illustrated earlier.

- Alternatively, the worker threads can be distributed over the available processors.

- Different classes of worker threads can be allocated to different processors.

System, Process, and Thread Affinity Masks

Each process has its own process affinity mask, which is a bit vector. There is also a system affinity mask.

- The system mask indicates the processors configured on this system.

- The system mask indicates the processors that can be used by the process's threads. By default, its value is the same as the system mask.

- Each individual thread has a thread affinity mask, which must be a subset of the process affinity mask. Initially, a thread's affinity mask is the same as the process mask.

There are functions to get and set the masks, although you can only read (get) the system mask and can only set thread masks. The set functions use thread and process handles, so one process or thread can set the affinity mask for another, assuming access rights, or for itself. Setting a mask has no effect on a thread that might already be running on a processor that is masked out; only future scheduling is affected.

A single function, `GetProcessAffinityMask`, reads both the system and process affinity masks. On a single-processor system, including any Windows 9x system, the mask values will be 1.

```
BOOL GetProcessAffinityMask (
    HANDLE hProcess,
    LPDWORD lpProcessAffinityMask,
    LPDWORD lpSystemAffinityMask)
```

The process affinity mask, which will be inherited by any child process, is set with `SetProcessAffinityMask`.

```
BOOL SetProcessAffinityMask (
    HANDLE hProcess,
    DWORD dwProcessAffinityMask)
```

The Microsoft documentation says that the new mask must be a *proper subset* of the values obtained from `GetProcessAffinityMask`. A quick experiment, included in the `TimedMutualExclusion` code, shows that the new mask can be the same as the system or preceding process mask. Such a limitation would not make sense because you would not be able to restore a system mask to a previous value.

Windows 9x does not support SMP and also does not support the process mask functions. The new value affects all the threads belonging to this process.

Thread masks are set with a similar function.

```
DWORD SetThreadAffinityMask (
    HANDLE hThread,
    DWORD dwThreadAffinityMask)
```

These functions are not designed consistently. `SetThreadAffinityMask` returns a `DWORD` rather than a `BOOL`, but the effect is the same (1 for success, 0 for failure). `SetThreadAffinityMask` also works on Windows 9x, but the mask must be 1, which has no utility whatsoever. Also, despite the documentation, the new mask does not need to be a proper subset of the system mask.

`SetThreadIdealProcessor` is a variation of `SetThreadAffinityMask`. You specify the preferred ("ideal") processor number (not a mask), and the scheduler will assign that processor to the thread if possible, but it will use a different processor if the preferred processor is not available. The return value gives the previous preferred processor number, if any.

Finding the Number of Processors

The system affinity mask does indicate the number of processors on the system; all that is necessary is to count the number of bits that are set. It is easier, however, to call `GetSystemInfo`, which returns a `SYSTEM_INFO` structure whose fields include the number of processors and the active processor mask, which is the same as the system mask. A simple program and project, `Version`, on the book's Web site, displays this information along with the Windows version.

Hyperthreading and the Processor Count

The Intel Pentium 4 and Xeon processors have a feature called HyperTreading whereby wait states during a thread's execution are used to run a different thread. A second register file is used to support this feature, which is feasible because the x86 architecture has a relatively small number of registers. A Xeon or other hyperthreading processor is regarded as a single processor by `GetSystem-Info` and `GetProcessAffinityMask`.

I/O Completion Ports

Chapter 14 describes I/O completion ports, which provide another mechanism to avoid thread contention by limiting the number of threads. I/O completion ports allow a small number of threads to manage a large number of concurrent I/O operations. Individual I/O operations are started asynchronously so that the operation is, in general, not complete when the read or write call returns. However, as outstanding operations complete, data processing is handed off to one of a small number of worker threads. Chapter 14 has an example using a server communicating with remote clients (Program 14–4).

Performance Guidelines and Pitfalls

Multiple threads can provide significant programming advantages, including simpler programming models and performance improvement. However, there are several performance pitfalls that can have drastic and unexpected negative performance impact, and the impact is not always consistent on different computers, even when they are running the same Windows version. Some simple guidelines, summarizing the experience in this chapter, will help to avoid these pitfalls. Some of these guidelines are adapted from Butenhof's *Programming with POSIX Pthreads*, as are many of the designing, debugging, and testing hints in the next chapter.

- Beware of conjecture and theoretical arguments about performance, which often sound convincing but can be wrong in practice. Test the conjecture with a simple prototype, such as `TimedMutualExclusion`, or with alternative implementations of your application.

- Test application performance on as wide a variety of systems as are available to you. It is helpful to run with different memory configurations, processor types, Windows versions, and number of processors. *An application may perform very well on one system and then have extremely poor performance on a similar one*; see the discussion of Program 9–1.

- Locking is expensive; use it only as required. Hold (own) a mutex or CS only as long as required and no longer. Setting the `TimedMutualExclusion` delay or sleep point parameters shows the impact of holding a lock for a long period of time.

- Use distinct mutexes for distinct resources so that locking is as granular as possible. In particular, avoid global locks.

- High lock contention hinders good performance. The greater the frequency of thread locking and unlocking, and the larger the number of threads, the greater the performance impact. Performance degradation can be drastic and is not just linear in the number of threads.

- CSs provide an efficient, lightweight locking mechanism when the number of contending threads is small, but mutexes sometimes provide better performance. When using CSs in a performance-critical SMP application, tune performance with the CS spin counts.

- Semaphores can reduce the number of active contending threads without forcing you to change your programming model.

- SMP can cause severe, often unexpected, performance impacts in cases where you might expect improved performance. Reducing contention and using thread affinity are techniques to maintain good performance.

- Choices such as whether to use a signal or broadcast model, explained in Chapter 10, also affect performance significantly.

- Investigate using commercially available profiling and performance analysis tools, which can help clarify the behavior of the threads in your program and locate time-consuming code segments.

Summary

Synchronization can impact program performance on both single-processor and SMP systems; in some cases, the impact can be severe. Careful program design and selection of the appropriate synchronization objects can help assure good performance. This chapter has discussed a number of useful techniques and guidelines and has illustrated performance issues with a simple test program that captures the essential characteristics of many real programming situations.

Looking Ahead

Chapter 10 shows how to use Windows synchronization in more general ways, and it discusses several programming models that help ensure correctness and maintainability, as well as good performance. Chapter 10 also creates several compound synchronization objects that are useful for solving a number of important problems. Subsequent chapters use threads and synchronization as required for applications, such as servers. There are also a few more basic threading topics; for example, Chapter 12 illustrates and discusses thread safety and reentrancy in DLLs.

Additional Reading

Chapter 10 provides information sources that apply to this chapter as well.

Exercises

9–1. Experiment with `statsMX` on your own system and on as many different systems (both hardware and Windows versions) as are available to you. Do you obtain similar results as those reported in this chapter? What happens on an SMP system?

9–2. Use `TimedMutualExclusionSC` to experiment with `CRITICAL_SECTION` spin counts to see whether adjusting the count can improve and tune SMP performance when you have a large number of threads. Results will vary from system to system, and I have found approximately optimal points ranging from 2,000 to 10,000.

9–3. Use `TimedMutualExclusion`, included on the book's Web site, to experiment with delay and sleep point counts.

9–4. `TimedMutualExclusion` also uses a semaphore throttle to limit the number of running threads. Experiment with the count on both single-processor and SMP systems. Can you reproduce the result reported earlier in this chapter?

9–5. Apply the semaphore throttle technique to `statsMX` (`statsCS.c`, `statsMX.c`).

9–6. *Advanced exercise*: Do the four variations of `statsMX` all operate correctly, ignoring performance, on SMP systems? Experiment with a large number of worker threads. If at all possible, run on an SMP Windows 2000 or 2003 server. Can you reproduce the "word tearing" or "cache line conflict" problem described earlier and also in Butenhof's *Programming with POSIX Threads*? You may need to use a 16-bit (short integer) count to reproduce the problem.

9–7. Use processor affinity as a performance enhancement technique by modifying this chapter's programs.

9–8. Determine the effect of hyperthreading on application performance. The Intel Xeon processor, for example, provides hyperthreading.

10 | Advanced Thread Synchronization

The preceding chapter described Windows performance issues and how to deal with them in realistic situations. Chapter 8 described several simple problems that require synchronization. This chapter will solve additional real but more complex problems, relying on the ideas introduced Chapters 8 and 9.

The first step is to combine two or more synchronization objects and data to create compound objects. The most useful combination is the condition variable model involving a mutex and one or more events. The condition variable model is essential in numerous practical situations, and many serious program race condition defects occur when programmers do not use the Windows synchronization objects, especially events, properly. Events are complex, and their behavior varies depending on the choices illustrated in Table 8–1, so they should be used according to well-understood models.

Subsequent sections show how to use asynchronous procedure calls (APCs) so that individual, cooperating threads can be controlled and canceled in an orderly manner.

Additional performance issues are discussed as appropriate.

The Condition Variable Model and Safety Properties

Threaded programs are much easier to develop, understand, and maintain if we use well-understood and familiar techniques and models. Chapter 7 discussed this and introduced the boss/worker and work crew models to establish a useful framework for understanding many threaded programs. The critical section concept is essential when using mutexes, and describing the invariants of your data structure is very useful. Finally, even defects have models, as we saw with the deadlock example. *Note*: Microsoft has its own set of models, such as the apartment model and free threading. These terms are most often used with COM and are discussed briefly at the end of Chapter 11.

Using Events and Mutexes Together

The next step is to describe how to use mutexes and events together, generalizing Program 8–2, where we had the following situation, which will occur over and over again. *Note*: This discussion applies to CRITICAL_SECTIONs as well as to mutexes.

- The mutex and event are both associated with the message block or other data structure.

- The mutex defines the critical code section for accessing the data structure object.

- The event is used to signal the fact that there is a new message.

- Generalizing, the mutex ensures the object's invariants (or safety properties), and the event signals that the object has changed state (e.g., a message has been added or removed from a message buffer), possibly being put into a known state (e.g., there is at least one message in the message buffer).

- One thread (the producer in Program 8–2) locks the data structure, changes the object's state by creating a new message, and sets or pulses the event associated with the fact that there is a new message.

- At least one other thread (the consumer in this example) waits on the event for the object to reach the desired state. The wait must occur outside the critical section so that the producer can access the object.

- A consumer thread can also lock the mutex, test the object's state (e.g., is there a new message in the buffer?), and avoid the event wait if the object is already in the desired state.

The Condition Variable Model

Now let's combine all of this into a single code fragment that represents what we will call the *condition variable model* (CV model) with two variations, the *signal* and *broadcast* CV models. The first examples use the broadcast variation. The result is a program model that will occur many times and can be used to solve a wide variety of synchronization problems. For convenience, the example is stated in terms of a producer and a consumer.

The discussion may seem a bit abstract, but once the techniques are understood, we will be able to solve a number of synchronization problems that would be very difficult without a good model.

The code fragment has several key elements.

- A data structure of type STATE_TYPE that contains all the data or *state variables* such as the messages, checksums, and counters used in Program 8–2.

- A mutex and one or more events associated with, and usually a part of, the data structure.

- One or more Boolean functions to evaluate the *condition variable predicates*, which are the conditions (states) on which a thread might wait. Examples include "a new message is ready," "there is available space in the buffer," and "the queue is not empty." A distinct event may be associated with each condition variable predicate, or one event may be used to represent simply a change of state or a combination (logical "or") of several predicates. In the latter case, individual predicate functions must be tested, with the mutex locked, to determine the actual state. If the predicate (logical expression) is simple, there is no need for a separate function.

The following code segment shows a producer and consumer using these principles, with a single event and condition variable predicate (implemented with a function, cvp, that is assumed but not shown). When the producer signals that a desired state has been reached, this example assumes that it is appropriate to release several consumer threads—that is, the signal should be broadcast to all waiting consumers. For instance, the producer may have created several messages, and the state is changed by increasing the message count. In many situations, you want to release only a single thread, as will be discussed after the code fragment.

This code segment is designed to operate under Windows 9x as well as all NT versions. SignalObjectAndWait will then be used to simplify the solution.

Note and caution: This example deliberately and consciously uses PulseEvent, even though some writers and some of the Microsoft documentation warn against its use (see the remarks section in the MSDN entry). The choice will be justified in the ensuing discussion and the examples, and the reader is invited to attempt to solve the problem (correctly) by using SetEvent.

```
typedef struct _state_t {
    HANDLE Guard; /* Mutex to protect the object. */
    HANDLE CvpSet; /* Manual-reset event -- cvp () holds. */
    ... other condition variables ...
```

```
    /* State structure with counts, checksums, etc. */
    struct STATE_VAR_TYPE StateVar;
} STATE_TYPE State;
...
/* Initialize State, creating the mutex and event. */
...
/* PRODUCER thread that modifies State. */
WaitForSingleObject (State.Guard, INFINITE);
/* Change state so that the CV predicate holds. */
/* Example: one or more messages are now ready. */
State.StateVar.MsgCount += N;
PulseEvent (State.CvpSet);
ReleaseMutex (State.Guard);
/* End of the interesting part of the producer. */
...
/* CONSUMER thread function waits for a particular state. */
WaitForSingleObject (State.Guard, INFINITE);
while (!cvp (&State)) {
    ReleaseMutex (State.Guard);
    WaitForSingleObject (State.CvpSet, TimeOut);
    WaitForSingleObject (State.Guard, INFINITE);
}
/* This thread now owns the mutex and cvp (&State) holds. */
/* Take appropriate action, perhaps modifying State. */
...
    ReleaseMutex (State.Guard);
/* End of the interesting part of the consumer. */
```

Comments on the Condition Variable Model

The essential feature in the code segment is the loop in the consumer. The loop body consists of three steps: (1) unlock the mutex that was locked prior to entering the loop, (2) wait on the event, and (3) lock the mutex again. *The event wait time-out is significant*, as explained later.

Pthreads, as implemented in many UNIX and other systems, combine these three steps into a single function, `pthread_cond_wait`, combining a mutex and a condition variable (which is similar but not identical to the Windows event). This is the reason for using the term condition variable model. There is also a timed version, which allows a time-out on the event wait.

Importantly, the single Pthreads function implements the first two steps (the mutex release and event wait) as an atomic operation so that no other thread can run before the calling thread waits on the event (or condition variable).

The Pthreads designers made a wise choice; the two functions (with and without a time-out) are the only ways to wait on a condition variable in Pthreads, so a condition variable must always be used with a mutex. Windows forces you to use two or three separate function calls, and you need to do it in just the right way to avoid problems.

Another motivation for learning the CV model, besides the fact that it simplifies programs and is essential if you ever need to use Pthreads, is that several third parties implement OS-independent thread and synchronization classes based on the CV model. With the material here, you will be able to understand those implementations quickly.

Note: Windows NT Version 4.0 introduced a new function, `Signal-ObjectAndWait` (SOAW), that performs the first two steps atomically. The later examples assume that this function is available, which means that the programs will not run on Windows 9x. Nonetheless, the CV model introduction does not use SOAW in order to motivate its later usage, and a few examples have alternative implementations on the book's Web site that use a CS in place of a mutex. (SOAW cannot be used with a CS.) Appendix C (Table C–5) shows that `Signal-ObjectAndWait` provides significant performance advantages.

Using the Condition Variable Model

The condition variable model, when implemented properly, works as follows.

- The producer locks the mutex, changes state, pulses the event when appropriate, and unlocks the mutex. For example, the producer pulses the event when one or more messages are ready.

- The event should be pulsed with the mutex locked so that no other thread can modify the object, perhaps invalidating the condition variable predicate.

- The consumer tests the condition variable predicate *with the mutex locked*. If the predicate holds, there is no need to wait.

- If the predicate does not hold, the consumer must unlock the mutex before waiting on the event. Otherwise, no thread could ever modify the state and set the event.

- The event wait must have a time-out just in case the producer pulses the event in the interval between the mutex release (step 1) and the event wait (step 2). That is, without the *finite* time-out, there could be a lost signal, which is another example of a race condition. APCs, described later in this chapter, can also cause lost signals. The time-out value used in the producer/consumer segment is a tunable parameter. (See Appendix C for comments on optimal values.)

- The consumer always retests the predicate after the event wait. Among other things, this is necessary in case the event wait has timed out. Also, the state may have changed. For example, the producer may have produced two messages and then released three waiting consumers, so one of the consumers will test the state, find no more messages, and wait again. Finally, the retest protects against spurious wakeups that might result from a thread setting or pulsing the event without the mutex locked.

- The consumer always owns the mutex when it leaves the loop, regardless of whether the loop body was executed.

Condition Variable Model Variations

Notice, first, that the preceding code fragment uses a manual-reset event and calls `PulseEvent` rather than `SetEvent`. Is this the correct choice, and could the event be used differently? The answer is "yes" to both questions.

Referring back to Table 8–1, we see that the example has the property that *multiple threads* will be released. This is correct in this example, where several messages are produced and there are multiple consuming threads, and we need to broadcast the change. However, if the producer creates just one message and there are multiple consuming threads, the event should be auto-reset and the producer should call `SetEvent` to ensure that exactly one thread is released. This variation is the signal CV model rather than the broadcast CV model. It is still essential for the released consumer thread, which will then own the mutex, to modify the object to indicate that there is no available message (that is, the condition variable predicate will no longer hold).

Of the four combinations in Table 8–1, two are useful in the condition variable model. Considering the other two combinations, auto-reset/`PulseEvent` would have the same effect as auto-reset/`SetEvent` (the signal CV model) because of the time-out, but the dependence on the time-out would reduce responsiveness. The manual-reset/`SetEvent` combination causes spurious signals (the condition variable predicate test offers protection, however), because some thread must reset the event, and there will be a race among the threads before the event is reset.

In summary, auto-reset/`SetEvent` is the signal CV model, which releases a single waiting thread, while manual-reset/`PulseEvent` is the broadcast CV model, which releases all waiting threads. Pthreads has the same distinction but does not require the finite time-out in the event wait for the broadcast model, whereas the time-out is essential in Windows because the mutex release and event wait are not performed atomically. This will change, however, when we introduce `SignalObjectAndWait`.

An Example Condition Variable Predicate

Consider the condition variable predicate:

```
State.StateVar.Count >= K;
```

In this case, a consumer thread will wait until the count is sufficiently large, and the producer can increment the count by an arbitrary amount. This shows, for example, how to implement a multiple-wait semaphore; recall that normal semaphores do not have an atomic wait for multiple units. The consumer thread would then decrement the count by K after leaving the loop but before releasing the mutex.

Notice that the broadcast CV model is appropriate in this case because a single producer may increase the count so as to satisfy several but not all of the waiting consumers.

Semaphores and the Condition Variable Model

In some cases, a semaphore would be appropriate rather than an event, and semaphores have the advantage of specifying the exact number of threads to be released. For example, if each consumer were known to consume exactly one message, the producer could call `ReleaseSemaphore` with the exact number of messages produced. In the more general case, however, the producer does not know how the individual consumers will modify the state variable structure, so the condition variable model can be used to solve a wider class of problems.

The CV model is powerful enough to implement semaphores. As described earlier, the basic technique is to define a predicate stating that "the semaphore count is nonzero" and create a state structure containing the count and maximum value. Exercise 10–11 shows a complete solution that allows for an atomic wait for multiple units. Pthreads do not provide semaphores because condition variables are sufficiently powerful.

Using `SignalObjectAndWait`

The consumer loop in the preceding code segment is critical to the CV model because it waits for a state change and then tests to see if the desired state holds. The state may not hold if the event is too *coarse*, indicating, for example, that there was simply some state change, not necessarily the one that is required. Furthermore, a different consumer thread might have made some other state change, such as emptying the message buffer. The loop required two waits and a mutex release, as follows:

```
while (!cvp (&State)) {
    ReleaseMutex (State.Guard);
    WaitForSingleObject (State.CvpSet, TimeOut);
    WaitForSingleObject (State.Guard, INFINITE);
}
```

The time-out on the first wait (the event wait) is required to avoid missed signals and other potential problems. This code will work under Windows 9x as well as NT 3.5 (another obsolete Windows version), and the code segment will also work if you replace the mutexes with CSs.

However, with Windows NT 5.x (XP, 2000, and 2003) and even NT 4.0, we can use `SignalObjectAndWait`, an important enhancement that eliminates the need for the time-out and combines the mutex release with the event wait. In addition to the program simplicity benefit, performance generally improves because a system call is eliminated and there is no need to tune the wait time-out period.

```
DWORD SignalObjectAndWait (
    HANDLE hObjectToSignal,
    HANDLE hObjectToWaitOn,
    DWORD dwMilliseconds,
    BOOL bAlertable)
```

This function simplifies the consumer loop, where the two handles are the mutex and event handles, respectively. There is no time-out because the calling thread waits on the second handle *immediately* after the first handle is signaled (which, in this case, means that the mutex is released). The signal and wait are atomic so that no other thread can possibly signal the event between the time that the calling thread releases the mutex and the thread waits on the second handle. The simplified consumer loop, then, is as follows.

```
while (!cvp (&State)) {
    SignalObjectAndWait (State.Guard, State.CvpSet,
        INFINITE, FALSE);
    WaitForSingleObject (State.Guard, INFINITE);
}
```

The final argument, `bAlertable`, is FALSE here but will be set to TRUE in the later sections on APCs.

In general, the two handles can be for any appropriate synchronization objects. You cannot, however, use a CRITICAL_SECTION as the signaled object; kernel objects are necessary.

All program examples, both in the book and on the Web site, use Signal-ObjectAndWait, although some alternative solutions are also included on the Web site and are mentioned in the text. If Windows 9x operation is required, replace it with the signal/wait pair in the original code segment, and be certain to have a finite time-out period on the wait.

The section on APCs shows a different technique to signal waiting threads which has the additional advantage of signaling a specific waiting thread, whereas, when using events, there is no easy way to control which thread is signaled.

Example: A Threshold Barrier Object

Suppose that you wish to have the worker threads wait until there are enough workers to form a work crew so that work can proceed. Once the threshold is reached, all the workers start operation and, if any other workers arrive later, they do not wait. This problem can be solved by creating a threshold barrier compound object.

Programs 10–1 and 10–2 show the implementation of the three functions that support the threshold barrier compound object. Two of the functions, Create-ThresholdBarrier and CloseThresholdBarrier, manage a THB_HANDLE, which is similar to the handles that we have used all along for kernel objects. The threshold number of threads is a parameter to CreateThresholdBarrier.

Program 10–1 shows the appropriate part of the header file, SynchObj.h, while Program 10–2 shows the implementation of the three functions. Notice that the barrier object has a mutex, an event, a counter, and a threshold. The condition variable predicate is documented in the header file—that is, the event is to be set exactly when the count is greater than or equal to the threshold.

Program 10–1   SynchObj.h: Part 1—Threshold Barrier Definitions

```
/* Chapter 10. Compound synchronization objects. */

#define CV_TIMEOUT 50 /* Tunable parameter for the CV model. */

/* THRESHOLD BARRIER -- TYPE DEFINITION AND FUNCTIONS. */
typedef struct THRESHOLD_BARRIER_TAG { /* Threshold barrier. */
    HANDLE b_guard; /* Mutex for the object. */
    HANDLE b_broadcast; /* Manual-reset evt: b_count >= b_threshold. */
    volatile DWORD b_destroyed; /* Set when closed. */
    volatile DWORD b_count; /* # of threads at the barrier. */
```

```
    volatile DWORD b_threshold; /* Barrier threshold. */
} THRESHOLD_BARRIER, *THB_HANDLE;

/* Error values. */
#define SYNCH_OBJ_NOMEM 1 /* Unable to allocate resources. */
#define SYNCH_OBJ_BUSY 2 /* Object is in use and cannot be closed. */
#define SYNCH_OBJ_INVALID 3 /* Object is no longer valid. */

DWORD CreateThresholdBarrier (THB_HANDLE *, DWORD /* Threshold. */);
DWORD WaitThresholdBarrier (THB_HANDLE);
DWORD CloseThresholdBarrier (THB_HANDLE);
```

Program 10–2 now shows the implementation of the three functions. A test program, `testTHB.c`, is included on the book's Web site. Notice how the `Wait-ThresholdBarrier` function contains the familiar condition variable loop. Also notice that the wait function not only waits on the event but also signals the event using `PulseEvent`. The previous producer/consumer discussion assumed that distinct thread functions were involved.

Finally, the condition variable predicate is, in this case, persistent. Once it becomes true, it will never change, so there is no danger from signaling the event more than once.

Program 10–2 `ThbObject.c`: Implementing the Threshold Barrier

```
/* Chapter 10. Program 10-2. */
/* Threshold barrier compound synch objects library. */

#include "EvryThng.h"
#include "synchobj.h"

/********************************/
/* THRESHOLD BARRIER OBJECTS */
/********************************/

DWORD CreateThresholdBarrier (THB_HANDLE *pthb, DWORD b_value)
{
    THB_HANDLE hthb;
    /* Initialize a barrier object. Full error testing is on Web site.*/
    hthb = malloc (sizeof (THRESHOLD_BARRIER));
    hthb->b_guard = CreateMutex (NULL, FALSE, NULL);
    hthb->b_broadcast = CreateEvent (NULL, FALSE /* Auto-reset. */,
        FALSE, NULL);

    hthb->b_threshold = b_value;
    hthb->b_count = 0;
    hthb->b_destroyed = 0;
```

```
    *pthb = hthb;
    return 0;
}

DWORD WaitThresholdBarrier (THB_HANDLE thb)
{
    /* Wait for the specified number of threads to reach */
    /* the barrier, then set the event. */
    if (thb->b_destroyed == 1) return SYNCH_OBJ_INVALID;
    WaitForSingleObject (thb->b_guard, INFINITE);
    thb->b_count++; /* A new thread has arrived. */
    while (thb->b_count < thb->b_threshold) {
        SignalObjectAndWait (thb->b_guard, thb->b_broadcast,
                INFINITE, FALSE);
        WaitForSingleObject (thb->b_guard, INFINITE);
    }
    PulseEvent (thb->b_broadcast);
    /* Broadcast CV model, releasing all waiting threads. */
    ReleaseMutex (thb->b_guard);
    return 0;
}

DWORD CloseThresholdBarrier (THB_HANDLE thb)
{
    /* Destroy the component mutex and event. */
    /* Be certain that no thread is waiting on the object. */
    if (thb->b_destroyed == 1) return SYNCH_OBJ_INVALID;
    WaitForSingleObject (thb->b_guard, INFINITE);
    if (thb->b_count < thb->b_threshold) {
        ReleaseMutex (thb->b_guard);
        return SYNCH_OBJ_BUSY;
    }
    ReleaseMutex (thb->b_guard);
    CloseHandle (thb->b_guard);
    CloseHandle (thb->b_broadcast);
    free (thb);
    return 0;
}
```

Comments on the Threshold Barrier Implementation

The threshold barrier object implemented here is limited for simplicity. In general, we would want to emulate Windows objects by:

- Allowing the object to have security attributes (Chapter 15)
- Allowing the object to be named

- Permitting multiple "handles" on the object and not destroying it until the reference count is 0

- Allowing the object to be shared between processes

The Web site contains a full implementation of one such object, a multiple wait semaphore, and the techniques used there can then be used for any of the objects in this chapter.

A Queue Object

So far, we have associated a single event with each mutex, but in general there might be more than one condition variable predicate. For example, in implementing a first in, first out (FIFO) queue, a thread that removes an element from the queue needs to wait on an event signifying that the queue is not empty, while a thread placing an element in the queue must wait until the queue is not full. The solution is to provide two events, one for each condition.

Program 10–3 shows the definitions of a queue object and its functions. The definitions intentionally demonstrate a different naming style from the Windows style used up to now. The original program was converted from a Pthreads implementation under UNIX, which encourages the conventions used here. In this way, you can sample a different style and, perhaps, determine one that is suitable for your own tastes and organizational requirements. Exercise 10–7 suggests making the conversion to Windows style.

Programs 10–4 and 10–5 show the queue functions and a program that uses them.

Program 10–3   SynchObj.h: Part 2—Queue Definitions

```
/* Definitions of synchronized, general bounded queue structure. */
/* Queues are implemented as arrays with indices to youngest */
/* and oldest messages, with wrap around. */
/* Each queue also contains a guard mutex and */
/* "not empty" and "not full" condition variables. */
/* Finally, there is a pointer to an array of messages of */
/* arbitrary type. */

typedef struct queue_tag { /* General-purpose queue. */
    HANDLE q_guard; /* Guard the message block. */
    HANDLE q_ne; /* Queue is not empty. MR event
                    (AR for "signal model"). */
    HANDLE q_nf; /* Queue is not full. MR event.
                    (AR for "signal model"). */
```

```
    volatile DWORD q_size; /* Queue max size. */
    volatile DWORD q_first; /* Index of oldest message. */
    volatile DWORD q_last; /* Index of youngest message. */
    volatile DWORD q_destroyed; /* Q receiver has terminated. */
    PVOID msg_array; /* Array of q_size messages. */
} queue_t;

/* Queue management functions. */
DWORD q_initialize (queue_t *, DWORD, DWORD);
DWORD q_destroy (queue_t *);
DWORD q_destroyed (queue_t *);
DWORD q_empty (queue_t *);
DWORD q_full (queue_t *);
DWORD q_get (queue_t *, PVOID, DWORD, DWORD);
DWORD q_put (queue_t *, PVOID, DWORD, DWORD);
DWORD q_remove (queue_t *, PVOID, DWORD);
DWORD q_insert (queue_t *, PVOID, DWORD);
```

Program 10–4 shows the functions, such as q_initialize and q_get, that are defined at the end of Program 10–3. Notice that q_get and q_put provide synchronized access, while q_remove and q_insert, which the first two functions call, are not themselves synchronized and could be used in a single-threaded program. The first two functions provide for a time-out, so the normal condition variable model is extended slightly.

q_empty and q_full are two other essential functions used to implement condition variable predicates.

This implementation uses PulseEvent and manual-reset events (the broadcast model) so that multiple threads are notified when the queue is not empty or not full.

A nice feature of the implementation is the symmetry of the q_get and q_put functions. Note, for instance, how they use the empty and full predicates and how they use the events. This simplicity is not only pleasing in its own right, but it also has the very practical benefit of making the code easier to write, understand, and maintain. The condition variable model enables this simplicity and its benefits.

Finally, C++ programmers will notice that a synchronized queue class could be constructed from this code; Exercise 10–8 suggests doing this.

Program 10–4 QueueObj.c: The Queue Management Functions

```c
/* Chapter 10. QueueObj.c. */
/* Queue function */

#include "EvryThng.h"
#include "SynchObj.h"

/* Finite bounded queue management functions. */

DWORD q_get (queue_t *q, PVOID msg, DWORD msize, DWORD MaxWait)
{

   if (q_destroyed (q)) return 1;
   WaitForSingleObject (q->q_guard, INFINITE);
   while (q_empty (q) {
       SignalObjectAndWait (q->q_guard, q->q_ne, INFINITE, FALSE);
       WaitForSingleObject (q->q_guard, INFINITE);
   }

   /* Remove the message from the queue. */
   q_remove (q, msg, msize);
   /* Signal that queue is not full as we've removed a message. */
   PulseEvent (q->q_nf);
   ReleaseMutex (q->q_guard);
   return 0;

}

DWORD q_put (queue_t *q, PVOID msg, DWORD msize, DWORD MaxWait)
{

   if (q_destroyed (q)) return 1;
   WaitForSingleObject (q->q_guard, INFINITE);
   while (q_full (q) {
       SignalObjectAndWait (q->q_guard, q->q_nf, INFINITE, FALSE);
       WaitForSingleObject (q->q_guard, INFINITE);
   }

   /* Put the message in the queue. */
   q_insert (q, msg, msize);
   /* Signal that queue is not empty; we've inserted a message. */
   PulseEvent (q->q_ne); /* Broadcast CV model. */
   ReleaseMutex (q->q_guard);
   return 0;

}
```

```
DWORD q_initialize (queue_t *q, DWORD msize, DWORD nmsgs)
{
    /* Initialize queue, including its mutex and events. */
    /* Allocate storage for all messages. */

    q->q_first = q->q_last = 0;
    q->q_size = nmsgs;
    q->q_destroyed = 0;

    q->q_guard = CreateMutex (NULL, FALSE, NULL);
    q->q_ne = CreateEvent (NULL, TRUE, FALSE, NULL);
    q->q_nf = CreateEvent (NULL, TRUE, FALSE, NULL);

    if ((q->msg_array = calloc (nmsgs, msize)) == NULL) return 1;
    return 0; /* No error. */
}

DWORD q_destroy (queue_t *q)
{
    if (q_destroyed (q)) return 1;
    /* Free all the resources created by q_initialize. */
    WaitForSingleObject (q->q_guard, INFINITE);
    q->q_destroyed = 1;
    free (q->msg_array);
    CloseHandle (q->q_ne);
    CloseHandle (q->q_nf);
    ReleaseMutex (q->q_guard);
    CloseHandle (q->q_guard);
    return 0;
}

DWORD q_destroyed (queue_t *q)
{
    return (q->q_destroyed);
}

DWORD q_empty (queue_t *q)
{
    return (q->q_first == q->q_last);
}

DWORD q_full (queue_t *q)
{
    return ((q->q_last - q->q_first) == 1 ||
            (q->q_first == q->q_size-1 && q->q_last == 0));
}
```

```
DWORD q_remove (queue_t *q, PVOID msg, DWORD msize)
{
    char *pm;

    pm = (char *)q->msg_array;
    /* Remove oldest ("first") message. */
    memcpy (msg, pm + (q->q_first * msize), msize);
    q->q_first = ((q->q_first + 1) % q->q_size);
    return 0; /* No error. */
}

DWORD q_insert (queue_t *q, PVOID msg, DWORD msize)
{
    char *pm;
    pm = (char *) q->msg_array;
    /* Add a new youngest ("last") message. */
    if (q_full (q)) return 1; /* Error - Q is full. */
    memcpy (pm + (q->q_last * msize), msg, msize);
    q->q_last = ((q->q_last + 1) % q->q_size);
    return 0;
}
```

Comments on the Queue Management Functions and Performance

Appendix C contains performance data, based on Program 10–5, which uses the queue management functions. The following comments that refer to performance are based on that data. The book's Web site contains code for all the implementation variations.

- This implementation uses the broadcast model (manual-reset/PulseEvent) to allow for the general case in which multiple messages may be requested or created by a single thread. The signal model (auto-reset/SetEvent) will work if this generality is not required, and there are significant performance advantages because only a single thread is released to test the predicate. The Web site contains QueueObj_Sig.c, a source file that uses signaling rather than broadcasting.

- Using a CRITICAL_SECTION, rather than a mutex, to protect the queue object can also improve performance. However, you must use an EnterCritical-Section followed by an event wait rather than SignalObjectAndWait. Two files provided on the Web site, QueueObjCS.c and QueueObjCS_Sig.c, illustrate this alternative approach.

- `QueueObj_noSOAW.c` and `QueueObj_noSOAW.c` are two additional source files provided on the Web site that build executable programs that will run on Windows 9x and do not use `SignalObjectAndWait`.

- Appendix C also shows the nonlinear performance impact when a large number of threads contend for a queue. The Web site contains projects for each of the alternative strategies; the projects are variations of the `ThreeStage` pipeline system described in the following sections.

- In summary, the queues can be extended to be process-sharable and to get and put multiple messages atomically. Some performance gains may be realized, however, by using the signal model, a `CRITICAL_SECTION`, or `SignalObjectAndWait`. Appendix C gives some performance results.

Example: Using Queues in a Multistage Pipeline

The boss/worker model, along with its variations, is one popular multithreaded programming model, and Program 8–2 is a simple producer/consumer model, a special case of the more general pipeline model.

Another important special case consists of a single boss thread that produces work items for a limited number of worker threads, placing the work items in a queue. This technique can be helpful when creating a scalable server that has a large number (perhaps thousands) of clients and it is not feasible to have a worker thread for each client. Chapter 14 discusses the scalable server problem in the context of I/O completion ports.

In the pipeline model, each thread, or group of threads, does some work on work items, such as messages, and passes the work items on to other threads for additional processing. A manufacturing assembly line is analogous to a thread pipeline. Queues are an ideal mechanism for pipeline implementations.

Program 10–5, `ThreeStage.c`, creates multiple production and consumption stages, and each stage maintains a queue of work to perform. Each queue has a bounded, finite length. There are three pipeline stages in total connecting the four work stages. The program structure is as follows.

- Producers create checksummed unit messages periodically, using the same message creation function as in Program 8–2, except that each message has a destination field indicating which consumer thread is to receive the message; each producer communicates with a single consumer. The number of producer/consumer pairs is a command line parameter. The producer then sends the unit message to the transmitter thread by placing the message in the transmission queue. If the queue is full, the producer waits until the queue state changes.

- The transmitter thread gathers all the available unit messages (but no more than five at a time) and creates a transmission message that contains a header block with the number of unit messages. The transmitter then puts each transmission message in the receiver queue, blocking if the queue is full. The transmitter and receiver might, in general, communicate over a network connection. The arbitrary 5:1 blocking factor is easy to adjust.

- The receiver thread processes the unit messages in each transmission message, putting each unit message in the appropriate consumer queue, if the queue is not full.

- Each consumer thread receives unit messages as they are available and puts the message in a log file.

Figure 10–1 shows the system. Notice how it models networking communication where messages between several sender/receiver pairs are combined and transmitted over a shared facility.

Program 10–5 shows the implementation, which uses the queue functions in Program 10–4. The message generation and display functions are not shown; they were first seen in Program 8–1. The message blocks have been augmented, however, to contain source and destination fields along with the checksum and data.

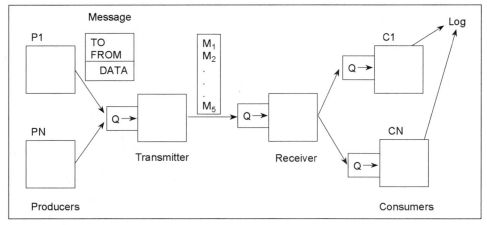

Figure 10–1 Multistage Pipeline

Program 10–5   `ThreeStage.c`: A Multistage Pipeline

```
/* Chapter 10. ThreeStage.c */
/* Three-stage producer/consumer system. */

/* Usage: ThreeStage npc goal. */
/* Start up "npc" paired producer and consumer threads. */
/* Each producer must produce a total of */
/* "goal" messages, where each message is tagged */
/* with the consumer that should receive it. */
/* Messages are sent to a "transmitter thread," which performs */
/* additional processing before sending message groups to the */
/* "receiver thread." Finally, the receiver thread sends */
/* the messages to the consumer threads. */

#include "EvryThng.h"
#include "SynchObj.h"
#include "messages.h"
#include <time.h>

#define DELAY_COUNT 1000
#define MAX_THREADS 1024

/* Q lengths and blocking factors. These are arbitrary and */
/* can be adjusted for performance tuning. The current values are */
/* not well balanced. */

#define TBLOCK_SIZE 5 /* Trsmttr combines 5 messages at a time. */
#define TBLOCK_TIMEOUT 50 /* Trsmttr time-out waiting for messages. */
#define P2T_QLEN 10 /* Producer to transmitter queue length. */
#define T2R_QLEN 4 /* Transmitter to receiver queue length. */
#define R2C_QLEN 4 /* Receiver to consumer queue length --
                      there is one such queue for each consumer. */

DWORD WINAPI producer (PVOID);
DWORD WINAPI consumer (PVOID);
DWORD WINAPI transmitter (PVOID);
DWORD WINAPI receiver (PVOID);

typedef struct _THARG {
    volatile DWORD thread_number;
    volatile DWORD work_goal; /* Used by producers. */
    volatile DWORD work_done; /* Used by producers & consumers. */
    char future [8];
} THARG;
```

```
/* Grouped messages sent by the transmitter to receiver. */
typedef struct t2r_msg_tag {
    volatile DWORD num_msgs; /* Number of messages contained. */
    msg_block_t messages [TBLOCK_SIZE];
} t2r_msg_t;

queue_t p2tq, t2rq, *r2cq_array;

static volatile DWORD ShutDown = 0;
static DWORD EventTimeout = 50;

DWORD _tmain (DWORD argc, LPTSTR * argv [])
{
    DWORD tstatus, nthread, ithread, goal, thid;
    HANDLE *producer_th, *consumer_th, transmitter_th, receiver_th;
    THARG *producer_arg, *consumer_arg;

    nthread = atoi (argv [1]);
    goal = atoi (argv [2]);
    producer_th = malloc (nthread * sizeof (HANDLE));
    producer_arg = calloc (nthread, sizeof (THARG));
    consumer_th = malloc (nthread * sizeof (HANDLE));
    consumer_arg = calloc (nthread, sizeof (THARG));

    q_initialize (&p2tq, sizeof (msg_block_t), P2T_QLEN);
    q_initialize (&t2rq, sizeof (t2r_msg_t), T2R_QLEN);
    /* Allocate, initialize Rec-Cons queue for each consumer. */
    r2cq_array = calloc (nthread, sizeof (queue_t));

    for (ithread = 0; ithread < nthread; ithread++) {
        /* Initialize r2c queue for this consumer thread. */
        q_initialize (&r2cq_array [ithread], sizeof (msg_block_t),
                R2C_QLEN);
        /* Fill in the thread arg. */
        consumer_arg [ithread].thread_number = ithread;
        consumer_arg [ithread].work_goal = goal;
        consumer_arg [ithread].work_done = 0;

        consumer_th [ithread] = (HANDLE)_beginthreadex (NULL, 0,
                consumer, (PVOID) &consumer_arg [ithread], 0, &thid);

        producer_arg [ithread].thread_number = ithread;
        producer_arg [ithread].work_goal = goal;
        producer_arg [ithread].work_done = 0;
        producer_th [ithread] = (HANDLE) _beginthreadex (NULL, 0,
                producer, (PVOID) &producer_arg [ithread], 0, &thid);
    }

    transmitter_th = (HANDLE) _beginthreadex (NULL, 0,
            transmitter, NULL, 0, &thid);
```

```
     receiver_th = (HANDLE) _beginthreadex (NULL, 0,
           receiver, NULL, 0, &thid);

     _tprintf _T ("BOSS: All threads are running\n");
     /* Wait for the producers to complete. */
     for (ithread = 0; ithread < nthread; ithread++) {
        WaitForSingleObject (producer_th [ithread], INFINITE);
        _tprintf _T ("BOSS: Producer %d produced %d work units\n",
              ithread, producer_arg [ithread].work_done);
     }
     /* Producers have completed their work. */
     _tprintf _T ("BOSS: All producers have completed their work.\n");

     /* Wait for the consumers to complete. */
     for (ithread = 0; ithread < nthread; ithread++) {
        WaitForSingleObject (consumer_th [ithread], INFINITE);
        _tprintf _T ("BOSS: consumer %d consumed %d work units\n",
              ithread, consumer_arg [ithread].work_done);
     }

     _tprintf _T ("BOSS: All consumers have completed their work.\n");
     ShutDown = 1; /* Set a shutdown flag. */

     /* Terminate, and wait for, the transmitter and receiver. */
     /* This thread termination is OK as the transmitter and */
     /* receiver cannot hold any resources other than a mutex, */
     /* which will be abandoned. Can you do this a better way? */

     TerminateThread (transmitter_th, 0);
     TerminateThread (receiver_th, 0);
     WaitForSingleObject (transmitter_th, INFINITE);
     WaitForSingleObject (receiver_th, INFINITE);

     q_destroy (&p2tq);
     q_destroy (&t2rq);
     for (ithread = 0; ithread < nthread; ithread++)
        q_destroy (&r2cq_array [ithread]);

     free (r2cq_array);
     free (producer_th); free (consumer_th);
     free (producer_arg); free (consumer_arg);
     _tprintf _T ("System has finished. Shutting down\n");
     return 0;
}

DWORD WINAPI producer (PVOID arg)
{
     THARG * parg;
     DWORD ithread, tstatus;
     msg_block_t msg;
```

```
    parg = (THARG *) arg;
    ithread = parg->thread_number;

    while (parg->work_done < parg->work_goal) {

        /* Produce work units until the goal is satisfied. */
        /* Messages receive source, destination address, which are */
        /* the same here but could, in general, be different. */

        delay_cpu (DELAY_COUNT * rand () / RAND_MAX);
        message_fill (&msg, ithread, ithread, parg->work_done);

        /* Put the message in the queue. */
        tstatus = q_put (&p2tq, &msg, sizeof (msg), INFINITE);
        parg->work_done++;
    }
    return 0;
}

DWORD WINAPI transmitter (PVOID arg)
{
    /* Obtain multiple producer messages, combining into a single */
    /* compound message for the receiver. */
    DWORD tstatus, im;
    t2r_msg_t t2r_msg = {0};
    msg_block_t p2t_msg;

    while (!ShutDown) {
        t2r_msg.num_msgs = 0;
        /* Pack the messages for transmission to the receiver. */
        for (im = 0; im < TBLOCK_SIZE; im++) {
            tstatus = q_get (&p2tq, &p2t_msg,
                    sizeof (p2t_msg), INFINITE);
            if (tstatus != 0) break;
            memcpy (&t2r_msg.messages [im], &p2t_msg, sizeof (p2t_msg));
            t2r_msg.num_msgs++;
        }
        tstatus = q_put (&t2rq, &t2r_msg, sizeof (t2r_msg), INFINITE);
        if (tstatus != 0) return tstatus;
    }
    return 0;
}

DWORD WINAPI receiver (PVOID arg)
{
    /* Obtain compound messages from the transmitter; unblock */
    /* them and transmit to the designated consumer. */
```

```
    DWORD tstatus, im, ic;
    t2r_msg_t t2r_msg;
    msg_block_t r2c_msg;

    while (!ShutDown) {
        tstatus = q_get (&t2rq, &t2r_msg, sizeof (t2r_msg), INFINITE);
        if (tstatus != 0) return tstatus;

        /* Distribute the messages to the proper consumer. */
        for (im = 0; im < t2r_msg.num_msgs; im++) {
            memcpy (&r2c_msg, &t2r_msg.messages [im], sizeof (r2c_msg));
            ic = r2c_msg.destination; /* Destination consumer. */
            tstatus = q_put (&r2cq_array [ic], &r2c_msg,
                    sizeof (r2c_msg), INFINITE);
            if (tstatus != 0) return tstatus;
        }
    }
    return 0;
}

DWORD WINAPI consumer (PVOID arg)
{
    THARG * carg;
    DWORD tstatus, ithread;
    msg_block_t msg;
    queue_t *pr2cq;
    carg = (THARG *) arg;
    ithread = carg->thread_number;

    carg = (THARG *) arg;
    pr2cq = &r2cq_array [ithread];

    while (carg->work_done < carg->work_goal) {
        /* Receive and display (optionally -- not shown) messages. */
        tstatus = q_get (pr2cq, &msg, sizeof (msg), INFINITE);
        if (tstatus != 0) return tstatus;
        carg->work_done++;
    }
    return 0;
}
```

Comments on the Multistage Pipeline

There are several things to notice about this implementation, some of which are mentioned in the program comments. Exercises 10–6, 10–7, and 10–10 suggest addressing these issues.

- A significant objection could be the way that the main thread terminates the transmitter and receiver threads. A solution would be to use a time-out value in the inner transmitter and receiver loops and shut down when the global shutdown flag is detected. Another approach would be to cancel the threads, as described later in this chapter.

- Note the symmetry between the transmitter and receiver threads. As with the queue implementation, this facilitates program design, debugging, and maintenance.

- The implementation is not well balanced in terms of the match of the message production rates, the pipeline sizes, and the transmitter-receiver blocking factor.

- This implementation (Program 10–4) uses mutexes to guard the queues. Experiments with `CRITICAL_SECTION`s show no significant speed-up on a single-processor system (see Appendix C). The CS version is included on the Web site as `ThreeStageCS.c`. `SignalObjectAndWait` provides similar performance improvements.

Asynchronous Procedure Calls

One major objection to `ThreeStage.c` (Program 10–5), as it is currently written, is the use of `TerminateThread` at the end to end the transmitter and receiver threads. A code comment asks if there is a cleaner way to terminate threads so they can shut down in an orderly way and free resources.

Another open problem is that there is no general method (other than `TerminateThread`) to signal, or cause an action in, a specific thread. Events signal one thread waiting on an auto-reset event or all the threads waiting on a manual-reset event, but there is no way to assure that a particular thread is signaled. The solution used so far is simply to wake up all the waiting threads so they can individually determine whether it is time to proceed. An alternative solution, which is occasionally used, is to assign events to specific threads so that the signaling thread can determine which event to pulse or set.

APCs provide a solution to both of these problems. The sequence of events is as follows, where the boss thread needs to control a cooperating worker or target thread.

- The boss thread specifies an APC routine to the target thread by queuing the APC to the target. More than one APC can be queued to a specific thread.

- The target thread enters an alertable wait state indicating that the thread can safely execute the APC. The order of these first two steps is irrelevant so there is no concern here with race conditions.

- A thread in an alertable wait state will execute all queued APCs.

- An APC can carry out any appropriate action, such as freeing resources or raising an exception. In this way, the boss thread can cause an exception to occur in the target, although the exception will not occur until the target has entered an alertable state.

APC execution is asynchronous in the sense that a boss thread can queue an APC to a target at any time, but the execution is synchronous in the sense that it can occur only when the target thread enters an alertable wait state.

Alertable wait states will be discussed again in Chapter 14, which covers asynchronous I/O.

The following sections describe the required functions and illustrate their use with another variation of the `ThreeStage` program. On the book's Web site, the source file is `ThreeStageCancel.c` and the project to build this version is `ThreeStageCancel`.

Queuing Asynchronous Procedure Calls

One thread (the boss) queues an APC to a target thread using `QueueUserAPC`.

```
DWORD QueueUserAPC (
    PAPCFUNC pfnAPC,
    HANDLE hThread,
    DWORD dwData)
```

`hThread` is the handle of the target thread. `dwData` is an argument value that will be passed to the APC function when it is executed, and the value could represent a termination code or convey other information to the function.

`ThreeStageCancel.c`, in the main function (compare to Program 10–5), replaces `TerminateThread` calls with `QueueUserAPC` calls, as follows.

```
// TerminateThread (transmitter_th, 0); Replace with APC
// TerminateThread (receiver_th, 0); Replace with APC
   tstatus = QueueUserAPC
       (ShutDownTransmitter, transmitter_th, 1);
   if (tstatus == 0) ReportError (
       "Failed queuing APC for transmitter", 8, FALSE);
```

```
        tstatus = QueueUserAPC
            (ShutDownReceiver, receiver_th, 2);
        if (tstatus == 0) ReportError (...);
```

The `QueueUserAPC` return value is nonzero for success or zero for failure. `GetLastError()`, however, does not return a useful value, so the `ReportError` call does not request an error message (the last argument is `FALSE`).

`pfnAPC` is a pointer to the actual function that the target thread will execute, such as the following example used in `ThreeStageCancel.c`.

```
/* APC to shut down the receiver. */
void WINAPI ShutDownReceiver (DWORD n)
{
    printf ("In ShutDownReceiver. %d\n", n);
    /* Free any resource (none in this example). */
    return;
}
```

`ShutDownTransmitter` is identical, other than the message text. It's not immediately clear why this function, which does nothing, can cause the target receiver thread to shut down. The next section will explain the process.

APCs and Missed Signals

A kernel mode APC (used in asynchronous I/O) can momentarily move a waiting thread out of its wait state, potentially causing a missed `PulseEvent` signal. Some documentation warns against `PulseEvent` for this reason, even though this chapter has demonstrated its usefulness. This risk is not an issue in our examples, which do not use kernel mode APCs. Furthermore, using `SignalObjectAndWait` and testing its return value is sufficient protection against this sort of missed signal. Finally, should there be a situation where a missed signal could occur, simply include a finite time-out period on the appropriate wait calls.

Alertable Wait States

The last `SignalObjectAndWait` parameter, `bAlertable`, has been `FALSE` in previous examples. By using `TRUE` instead, we indicate that the wait is a so-called alertable wait and the thread enters an alertable wait state. The behavior is as follows.

- If one or more APCs are queued to the thread (as a `QueueUserAPC` target thread) *before* either `hObjectToWaitOn` (normally an event) is signaled or the time-out expires, then the APCs are executed (there is no guaranteed order) and `SignalObjectAndWait` returns with a return value of `WAIT_IO_COMPLETION`.

- If an APC is never queued, then `SignalObjectAndWait` behaves in the normal way; that is, it waits for the object to be signaled or the time-out period to expire.

Alterable wait states will be used again with asynchronous I/O (Chapter 14); the name `WAIT_IO_COMPLETION` comes from this usage. A thread can also enter an alterable wait state with other alertable wait functions such as `WaitForSingleObjectEx`, `WaitForMultipleObjectsEx`, and `SleepEx`, and these functions will be useful when performing asynchronous I/O.

`q_get` and `q_put` (see Program 10–4) can now be modified to perform an orderly shutdown after an APC is performed, even though the APC function does not do anything other than print a message and return. All that is required is to enter an alterable wait state and to test the `SignalObjectAndWait` return value, as shown by the following modified version of `q_get` (see `QueueObj-Cancel.c` on the Web site).

Program 10–6   `q_get` Modified for Cancellation

```
DWORD q_put (queue_t *q, PVOID msg, DWORD msize, DWORD MaxWait)
{
    BOOL Cancelled = FALSE;

    if (q_destroyed(q)) return 1;
    WaitForSingleObject (q->q_guard, INFINITE);
    while (q_full (q) && !Cancelled) {
        if (SignalObjectAndWait(q->q_guard, q->q_nf, INFINITE, TRUE)
                == WAIT_IO_COMPLETION) {
            Cancelled = TRUE;
            continue;
        }
        WaitForSingleObject (q->q_guard, INFINITE);
    }
    /* Put the message in the queue. */
    if (!Cancelled) {
        q_remove (q, msg, msize);
        /* Signal that queue is not full as we've removed a message. */
        PulseEvent (q->q_nf);
        ReleaseMutex (q->q_guard);
    }
    return Cancelled ? WAIT_TIMEOUT : 0;
}
```

The APC routine could be either `ShutDownReceiver` or `ShutDownTransmitter`, as the receiver and transmitter threads use both `q_get` and `q_put`. If it were necessary for the shutdown functions to know which thread they are executed from, use different APC argument values for the third `QueueUserAPC` arguments in the code segment preceding Program 10–6.

The thread exit code will be `WAIT_TIMEOUT` to maintain consistency with previous versions. Additional cleanup can be performed in a `DllMain` function if appropriate.

An alternative to testing the return value for `WAIT_IO_COMPLETION` would be for the shutdown functions to raise an exception, place the `q_put` body in a try block, and add an exception handler.

Safe Thread Cancellation

The preceding example and discussion show how we can safely cancel a target thread that uses alertable wait states. Such cancellation is sometimes called *synchronous cancellation*, despite the use of APCs, because the cancellation, which is caused by the boss's `QueueUserAPC` call, can only take effect when the target thread reaches a safe alertable wait state.

Synchronous cancellation requires the target thread to cooperate and allow itself to be canceled from time to time. Event waits are a natural place to enter an alertable wait state because, as a system shuts down, the event may never be signaled again. Mutex waits could also be alertable to allow thread waiting on a resource that may not become available again. For example, a boss thread could break deadlocks with this technique.

Asynchronous thread cancellation is useful if it is necessary to signal a compute-bound thread that seldom, if ever, waits for I/O or events. Windows does not allow asynchronous cancellation, although there are techniques, using processor-specific code, to interrupt a specified thread.

Pthreads for Application Portability

Pthreads have been mentioned several times as the alternative threading and synchronization model available with UNIX, Linux, and other non-Windows systems. There is an open source Windows Pthreads library, and, by using this library, it is possible to write portable threaded applications that can run on a wide variety of systems. The book's Web site discusses this subject in more detail. The `ThreeStagePthreads` project uses the open source library and points to the download site.

Thread Stacks and the Number of Threads

Two more cautions, which are related, are in order. First, give some thought to the thread stack size, where 1MB is the default. This should be sufficient in most cases, but if there is any doubt, determine the maximum amount of stack space each thread will require, including the requirements of any library functions or recursive functions that the thread calls. A stack overflow will corrupt other memory or cause an exception.

Second, a large number of threads with large stacks will require large amounts of virtual memory for the process and could affect paging behavior and the paging file. For example, using 1,000 threads would not be unreasonable in some of the examples in this and later chapters. Allowing 1MB per thread stack results in 1GB of virtual address space. Preventive measures include careful stack sizing, I/O completion ports, and multiplexing operations within a single thread.

Hints for Designing, Debugging, and Testing

At the risk of presenting advice that is contrary to that given in many other books and technical articles, which stress testing and little else, my personal advice is to balance your efforts so that you pay attention to design, implementation, and use of familiar programming models. The best debugging technique is not to create the bugs in the first place; this advice, of course, is easier to give than to follow. Nonetheless, when defects do occur, as they will, code inspection, balanced with debugging, often is most effective in finding and fixing the defects' root causes.

Overdependence on testing is not advisable because many serious defects will elude the most extensive and expensive testing. Testing can only reveal defects; it cannot prove they do not exist, and testing shows only defect symptoms, not root causes. As a personal example, I ran a version of a multiple semaphore wait function that used the CV model without the finite time-out on the event variable wait. The defect, which could cause a thread to block indefinitely, did not show up in over a year of use; eventually, however, something would have failed. Simple code inspection and knowledge of the condition variable model revealed the error.

Debugging is also problematic because debuggers change timing behavior, masking the very race conditions you wish to expose. For example, debugging is unlikely to find a problem with an incorrect choice of event type (auto-reset or manual-reset) and `SetEvent/PulseEvent`. You have to think carefully about what you wish to achieve.

Having said all that, testing on a wide variety of platforms, including SMP, is an essential part of any multithreaded software development project.

Avoiding Incorrect Code

Every bug you don't put in your code in the first place is one more bug you won't find in testing or production. Here are some hints, most of which are taken, although rephrased, from Butenhof's *Programming with POSIX Threads* (*PWPT*).

- **Avoid relying on thread inertia.** Threads are asynchronous, but we often assume, for example, that a parent thread will continue running after creating one or more child threads. The assumption is that the parent's "inertia" will keep it running before the children run. This assumption is especially dangerous on an SMP system, but it can also lead to problems on single-processor systems.

- **Never bet on a thread race.** Nearly anything can happen in terms of thread scheduling. Your program has to assume that any ready thread can start running at any time and that any running thread can be preempted at any time. "No ordering exists between threads unless you cause ordering" (*PWPT*, p. 294).

- **Scheduling is not the same as synchronization.** Scheduling policy and priorities cannot ensure proper synchronization. Use synchronization objects instead.

- **Sequence races can occur even when you use mutexes to protect shared data.** Just because data is protected, there is no assurance as to the order in which different threads will access the shared data. For example, if one thread adds money to a bank account and another makes a withdrawal, there is no assurance, using a mutex guard alone, that the deposit will be made before the withdrawal. Exercise 10–14 shows how to control thread execution order.

- **Cooperate to avoid deadlocks.** You need a well-understood lock hierarchy, used by all threads, to ensure that deadlocks will not occur.

- **Never share events between predicates.** Each event used in a condition variable implementation should be associated with a distinct predicate. Furthermore, an event should always be used with the same mutex.

- **Beware of sharing stacks and related memory corrupters.** Always remember that when you return from a function or when a thread terminates, memory local to the function or thread is no longer valid. Memory on a thread's stack can be used by other threads, but you have to be sure that the first thread continues to exist.

- **Be sure to use the `volatile` storage modifier.** Whenever a shared variable can be changed in one thread and accessed in another, the variable should be `volatile` to ensure that each thread stores and fetches the variable to and from memory, rather than assuming that the variable is held in a register that is specific to the thread.

Here are some additional guidelines and rules of thumb that can be helpful.

- **Use the condition variable model properly,** being certain not to use two distinct mutexes with the same event. Understand the condition variable model on which you depend. Be certain that the invariant holds before waiting on a condition variable.

- **Understand your invariants and condition variable predicates,** even if they are stated only informally. Be certain that the invariant always holds outside the critical code section.

- **Keep it simple.** Multithreaded programming is complex enough without the burden of additional complex, poorly understood thread models and logic. If a program becomes overly complex, assess whether the complexity is really necessary or is the result of poor design. Careful use of standard threading models can simplify your program and make it easier to understand, and lack of a good model may be a symptom of a poorly designed program.

- **Test on both single-processor and multiprocessor systems and on systems with different clock rates and other characteristics.** Some defects will never, or rarely, show up on a single-processor system but will occur immediately on an SMP system, and conversely. Likewise, a variety of system characteristics helps ensure that a defective program has more opportunity to fail.

- **Testing is necessary but not sufficient to ensure correct behavior.** There have been a number of examples of programs, known to be defective, that seldom fail in routine or even extensive tests.

- **Be humble.** After all these precautions, bugs will still occur. This is true even with single-threaded programs; threads simply give us more, different, and very interesting ways to cause problems.

Beyond the Windows API

We have intentionally limited coverage to the Windows API. Microsoft does, however, provide additional access to kernel objects, such as threads. For example, the `ThreadPool` class, accessible through C++, C#, and other languages, allows you to create a pool of threads and to queue work items to the threads (the `Thread-Pool` method is `QueueUserWorkItem`).

Microsoft also implements the Microsoft Message Queuing (MSMQ) service, which provides messaging services between networked systems. The examples in this chapter should help show the value of a general-purpose message queuing system. MSMQ is documented on the Microsoft Web site.

Summary

Multithreaded program development is much simpler if you use well-understood and familiar programming models and techniques. This chapter has shown the utility of the condition variable model and has solved several relatively complex but important programming problems. APCs allow one thread to signal and cause actions in another thread, which allows thread cancellation so that all threads in a system can shut down properly.

Synchronization and thread management are complex because there are multiple ways to solve a given problem, and the different techniques involve complexity and performance trade-offs. The three-stage pipeline example was implemented several different ways in order to illustrate the options.

Use of careful program design and implementation is the best way to improve program quality. Overdependence on testing and debugging, without attention to detail, can lead to serious problems that may be very difficult to detect and fix.

Looking Ahead

Chapter 11 shows how to use Windows named pipes and mailslots to communicate between processes and threads in those processes. The major example is a client/ server system where the server uses a pool of worker threads to service client requests. Chapter 12 then implements the same system using Windows Sockets, extending Chapter 11's client/server system to the use of standard protocols. The server also uses a DLL in-process server and creates thread-safe DLLs.

Additional Reading

David Butenhof's *Programming with POSIX Threads* was the source of much of the information and programming guidelines at the end of the chapter. The threshold barrier solution, Programs 10–1 and 10–2, was adapted from Butenhof as well.

"Strategies for Implementing POSIX Condition Variables in Win32," by Douglas Schmidt and Irfan Pyarali (posted at http://www.cs.wustl.edu/~schmidt/ win32-cv-1.html), discusses Win32 (Windows) event limitations along with condition variables emulation, thoroughly analyzing and evaluating several approaches. However, this material was written before `SignalObjectAndWait` became available, so a great deal of effort is expended in avoiding missed signals.

Reading this paper will increase your appreciation of the new function. Another paper by the same authors (http://www.cs.wustl.edu/~schmidt/win32-cv-2.html) builds object-oriented wrappers around Windows synchronization objects to achieve a platform-independent synchronization interface. The open source Pthreads implementation, which is based on the Schmidt and Pyarali work, is available at http://sources.redhat.com/pthreads-win32/.

Exercises

10–1. Revise Program 10–1 so that it does not use the `SignalObjectAndWait` function; test the result on a Windows 9x system.

10–2. Modify `eventPC` (Program 8–2) so that there can be multiple consumers and so that it uses the condition variable model. Which event type is appropriate?

10–3. Change the logic in Program 10–2 so that the event is signaled only once.

10–4. Replace the mutex in the queue object used in Program 10–2 with a CS. What are the effects on performance and throughput? The solution is on the book's Web site, and Appendix C contains experimental data.

10–5. Program 10–4 uses the broadcast CV model to indicate when the queue is either not empty or not full. Would the signal CV model work? Would the signal model even be preferable in any way? Appendix C contains experimental data.

10–6. Experiment with the queue lengths and the transmitter-receiver blocking factor in Program 10–5 to determine the effects on performance, throughput, and CPU load.

10–7. Modify Programs 10–3 through 10–5 to conform to the Windows naming style used elsewhere in this book.

10–8. *For C++ programmers*: The code in Programs 10–3 and 10–4 could be used to create a synchronized queue class in C++; create this class and modify Program 10–5 to test it. Which of the functions should be public and which should be private?

10–9. Study the performance behavior of Program 10–5 if `CRITICAL_SECTION`s are used instead of mutexes.

10–10. Improve Program 10–5 so that it is not necessary to terminate the transmitter and receiver threads. The threads should shut themselves down.

10–11. The Web site contains `MultiSem.c`, which implements a multiple-wait semaphore modeled after the Windows objects (they can be named, secured, and process shared, and there are two wait models), and `TestMultiSem.c` is a test program. Build and test this program. How does it use the condition variable model? Is performance improved by using a `CRITICAL_SECTION`? What are the invariants and condition variable predicates?

10–12. Illustrate the various guidelines at the end of this chapter in terms of bugs you have encountered or in the defective versions of the programs provided on the Web site.

10–13. Read *"Strategies for Implementing POSIX Condition Variables in Win32"* by Schmidt and Pyarali (see the Additional Reading section). Apply their fairness, correctness, serialization, and other analyses to the condition variable models (called "idioms" in their paper) in this chapter. Notice that this chapter does not directly emulate condition variables; rather, it emulates condition variable usage, whereas Schmidt and Pyarali emulate condition variables used in an arbitrary context.

10–14. Two projects on the Web site, `batons` and `batonsMultipleEvents`, show alternative solutions to the problem of serializing thread execution. The code comments give background and acknowledgments. The second solution associates a unique event with each thread so that specific threads can be signaled. The implementation uses C++ in order to take advantage of the C++ Standard Template Library (STL). Compare and contrast these two solutions, and use the second as a means to become familiar with the STL.

11 Interprocess Communication

Chapter 6 showed how to create and manage processes, and Chapters 7–10 showed how to manage and synchronize threads within processes. So far, however, we have not been able to perform direct process-to-process communication other than through shared memory.

The next step is to provide sequential interprocess communication (IPC) between processes[1] using filelike objects. Two primary Windows mechanisms for IPC are the anonymous pipe and the named pipe, both of which can be accessed with the familiar `ReadFile` and `WriteFile` functions. Simple anonymous pipes are character-based and half-duplex. As such, they are well suited for redirecting the output of one program to the input of another, as is commonly done between UNIX programs. The first example shows how to do this.

Named pipes are much more powerful than anonymous pipes. They are full-duplex and message-oriented, and they allow networked communication. Furthermore, there can be multiple open handles on the same pipe. These capabilities, coupled with convenient transaction-oriented named pipe functions, make named pipes appropriate for creating client/server systems. This capability is shown in this chapter's second example, a multithreaded client/server command processor, modeled after Figure 7–1, which was used to introduce threads. Each server thread manages communication with a different client, and each thread/client pair uses a distinct handle, or named pipe instance.

Finally, mailslots allow for one-to-many message broadcasting, and this chapter's final example enhances the command processor with mailslots.

---

[1] The Windows system services also allow processes to communicate through mapped files, as demonstrated in the semaphore exercise in Chapter 10 (Exercise 10–11). Additional mechanisms for IPC include files, sockets, remote procedure calls, COM, and message posting. Sockets are described in Chapter 12.

Anonymous Pipes

The Windows anonymous pipes allow one-way (half-duplex), character-based IPC. Each pipe has two handles: a read handle and a write handle. The `CreatePipe` function is as follows.

```
BOOL CreatePipe (
    PHANDLE phRead,
    PHANDLE phWrite,
    LPSECURITY_ATTRIBUTES lpsa,
    DWORD cbPipe)
```

The pipe handles are often inheritable; the next example shows the reasons. `cbPipe`, the pipe byte size, is only a suggestion, and 0 specifies the default value.

In order for the pipe to be used for IPC, there must be another process, and that process requires one of the pipe handles. Assume that the parent process, which calls `CreatePipe`, wishes to write data for a child to use. The problem, then, is to communicate the read handle (`phRead`) to the child. The parent achieves this by setting the child procedure's input handle in the start-up structure to `*phRead`.

Reading a pipe read handle will block if the pipe is empty. Otherwise, the read will accept as many bytes as are in the pipe, up to the number specified in the `ReadFile` call. A write operation to a full pipe, which is implemented in a memory buffer, will also block.

Finally, anonymous pipes are one-way. Two pipes are required for bidirectional communication.

Example: I/O Redirection Using an Anonymous Pipe

Program 11–1 shows a parent process, `Pipe`, that creates two processes from the command line and pipes them together. The parent process sets up the pipe and redirects standard input and output. Notice how the anonymous pipe handles are inheritable and how standard I/O is redirected to the two child processes; these techniques were described in Chapter 6.

The location of `WriteFile` in `Program2` on the right side of Figure 11–1 assumes that the program reads a large amount of data, processes it, and then writes out results. Alternatively, the write could be inside the loop, putting out results after each read.

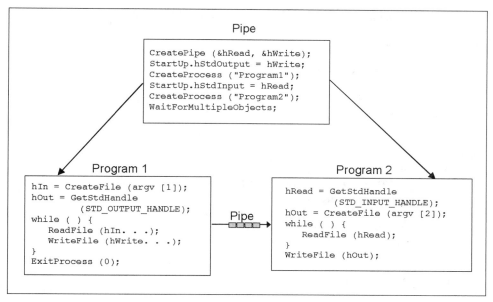

Figure 11-1   Process-to-Process Communication Using an Anonymous Pipe

The pipe and thread handles are closed at the earliest possible point. Figure 11–1 does not show the handle closings, but Program 11–1 does. It is necessary for the parent to close the standard output handle immediately after creating the first child process so that the second process will be able to recognize an end of file when the first process terminates. If there were still an open handle, the second process might not terminate because the system would not indicate an end of file.

Program 11–1 uses an unusual syntax; the = sign is the pipe symbol separating the two commands. The vertical bar (|) would conflict with the command processor. Figure 11–1 schematically shows the execution of the command:

```
$ pipe Program1 arguments = Program2 arguments
```

In UNIX or the Windows command prompt, the corresponding command would be:

```
$ Program1 arguments | Program2 arguments
```

Program 11-1   pipe: Interprocess Communication with Anonymous Pipes

```
#include "EvryThng.h"

int _tmain (int argc, LPTSTR argv [])

/* Pipe together two programs on the command line:
     pipe command1 = command2 */
{
   DWORD i = 0;
   HANDLE hReadPipe, hWritePipe;
   TCHAR Command1 [MAX_PATH];
   SECURITY_ATTRIBUTES PipeSA = /* For inheritable handles. */
         {sizeof (SECURITY_ATTRIBUTES), NULL, TRUE};
   PROCESS_INFORMATION ProcInfo1, ProcInfo2;
   STARTUPINFO StartInfoCh1, StartInfoCh2;
   LPTSTR targv = SkipArg (GetCommandLine ());

   GetStartupInfo (&StartInfoCh1);
   GetStartupInfo (&StartInfoCh2);

   /* Find the = separating the two commands. */
   while (*targv != '=' && *targv != '\0') {
      Command1 [i] = *targv;
      targv++;
      i++;
   }

   Command1 [i] = '\0';

   /* Skip to start of second command. */
   targv = SkipArg (targv);

   CreatePipe (&hReadPipe, &hWritePipe, &PipeSA, 0);

   /* Redirect standard output & create first process. */

   StartInfoCh1.hStdInput = GetStdHandle (STD_INPUT_HANDLE);
   StartInfoCh1.hStdError = GetStdHandle (STD_ERROR_HANDLE);
   StartInfoCh1.hStdOutput = hWritePipe;
   StartInfoCh1.dwFlags = STARTF_USESTDHANDLES;

   CreateProcess (NULL, (LPTSTR)Command1, NULL, NULL,
         TRUE /* Inherit handles. */, 0, NULL, NULL,
         &StartInfoCh1, &ProcInfo1);
   CloseHandle (ProcInfo1.hThread);

   /* Close the pipe's write handle as it is no longer needed
      and to ensure the second command detects a file end. */
```

```
CloseHandle (hWritePipe);

/* Repeat (symmetrically) for the second process. */
StartInfoCh2.hStdInput = hReadPipe;
StartInfoCh2.hStdOutput = GetStdHandle (STD_OUTPUT_HANDLE);
StartInfoCh2.hStdError = GetStdHandle (STD_ERROR_HANDLE);
StartInfoCh2.dwFlags = STARTF_USESTDHANDLES;

CreateProcess (NULL, (LPTSTR) targv, NULL, NULL, TRUE, 0, NULL,
       NULL, &StartInfoCh2, &ProcInfo2);
CloseHandle (ProcInfo2.hThread);
CloseHandle (hReadPipe);

/* Wait for the first and second processes to terminate. */
WaitForSingleObject (ProcInfo1.hProcess, INFINITE);
CloseHandle (ProcInfo1.hProcess);

WaitForSingleObject (ProcInfo2.hProcess, INFINITE);
CloseHandle (ProcInfo2.hProcess);

return 0;
}
```

Named Pipes

Named pipes have several features that make them an appropriate general-purpose mechanism for implementing IPC-based applications, including networked file access and client/server systems,[2] although anonymous pipes remain a good choice for simple byte-stream IPC, such as the preceding example, where communication is within a single system. Named pipe features (some are optional) include the following.

- Named pipes are message-oriented, so the reading process can read varying-length messages precisely as sent by the writing process.

- Named pipes are bidirectional, so two processes can exchange messages over the same pipe.

- There can be multiple, independent instances of pipes with the same name. For example, several clients can communicate concurrently with a single

---

[2] This statement requires a major qualification. Windows Sockets (Chapter 12) is the preferred API for most networking applications and higher-level protocols (http, ftp, and so on), especially where TCP/IP-based interoperability with non-Windows systems is required. Many developers prefer to limit named pipe usage to IPC within a single system or to communication within Windows networks.

server system using pipes with the same name. Each client can have its own named pipe instance, and the server can respond to a client using the same instance.

- The pipe name can be accessed by systems on a network. Named pipe communication is the same whether the two processes are on the same machine or on different machines.

- Several convenience and connection functions simplify named pipe request/response interaction and client/server connection.

Named pipes are generally preferable to anonymous pipes, although Program 11–1 and Figure 11–1 did illustrate a situation in which anonymous pipes are useful. Named pipes should be used any time your communication channel needs to be bidirectional, message oriented, or available to multiple client processes. The upcoming examples could not be implemented using anonymous pipes without a great deal of difficulty.

Using Named Pipes

`CreateNamedPipe` creates the first instance of a named pipe and returns a handle. The function also specifies the maximum number of pipe instances and, hence, the number of clients that can be supported simultaneously.

Normally, the creating process is regarded as the *server*. *Client* processes, possibly on other systems, open the pipe with `CreateFile`.

Figure 11–2 shows an illustrative client/server relationship, and the pseudocode shows one scheme for using named pipes. Notice that the server creates multiple instances of the same pipe, each of which can support a client. The server also creates a thread for each named pipe instance, so that each client has a dedicated thread and named pipe instance. Figure 11–2, then, shows how to implement the multithreaded server model, first shown in Figure 7–1.

Creating Named Pipes

Only Windows NT (that is, as always, Version 4.0 and above) systems can act as named pipe servers; Windows 9x systems can only be clients.

Here is the specification of the `CreateNamedPipe` function.

```
HANDLE CreateNamedPipe (
    LPCTSTR lpName,
    DWORD dwOpenMode,
    DWORD dwPipeMode,
    DWORD nMaxInstances,
    DWORD nOutBufferSize,
    DWORD nInBufferSize,
    DWORD nDefaultTimeOut,
    LPSECURITY_ATTRIBUTES lpSecurityAttributes)
```

Parameters

`lpName` indicates the pipe name, which must be of the form:

```
\\.\pipe\[path]pipename
```

The period (`.`) stands for the local machine; thus, it is not possible to create a pipe on a remote machine.

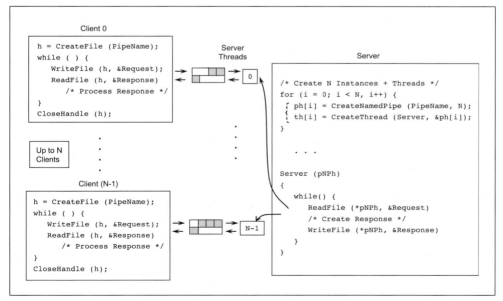

Figure 11-2 Clients and Servers Using Named Pipes

`dwOpenMode` specifies one of the following flags.

- `PIPE_ACCESS_DUPLEX`—This flag is equivalent to the combination of `GENERIC_READ` and `GENERIC_WRITE`.

- `PIPE_ACCESS_INBOUND`—Data flow is from the client to the server only, equivalent to `GENERIC_READ`.

- `PIPE_ACCESS_OUTBOUND`—This flag is equivalent to `GENERIC_WRITE`.

The mode can also specify `FILE_FLAG_WRITE_THROUGH` (not used with message pipes) and `FILE_FLAG_OVERLAPPED` (overlapped operations are discussed in Chapter 14).

`dwPipeMode` has three mutually exclusive flag pairs. They indicate whether writing is message-oriented or byte-oriented, whether reading is by messages or blocks, and whether read operations block.

- `PIPE_TYPE_BYTE` and `PIPE_TYPE_MESSAGE` indicate whether data is written to the pipe as a stream of bytes or messages. Use the same type value for all pipe instances with the same name.

- `PIPE_READMODE_BYTE` and `PIPE_READMODE_MESSAGE` indicate whether data is read as a stream of bytes or messages. `PIPE_READMODE_MESSAGE` requires `PIPE_TYPE_MESSAGE`.

- `PIPE_WAIT` and `PIPE_NOWAIT` determine whether `ReadFile` will block. Use `PIPE_WAIT` because there are better ways to achieve asynchronous I/O.

`nMaxInstances` determines the number of pipe instances and, therefore, the number of simultaneous clients. As Figure 11–2 shows, this same value must be used for every `CreateNamedPipe` call for a given pipe. Use the value `PIPE_UNLIMITED_INSTANCES` to have the OS base the number on available system resources.

`nOutBufferSize` and `nInBufferSize` give the sizes, in bytes, of the input and output buffers used for the named pipes. Specify 0 to get default values.

`nDefaultTimeOut` is a default time-out period (in milliseconds) for the `WaitNamedPipe` function, which is discussed in an upcoming section. This situation, in which the create function specifies a time-out for a related function, is unique.

The return value in case of error is `INVALID_HANDLE_VALUE` because pipe handles are similar to file handles. If you inadvertently attempt to create a named pipe on Windows 9x, which cannot act as a named pipe server, the return value will be `NULL`, possibly causing confusion.

`lpSecurityAttributes` operates as in all the other create functions.

The first `CreateNamedPipe` call actually creates the named pipe rather than just an instance. Closing the last handle to an instance will delete the instance (usually, there is only one handle per instance). Deleting the last instance of a named pipe will delete the pipe itself, making the pipe name available for reuse.

Named Pipe Client Connections

Figure 11–2 shows that a client can connect to a named pipe using `CreateFile` with the named pipe name. In many cases, the client and server are on the same machine, and the name would take this form:

    \\.\pipe*[path]pipename*

If the server is on a different machine, the name would take this form:

    servername\pipe*[path]pipename*

Using the name period (`.`) when the server is local—rather than using the local machine name—delivers significantly better connection-time performance.

Named Pipe Status Functions

Two functions are provided to interrogate pipe status information, and a third is provided to set state information. They are mentioned briefly, and one of the functions is used in Program 11–2.

- `GetNamedPipeHandleState` returns information, given an open handle, on whether the pipe is in blocking or nonblocking mode, whether it is message-oriented or byte-oriented, the number of pipe instances, and so on.

- `SetNamedPipeHandleState` allows the program to set the same state attributes. The mode value is passed by address, rather than by value, which can be confusing. This is shown in Program 11–2.

- `GetNamedPipeInfo` determines whether the handle is for a client or server instance, the buffer sizes, and so on.

Named Pipe Connection Functions

The server, after creating a named pipe instance, can wait for a client connection (`CreateFile` or `CallNamedPipe`, described in a subsequent function) using `ConnectNamedPipe`, which is a server function for NT only.

```
BOOL ConnectNamedPipe (
    HANDLE hNamedPipe,
    LPOVERLAPPED lpOverlapped)
```

With lpOverlapped set to NULL, ConnectNamedPipe will return as soon as there is a client connection. Normally, the return value is TRUE. However, it would be FALSE if the client connected between the server's CreateNamedPipe call and the Connect-NamedPipe call. In this case, GetLastError returns ERROR_PIPE_CONNECTED.

Following the return from ConnectNamedPipe, the server can read requests using ReadFile and write responses using WriteFile. Finally, the server should call DisconnectNamedPipe to free the handle (pipe instance) for connection with another client.

WaitNamedPipe, the final function, is for use by the client to synchronize connections to the server. The call will return successfully as soon as the server has a pending ConnectNamedPipe call, indicating that there is an available named pipe instance. By using WaitNamedPipe, the client can be certain that the server is ready for a connection and the client can then call CreateFile. Nonetheless, the client's CreateFile call could fail if some other client opens the named pipe instance or if the server closes the instance's handle. The server's ConnectNamedPipe call will not fail. Notice that there is a time-out period for WaitNamedPipe that, if specified, will override the time-out period specified with the server's CreateNamedPipe call.

Client and Server Named Pipe Connection

The proper connection sequences for the client and server are as follows. First is the server sequence, in which the server makes a client connection, communicates with the client until the client disconnects (causing ReadFile to return FALSE), disconnects the server-side connection, and then connects to another client.

```
/* Named pipe server connection sequence. */
hNp = CreateNamedPipe ("\\\\.\\pipe\\my_pipe", ...);
while (... /* Continue until server shuts down. */) {
    ConnectNamedPipe (hNp, NULL);
    while (ReadFile (hNp, Request, ...) {
        ...
        WriteFile (hNp, Response, ...);
    }
    DisconnectNamedPipe (hNp);
```

```
}
CloseHandle (hNp);
```

The client connection sequence is as follows, where the client terminates after it finishes, allowing another client to connect on the same named pipe instance. As shown, the client can connect to a networked server if it knows the server name.

```
/* Named pipe client connection sequence. */
WaitNamedPipe ("\\\\ServerName\\pipe\\my_pipe",
        NMPWAIT_WAIT_FOREVER);
hNp =
        CreateFile ("\\\\ServerName\\pipe\\my_pipe", ...);
while (... /* Run until there are no more requests. */ {
        WriteFile (hNp, Request, ...);
        ...
        ReadFile (hNp, Response);
}
CloseHandle (hNp); /* Disconnect from the server. */
```

Notice that there are race conditions between the client and the server. First, the client's `WaitNamedPipe` call will fail if the server has not yet created the named pipe; the failure test is omitted for brevity but is included in the sample programs on the book's Web site. Next, the client may, in rare circumstances, complete its `CreateFile` call before the server calls `ConnectNamedPipe`. In that case, `ConnectNamedPipe` will return `FALSE` to the server, but the named pipe communication will still function properly.

The named pipe instance is a global resource, so once the client disconnects, another client can connect with the server.

Named Pipe Transaction Functions

Figure 11–2 shows a typical client configuration in which the client does the following:

- Opens an instance of the pipe, creating a long-lived connection to the server and consuming a pipe instance
- Repetitively sends requests and waits for responses
- Closes the connection

The common `WriteFile`, `ReadFile` sequence could be regarded as a single client transaction, and Windows provides such a function for message pipes.

```
BOOL TransactNamedPipe (
    HANDLE hNamedPipe,
    LPVOID lpWriteBuf,
    DWORD cbWriteBuf,
    LPVOID lpReadBuf,
    DWORD cbReadBuf,
    LPDWORD lpcbRead,
    LPOVERLAPPED lpOverlapped)
```

The parameter usage is clear because this function combines `WriteFile` and `ReadFile` on the named pipe handle. Both the output and input buffers are specified, and `*lpcbRead` gives the message length. Overlapped operations (Chapter 14) are possible. More typically, the function waits for the response.

`TransactNamedPipe` is convenient, but, as in Figure 11–2, it requires a permanent connection, which limits the number of clients.[3]

`CallNamedPipe` is the second client convenience function:

```
BOOL CallNamedPipe (
    LPCTSTR lpPipeName,
    LPVOID lpWriteBuf,
    DWORD cbWriteBuf,
    LPVOID lpReadBuf,
    DWORD cbReadBuf,
    LPDWORD lpcbRead,
    DWORD dwTimeOut)
```

`CallNamedPipe` does not require a permanent connection; instead it makes a temporary connection by combining the following complete sequence:

---

[3] Note that `TransactNamedPipe` is more than a mere convenience compared with `WriteFile` and `ReadFile` and can provide some performance advantages. One experiment shows throughput enhancements ranging from 57 percent (small messages) to 24 percent (large messages).

```
CreateFile
WriteFile
ReadFile
CloseHandle
```

into a single function. The benefit is better pipe utilization at the cost of per-request connection overhead.

The parameter usage is similar to that of `TransactNamedPipe` except that a pipe name, rather than a handle, is used to specify the pipe. `CallNamedPipe` is synchronous (there is no overlapped structure). It specifies a time-out period, in milliseconds, for the connection but not for the transaction. There are three special values for `dwTimeOut`:

- `NMPWAIT_NOWAIT`

- `NMPWAIT_WAIT_FOREVER`

- `NMPWAIT_USE_DEFAULT_WAIT`, which uses the default time-out period specified by `CreateNamedPipe`

Peeking at Named Pipe Messages

In addition to reading a named pipe using `ReadFile`, you can also determine whether there is actually a message to read using `PeekNamedPipe`. This can be used to poll the named pipe (an inefficient operation), determine the message length so as to allocate a buffer before reading, or look at the incoming data so as to prioritize its processing.

```
BOOL PeekNamedPipe (
    HANDLE hPipe,
    LPVOID lpBuffer,
    DWORD cbBuffer,
    LPDWORD lpcbRead,
    LPDWORD lpcbAvail,
    LPDWORD lpcbMessage)
```

`PeekNamedPipe` nondestructively reads any bytes or messages in the pipe, but it does not block; it returns immediately.

Test `*lpcbAvail` to determine whether there is data in the pipe; if there is, `*lpcbAvail` will be greater than 0. In this case, `lpBuffer` and `lpcbRead` can be `NULL`. If a buffer is specified with `lpBuffer` and `cbBuffer`, then `*lpcbMessage` will tell whether there are leftover message bytes that could not fit into the buffer, allowing you to allocate a large buffer before reading from the named pipe. This value is 0 for a byte mode pipe.

Again, `PeekNamedPipe` reads nondestructively, so a subsequent `ReadFile` is required to remove messages or bytes from the pipe.

The UNIX FIFO is similar to a named pipe, thus allowing communication between unrelated processes. There are limitations compared with Windows named pipes.

- FIFOs are half-duplex.

- FIFOs are limited to a single machine.

- FIFOs are still byte-oriented, so it is easiest to use fixed-size records in client/server applications. Nonetheless, individual read and write operations are atomic.

A server using FIFOs must use a separate FIFO for each client's response, although all clients can send requests to a single, well-known FIFO. A common practice is for the client to include a FIFO name in a connect request.

`mkfifo` is the UNIX function that is a limited version of `CreateNamedPipe`.

If the clients and server are to be networked, use sockets or a similar transport mechanism. Sockets are full-duplex, but there must still be one separate connection per client.

Example: A Client/Server Command Line Processor

Everything required to build a request/response client/server system is now available. This example is a command line server that executes a command on behalf of the client. Features of the system include the following.

- Multiple clients can interact with the server.

- The clients can be on different systems on the network, although the clients can also be on the server machine.

- The server is multithreaded, with a thread dedicated to each named pipe instance. That is, there is a *thread pool* of worker threads ready for use by connecting clients. Worker threads are allocated to a client on the basis of the named pipe instance that the system allocates to the client.

- The individual server threads process a single request at a time, simplifying concurrency control. Each thread handles its own requests independently.

Nonetheless, the normal precautions are required if different server threads are accessing the same file or other resource.

Program 11–2 shows the single-threaded client, and its server is Program 11–3. The server corresponds to the model in Figures 7–1 and 11–2. The client request is simply the command line. The server response is the resulting output, which is sent in several messages. The programs also use the include file `ClntSrvr.h`, which is included on the book's Web site and defines the request and response data structures as well as the client and server pipe names.

The client in Program 11–2 also calls a function, `LocateServer`, which finds the name of a server's pipe. `LocateServer` uses a mailslot, as will be described in a later section and shown in Program 11–5.

The defined records have length fields that are defined as `DWORD32`; this is done so that these programs can be ported to Win64 in the future but will interoperate with servers or clients running on any Windows system.

Program 11–2   `clientNP`: Named Pipe Connection-Oriented Client

```
/* Chapter 11. Client/server system. CLIENT VERSION.
   clientNP -- connection-oriented client. */
/* Execute a command line (on the server); display the response. */
/* The client creates a long-lived connection with the server
   (consuming a pipe instance) and prompts user for a command. */

#include "EvryThng.h"
#include "ClntSrvr.h" /* Defines the request, records. */

int _tmain (int argc, LPTSTR argv [])
{
    HANDLE hNamedPipe = INVALID_HANDLE_VALUE;
    TCHAR PromptMsg [] = _T ("\nEnter Command: ");
    TCHAR QuitMsg [] = _T ("$Quit");
    TCHAR ServerPipeName [MAX_PATH];
    REQUEST Request; /* See ClntSrvr.h. */
    RESPONSE Response; /* See ClntSrvr.h. */
    DWORD nRead, nWrite, NpMode = PIPE_READMODE_MESSAGE | PIPE_WAIT;

    LocateServer (ServerPipeName);
    /* Wait for an NP instance and "race" to open it. */
    while (INVALID_HANDLE_VALUE == hNamedPipe) {
        WaitNamedPipe (ServerPipeName, NMPWAIT_WAIT_FOREVER);
        hNamedPipe = CreateFile (ServerPipeName,
            GENERIC_READ | GENERIC_WRITE, 0, NULL,
            OPEN_EXISTING, FILE_ATTRIBUTE_NORMAL, NULL);
    }
```

```
    /* Set NP handle to blocking, message mode. */
    SetNamedPipeHandleState (hNamedPipe, &NpMode, NULL, NULL);

    /* Prompt the user for commands. Terminate on "$quit." */
    while (ConsolePrompt (PromptMsg, Request.Record,
            MAX_RQRS_LEN, TRUE)
            && (_tcscmp (Request.Record, QuitMsg) != 0)) {
        WriteFile (hNamedPipe, &Request, RQ_SIZE, &nWrite, NULL);
        /* Read each response and send it to std out.
            Response.Status == 0 indicates "end of response." */

        while (ReadFile (hNamedPipe, &Response, RS_SIZE,
            &nRead, NULL) && (Response.Status == 0))
                _tprintf (_T ("%s"), Response.Record);
    }

    _tprintf (_T ("Quit command received. Disconnect."));
    CloseHandle (hNamedPipe);
    return 0;
}
```

Program 11–3 is the server program, including the server thread function, that processes the requests from Program 11–2. The server also creates a "server broadcast" thread (see Program 11–4) to broadcast its pipe name on a mailslot to clients that want to connect. Program 11–2 calls the LocateServer function, shown in Program 11–5, which reads the information sent by this process. Mailslots are described later in this chapter.

While the code is omitted in Program 11–4, the server (on the Web site) optionally secures its named pipe to prevent access by unauthorized clients. Chapter 15 will describe object security and how to use this option.

Program 11–3   serverNP: Multithreaded Named Pipe Server Program

```
/* Chapter 11. ServerNP.
 * Multithreaded command line server. Named pipe version. */

#include "EvryThng.h"
#include "ClntSrvr.h" /* Request and response message definitions. */

typedef struct { /* Argument to a server thread. */
    HANDLE hNamedPipe; /* Named pipe instance. */
    DWORD ThreadNo;
    TCHAR TmpFileName [MAX_PATH]; /* Temporary file name. */
} THREAD_ARG;
typedef THREAD_ARG *LPTHREAD_ARG;
```

```
volatile static BOOL ShutDown = FALSE;
static DWORD WINAPI Server (LPTHREAD_ARG);
static DWORD WINAPI Connect (LPTHREAD_ARG);
static DWORD WINAPI ServerBroadcast (LPLONG);
static BOOL WINAPI Handler (DWORD);
static TCHAR ShutRqst [] = _T ("$ShutDownServer");
_tmain (int argc, LPTSTR argv [])
{
    /* MAX_CLIENTS is defined in ClntSrvr.h. */

    HANDLE hNp, hMonitor, hSrvrThread [MAX_CLIENTS];
    DWORD iNp, MonitorId, ThreadId;
    LPSECURITY_ATTRIBUTES pNPSA = NULL;
    THREAD_ARG ThArgs [MAX_CLIENTS];

    /* Console control handler to permit server shutdown. */
    SetConsoleCtrlHandler (Handler, TRUE);

    /* Create a thread broadcast pipe name periodically. */
    hMonitor = (HANDLE) _beginthreadex (NULL, 0,
            ServerBroadcast, NULL, 0, &MonitorId);

    /* Create pipe instance & temp file for every server thread. */

    for (iNp = 0; iNp < MAX_CLIENTS; iNp++) {
        hNp = CreateNamedPipe ( SERVER_PIPE, PIPE_ACCESS_DUPLEX,
                PIPE_READMODE_MESSAGE | PIPE_TYPE_MESSAGE | PIPE_WAIT,
                MAX_CLIENTS, 0, 0, INFINITE, pNPSA);
        ThArgs [iNp].hNamedPipe = hNp;
        ThArgs [iNp].ThreadNo = iNp;
        GetTempFileName (_T ("."), _T ("CLP"), 0,
            ThArgs [iNp].TmpFileName);
        hSrvrThread [iNp] = (HANDLE)_beginthreadex (NULL, 0, Server,
                &ThArgs [iNp], 0, &ThreadId);
    }

    /* Wait for all the threads to terminate. */
    WaitForMultipleObjects (MAX_CLIENTS, hSrvrThread,
            TRUE, INFINITE);
    WaitForSingleObject (hMonitor, INFINITE);
    CloseHandle (hMonitor);
    for (iNp = 0; iNp < MAX_CLIENTS; iNp++) {
        /* Close pipe handles and delete temp files. */
        CloseHandle (hSrvrThread [iNp]);
        DeleteFile (ThArgs [iNp].TmpFileName);
    }

    _tprintf (_T ("Server process has shut down.\n"));
    return 0;
}
```

```
static DWORD WINAPI Server (LPTHREAD_ARG pThArg)

/* Server thread function; one for every potential client. */
{
    HANDLE hNamedPipe, hTmpFile = INVALID_HANDLE_VALUE,
            hConTh, hClient;
    DWORD nXfer, ConThId, ConThStatus;
    STARTUPINFO StartInfoCh;
    SECURITY_ATTRIBUTES TempSA =
            {sizeof (SECURITY_ATTRIBUTES), NULL, TRUE};
    PROCESS_INFORMATION ProcInfo;
    FILE *fp;
    REQUEST Request;
    RESPONSE Response;

    GetStartupInfo (&StartInfoCh);
    hNamedPipe = pThArg->hNamedPipe;
    hTmpFile = CreateFile (pThArg->TmpFileName,
            GENERIC_READ | GENERIC_WRITE,
            FILE_SHARE_READ | FILE_SHARE_WRITE, &TempSA,
            CREATE_ALWAYS, FILE_ATTRIBUTE_TEMPORARY, NULL);

    while (!ShutDown) { /* Connection loop. */
        /* Create connection thread; wait for it to terminate. */
        hConTh = (HANDLE)_beginthreadex (NULL, 0,
                Connect, pThArg, 0, &ConThId);

        /* Wait for a client connection & test shutdown flag. */
        while (!ShutDown && WaitForSingleObject
                (hConTh, CS_TIMEOUT) == WAIT_TIMEOUT)
                    { /* Empty loop body. */};
        if (ShutDown) continue; /* Flag can be set by any thread. */
        CloseHandle (hConTh);
        /* A connection now exists. */

        while (!ShutDown && ReadFile
                (hNamedPipe, &Request, RQ_SIZE, &nXfer, NULL)) {
            /* Receive new commands until the client disconnects. */
            ShutDown = ShutDown ||
                    (_tcscmp (Request.Record, ShutRqst) == 0);
            if (ShutDown) continue; /* Tested on each iteration. */

            /* Create a process to carry out the command. */
            StartInfoCh.hStdOutput = hTmpFile;
            StartInfoCh.hStdError = hTmpFile;
            StartInfoCh.hStdInput = GetStdHandle (STD_INPUT_HANDLE);
            StartInfoCh.dwFlags = STARTF_USESTDHANDLES;
```

```
        CreateProcess (NULL, Request.Record, NULL,
            NULL, TRUE, /* Inherit handles. */
            0, NULL, NULL, &StartInfoCh, &ProcInfo);

        /* Server process is running. */
        CloseHandle (ProcInfo.hThread);
        WaitForSingleObject (ProcInfo.hProcess, INFINITE);
        CloseHandle (ProcInfo.hProcess);

        /* Respond a line at a time. It is convenient to use
           C library line-oriented routines at this point. */

        fp = _tfopen (pThArg->TmpFileName, _T ("r"));
        Response.Status = 0;
        while (_fgetts (Response.Record, MAX_RQRS_LEN, fp)
            != NULL)
            WriteFile (hNamedPipe, &Response, RS_SIZE,
                &nXfer, NULL);

        FlushFileBuffers (hNamedPipe);
        fclose (fp);

        /* Erase temp file contents. */
        SetFilePointer (hTmpFile, 0, NULL, FILE_BEGIN);
        SetEndOfFile (hTmpFile);

        /* Send an end of response indicator. */
        Response.Status = 1; strcpy (Response.Record, "");
        WriteFile (hNamedPipe, &Response, RS_SIZE, &nXfer, NULL);
    }
    /* End of main command loop. Get next command. */

/* Shut down active connection thread - see comments on the disk. */
    GetExitCodeThread (hConTh, &ConThStatus);
    if (ConThStatus == STILL_ACTIVE) {
        hClient = CreateFile (SERVER_PIPE,
            GENERIC_READ | GENERIC_WRITE, 0, NULL,
            OPEN_EXISTING, FILE_ATTRIBUTE_NORMAL, NULL);
        if (hClient != INVALID_HANDLE_VALUE)
            CloseHandle (hClient);
        WaitForSingleObject (hConTh, INFINITE);
    }

    /* Client disconnected or there is a shutdown request. */
    FlushFileBuffers (hNamedPipe);
    DisconnectNamedPipe (hNamedPipe);
}
```

```
    /* End of command loop. Free resources; exit from the thread. */
    if (hTmpFile != INVALID_HANDLE_VALUE)
        CloseHandle (hTmpFile);
    DeleteFile (pThArg->TmpFileName);
    _tprintf (_T ("Exiting thread number %d\n"), pThArg->ThreadNo);
    _endthreadex (0);
}

static DWORD WINAPI Connect (LPTHREAD_ARG pThArg)
{
    /* Connection thread allowing server to poll ShutDown flag. */
    ConnectNamedPipe (pThArg->hNamedPipe, NULL);
    _endthreadex (0);
    return 0;
}

BOOL WINAPI Handler (DWORD CtrlEvent)
{
    /* Shut down the system. */
    ShutDown = TRUE;
    return TRUE;
}
```

Comments on the Client/Server Command Line Processor

This solution includes a number of features as well as limitations that will be addressed in later chapters.

- Multiple client processes can connect with the server and perform concurrent requests; each client has a dedicated server (or worker) thread allocated from the thread pool.

- The server and clients can be run from separate command prompts or can be run under control of JobShell (Program 6–3).

- If all the named pipe instances are in use when a client attempts to connect, the new client will wait until a different client disconnects on receiving a $Quit command, making a pipe instance available for another client. Several new clients may be attempting to connect concurrently and will race to open the available instance; any threads that lose this race will need to wait again.

- Each server thread performs synchronous I/O, but some server threads can be processing requests while others are waiting for connections or client requests.

- Extension to networked clients is straightforward, subject to the limitations of named pipes discussed earlier in this chapter. Simply change the pipe names in the header file, or add a client command line parameter for the server name.

- Each server worker thread creates a simple connection thread, which calls `ConnectNamedPipe` and terminates as soon as a client connects. This allows a worker thread to wait, with a time-out, on the connection thread handle and test the global shutdown flag periodically. If the worker threads blocked on `ConnectNamedPipe`, they could not test the flag and the server could not shut down. For this reason, the server thread performs a `CreateFile` on the named pipe in order to force the connection thread to resume and shut down. An alternative would be to use asynchronous I/O (Chapter 14) so that an event could be associated with the `ConnectNamedPipe` call. The comments in the book's Web site source file provide additional alternatives and information. Without this solution, connection threads might never terminate by themselves, resulting in resource leaks in DLLs. This subject is discussed in Chapter 12.

- There are a number of opportunities to enhance the system. For example, there could be an option to execute an in-process server by using a DLL that implements some of the commands. This enhancement is added in Chapter 12.

- The number of server threads is limited by the `WaitForMultipleObjects` call in the main thread. While this limitation is easily overcome, the system here is not truly scalable; too many threads will impair performance, as we saw in Chapter 10. Chapter 14 uses asynchronous I/O ports to address this issue.

Mailslots

A Windows mailslot, like a named pipe, has a name that unrelated processes can use for communication. Mailslots are a broadcast mechanism, based on datagrams (described in Chapter 12), and behave differently from named pipes, making them useful in some important but limited situations. Here are the significant characteristics of mailslots.

- A mailslot is one-directional.

- A mailslot can have multiple writers and multiple readers, but frequently it will be one-to-many of one form or the other.

- A writer (client) does not know for certain that all, some, or any readers (servers) actually received the message.

- Mailslots can be located over a network domain.

- Message lengths are limited.

Using a mailslot requires the following operations.

- Each server creates a mailslot handle with `CreateMailslot`.
- The server then waits to receive a mailslot message with a `ReadFile` call.
- A write-only client should open the mailslot with `CreateFile` and write messages with `WriteFile`. The open will fail (name not found) if there are no waiting readers.

A client's message can be read by *all* servers; all of them receive the same message.

There is one further possibility. The client, in performing the `CreateFile`, can specify a name of this form:

```
\\*\mailslot\mailslotname
```

In this way, the * acts as a wildcard, and the client can locate every server in the *name domain*, a networked group of systems assigned a common name by the network administrator.

Using Mailslots

The preceding client/server command processor suggests several ways that mailslots might be useful. Here is one scenario that will solve the server location problem in the preceding client/server system (Programs 11–2 and 11–3).

The *application server*, acting as a *mailslot client*, periodically broadcasts its name and a named pipe name. Any *application client* that wants to find a server can receive this name by being a *mailslot server*. In a similar manner, the command line server can periodically broadcast its status, including information such as utilization, to the clients. This situation could be described as a single writer (the mailslot client) and multiple readers (the mailslot servers). If there were multiple mailslot clients (that is, multiple application servers), there would be a many-to-many situation.

Alternatively, a single reader could receive messages from numerous writers, perhaps giving their status—that is, there would be multiple writers and a single reader. This usage, for example, in a bulletin board application, justifies the term *mailslot*. These first two uses—name and status broadcast—can be combined so that a client can select the most appropriate server.

The inversion of the terms *client* and *server* is confusing in this context, but notice that both named pipe and mailslot servers perform the `CreateNamedPipe` (or `CreateMailSlot`) calls, while the client (named pipe or mailslot) connects using `CreateFile`. Also, in both cases, the client performs the first `WriteFile` and the server performs the first `ReadFile`.

Figure 11–3 shows the use of mailslots for the first approach.

Creating and Opening a Mailslot

The mailslot servers (readers) use `CreateMailslot` to create a mailslot and to get a handle for use with `ReadFile`. There can be only one mailslot of a given name on a specific machine, but several systems in a network can use the same name to take advantage of mailslots in a multireader situation.

```
HANDLE CreateMailslot (LPCTSTR lpName,
    DWORD cbMaxMsg,
    DWORD dwReadTimeout,
    LPSECURITY_ATTRIBUTES lpsa)
```

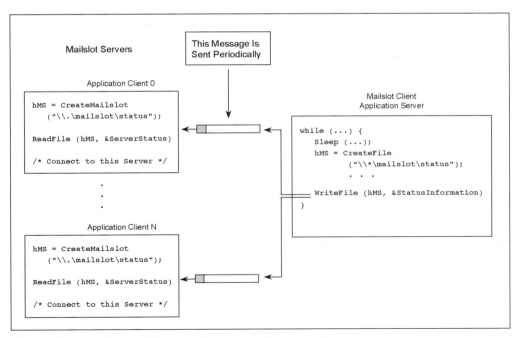

Figure 11–3 Clients Using a Mailslot to Locate a Server

Parameters

`lpName` points to a mailslot name of this form:

```
\\.\mailslot\[path]name
```

The name must be unique. The period (`.`) indicates that the mailslot is created on the current machine.

`cbMaxMsg` is the maximum size (in bytes) for messages that a client can write. A value of 0 means no limit.

`dwReadTimeout` is the number of milliseconds that a read operation will wait. A value of 0 causes an immediate return, and `MAILSLOT_WAIT_FOREVER` is an infinite wait (no time-out).

The client (writer), when opening a mailslot with `CreateFile`, can use the following name forms.

`\\.\mailslot\[path]name` specifies a local mailslot. *Note*: Windows 95 limits the name length to 11 characters.

`\\computername\mailslot\[path]name` specifies a mailslot on a specified machine.

`\\domainname\mailslot\[path]name` specifies all mailslots on machines in the domain. In this case, the maximum message length is 424 bytes.

`\\*\mailslot\[path]name` specifies all mailslots on machines in the system's primary domain. In this case, the maximum message length is also 424 bytes.

Finally, the client must specify the `FILE_SHARE_READ` flag.

The functions `GetMailslotInfo` and `SetMailslotInfo` are similar to their named pipe counterparts.

UNIX does not have a facility comparable to mailslots. A broadcast or multicast TCP/IP datagram, however, could be used for this purpose.

Pipe and Mailslot Creation, Connection, and Naming

Table 11–1 summarizes the valid pipe names that can be used by application clients and servers. It also summarizes the functions that should be used to create and connect with named pipes.

Table 11–2 gives similar information for mailslots. Recall that the mailslot client (or server) may not be the same process or even on the same system as the application client (or server).

Example: A Server That Clients Can Locate

Program 11–4 shows the thread function that the command line server (Program 11–3), *acting as a mailslot client*, uses to broadcast its pipe name to waiting clients. There can be multiple servers with different characteristics and pipe names, and the clients obtain their names from the well-known mailslot name. This function is started as a thread by Program 11–3.

Table 11-1   Named Pipes: Creating, Connecting, and Naming

	Application Client	Application Server
Named Pipe Handle or Connection	CreateFile	CreateNamedPipe
	CallNamedPipe, TransactNamedPipe	
Pipe Name	\\.*pipename* (pipe is local)	\\.*pipename* (pipe is created locally)
	*sys_name**pipename* (pipe is local or remote)	

Table 11-2   Mailslots: Creating, Connecting, and Naming

	Mailslot Client	Mailslot Server
Mailslot Handle	CreateFile	CreateMailslot
Mailslot Name	\\.*msname* (mailslot is local)	\\.*msname* (mailslot is created locally)
	*sys_name**msname* (mailslot is on a specific remote system)	
	**msname* (all mailslots with this name)	

Note: In practice, many client/server systems invert the location logic used here. The alternative is to have the application client also act as the mailslot client and broadcast a message requesting a server to respond on a specified named pipe (the client determines the pipe name and includes that name in the message). The application server, acting as a mailslot server, then reads the request and creates a connection on the specified named pipe.

Program 11–4   SrvrBcst: Mailslot Client Thread Function

```
static DWORD WINAPI ServerBroadcast (LPLONG pNull)
{
    MS_MESSAGE MsNotify;
    DWORD nXfer;
    HANDLE hMsFile;

    /* Open the mailslot for the MS "client" writer. */
    while (!ShutDown) { /* Run as long as there are server threads. */
        /* Wait for another client to open a mailslot. */
        Sleep (CS_TIMEOUT);
        hMsFile = CreateFile (MS_CLTNAME,
                GENERIC_WRITE, FILE_SHARE_READ,
                NULL, OPEN_EXISTING, FILE_ATTRIBUTE_NORMAL, NULL);
        if (hMsFile == INVALID_HANDLE_VALUE) continue;

        /* Send out the message to the mailslot. */

        MsNotify.msStatus = 0;
        MsNotify.msUtilization = 0;
        _tcscpy (MsNotify.msName, SERVER_PIPE);
        if (!WriteFile (hMsFile, &MsNotify, MSM_SIZE, &nXfer, NULL))
            ReportError (_T ("Server MS Write error."), 13, TRUE);
        CloseHandle (hMsFile);
    }
    _tprintf (_T ("Shutting down monitor thread.\n"));

    _endthreadex (0);
    return 0;
}
```

Program 11–5 shows the function called by the client (see Program 11–2) so that it can locate the server.

Program 11–5   `LocSrver`: Mailslot Server

```
/* Chapter 11. LocSrver.c */
/* Find a server by reading the mailslot
   used to broadcast server names. */

#include "EvryThng.h"
#include "ClntSrvr.h" /* Defines mailslot name. */

BOOL LocateServer (LPTSTR pPipeName)
{
    HANDLE MsFile;
    MS_MESSAGE ServerMsg;
    BOOL Found = FALSE;
    DWORD cbRead;

    MsFile = CreateMailslot (MS_SRVNAME, 0, CS_TIMEOUT, NULL);
    while (!Found) {
        _tprintf (_T ("Looking for a server.\n"));
        Found = ReadFile (MsFile, &ServerMsg, MSM_SIZE,
                &cbRead, NULL);
    }
    _tprintf (_T ("Server has been located.\n"));
    CloseHandle (MsFile);

    /* Name of the server pipe. */
    _tcscpy (pPipeName, ServerMsg.msName);
    return TRUE;
}
```

Comments on Thread Models

Terms such as *thread pool, symmetric threads*, and *asymmetric threading* have been used to describe methods for designing threaded programs, and we have relied on the boss/worker, pipeline, and other classical threading models.

This section briefly describes some descriptive and helpful terms used as integral parts of Microsoft's Component Object Model (COM; see *Essential COM* by Don Box) object-oriented technology: *single threading, apartment model threading*, and *free threading*. COM implements these models using Windows thread management and synchronization functions. Each of these models has unique performance characteristics and synchronization requirements.

- A thread pool is a collection of threads that are available for use as required. Figure 7–1 and Program 11–3 illustrate a pool of threads that can be assigned to new clients that attach by connecting to an associated named pipe. When the client disconnects, the thread is returned to the pool.

- The thread model is symmetric when a group of threads perform the same task using exactly the same thread function. grepMT, Program 7–1, uses symmetric threading: all the threads execute the same pattern searching code. Note that the threads are not in a pool; all of them are created to perform specific tasks and terminate when the task is complete. Program 11–3 creates a pool of symmetric threads.

- The thread model is asymmetric when different threads perform different tasks using separate thread functions. The broadcast function, shown in Figure 7–1 and Program 11–4, and the server function are asymmetric.

- In COM terminology, an object is single-threaded when only one thread can access it. This means that access is serialized. In the case of a database server, the object would be the database itself. The examples in this chapter use a multithreaded model to access the object, which could be considered to be the programs and files on the server machine.

- In COM terminology, apartment model threading occurs when a unique thread is assigned to each instance of an object. For example, individual threads could be assigned to access a distinct database or portion of a database. Access to the object is serialized through the single thread.

- A free-threaded object will have a thread, generally from a thread pool, assigned to it when a request is made. The server in this chapter is free-threaded if the connection is regarded as the request. Similarly, if the threads supported a database server, the database would be free-threaded.

Some programs, such as sortMT (Program 7–2), do not fit any of these models exactly. Also, recall that we have already used other thread models—namely, the boss/worker, pipeline, and client/server models—in conformance with common non-Microsoft usage.

These threading models are also appropriate in Chapter 12, which introduces in-process servers, and the terms are used in some of the Microsoft documentation. Remember that these terms are defined specifically for COM; the preceding discussion shows how they might be used in a more general context. COM is a large and complex subject, beyond the scope of this book. The bibliography lists several references you can consult.

Summary

Windows pipes and mailslots, which are accessed with file I/O operations, provide stream-oriented interprocess and networked communication. The examples show how to pipe data from one process to another and a simple, multithreaded client/server system. Pipes also provide another thread synchronization method because a reading thread blocks until another thread writes to the pipe.

Looking Ahead

Chapter 12 shows how to use standard, rather than Windows proprietary, interprocess and networking communication. The same client/server system, with some server enhancements, will be rewritten to use the standard methods.

Exercises

11–1. Carry out experiments to determine the accuracy of the performance advantages cited for `TransactNamedPipe`. You will need to make some changes to the server code as given. Also compare the results with the current implementation.

11–2. Use the `JobShell` program from Chapter 6 to start the server and several clients, where each client is created using the "detached" option. Eventually, shut down the server by sending a console control event through the `kill` command. Can you suggest any improvements to the `serverNP` shutdown logic so that a connected server thread can test the shutdown flag while blocked waiting for a client request? *Hint*: Create a read thread similar to the connection thread.

11–3. Enhance the server so that the name of its named pipe is an argument on the command line. Bring up multiple server processes with different pipe names using the job management programs in Chapter 6. Verify that multiple clients simultaneously access this multiprocess server system.

11–4. Run the client and server on different systems to confirm correct network operation. Modify `SrvrBcst` (Program 11–4) so that it includes the server machine name in the named pipe. Also, modify the mailslot name used in Program 11–4.

11–5. Modify the server so that you measure the server's utilization. (In other words, what percentage of elapsed time is spent in the server?) Maintain performance information and report this information to the client on request. The `Request.Command` field could be used.

11–6. Enhance the server location programs so that the client will find the server with the lowest utilization rate.

11–7. Enhance the server so that the request includes a working directory. The server should set its working directory, carry out the command, and then restore the working directory to the old value. *Caution*: The server thread should not set the process working directory; instead, each thread should maintain a string representing its working directory and concatenate that string to the start of relative pathnames.

11–8. `serverNP` is designed to run indefinitely as a server, allowing clients to connect, obtain services, and disconnect. When a client disconnects, it is important for the server to free *all* associated resources, such as memory, file handles, and thread handles. Any remaining resource leaks will ultimately exhaust system resources, causing the server to fail, and before failure there will probably be significant performance degradation. Carefully examine `serverNP` to ensure that there are no resource leaks, and, if you find any, fix them. (Also, please inform the author using the e-mail address in the preface.) *Note*: Resource leaks are a common and serious defect in many production systems. No "industry-strength" quality assurance effort is complete if it has not addressed this issue.

11–9. *Extended exercise*: Synchronization objects can be used to synchronize threads in different processes on the same machine, but they cannot synchronize threads running in processes on different machines. Use named pipes and mailslots to create emulated mutexes, events, and semaphores to overcome this limitation.

12 | Network Programming with Windows Sockets

Named pipes and mailslots are suitable for interprocess communication between processes on the same system or processes on machines connected by a local or wide area network. The client/server system developed in Chapter 11, starting with Program 11–2, demonstrated these capabilities.

Named pipes and mailslots (more simply referred to here as "named pipes," unless the distinction is important) have the distinct drawback, however, of not being an industry standard. Therefore, programs such as those in Chapter 11 will not port easily to non-Windows systems, nor will they interoperate with non-Windows systems. This is the case even though named pipes are protocol-independent and can run over industry-standard protocols such as TCP/IP.

Windows provides interoperability by supporting Windows Sockets, which are nearly the same as, and interoperable with, Berkeley Sockets, a *de facto* industry standard. This chapter shows how to use the Windows Sockets (or "Winsock") API by modifying Chapter 11's client/server system. The resulting system can operate over TCP/IP-based wide area networks, and the server, for instance, can accept requests from UNIX and other non-Windows clients.

Readers who are familiar with Berkeley Sockets may want to proceed directly to the programming examples, where not only are sockets used but new server features are added and additional thread-safe library techniques are demonstrated.

Winsock, by enabling standards-based interoperability, allows programmers to exploit higher-level protocols and applications, such as ftp, http, RPCs, and COM, all of which provide different, and higher-level, models for standard, interoperable, networked interprocess communication.

In this chapter, the client/server system is used as a vehicle for demonstrating Winsock, and, in the course of modifying the server, interesting new features are added. In particular, *DLL entry points* (Chapter 5) and *in-process DLL servers* are used for the first time. (These new features could have been incorporated in the initial Chapter 11 version, but doing so would have distracted from the development and understanding of the basic system architecture.) Finally, additional examples show how to create reentrant thread-safe libraries.

Winsock, because of conformance to industry standards, has naming conventions and programming characteristics somewhat different from the Windows functions described so far. The Winsock API is not strictly a part of Win32/64. Winsock also provides additional functions that are not part of the standard; these functions are used only as absolutely required. Among other advantages, programs will be more portable to other systems.

Windows Sockets

The Winsock API was developed as an extension of the Berkeley Sockets API into the Windows environment, and Winsock is supported by all Windows systems. Winsock's benefits include the following.

- Porting of code already written for Berkeley Sockets is straightforward.

- Windows systems easily integrate into TCP/IP networks, both IPv4 and the emerging IPv6. IPv6, among other features, allows for longer IP addresses, overcoming the 4-byte address limit of IPv4.

- Sockets can be used with Windows overlapped I/O (Chapter 14), which, among other things, allows servers to scale when there is a large number of active clients.

- Sockets can be treated as file `HANDLE`s for use with `ReadFile`, `WriteFile`, and, with some limitations, other Windows functions, just as UNIX allows sockets to be used as file descriptors. This capability is convenient whenever there is a need to use asynchronous I/O and I/O completion ports (Chapter 14).

- Extended, nonportable extensions are also available.

Winsock Initialization

The Winsock API is supported by a DLL (`WS2_32.DLL`) that can be accessed by linking `WS2_32.LIB` with your program. The DLL needs to be initialized with a nonstandard, Winsock-specific function, `WSAStartup`, which must be the first Winsock function a program calls. `WSACleanup` should be called when the program no longer needs to use Winsock functionality. *Note*: The prefix `WSA` denotes

"Windows Sockets asynchronous. . . ." The asynchronous capabilities will not be used here because threads can and will be used where asynchronous operation is required.

WSAStartup and WSACleanup, while always required, may be the only non-standard functions you will use. A common practice is to use #ifdef statements to test the _WIN32 macro (normally defined at compile time by Visual C++) so that the WSA functions are called only if you are building on Windows. This approach assumes, of course, that the rest of your code is platform-independent.

```
int WSAStartup (
    WORD wVersionRequired,
    LPWSADATA lpWSAData);
```

Parameters

wVersionRequired indicates the highest version of the Winsock DLL that you need and can use. Version 1.1 is generally adequate and ensures the widest possible Windows interoperability. Nonetheless, Version 2.0 is available on all Windows systems, including 9x, and is used in the examples. Version 1.1 is obsolete.

The return value is nonzero if the DLL cannot support the version you want.

The low byte of wVersionRequired specifies the major version; the high byte specifies the minor version. The MAKEWORD macro is usually used; thus, MAKEWORD (2, 0) represents Version 2.0.

lpWSAData points to a WSADATA structure that returns information on the configuration of the DLL, including the highest version available. The Visual Studio on-line help shows how to interpret the results.

WSAGetLastError can be used to get the error, but GetLastError also works, as does the ReportError function developed in Chapter 2.

When a program has completed or no longer needs to use sockets, it should call WSACleanup so that WS2_32.DLL, the sockets DLL, can free resources allocated for this process.

Creating a Socket

Once the Winsock DLL has been initialized, you can use the standard (i.e., Berkeley Sockets) functions to create sockets and connect for client/server or peer-to-peer communication.

A Winsock SOCKET data type is analogous to the Windows HANDLE and can even be used with ReadFile and other Windows functions requiring a HANDLE.

The `socket` function is called in order to create (or open) a `SOCKET` and returns its value.

```
SOCKET socket (int af, int type, int protocol);
```

Parameters

The type `SOCKET` is actually defined as an `int`, so UNIX code will port without the necessity of using the Windows type definitions.

`af` denotes the address family, or protocol; use `PF_INET` (or `AF_INET`, which has the same value but is more properly used with the `bind` call) to designate IP (the Internet protocol component of TCP/IP).

`type` specifies connection-oriented (`SOCK_STREAM`) or datagram communications (`SOCK_DGRAM`), slightly analogous to named pipes and mailslots, respectively.

`protocol` is unnecessary when `af` is `AF_INET`; use 0.

`socket` returns `INVALID_SOCKET` on failure.

You can use Winsock with protocols other than TCP/IP by specifying different protocol values; we will use only TCP/IP.

`socket`, like all the other standard functions, does not use uppercase letters in the function name. This is a departure from the Windows convention and is mandated by the need to conform to industry standards.

Socket Server Functions

In this discussion, a *server* is a process that accepts connections on a specified port. While sockets, like named pipes, can be used for peer-to-peer communication, this distinction is convenient and reflects the manner in which two systems connect to one another.

Unless specifically mentioned, the socket type will always be `SOCK_STREAM` in the examples. `SOCK_DGRAM` will be described later in this chapter.

Binding a Socket

The next step is to bind the socket to its address and *endpoint* (the communication path from the application to a service). The `socket` call, followed by the `bind`, is analogous to creating a named pipe. There is, however, no name to distinguish sockets on a given machine. A *port number* is used instead as the service endpoint. A given server can have multiple endpoints. The `bind` function is shown here.

```
int bind (
   SOCKET s,
   const struct sockaddr *saddr,
   int namelen);
```

Parameters

s is an unbound SOCKET returned by socket.

saddr, filled in before the call, specifies the protocol and protocol-specific information, as described next. Among other things, the port number is included in this structure.

namelen is sizeof(sockaddr).

The return value is normally 0 or SOCKET_ERROR in case of error. The sockaddr structure is defined as follows.

```
struct sockaddr {
   u_short sa_family;
   char sa_data [14];
   };
typedef struct sockaddr SOCKADDR, *PSOCKADDR;
```

The first member, sa_family, is the protocol. The second member, sa_data, is protocol-specific. The Internet version of sockaddr is sockaddr_in.

```
struct sockaddr_in {
   short sin_family; /* AF_INET */
   u_short sin_port;
   struct in_addr sin_addr; /* 4-byte IP addr */
   char sin_zero [8];
   };

typedef struct sockaddr_in SOCKADDR_IN,
   *PSOCKADDR_IN;
```

Note the use of a short integer for the port number. The port number and other information must also be in the proper byte order, big-endian, so as to allow interoperability. The `sin_addr` member has a submember, `s_addr`, which is filled in with the familiar 4-byte IP address, such as `127.0.0.1`, to indicate the system from which connections will be accepted. Normally, connections from any system will be accepted, so the value `INADDR_ANY` is used, although this symbolic value must be converted to the correct form, as shown in the next code fragment.

The `inet_addr` function can be used to convert an IP address text string into the form required, so that you can initialize the `sin_addr.s_addr` member of a `sockaddr_in` variable, as follows:

```
sa.sin_addr.s_addr = inet_addr ("192.13.12.1");
```

A bound socket, with a protocol, port number, and IP address, is sometimes said to be a *named socket*.

Putting a Bound Socket into the Listening State

`listen` makes a server socket available for client connection. There is no analogous named pipe function.

```
int listen (SOCKET s, int nQueueSize);
```

`nQueueSize` indicates the number of connection requests you are willing to have queued at the socket. There is no upper bound in Winsock Version 2.0, but Version 1.1 has a limit of `SOMAXCON` (which is 5).

Accepting a Client Connection

Finally, a server can wait for a client to connect, using the `accept` function, which returns a new connected socket that is used in the I/O operations. Notice that the original socket, now in the listening state, is used solely as an `accept` parameter and is not used directly for I/O.

`accept` blocks until a client connection request arrives, and then it returns the new I/O socket. It is possible, but out of scope, to make a socket be nonblocking, and the server (Program 12–2) uses a separate accepting thread to allow for nonblocking servers.

```
SOCKET accept (
    SOCKET s,
    LPSOCKADDR lpAddr,
    LPINT lpAddrLen);
```

Parameters

s, the first argument, is the listening socket. Preceding socket, bind, and listen calls are required to put the socket into the listening state.

lpAddr points to a sockaddr_in structure that gives the address of the client system.

lpAddrLen points to a variable that will contain the length of the returned sockaddr_in structure. It is necessary to initialize this variable to sizeof (struct sockaddr_in) before the accept call.

Disconnecting and Closing Sockets

Disconnect a socket using shutdown (s, how). The how argument is either 1 or 2 to indicate whether sending only (1) or both sending and receiving (2) are to be disconnected. shutdown does not free resources associated with the socket, but it does assure that all data is sent or received before the socket is closed. Nonetheless, an application should not reuse a socket after calling shutdown.

Once you are finished with a socket, you can close it with the closesocket (SOCKET s) function. The server first closes the socket created by accept, not the listening socket. The server should not close the listening socket until the server shuts down or will no longer accept client connections. Even if you are treating a socket as a HANDLE and using ReadFile and WriteFile, Close-Handle alone will not destroy the socket; use closesocket.

Example: Preparing for and Accepting a Client Connection

The following code fragment shows how to create a socket and then accept client connections.

This example uses two standard functions, htons ("host to network short") and htonl ("host to network long") that convert integers to big-endian form, as required by IP.

The server port can be any short integer, but user-defined services are normally in the range 1025–5000. Lower port numbers are reserved for well-known services such as `telnet` and `ftp`, while higher numbers are likely to be assigned to other standard services.

```
struct sockaddr_in SrvSAddr; /* Server address struct. */
struct sockaddr_in ConnectAddr;
SOCKET SrvSock, sockio;
...
SrvSock = socket (AF_INET, SOCK_STREAM, 0);
SrvSAddr.sin_family = AF_INET;
SrvSAddr.sin_addr.s_addr = htonl (INADDR_ANY);
SrvSAddr.sin_port = htons (SERVER_PORT);
bind (SrvSock, (struct sockaddr *) &SrvSAddr,
        sizeof SrvSAddr);
listen (SrvSock, 5);
AddrLen = sizeof (ConnectAddr);
sockio = accept (SrvSock,
        (struct sockaddr *) &ConnectAddr, &AddrLen);
... Receive requests and send responses ...
shutdown (sockio);
closesocket (sockio);
```

Socket Client Functions

A client station wishing to connect to a server must also create a socket by calling the `socket` function. The next step is to connect with a server, and it is necessary to specify a port, host address, and other information. There is just one additional function, `connect`.

Connecting to a Server

If there is a server with a listening socket, the client connects with the `connect` function.

```
int connect (
    SOCKET s,
    LPSOCKADDR lpName,
    int nNameLen);
```

Parameters

s is a socket created with the socket function.

lpName points to a sockaddr_in structure that has been initialized with the port and IP address of a system with a socket, bound to the specified port, that is in listening mode.

Initialize nNameLen with sizeof (struct sockaddr_in).

A return value of 0 indicates a successful connection, whereas SOCKET_ERROR indicates failure, possibly because there is no listening socket at the specified address.

The socket, s, does not need to be bound to a port before the connect call, although it can be. The system allocates a port if required and determines the protocol.

Example: Client Connecting to a Server

The following code sequence allows a client to connect to a server. Just two function calls are required, but the address structure must be initialized before the connect call. Error testing is omitted here but should be included in actual programs. In the example, it is assumed that the IP address (a text string such as "192.76.33.4") is given in argv [1] on the command line.

```
SOCKET ClientSock;
. . .
ClientSock = socket (AF_INET, SOCK_STREAM, 0);
memset (&ClientSAddr, 0, sizeof (ClientSAddr));
ClientSAddr.sin_family = AF_INET;
ClientSAddr.sin_addr.s_addr = inet_addr (argv [1]);
ClientSAddr.sin_port = htons (SERVER_PORT);
ConVal = connect (ClientSock,
      (struct sockaddr *) &ClientSAddr,
      sizeof (ClientSAddr));
```

Sending and Receiving Data

Socket programs exchange data using send and recv, which have nearly identical argument forms (the send buffer has the const modifier). Only send is shown here.

```
int send (
   SOCKET s,
   const char * lpBuffer,
   int nBufferLen,
   int nFlags);
```

The return value is the actual number of bytes transmitted. An error is indicated by the value SOCKET_ERROR.

nFlags can be used to indicate urgency (such as out-of-band data), and MSG_PEEK can be used to look at incoming data without reading it.

The most important fact to remember is that send and recv *are not atomic*, and there is no assurance that all the requested data has been received or sent. "Short sends" are extremely rare but possible, as are "short receives." There is no concept of a message as with named pipes; therefore, you need to test the return value and resend or transmit until all data has been transmitted.

You can also use ReadFile and WriteFile with sockets by casting the socket to a HANDLE in the function call.

Comparing Named Pipes and Sockets

Named pipes, described in Chapter 11, are very similar to sockets, but there are significant differences in how they are used.

- Named pipes can be message-oriented, which can simplify programs.

- Named pipes require ReadFile and WriteFile, whereas sockets can also use send and recv.

- Sockets, unlike named pipes, are flexible so that a user can select the protocol to be used with a socket, such as TCP or UDP. The user can also select protocols based on quality of service and other factors.

- Sockets are based on an industry standard, allowing interoperability with non-Windows systems.

There are also differences in the server and client programming models.

Comparing Named Pipes and Socket Servers

When using sockets, call `accept` repetitively to connect to multiple clients. Each call will return a different connected socket. Note the following differences relative to named pipes.

- Named pipes require you to create each named pipe instance and `HANDLE` with `CreateNamedPipe`, whereas socket instances are created by `accept`.

- There is no upper bound on the number of socket clients (`listen` limits only the number of queued clients), but there can be a limit on the number of named pipe instances, depending on the first call to `CreateNamedPipe`.

- There are no sockets convenience functions comparable to `TransactNamed-Pipe`.

- Named pipes do not have explicit port numbers and are distinguished by name.

A named pipe server requires two function calls (`CreateNamedPipe` and `ConnectNamedPipe`) to obtain a usable `HANDLE`, whereas socket servers require four function calls (`socket`, `bind`, `listen`, and `accept`).

Comparing Named Pipes and Socket Clients

Named pipes use `WaitNamedPipe` followed by `CreateFile`. The socket sequence is in the opposite order because the `socket` function can be regarded as the creation function, while `connect` is the blocking function.

An additional distinction is that `connect` is a socket client function, while a named pipe server uses `ConnectNamedPipe`.

Example: A Socket Message Receive Function

It is frequently convenient to send and receive messages as a single unit. Named pipes can do this, as shown in Chapter 11. Sockets, however, require that you create a message header with a length field, followed by the message itself. The following function, `ReceiveMessage`, receives such a message and will be used in the examples. The `SendMessage` function is similar.

Notice that the message is received in two parts: the header and the contents. A user-defined `MESSAGE` type with a 4-byte message length header is assumed. Even the 4-byte header requires repetitive `recv` calls to ensure that it is read in its entirety because `recv` is not atomic.

Win64 note: The message length variables have the fixed-precision LONG32 type to ensure the length, which is included in messages that may be transferred to and from non-Windows systems, and have a well-defined length, even after future recompilation for Win64 (see Chapter 16).

```
DWORD ReceiveMessage (MESSAGE *pMsg, SOCKET sd)
{
    /* A message has a 4-byte length field, followed
       by the message contents. */
    DWORD Disconnect = 0;
    LONG32 nRemainRecv, nXfer;
    LPBYTE pBuffer;
    /* Read message. */
    /* First the length header, then contents. */
    nRemainRecv = 4; /* Header field length. */
    pBuffer = (LPBYTE) pMsg; /* recv may not */
    /* transmit the number of bytes requested. */
    while (nRemainRecv > 0 && !Disconnect) {
        nXfer = recv (sd, pBuffer, nRemainRecv, 0);
        Disconnect = (nXfer == 0);
        nRemainRecv -=nXfer; pBuffer += nXfer;
    }
    /* Read the message contents. */
    nRemainRecv = pMsg->RqLen;
    while (nRemainRecv > 0 && !Disconnect) {
        nXfer = recv (sd, pBuffer, nRemainRecv, 0);
        Disconnect = (nXfer == 0);
        nRemainRecv -=nXfer; pBuffer += nXfer;
    }
    return Disconnect;
}
```

Example: A Socket-Based Client

Program 12–1 reimplements the client program, which in named pipe form is Program 11–2, clientNP. The conversion is straightforward, with several small differences.

- Rather than locating a server using mailslots, the user enters the IP address on the command line. If the IP address is not specified, the default address is 127.0.0.1, which indicates the current system.

- Functions for sending and receiving messages, such as `ReceiveMessage`, are used but are not shown here.

- The port number, `SERVER_PORT`, is defined in the header file, `ClntSrvr.h`.

While the code is written for Windows, there are no Windows dependencies other than the `WSA` calls.

Program 12–1 `clientSK`: Socket-Based Client

```
/* Chapter 12. clientSK.c */
/* Single-threaded command line client. */
/* WINDOWS SOCKETS VERSION. */
/* Reads a sequence of commands to send to a server process */
/* over a socket connection. Wait for and display response. */

#define _NOEXCLUSIONS /* Required to include socket definitions. */
#include "EvryThng.h"
#include "ClntSrvr.h" /* Defines request and response records. */
/* Message functions for request and response. */
/* ReceiveResponseMessage also prints the received messages. */
static DWORD SendRequestMessage (REQUEST *, SOCKET);
static DWORD ReceiveResponseMessage (RESPONSE *, SOCKET);

struct sockaddr_in ClientSAddr; /* Clients's socket address. */

int _tmain (DWORD argc, LPTSTR argv [])
{
    SOCKET ClientSock = INVALID_SOCKET;
    REQUEST Request; /* See ClntSrvr.h. */
    RESPONSE Response; /* See ClntSrvr.h. */
    WSADATA WSStartData; /* Socket library data structure. */
    BOOL Quit = FALSE;
    DWORD ConVal, j;
    TCHAR PromptMsg [] = _T ("\nEnter Command> ");
    TCHAR Req [MAX_RQRS_LEN];
    TCHAR QuitMsg [] = _T ("$Quit");
                /* Request: shut down client. */
    TCHAR ShutMsg [] = _T ("$ShutDownServer");
                /* Stop all threads. */
    CHAR DefaultIPAddr [] = "127.0.0.1"; /* Local system. */

    /* Initialize the WSA library, Ver 2.0, although 1.1 will work. */
    WSAStartup (MAKEWORD (2, 0), &WSStartData);

    /* Connect to the server. */
    /* Follow the standard client socket/connect sequence. */
    ClientSock = socket (AF_INET, SOCK_STREAM, 0);
```

```
memset (&ClientSAddr, 0, sizeof (ClientSAddr));
ClientSAddr.sin_family = AF_INET;
if (argc >= 2)
    ClientSAddr.sin_addr.s_addr = inet_addr (argv [1]);
else
    ClientSAddr.sin_addr.s_addr = inet_addr (DefaultIPAddr);
ClientSAddr.sin_port = htons (SERVER_PORT);
            /* Defined as 1070. */
connect (ClientSock,
    (struct sockaddr *) &ClientSAddr, sizeof (ClientSAddr));
/* Main loop to prompt user, send request, receive response. */
while (!Quit) {
    _tprintf (_T ("%s"), PromptMsg);
    /* Generic input, but command to server must be ASCII. */
    _fgetts (Req, MAX_RQRS_LEN-1, stdin);
    for (j = 0; j <= _tcslen (Req); j++)
        Request.Record [j] = Req [j];
    /* Get rid of the new line at the end. */
    Request.Record [strlen (Request.Record) - 1] = '\0';
    if (strcmp (Request.Record, QuitMsg) == 0 ||
            strcmp (Request.Record, ShutMsg) == 0) Quit = TRUE;
    SendRequestMessage (&Request, ClientSock);
    ReceiveResponseMessage (&Response, ClientSock);
}

shutdown (ClientSock, 2); /* Disallow sends and receives. */
closesocket (ClientSock);
WSACleanup ();
_tprintf (_T ("\n****Leaving client\n"));
return 0;
}
```

Example: A Socket-Based Server with New Features

serverSK, Program 12–2, is similar to serverNP, Program 11–3, but there are several changes and improvements.

- Rather than creating a fixed-size thread pool, we now create *server threads on demand*. Every time the server accepts a client connection, it creates a server worker thread, and the thread terminates when the client quits.

- The server creates a separate *accept thread* so that the main thread can poll the global shutdown flag while the accept call is blocked. While it is possible to specify nonblocking sockets, threads provide a convenient and uniform solution. It's worth noting that a lot of the extended Winsock functionality is designed to support asynchronous operation, and Windows threads allow you to use the much simpler and more standard synchronous socket functionality.

- The thread management is improved, at the cost of some complexity, so that the state of each thread is maintained.

- This server also supports *in-process servers* by loading a DLL during initialization. The DLL name is a command line option, and the server thread first tries to locate an entry point in the DLL. If successful, the server thread calls the DLL entry point; otherwise, the server creates a process, as in serverNP. A sample DLL is shown in Program 12–3. If the DLL were to generate an exception, the entire server process would be destroyed, so the DLL function call is protected by a simple exception handler.

In-process servers could have been included in serverNP if desired. The biggest advantage of in-process servers is that no context switch to a different process is required, potentially improving performance.

The server code is Windows-specific, unlike the client, due to thread management and other Windows dependencies.

Program 12–2   serverSK: Socket-Based Server with In-Process Servers

```
/* Chapter 12. Client/server. SERVER PROGRAM. SOCKET VERSION. */
/* Execute the command in the request and return a response. */
/* Commands will be executed in process if a shared library */
/* entry point can be located, and out of process otherwise. */
/* ADDITIONAL FEATURE: argv [1] can be name of a DLL supporting */
/* in-process servers. */

#define _NOEXCLUSIONS
#include "EvryThng.h"
#include "ClntSrvr.h" /* Defines request and response records. */

struct sockaddr_in SrvSAddr;
/* Server's socket address structure. */
struct sockaddr_in ConnectSAddr; /* Connected socket. */
WSADATA WSStartData; /* Socket library data structure. */

typedef struct SERVER_ARG_TAG { /* Server thread arguments. */
    volatile DWORD number;
    volatile SOCKET sock;
    volatile DWORD status;
    /* Explained in main thread comments. */
    volatile HANDLE srv_thd;
    HINSTANCE dlhandle; /* Shared library handle. */
} SERVER_ARG;
```

```
volatile static ShutFlag = FALSE;
static SOCKET SrvSock, ConnectSock;

int _tmain (DWORD argc, LPCTSTR argv [])
{
   /* Server listening and connected sockets. */
   BOOL Done = FALSE;
   DWORD ith, tstatus, ThId;
   SERVER_ARG srv_arg [MAX_CLIENTS];
   HANDLE hAcceptTh = NULL;
   HINSTANCE hDll = NULL;

   /* Initialize the WSA library, Ver 2.0, although 1.1 will work. */
   WSAStartup (MAKEWORD (2, 0), &WSStartData);

   /* Open command library DLL if specified on command line. */
   if (argc > 1) hDll = LoadLibrary (argv [1]);
   /* Initialize thread arg array. */
   for (ith = 0; ith < MAX_CLIENTS; ith++) {
      srv_arg [ith].number = ith;
      srv_arg [ith].status = 0; srv_arg [ith].sock = 0;
      srv_arg [ith].dlhandle = hDll; srv_arg [ith].srv_thd = NULL;
   }
   /* Follow standard server socket/bind/listen/accept sequence. */
   SrvSock = socket (AF_INET, SOCK_STREAM, 0);
   SrvSAddr.sin_family = AF_INET;
   SrvSAddr.sin_addr.s_addr = htonl ( INADDR_ANY );
   SrvSAddr.sin_port = htons ( SERVER_PORT );
   bind (SrvSock, (struct sockaddr *) &SrvSAddr,
         sizeof SrvSAddr);
   listen (SrvSock, MAX_CLIENTS);

   /* Main thread becomes listening/connecting/monitoring thread. */
   /* Find an empty slot in the server thread arg array. */
   /* status values: 0 -- slot is free; 1 -- thread stopped;
      2 -- thread running; 3 -- stop entire system. */
   while (!ShutFlag) {
      for (ith = 0; ith < MAX_CLIENTS && !ShutFlag; ) {
         if (srv_arg [ith].status==1 || srv_arg [ith].status==3) {
            /* Thread stopped, normally or by shutdown request. */
            WaitForSingleObject (srv_arg[ith].srv_thd INFINITE);
            CloseHandle (srv_arg[ith].srv_thd);
            if (srv_arg [ith].status == 3) ShutFlag = TRUE;
            else srv_arg [ith].status = 0;
                      /* Free thread slot. */
         }
         if (srv_arg [ith].status == 0 || ShutFlag) break;
         ith = (ith + 1) % MAX_CLIENTS;
         if (ith == 0) Sleep (1000);
         /* Break the polling loop. */
```

```
            /* Alternative: use an event to signal a free slot. */
        }

        /* Wait for a connection on this socket. */
        /* Separate thread so we can poll the ShutFlag flag. */
        hAcceptTh = (HANDLE)_beginthreadex (NULL, 0, AcceptTh,
                &srv_arg [ith], 0, &ThId);
        while (!ShutFlag) {
            tstatus = WaitForSingleObject (hAcceptTh, CS_TIMEOUT);
            if (tstatus == WAIT_OBJECT_0) break;
            /* Connection made. */
        }
        CloseHandle (hAcceptTh);
        hAcceptTh = NULL; /* Prepare for next connection. */
    }

    _tprintf (_T ("Server shutdown. Wait for all srvr threads\n"));
    /* Terminate the accept thread if it is still running.
     * See the Web site for more detail on this shutdown logic. */
    if (hDll != NULL) FreeLibrary (hDll);
    if (hAcceptTh != NULL) TerminateThread (hAcceptTh, 0);
    /* Wait for any active server threads to terminate. */
    for (ith = 0; ith < MAX_CLIENTS; ith++)
        if (srv_arg [ith].status != 0) {
            WaitForSingleObject (srv_arg[ith].srv_thd, INFINITE);
            CloseHandle (srv_arg[ith].srv_thd);
        }
    shutdown (SrvSock, 2);
    closesocket (SrvSock);
    WSACleanup ();
    return 0;
}

static DWORD WINAPI AcceptTh (SERVER_ARG * pThArg)
{
    /* Accepting thread that allows the main thread to poll the */
    /* shutdown flag. This thread also creates the server thread. */
    LONG AddrLen, ThId;

    AddrLen = sizeof (ConnectSAddr);
    pThArg->sock = accept (SrvSock, /* This is a blocking call. */
        (struct sockaddr *) &ConnectSAddr, &AddrLen);
        /* A new connection. Create a server thread. */
    pThArg->status = 2;
    pThArg->srv_thd =
            (HANDLE) _beginthreadex (NULL, 0, Server, pThArg, 0, &ThId);
    return 0; /* Server thread remains running. */
}
```

```
static DWORD WINAPI Server (SERVER_ARG * pThArg)
/* Server thread function. Thread created on demand. */
{
    /* Each thread keeps its own request, response,
       and bookkeeping data structures on the stack. */
    /* ... Standard declarations from serverNP omitted ... */
    SOCKET ConnectSock;
    int Disconnect = 0, i;
    int (*dl_addr)(char *, char *);
    char *ws = " \0\t\n"; /* White space. */

    GetStartupInfo (&StartInfoCh);
    ConnectSock = pThArg->sock;
    /* Create a temp file name. */
    sprintf (TempFile, "%s%d%s", "ServerTemp",
            pThArg->number, ".tmp");

    while (!Done && !ShutFlag) { /* Main command loop. */
        Disconnect = ReceiveRequestMessage (&Request, ConnectSock);
        Done = Disconnect || (strcmp (Request.Record, "$Quit") == 0)
                || (strcmp (Request.Record, "$ShutDownServer") == 0);
        if (Done) continue;
        /* Stop this thread on "$Quit" or "$ShutDownServer". */
        hTmpFile = CreateFile (TempFile,
                GENERIC_READ | GENERIC_WRITE,
                FILE_SHARE_READ | FILE_SHARE_WRITE, &TempSA,
                CREATE_ALWAYS, FILE_ATTRIBUTE_NORMAL, NULL);

        /* Check for a DLL command. For simplicity, shared */
        /* library commands take precedence over process
           commands. First, extract the command name. */

        i = strcspn (Request.Record, ws); /* Length of token. */
        memcpy (sys_command, Request.Record, i);
        sys_command [i] = '\0';

        dl_addr = NULL; /* Will be set if GetProcAddress succeeds. */
        if (pThArg->dlhandle != NULL) { /* Try server "in process." */
            dl_addr = (int (*)(char *, char *))
                    GetProcAddress (pThArg->dlhandle, sys_command);
            if (dl_addr != NULL) __try {
                /* Protect server process from exceptions in DLL. */
                (*dl_addr) (Request.Record, TempFile);
            } __except (EXCEPTION_EXECUTE_HANDLER {
                ReportError (_T ("Exception in DLL"), 0, FALSE);
            }
        }
```

```
    if (dl_addr == NULL) { /* No in-process support. */
    /* Create a process to carry out the command. */
    /* ... Same as in serverNP ... */
    }
    /* ... Same as in serverNP ... */

} /* End of main command loop. Get next command. */

/* End of command loop. Free resources; exit from the thread. */

_tprintf (_T ("Shutting down server# %d\n"), pThArg->number);
shutdown (ConnectSock, 2);
closesocket (ConnectSock);
pThArg->status = 1;
if (strcmp (Request.Record, "$ShutDownServer") == 0) {
    pThArg->status = 3;
    ShutFlag = TRUE;
}
return pThArg->status;
}
```

A Security Note

This client/server system, as presented, is *not* secure. If you are running the server on your system and someone else knows the port and your system name, your system is at risk. The other user, running the client, can run commands on your system that could, for example, delete or modify files.

A complete discussion of security solutions is well beyond this book's scope. Nonetheless, Chapter 15 shows how to secure Windows objects, and Exercise 12–14 suggests using SSL.

In-Process Servers

As mentioned previously, in-process servers are a major enhancement in serverSK. Program 12–3 shows how to write a DLL to provide these services. Two familiar functions are shown, a word counting function and a toupper function.

By convention, the first parameter is the command line, while the second is the name of the output file. Beyond that, always remember that the function will execute in the same thread as the server thread, so there are strict requirements for thread safety, including but not limited to the following.

- The functions should not change the process environment in any way. For example, if one of the functions changes the working directory, that change will affect the entire process.

- Similarly, the functions should not redirect standard input or output.

- Programming errors, such as allowing a subscript or pointer to go out of bounds or the stack to overflow, could corrupt another thread or the server process itself.

- Resource leaks, such as failing to deallocate memory or to close handles, will ultimately affect the server system.

Processes do not have such stringent requirements because a process cannot normally corrupt other processes, and resources are freed when the process terminates. A typical development methodology, then, is to develop and debug a service as a process, and when it is judged to be reliable, it can be converted to a DLL.

Program 12–3 shows a small DLL library with two functions.

Program 12–3   command: Sample In-Process Servers

```
/* Chapter 12. commands.c. */
/* In-process server commands to use with serverSK, etc. */

/* There are several commands implemented as DLLs. */
/* Each command function must be a thread-safe function */
/* and take two parameters. The first is a string: */
/* command arg1 arg2 ... argn (i.e., a normal command line) */
/* and the second is the file name for the output.
   ... */
static void extract_token (int, char *, char *);

_declspec (dllexport)
int wcip (char * command, char * output_file)
/* Word count; in process. */
/* NOTE: Simple version; results may differ from wc utility. */
{
    . . .

    extract_token (1, command, input_file);

    fin = fopen (input_file, "r");
    /* ... */
    ch = nw = nc = nl = 0;
    while ((c = fgetc (fin)) != EOF) {
    /* ... Standard code -- not important for example ... */
    }
    fclose (fin);
```

```
    /* Write the results. */
    fout = fopen (output_file, "w");
    if (fout == NULL) return 2;
    fprintf (fout, " %9d %9d %9d %s\n", nl, nw, nc, input_file);
    fclose (fout);
    return 0;
}

_declspec (dllexport)
int toupperip (char * command, char * output_file)
/* Convert input to uppercase; in process. */
/* Input file is the second token ("toupperip" is the first). */
{
    /* ... */
    extract_token (1, command, input_file);

    fin = fopen (input_file, "r");
    if (fin == NULL) return 1;
    fout = fopen (output_file, "w");
    if (fout == NULL) return 2;

    while ((c = fgetc (fin)) != EOF) {
        if (c == '\0') break;
        if (isalpha(c)) c = toupper(c);
        fputc (c, fout);
    }

    fclose (fin); fclose (fout);
    return 0;
}

static void extract_token (int it, char * command, char * token)
{
    /* Extract token number "it" (first token is number 0) */
    /* from "command." Result goes in "token." */
    /* Tokens are white space delimited.
        ... */
    return;
}
```

Line-Oriented Messages, DLL Entry Points, and TLS

`serverSK` and `clientSK` communicate using messages, where each message is composed of a 4-byte length header followed by the message content. A common alternative to this approach is to have the messages delimited by end-of-line (or new-line) characters.

The difficulty with delimited messages is that there is no way to know the message length in advance, and each incoming character must be examined. Receiving a single character at a time would be inefficient, however, so incoming characters are stored in a buffer, and the buffer contents might include one or more end-of-line characters and parts of one or more messages. *Buffer contents and state must be retained between calls to the message receive function.* In a single-threaded environment, static storage can be used, but multiple threads cannot share the same static storage.

In more general terms, we have a *multithreaded persistent state problem*. This problem occurs any time a thread-safe function must maintain information from one call to the next. The Standard C library `strtok` function, which scans a string for successive instances of a token, is a common alternative example of this problem.

Solving the Multithreaded Persistent State Problem

The solution requires a combination of the following components.

- A DLL for the message send and receive functions.

- An entry point function in the DLL.

- Thread Local Storage (TLS, Chapter 7). The DLL index is created when the process attaches, and it is destroyed when the process detaches. The index number is stored in static storage to be accessed by all the threads.

- A structure containing a buffer and its current state. A structure is allocated every time a thread attaches, and the address is stored in the TLS entry for that thread. A thread's structure is deallocated when the thread detaches.

The TLS, then, plays the role of static storage, and each thread has its own unique copy of the static storage.

Example: A Thread-Safe DLL for Socket Messages

Program 12–4 is the DLL containing two character string ("CS" in names in this example) or socket streaming functions: `SendCSMessage` and `ReceiveCSMessage`, along with a `DllMain` entry point (see Chapter 5). These two functions are similar to and essentially replace `ReceiveMessage`, listed earlier in this chapter, and the functions used in Programs 12–1 and 12–2.

The DllMain function is a representative solution of a multithreaded persistent state problem, and it combines TLS and DLLs. The resource deallocation in the DLL_THREAD_DETACH case is especially important in a server environment; without it, the server would eventually exhaust resources, typically resulting in either failure or performance degradation or both. *Note*: This example illustrates concepts that are not directly related to sockets, but it is included here, rather than in earlier chapters, because this is a convenient place to illustrate thread-safe DLL techniques in a realistic example.

The book's Web site contains client and server code, slightly modified from Programs 12–1 and 12–2, that uses this DLL.

Program 12–4   SendReceiveSKST: Thread-Safe DLL

```
/* SendReceiveSKST.c -- Multithreaded streaming socket DLL. */
/* Messages are delimited by end-of-line characters ('\0') */
/* so the message length is not known ahead of time. Incoming */
/* data is buffered and preserved from one function call to */
/* the next. Therefore, use Thread Local Storage (TLS) */
/* so that each thread has its own private "static storage." */

#define _NOEXCLUSIONS
#include "EvryThng.h"
#include "ClntSrvr.h" /* Defines request and response records. */

typedef struct STATIC_BUF_T {
/* "static_buf" contains "static_buf_len" bytes of residual data. */
/* There may or may not be end-of-string (null) characters. */
   char static_buf [MAX_RQRS_LEN];
   LONG32 static_buf_len;
} STATIC_BUF;

static DWORD TlsIx = 0; /* TLS index -- EACH PROCESS HAS ITS OWN. */
/* A single-threaded library would use the following: */
   static char static_buf [MAX_RQRS_LEN];
   static LONG32 static_buf_len; */

/* DLL main function. */
BOOL WINAPI DllMain (HINSTANCE hinstDLL,
      DWORD fdwReason, LPVOID lpvReserved)
{
   STATIC_BUF * pBuf;

   switch (fdwReason) {
      case DLL_PROCESS_ATTACH:
         TlsIx = TlsAlloc ();
```

```
    /* There is no thread attach for the primary thread, so it is
    necessary to carry out the thread attach operations as well
    during process attach. */

    case DLL_THREAD_ATTACH:
        /* Indicate that memory has not been allocated. */
        TlsSetValue (TlsIx, NULL);
        return TRUE; /* This value is actually ignored. */

    case DLL_PROCESS_DETACH:
        /* Detach the primary thread as well. */
        pBuf = TlsGetValue (TlsIx);
        if (pBuf != NULL) {
            free (pBuf);
            pBuf = NULL;
        }
        return TRUE;

    case DLL_THREAD_DETACH:
        pBuf = TlsGetValue (TlsIx);
        if (pBuf != NULL) {
            free (pBuf);
            pBuf = NULL;
        }
        return TRUE;
    }
}


_declspec (dllexport)
BOOL ReceiveCSMessage (REQUEST *pRequest, SOCKET sd)
{
    /* TRUE return indicates an error or disconnect. */
    BOOL Disconnect = FALSE;
    LONG32 nRemainRecv = 0, nXfer, k; /* Must be signed integers. */
    LPSTR pBuffer, message;
    CHAR TempBuf [MAX_RQRS_LEN + 1];
    STATIC_BUF *p;

    p = (STATIC_BUF *) TlsGetValue (TlsIx);
    if (p == NULL) { /* First-time initialization. */
        /* Only threads that need this storage will allocate it. */
        /* Other thread types can use the TLS for other purposes. */
        p = malloc (sizeof (STATIC_BUF));
        TlsSetValue (TlsIx, p);
        if (p == NULL) return TRUE; /* Error. */
        p->static_buf_len = 0; /* Initialize state. */
    }
```

```
    message = pRequest->Record;
    /* Read up to the new-line character, leaving residual data
       in the static buffer. */

    for (k = 0;
        k < p->static_buf_len && p->static_buf [k] != '\0'; k++) {
            message [k] = p->static_buf [k];
    } /* k is the number of characters transferred. */

    if (k < p->static_buf_len) { /* A null was found in static buf. */
        message [k] = '\0';
        p->static_buf_len -= (k + 1); /* Adjust static buffer state. */
        memcpy (p->static_buf, &(p->static_buf [k + 1]),
                p->static_buf_len);
        return FALSE; /* No socket input required. */
    }

    /* The entire static buffer was transferred. No eol found. */
    nRemainRecv = sizeof (TempBuf) - 1 - p->static_buf_len;
    pBuffer = message + p->static_buf_len;
    p->static_buf_len = 0;

    while (nRemainRecv > 0 && !Disconnect) {
        nXfer = recv (sd, TempBuf, nRemainRecv, 0);
        if (nXfer <= 0) {
            Disconnect = TRUE;
            continue;
        }

        nRemainRecv -= nXfer;
        /* Transfer to target message up to null, if any. */
        for (k = 0; k < nXfer && TempBuf [k] != '\0'; k++) {
            *pBuffer = TempBuf [k];
            pBuffer++;
        }
        if (k >= nXfer) { /* End of line not found, read more. */
            nRemainRecv -= nXfer;
        } else { /* End of line has been found. */
            *pBuffer = '\0';
            nRemainRecv = 0;
            memcpy (p->static_buf, &TempBuf [k + 1], nXfer - k - 1);
            p->static_buf_len = nXfer - k - 1;
        }
    }
    return Disconnect;
}

_declspec (dllexport)
BOOL SendCSMessage (RESPONSE *pResponse, SOCKET sd)
```

```
{
        /* Send the request to the server on socket sd. */
    BOOL Disconnect = FALSE;
    LONG32 nRemainSend, nXfer;
    LPSTR pBuffer;

    pBuffer = pResponse->Record;
    nRemainSend = strlen (pBuffer) + 1;

    while (nRemainSend > 0 && !Disconnect) {
        /* Send does not guarantee that the entire message is sent. */
        nXfer = send (sd, pBuffer, nRemainSend, 0);
        if (nXfer <= 0) {
            fprintf (stderr,
                "\nServer disconnect before complete request sent");
            Disconnect = TRUE;
        }
        nRemainSend -=nXfer; pBuffer += nXfer;
    }

    return Disconnect;
}
```

Comments on the DLL and Thread Safety

- DllMain, with DLL_THREAD_ATTACH, is called whenever a new thread is created, but there is not a distinct DLL_THREAD_ATTACH call for the primary thread. The DLL_PROCESS_ATTACH case must handle the primary thread.

- In general, and even in this case (consider the accept thread), some threads may not require the allocated memory, but DllMain cannot distinguish the different thread types. Therefore, the DLL_THREAD_ATTACH case does not actually allocate any memory; it only initializes the TLS value. The ReceiveCSMessage entry point allocates the memory the first time it is called. In this way, the thread-specific memory is allocated only by threads that require it, and different thread types can allocate exactly the resources they require.

- While this DLL is thread-safe, a given thread can use these routines with only one socket at a time because the persistent state is associated with the thread, not the socket. The next example addresses this issue.

- The DLL source code on the Web site is instrumented to print the total number of DllMain calls by type.

- There is still a resource leak risk, even with this solution. Some threads, such as the accept thread, may never terminate and therefore will never be detached from the DLL. `ExitProcess` will call `DllMain` with `DLL_PROCESS_DETACH` but not with `DLL_THREAD_DETACH` for threads that are still active. This does not cause a problem in this case because the accept thread does not allocate any resources, and even memory is freed when the process terminates. There would, however, be an issue if threads allocated resources such as temporary files; the ultimate solution would be to create a globally accessible list of resources. The `DLL_PROCESS_DETACH` code would then have the task of scanning the list and deallocating the resources.

Example: An Alternative Thread-Safe DLL Strategy

Program 12–4, while typical of the way in which TLS and `DllMain` are combined to create thread-safe libraries, has a weakness that is noted in the comments in the previous section. In particular, the "state" is associated with the thread rather than with the socket, so a given thread can process only one socket at a time.

An effective alternative approach to thread-safe library functions is to create a handle-like structure that is passed to every function call. The state is then maintained in the structure. Many UNIX systems use this technique to create thread-safe C libraries; the main disadvantage is that the functions require an additional parameter for the state structure.

Program 12–5 modifies Program 12–4. Notice that `DllMain` is not necessary, but there are two new functions to initialize and free the state structure. The send and receive functions require only minimal changes. An associated server, `serverSKHA`, is included on the book's Web site and requires only slight changes in order to create and close the socket handle (`HA` denotes "handle").

Program 12–5   `SendReceiveSKHA`: Thread-Safe DLL with a State Structure

```
/* SendReceiveSKHA.c -- multithreaded streaming socket. */
/* This is a modification of SendReceiveSKST.c to illustrate a */
/* different thread-safe library technique. */
/* State is preserved in a HANDLE-like state structure rather than */
/* using TLS. This allows a thread to use several sockets at once. */
/* Messages are delimited by end-of-line characters ('\0'). */
#define _NOEXCLUSIONS
#include "EvryThng.h"
#include "ClntSrvr.h " /* Defines the request and response records. */

typedef struct SOCKET_HANDLE_T {
    /* Current socket state in a "handle" structure. */
```

```
    /* Structure contains "static_buf_len" characters of
       residual data. */
    /* There may or may not be end-of-string (null) characters. */
    SOCKET sk; /* Socket associated with this "handle." */
    char static_buf [MAX_RQRS_LEN];
    LONG32 static_buf_len;
} SOCKET_HANDLE, * PSOCKET_HANDLE;

/* Functions to create and close "streaming socket handles." */
_declspec (dllexport)
PVOID CreateCSSocketHandle (SOCKET s)
{
    PVOID p;
    PSOCKET_HANDLE ps;

    p = malloc (sizeof (SOCKET_HANDLE));
    if (p == NULL) return NULL;
    ps = (PSOCKET_HANDLE) p;
    ps->sk = s;
    ps->static_buf_len = 0; /* Initialize buffer state. */
    return p;
}

_declspec (dllexport)
BOOL CloseCSSocketHandle (PVOID p)
{
    if (p == NULL) return FALSE;
    free (p);
    return TRUE;
}

_declspec (dllexport)
BOOL ReceiveCSMessage (REQUEST *pRequest, PVOID sh)
/* Use PVOID so that calling program does not need to include */
/* the SOCKET_HANDLE definition. */
{
    /* TRUE return indicates an error or disconnect.
       ... */
    PSOCKET_HANDLE p;
    SOCKET sd;

    p = (PSOCKET_HANDLE) sh;
    if (p == NULL) return FALSE;
    sd = p->sk;
    /* This is all that's changed from SendReceiveSKST!
       ... */
}

_declspec (dllexport)
BOOL SendCSMessage (RESPONSE *pResponse, PVOID sh)
```

```
{
    /* Send the request to the server on socket sd.
       ... */
    SOCKET sd;
    PSOCKET_HANDLE p;

    p = (PSOCKET_HANDLE) sh;
    if (p == NULL) return FALSE;
    sd = p->sk;

    /* That's all that's changed from SendReceiveSKST!
       ... */
}
```

Datagrams

Datagrams are similar to mailslots and are used in similar circumstances. There is no connection between the sender and receiver, and there can be multiple receivers. Delivery to the receiver is not ensured with either mailslots or datagrams, and successive messages will not necessarily be received in the order they were sent.

The first step in using datagrams is to specify SOCK_DGRAM in the type field when creating the socket with the socket function.

Next, use sendto and recvfrom, which take the same arguments as send and recv, but add two arguments to designate the partner station. Thus, the sendto function is as follows.

```
int sendto (
    SOCKET s,
    LPSTR lpBuffer,
    int nBufferLen,
    int nFlags,
    LPSOCKADDR lpAddr,
    int nAddrLen);
```

lpAddr points to an address structure where you can specify the name of a specific system and port, or you can specify that the datagram is to be broadcast to a specific set of systems.

When using recvfrom, you specify which system or systems (perhaps all) from which you are willing to accept datagrams.

Using Datagrams for Remote Procedure Calls

A common use of datagrams is in the implementation of RPCs. Essentially, in the most common situation, a client sends a request to a server using a datagram. Because delivery is not ensured, the client will retransmit the request if a response (also using a datagram) is not received from the server after a wait period. The server must be prepared to receive the same request several times.

The important point is that the RPC client and server do not require the overhead of a stream socket connection; instead, they communicate with simple requests and responses. As an option, the RPC implementation ensures reliability through time-outs and retransmissions, simplifying the application program. Alternatively, the client and server are frequently said to be *stateless* (they do not maintain any state information about current or pending requests). This means that the effect on the server of executing multiple identical client requests is the same as executing a single request. Again, application design and implementation logic are greatly simplified.

Berkeley Sockets vs. Windows Sockets

Programs that use standard Berkeley Sockets calls will port to Windows Sockets, with the following important exceptions.

- You must call `WSAStartup` to initialize the Winsock DLL.

- You must use `closesocket` (which is not portable), rather than `close` (which is), to close a socket.

- You must call `WSACleanup` to shut down the DLL.

Optionally, you can use the Windows data types such as `SOCKET` and `LONG` in place of `int`, as was done in this chapter. Programs 12–1 and 12–2 were ported from UNIX, and the effort was minimal. It was necessary, however, to modify the DLL and process management sections. Exercise 12–13 suggests that you port these two programs back to UNIX.

Overlapped I/O with Windows Sockets

Chapter 14 describes asynchronous I/O, which allows a thread to continue running while an I/O operation is in process. Sockets with Windows asynchronous I/O are discussed in that chapter.

Most asynchronous programming can be achieved uniformly and easily using threads. For example, serverSK uses an accept thread rather than a nonblocking socket. Nonetheless, I/O completion ports, which are associated with asynchronous I/O, are important for scalability when there is a large number of clients. This topic is also described in Chapter 14.

Windows Sockets 2

Windows Sockets 2 adds several areas of functionality and is available on all Windows systems, although 9x systems require an installable update. The examples used Version 2.0, but Version 1.1 also works in the event that interoperability is required with 9x systems that have not been updated. Furthermore, Version 1.1 is adequate for most purposes.

Version 2.0 features include those listed here.

- Standardized support for overlapped I/O (see Chapter 14). This is considered to be the most important enhancement.

- Scatter/gather I/O (sending and receiving from noncontiguous buffers in memory).

- The ability to request quality of service (speed and reliability of transmission).

- The ability to organize sockets into groups. The quality of service of a socket group can be configured, so it does not have to be done on a socket-by-socket basis. Also, the sockets belonging to a group can be prioritized.

- Piggybacking of data onto connection requests.

- Multipoint connections (comparable to conference calls).

Summary

Windows Sockets allows the use of an industry-standard API, so that your programs can be interoperable and nearly portable in source code form. Winsock is capable of supporting nearly any network protocol, but TCP/IP is the most common.

Winsock is comparable to named pipes (and mailslots) in both functionality and performance, but portability and interoperability are important reasons for considering sockets. Keep in mind that socket I/O is not atomic, so it is necessary to take care to ensure that a complete message is transmitted.

This chapter has covered the Winsock essentials, which are enough to build a workable system. There is, however, much more, including asynchronous usage; see the Additional Reading references for more information.

This chapter also provided examples of using DLLs for in-process servers and for creating thread-safe libraries.

Looking Ahead

Chapters 11 and 12 have shown how to develop servers that respond to client requests. Servers, in various forms, are common Windows applications. Chapter 13 describes Windows Services, which provide a standard way to create and manage servers, in the form of services, permitting automated service start-up, shutdown, and monitoring. Chapter 13 shows how to turn a server into a manageable service.

Additional Reading

Windows Sockets

Windows Sockets Network Programming, by Bob Quinn and Dave Shute, and its supporting site, http://www.sockets.com, are dedicated to Windows sockets. However, the book is outdated in many ways, and threads are never used. Many readers will find the following books more helpful.

Berkeley Sockets and TCP/IP

W. R. Stevens' *TCP/IP Illustrated, Volume 3*, covers sockets and much more, while the first two volumes in the series describe the protocols and their implementation. The same author's *UNIX Network Programming* provides comprehensive coverage that is valuable even for non-UNIX systems. Other good references are Douglas E. Comer and David L. Stevens, *Internetworking with TCP/IP, Volume III*, and Michael Donahoo and Kenneth Calvert, *TCP/IP Sockets in C: Practical Guide for Programmers*.

Exercises

12–1. Use `WSAStartup` to determine the highest and lowest Winsock version numbers supported on the systems accessible to you.

12–2. Use the `JobShell` program from Chapter 6 to start the server and several clients, where each client is created using the "detached" option. Eventually, shut down the server by sending a console control event through the `kill` command. Can you suggest any improvements in the `serverSK` shutdown logic?

12–3. Modify the client and server programs (Programs 12–1 and 12–2) so that they use datagrams to locate a server. The mailslot solution in Chapter 11 could be used as a starting point.

12–4. Modify the named pipe server in Chapter 11 (Program 11–3) so that it creates threads on demand instead of a server thread pool. Rather than predefining a fixed maximum for the number of named pipe instances, allow the system to determine the maximum.

12–5. Perform experiments to determine whether in-process servers are faster than out-of-process servers. For example, you can use the word count example (Program 12–3); there is an executable wc program as well as the DLL function shown in Program 12–3.

12–6. The number of clients that `serverSK` can support is bounded by the array of server thread arguments. Modify the program so that there is no such bound. You will need to create a data structure that allows you to add and delete thread arguments, and you also need to be able to scan the structure for terminated server threads.

12–7. Develop additional in-process servers. For example, convert the `grep` program (see Chapter 6).

12–8. Enhance the server (Program 12–2) so that you can specify multiple DLLs on the command line. If the DLLs do not all fit into memory, develop a strategy for loading and unloading them.

12–9. Investigate the `setsockopt` function and the `SO_LINGER` option. Apply the option to one of the server examples.

12–10. Use the scatter/gather feature of Windows Sockets 2.0 to simplify the message sending and receiving functions in Programs 12–1 and 12–2.

12–11. Ensure that `serverSK` is free of resource leaks (see Exercise 11–8 for more explanation). Do the same with `serverSKST`, which was modified to use the DLL in Program 12–4.

12–12. Extend the exception handler in Program 12–3 so that it reports the exception and exception type at the end of the temporary file used for the server results.

12–13. *Extended exercise (requires extra equipment)*: If you have access to a UNIX system that is networked to your Windows system, port clientSK to the UNIX system and have it access serverSK to run Windows programs. You will, of course, need to convert data types such as DWORD and SOCKET to other types (unsigned int and int, respectively, in these two cases). Also, you will need to ensure that the message length is transmitted in big-endian format. Use functions such as htonl to convert the message lengths. Finally, port serverSK to UNIX so that Windows systems can execute UNIX commands. Convert the DLL calls to shared library calls.

12–14. Read about the Secure Sockets Layer (SSL) in MSDN and the Additional Reading references. Enhance the programs to use SSL for secure client/ server communication.

13 | Windows Services

The server programs in Chapters 11 and 12 were console applications written to run in the background. In principle, the servers could run indefinitely, serving numerous clients as they connect, send requests, receive responses, and disconnect. That is, these servers could provide continuous services, but to be fully effective, the services must be manageable.

Windows Services,[1] previously known as NT Services, provide the management capabilities required to convert our servers into services that can be initiated on command or, at system boot time, before any user logs in, and can also be paused, resumed, and terminated. Services even make it possible to monitor the health of a service. Information about services is maintained in the registry.

Ultimately, any server system, such as those developed in Chapters 11 and 12, should be converted to a service, especially if it is to be widely used by customers or within an organization.

Windows provides a number of services; examples include the telnet, fax, and security accounts' management services as well as device drivers. There is an administrative tool, accessible from the control panel, that will display the full set of services.

Chapter 6's JobShell (Program 6–3) provides rudimentary server management by allowing you to bring up a server under job control and send a termination signal. Windows Services, however, are much more comprehensive and robust, and the main example is a conversion of JobShell so that it can control Windows Services.

This chapter also shows how to convert an existing console application into a Windows service and how to install, monitor, and control the service. Event logging, which allows a service to log its actions, is also described.

---

[1] This terminology can be confusing as the Windows systems provides numerous services that are not the Windows Services described here. However, using the term "Windows" throughout the book when talking specifically about the API is equally confusing.

Writing Windows Services—Overview

Windows services run under the control of a Service Control Manager (SCM). Converting a console application, such as serverNP or serverSK, to a Windows service requires three major steps to place the program under the SCM.

1. Create a new main() entry point that registers the service with the SCM, supplying the logical service entry points and names.

2. Convert the old main() entry point function to *ServiceMain()*, which registers a service control handler and informs the SCM of its status. The remaining code is essentially that of the existing program, although event logging commands can be added. The name *ServiceMain()* is a placeholder for the name of a logical service, and there can be one or more logical services.

3. Write the service control handler function to respond to commands from the SCM.

As these three steps are described, there will be several references to creating, starting, and controlling services. The specifics are described in later sections, and Figure 13–1, later in the chapter, illustrates the component interactions.

The main() Function

The new main() function, which is called by the SCM, has the task of registering the service with the SCM and starting the service control dispatcher. This requires a call to the StartServiceCtrlDispatcher function with the name(s) and entry point(s) of one or more logical services.

```
BOOL StartServiceCtrlDispatcher (
    LPSERVICE_TABLE_ENTRY lpServiceStartTable)
```

The single parameter, lpServiceStartTable, is the address of an array of SERVICE_TABLE_ENTRY items, where each item is a logical service name and entry point. The end of the array is indicated by a pair of NULL entries.

The return is TRUE if the registration was successful. Errors, which can be processed in the usual way, will occur if the service is already running or if there is a problem updating the registry (HKEY_LOCAL_MACHINE\SYSTEM\Current-ControlSet\Services).

The main thread of the service process that calls `StartServiceCtrl-Dispatcher` connects the thread to the SCM. The SCM registers the service with the calling thread as the service control dispatcher thread. The SCM does not return to the calling thread until all services have terminated. Notice, however, that the logical services are not actually started at this time; starting the service requires the `StartService` function, which is described later in the chapter.

Program 13–1 shows a typical service main program with a single logical service.

Program 13–1 `main`: The Main Service Entry Point

```
#include "EvryThng.h"

void WINAPI ServiceMain (DWORD argc, LPTSTR argv []);
static LPTSTR ServiceName = _T ("SocketCommandLineService");

/* Main routine that starts the service control dispatcher. */
VOID _tmain (int argc, LPTSTR argv [])
{
    SERVICE_TABLE_ENTRY DispatchTable [] =
    {
        { ServiceName, ServiceMain },
        { NULL, NULL }
    };

    if (!StartServiceCtrlDispatcher (DispatchTable))
        ReportError (_T ("Failed to start srvc ctrl dis."), 1, TRUE);
    /* ServiceMain () will not run until started by the SCM. */
    /* Return here only when all services have terminated. */
    return;
}
```

The *ServiceMain()* Functions

These functions are specified in the dispatch table, as shown in Program 13–1, and represent logical services. The functions are essentially enhanced versions of the base program that is being converted to a service, and each logical service will be invoked on its own thread by the SCM. A logical service may, in turn, start up additional threads, such as the server worker threads that were used in `serverSK` and `serverNP`. Frequently, there is just one logical service within a service. In Program 13–2, the logical service is adapted from the main server shown in Program 12–2. It would be possible, however, to run both socket and named pipe logical services under the same Windows service, in which case two service main functions would be supplied.

While the *ServiceMain()* function is an adaptation of a main() function with argument count and argument string parameters, there is one small change. The function should be declared void rather than having an int return value the way that a normal main() function would.

Extra code is required to register the service control handler, which is a function called by the SCM to control the services.

Registering the Service Control Handler

A service control handler, called by the SCM, must be able to control the associated logical service. The console control handler in serverSK, which sets a global shutdown flag, illustrates, in limited form, what is expected of a handler. First, however, each logical service must immediately register a handler using the RegisterServiceCtrlHandlerEx function. The function call should be at the beginning of *ServiceMain()* and not called again. The SCM, after receiving a control request for the service, calls the handler.

```
SERVICE_STATUS_HANDLE
    RegisterServiceCtrlHandlerEx (
    LPCTSTR lpServiceName,
    LPHANDLER_FUNCTION_EX lpHandlerProc,
    LPVOID lpContext)
```

Parameters

lpServiceName is the user-supplied service name provided in the service table entry for this logical service.

lpHandlerProc is the address of the extended handler function, which will be described in a later section. The extended handler form was added to NT5, with RegisterServiceCtrlHandlerEx superseding RegisterServiceCtrl-Handler. The next parameter was also added to NT5.

lpContext is user-defined data passed to the control handler. This allows a single control handler to distinguish between multiple services using the same handler.

The return value, which is a SERVICE_STATUS_HANDLE object, is 0 if there is an error, and the usual methods can be used to analyze errors.

Setting the Service Status

Now that the handler is registered, the next immediate task is to set the service status to SERVICE_START_PENDING using SetServiceStatus. SetService-Status will also be used in several other places to set different values, informing the SCM of the service's current status. A later section and Table 13–3 describe the valid status values in addition to SERVICE_START_PENDING.

The service control handler must set the status every time it is called, even if there is no status change.

Furthermore, any of the service's threads can call SetServiceStatus at any time to report progress, errors, or other information, and services frequently have a thread dedicated to periodic status updates. The time period between status update calls is specified in a member field in a data structure parameter. The SCM can assume an error has occurred if a status update does not occur within this time period.

```
BOOL SetServiceStatus (
    SERVICE_STATUS_HANDLE hServiceStatus,
    LPSERVICE_STATUS lpServiceStatus)
```

Parameters

hServiceStatus is the SERVICE_STATUS_HANDLE returned by Register-ServiceCtrlHandlerEx. The RegisterServiceCtrlHandlerEx call must, therefore, precede the SetServiceStatus call.

lpServiceStatus, pointing to a SERVICE_STATUS structure, describes service properties, status, and capabilities.

The SERVICE_STATUS Structure

The SERVICE_STATUS structure is defined as follows:

```
typedef struct _SERVICE_STATUS {
    DWORD dwServiceType;
    DWORD dwCurrentState;
    DWORD dwControlsAccepted;
    DWORD dwWin32ExitCode;
    DWORD dwServiceSpecificExitCode;
    DWORD dwCheckPoint;
    DWORD dwWaitHint;
} SERVICE_STATUS, *LPSERVICE_STATUS;
```

Parameters

dwWin32ExitCode is the normal thread exit code for the logical service. The service must set this to NO_ERROR while running and on normal termination.

dwServiceSpecificExitCode can be used to indicate an error while the service is starting or stopping, but this value will be ignored unless dwWin32ExitCode is set to ERROR_SERVICE_SPECIFIC_ERROR.

dwCheckPoint should be incremented periodically by the service to report its progress during all steps, including initialization and shutdown. This value is invalid and should be 0 if the service does not have a start, stop, pause, or continue operation pending.

dwWaitHint, in milliseconds, is the elapsed time between calls to SetService-Status with either an incremented value of dwCheckPoint value or a change in dwCurrentState. As mentioned previously, the SCM can assume that an error has occurred if this time period passes without such a SetServiceStatus call.

The remaining SERVICE_STATUS members are now described in individual sections.

Service Type

dwServiceType must be one of the values described in Table 13–1.

For our purposes, the type is almost always SERVICE_WIN32_OWN_PROCESS, but the different values indicate that services play many different roles.

Table 13-1 Service Types

Value	Meaning
SERVICE_WIN32_OWN_PROCESS	Indicates that the Windows service runs in its own process with its own resources. *Used in Program 13–2.*
SERVICE_WIN32_SHARE_PROCESS	Indicates a Windows service that shares a process with other services so that several services can share resources, environment variables, and so on.
SERVICE_KERNEL_DRIVER	Indicates a Windows device driver.
SERVICE_FILE_SYSTEM_DRIVER	Specifies a Windows file system driver.
SERVICE_INTERACTIVE_PROCESS	Indicates a Windows Service process that can interact with the user through the desktop.

Service State

dwCurrentState indicates the current service state. Table 13–2 shows the different possible values.

Table 13-2 Service State Values

Value	Meaning
SERVICE_STOPPED	The service is not running.
SERVICE_START_PENDING	The service is in the process of starting but is not yet ready to respond to requests. For example, the worker threads have not yet been started.
SERVICE_STOP_PENDING	The service is stopping but has not yet completed shutdown. For example, a global shutdown flag may have been set, but the worker threads have not yet responded.
SERVICE_RUNNING	The service is running.
SERVICE_CONTINUE_PENDING	The service continue is pending after a service has been in the pause state.
SERVICE_PAUSE_PENDING	The service pause is pending, but the service is not yet safely in the pause state.
SERVICE_PAUSED	The service is paused.

Table 13–3 Controls That a Service Accepts (Partial List)

Value	Meaning
SERVICE_ACCEPT_STOP	Enables the SERVICE_CONTROL_STOP.
SERVICE_ACCEPT_PAUSE_CONTINUE	Enables SERVICE_CONTROL_PAUSE and SERVICE_CONTROL_CONTINUE.
SERVICE_ACCEPT_SHUTDOWN (The ControlService function cannot send this control code.)	Notifies the service when system shutdown occurs. This enables the system to send a SERVICE_CONTROL_SHUTDOWN value to the service.
SERVICE_ACCEPT_PARAMCHANGE	Requires NT5. The startup parameters can change without restarting. The notification is SERVICE_CONTROL_PARAMCHANGE.

Controls Accepted

dwControlsAccepted specifies the control codes that the service will accept and process through its service control handler (see the next section). Table 13–3 enumerates four of the possible values, and the appropriate values should be combined by bit-wise "or" (|). The service version of serverSK, developed later, will accept only the first three values. Additional values are described in the MSDN entry for SERVICE_STATUS.

Service-Specific Code

Once the handler has been registered and the service status has been set to SERVICE_START_PENDING, the service can initialize itself and set its status again. In the case of converting serverSK, once the sockets are initialized and the server is ready to accept clients, the status should be set to SERVICE_RUNNING.

The Service Control Handler

The service control handler, the callback function specified in Register-ServiceCtrlHandlerEx, has the following form:

```
DWORD WINAPI HandlerEx (
    DWORD dwControl,
    DWORD dwEventType,
    LPVOID lpEventData,
    LPVOID lpContext)
```

The `dwControl` parameter indicates the actual control signal sent by the SCM that should be processed. Prior to NT5 and the introduction of `Register-ServiceCtrlHandlerEx`, this was the handler's only parameter.

There are 14 possible values for `dwControl`, including the controls mentioned in Table 13–3, although some controls are supported only on NT5 or XP. Five control values of interest in the example are listed here:

`SERVICE_CONTROL_STOP`

`SERVICE_CONTROL_PAUSE`

`SERVICE_CONTROL_CONTINUE`

`SERVICE_CONTROL_INTERROGATE`

`SERVICE_CONTROL_SHUTDOWN`

User-defined values in the range `128–255` are also permitted but will not be used here.

`dwEventType` is usually `0`, but nonzero values are used for device management, which is out of scope for this book. `lpEventData` provides additional data required by some of these events.

Finally, `lpContext` is user-defined data passed to `RegisterServiceCtrl-HandlerEx` when the handler was registered.

The handler is invoked by the SCM in the same thread as the main program, and the function is usually written as a `switch` statement. This is shown in the examples.

Example: A Service "Wrapper"

Program 13–2 carries out the `serverSK` conversion discussed previously. The conversion to a service depends on carrying out all the tasks described earlier. The existing server code, with some very minor modifications, is placed in a function, `ServiceSpecific`. Therefore, the code shown here is essentially a wrapper around an existing server program whose entry point has been changed from main to ServiceSpecific.

Another addition, not shown here but included on the book's Web site, is the use of a log file because services frequently run "headless" without an interactive console. When a log file is specified on the command to ServiceMain, significant events will be logged to that file.

Program 13–2 SimpleService: A Service Wrapper

```
/* Chapter 13. serviceSK.c - See additional comments on the disk
   serverSK modified to be a Windows service.
   This is, however, a general-purpose wrapper. */

#include "EvryThng.h"
#include "ClntSrvr.h"
#define UPDATE_TIME 1000 /* One second between updates. */

VOID LogEvent (LPCTSTR, DWORD, BOOL);
void WINAPI ServiceMain (DWORD argc, LPTSTR argv []);
VOID WINAPI ServerCtrlHandlerEx(DWORD, DWORD, LPVOID, LPVOID);
void UpdateStatus (int, int); /* Calls SetServiceStatus. */
int ServiceSpecific (int, LPTSTR *); /* Former main program. */
volatile static BOOL ShutDown = FALSE, PauseFlag = FALSE;
static SERVICE_STATUS hServStatus;
static SERVICE_STATUS_HANDLE hSStat; /* Handle to set status. */

static LPTSTR ServiceName = _T ("SocketCommandLineService");
static LPTSTR LogFileName = _T ("CommandLineServiceLog.txt");

/* Main routine that starts the service control dispatcher. */
VOID _tmain (int argc, LPTSTR argv [])
{
    SERVICE_TABLE_ENTRY DispatchTable [] =
    {
        { ServiceName, ServiceMain },
        { NULL, NULL }
    };

    StartServiceCtrlDispatcher (DispatchTable);
    return 0;
}

/* ServiceMain entry point, called when the service is created. */
void WINAPI ServiceMain (DWORD argc, LPTSTR argv [])
{
    DWORD i, Context = 1;
```

```
    /* Set the current directory and open a log file, appending to
       an existing file. */

    /* Set all server status data members. */
    hServStatus.dwServiceType = SERVICE_WIN32_OWN_PROCESS;
    hServStatus.dwCurrentState = SERVICE_START_PENDING;
    hServStatus.dwControlsAccepted = SERVICE_ACCEPT_STOP |
        SERVICE_ACCEPT_SHUTDOWN | SERVICE_ACCEPT_PAUSE_CONTINUE;
    hServStatus.dwWin32ExitCode = ERROR_SERVICE_SPECIF0C_ERROR;
    hServStatus.dwServiceSpecificExitCode = 0;
    hServStatus.dwCheckPoint = 0;
    hServStatus.dwWaitHint = 2 * CS_TIMEOUT;

    hSStat = RegisterServiceCtrlHandlerEx (ServiceName,
        ServerCtrlHandler, &Context);
    SetServiceStatus (hSStat, &hServStatus);

    /* Start service-specific work; generic work is complete. */
    if (ServiceSpecific (argc, argv) != 0) {
        hServStatus.dwCurrentState = SERVICE_STOPPED;
        hServStatus.dwServiceSpecificExitCode = 1;
            /* Server initialization failed. */
        SetServiceStatus (hSStat, &hServStatus);
        return;
    }
    /* We will only return here when the ServiceSpecific function
       completes, indicating system shutdown. */
    UpdateStatus (SERVICE_STOPPED, 0);
    return;
}

void UpdateStatus (int NewStatus, int Check)
/* Set a new service status and checkpoint --
   either specific value or increment. */
{
    if (Check < 0) hServStatus.dwCheckPoint++;
    else hServStatus.dwCheckPoint = Check;
    if (NewStatus >= 0) hServStatus.dwCurrentState = NewStatus;
    SetServiceStatus (hSStat, &hServStatus);
    return;
}

/* Control handler function, invoked by the SCM to run */
/* in the same thread as the main program. */
/* The last three parameters are not used, and the pre-NT5 */
/* handlers would also work in this example. */
VOID WINAPI ServerCtrlHandlerEx (DWORD Control, DWORD EventType,
        LPVOID lpEventData, LPVOID lpContext)
```

```
{
    switch (Control) {
        case SERVICE_CONTROL_SHUTDOWN:
        case SERVICE_CONTROL_STOP:
            ShutDown = TRUE; /* Set the global shutdown flag. */
            UpdateStatus (SERVICE_STOP_PENDING, -1);
            break;
        case SERVICE_CONTROL_PAUSE:
            PauseFlag = TRUE; /* Interrogated periodically. */
            break;
        case SERVICE_CONTROL_CONTINUE:
            PauseFlag = FALSE;
            break;
        case SERVICE_CONTROL_INTERROGATE:
            break;
        default:
            if (Control > 127 && Control < 256) /* User defined. */
            break;
    }
    UpdateStatus (-1, -1); /* Increment checkpoint. */
    return;
}

/* This is the service-specific function, or "main," and is
   called from the more generic ServiceMain.
   In general, you can take any server, such as ServerNP.c, and
   rename "main" as "ServiceSpecific"; putting code right here.
   But some changes are required to update status. */

int ServiceSpecific (int argc, LPTSTR argv [])
{
    UpdateStatus (-1, -1); /* Increment the checkpoint. */
    /* ... Initialize system ... */
    /* Be sure to update the checkpoint periodically. */

    return 0;
}
```

Managing Windows Services

Once a service has been written, the next task is to put the service under the control of the SCM so that it can be started, stopped, and otherwise controlled.

Several steps are required to open the SCM, create a service under SCM control, and then start the service. These steps do not directly control the service; they are directives to the SCM, which in turn controls the specified service.

Opening the SCM

A separate process, running as "Administrator," is required to create the service, much as `JobShell` was used in Chapter 6 to start jobs. The first step is to open the SCM, obtaining a handle that then allows the service to be created.

```
SC_HANDLE OpenSCManager (
   LPCTSTR lpMachineName,
   LPCTSTR lpDatabaseName,
   DWORD dwDesiredAccess)
```

Parameters

`lpMachineName` is `NULL` if the SCM is on the local system, but you can also access the SCM on networked machines.

`lpDatabaseName` is also normally `NULL`.

`dwDesiredAccess` is normally `SC_MANAGER_ALL_ACCESS`, but you can specify more limited access rights, as described in the on-line documentation.

Creating and Deleting a Service

Call `CreateService` to register a service.

```
SC_HANDLE CreateService (
   SC_HANDLE hSCManager,
   LPCTSTR lpServiceName,
   LPCTSTR lpDisplayName,
   DWORD dwDesiredAccess,
   DWORD dwServiceType,
   DWORD dwStartType,
   DWORD dwErrorControl,
   LPCTSTR lpBinaryPathName,
   LPCTSTR lpLoadOrderGroup,
   LPDWORD lpdwTagId,
   LPCTSTR lpDependencies,
   LPCTSTR lpServiceStartName,
   LPCTSTR lpPassword);
```

New services are entered into the registry under:

HKEY_LOCAL_MACHINE\SYSTEM\CurrentControlSet\Services

Parameters

hSCManager is the SC_HANDLE obtained from OpenSCManager.

lpServiceName is the name that you use in future references to the service and is one of the logical service names specified in the dispatch table in the StartServiceCtrlDispatcher call. Notice that there is a separate Create-Service call for each logical service.

lpDisplayName is the name that will show up as a registry key and in the "Services" administrative tool (accessed from the control panel under Administrative Tools). You will see this name entered immediately after a successful Create-Service call.

dwDesiredAccess can be SERVICE_ALL_ACCESS or combinations of GENERIC_READ, GENERIC_WRITE, and GENERIC_EXECUTE. See the on-line documentation for additional details.

dwServiceType has values as in Table 13–1.

dwStartType specifies how the service is started. SERVICE_DEMAND_START is used in our examples, but other values (SERVICE_BOOT_START and SER-VICE_SYSTEM_START) allow device driver services to be started during bootup or at system start time, and SERVICE_AUTO_START specifies that a service is to be started at system start-up.

lpBinaryPathName gives the service's executable; the .exe extension is not required.

Other parameters specify account name and password, groups for combining services, and dependencies when there are several interdependent services.

Service configuration parameters of an existing service can be changed with ChangeServiceConfig and, for NT5, ChangeServiceConfig2. The service is identified by its handle, and you can specify new values for most of the parameters. For example, you can provide a new dwServiceType or dwStartType value, but not a new value for dwAccess.

There is also an OpenService function to obtain a handle to a named service. Use DeleteService to remove a service from the registry and CloseService-Handle to close SC_HANDLEs.

Starting a Service

A service, once created, is not running. Start the *ServiceMain()* function by specifying the handle obtained from CreateService along with the argc, argv command line parameters expected by the service's main function (that is, the function specified in the dispatch table).

```
BOOL StartService (
    SC_HANDLE hService,
    DWORD argc,
    LPTSTR argv [ ])
```

Controlling a Service

Control a service by telling the SCM to invoke the service's control handler with the specified control.

```
BOOL ControlService (
    SC_HANDLE hService,
    DWORD dwControlCode,
    LPSERVICE_STATUS lpServStat)
```

dw ControlCode, if access permits, is one of the following:

SERVICE_CONTROL_STOP

SERVICE_CONTROL_PAUSE

SERVICE_CONTROL_CONTINUE

SERVICE_CONTROL_INTERROGATE

SERVICE_CONTROL_SHUTDOWN

or a user-specified value in the range 128–255. These are the same values as those used with the dwControl flag in the ServerCtrlHandler function.

lpServStat points to a SERVICE_STATUS structure that receives the current status. This is the same structure as that used by the SetServiceStatus function.

Querying Service Status

Obtain a service's current status in a `SERVICE_STATUS` structure with the following:

```
BOOL QueryServiceStatus (
    SC_HANDLE hService,
    LPSERVICE_STATUS lpServiceStatus)
```

Summary: Service Operation and Management

Figure 13–1 shows the SCM and its relation to the services and to a service control program, such as the one in Program 13–3 in the next section. In particular, a service must register with the SCM, and all commands to the service pass through the SCM.

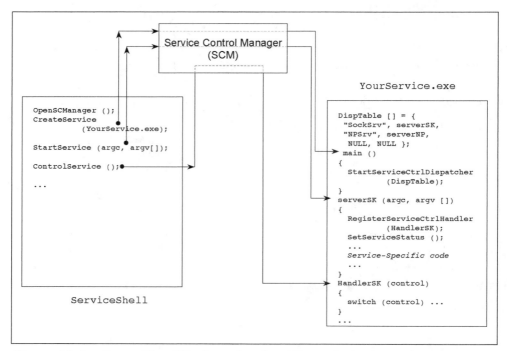

Figure 13-1   Controlling Windows Services Through the SCM

Example: A Service Control Shell

Services are frequently controlled from the Administrative Tools, where there is a "Services" icon. Alternatively, you can control user-developed services using ServiceShell (Program 13–3), which was developed by modifying Chapter 6's JobShell (Program 6–3).

Program 13–3   ServiceShell: A Service Control Program
_____

```
/* Chapter 13. */
/* ServiceShell.c Windows service management shell program.
   This program modifies Chapter 6's job management program,
   managing services rather than jobs. */
/* Commands supported are:
        create -- create a service
        delete -- delete a service
        start -- start a service
        control -- control a service */

#include "EvryThng.h"

static SC_HANDLE hScm;
static BOOL Debug;

int _tmain (int argc, LPTSTR argv [])
{
    BOOL Exit = FALSE;
    TCHAR Command [MAX_COMMAND_LINE + 10], *pc;
    DWORD i, LocArgc; /* Local argc. */
    TCHAR argstr [MAX_ARG] [MAX_COMMAND_LINE];
    LPTSTR pArgs [MAX_ARG];

    /* Prepare the local "argv" array as pointers to strings. */
    for (i = 0; i < MAX_ARG; i++) pArgs [i] = argstr [i];

    /* Open the SC Control Manager on the local machine. */
    hScm = OpenSCManager (NULL, NULL, SC_MANAGER_ALL_ACCESS);

    /* Main command processing loop. */
    _tprintf (_T ("\nWindows Service Management"));
    while (!Exit) {
        _tprintf (_T ("\nSM$"));
        _fgetts (Command, MAX_COMMAND_LINE, stdin);
        ... Similar to JobShell ...
        if (_tcscmp (argstr [0], _T ("create")) == 0) {
            Create (LocArgc, pArgs, Command);
        }
        ... Similarly for all commands ...
```

```
    }
    CloseServiceHandle (hScm);
    return 0;
}

int Create (int argc, LPTSTR argv [], LPTSTR Command)
{
    /* Create a new service as a "demand start" service:
        argv [1]: service Name
        argv [2]: display Name
        argv [3]: binary executable */
    SC_HANDLE hSc;
    TCHAR CurrentDir [MAX_PATH + 1], Executable [MAX_PATH + 1];

    hSc = CreateService (hScm, argv [1], argv [2],
            SERVICE_ALL_ACCESS, SERVICE_WIN32_OWN_PROCESS,
            SERVICE_DEMAND_START, SERVICE_ERROR_NORMAL,
            Executable, NULL, NULL, NULL, NULL, NULL);
    return 0;
}

/* Delete a service -- argv [1]: ServiceName to delete. */

int Delete (int argc, LPTSTR argv [], LPTSTR Command)
{
    SC_HANDLE hSc;
    hSc = OpenService (hScm, argv [1], DELETE);
    DeleteService (hSc);
    CloseServiceHandle (hSc);
    return 0;
}

/* Start a named service -- argv [1]: service name to start. */
int Start (int argc, LPTSTR argv [], LPTSTR Command)
{
    SC_HANDLE hSc;
    TCHAR WorkingDir [MAX_PATH + 1];
    LPTSTR pWorkingDir = WorkingDir;
    LPTSTR argvStart [] = {argv [1], WorkingDir};

    GetCurrentDirectory (MAX_PATH + 1, WorkingDir);
    hSc = OpenService(hScm, argv [1], SERVICE_ALL_ACCESS);
    /* Start the service with one arg, the working directory. */
    /* Note: The service name agrees, by default, with the name */
    /*     associated with the handle, hSc, by OpenService. */
    /*     But, the ServiceMain function does not verify this. */
    StartService (hSc, 2, argvStart);
    CloseServiceHandle (hSc);
    return 0;
}
```

```
/* Control a named service. argv [1]: service name to control.
   argv [2]: Control command: stop, pause, resume, interrogate. */
   static LPCTSTR Commands [] =
       {"stop," "pause," "resume," "interrogate," "user"};
   static DWORD Controls [] = {
       SERVICE_CONTROL_STOP, SERVICE_CONTROL_PAUSE,
       SERVICE_CONTROL_CONTINUE, SERVICE_CONTROL_INTERROGATE, 128};

int Control (int argc, LPTSTR argv [], LPTSTR Command)
{
    SC_HANDLE hSc;
    SERVICE_STATUS ServiceStatus;
    DWORD dwControl, i;
    BOOL Found = FALSE;

    for (i= 0; i < sizeof (Controls)/sizeof (DWORD) && !Found; i++)
        Found = (_tcscmp (Commands [i], argv [2]) == 0);
    if (!Found) {
        _tprintf (_T ("\nIllegal Control Command %s"), argv [1]);
        return 1;
    }
    dwControl = Controls [i - 1];
    hSc = OpenService(hScm, argv [1],
        SERVICE_INTERROGATE | SERVICE_PAUSE_CONTINUE |
        SERVICE_STOP | SERVICE_USER_DEFINED_CONTROL |
        SERVICE_QUERY_STATUS );
    ControlService (hSc, dwControl, &ServiceStatus );

    if (dwControl == SERVICE_CONTROL_INTERROGATE) {
        QueryServiceStatus (hSc, &ServiceStatus );
        printf (_T ("Status from QueryServiceStatus\n"));
        printf (_T ("Service Status\n"));
            ... Print all other status information ...
    }
    if (hSc != NULL) CloseServiceHandle (hSc);
    return 0;
}
```

Sharing Kernel Objects with a Service

There can be situations in which a service and applications share a kernel object.
For example, the service might use a named mutex to protect a shared memory
region used to communicate with applications. Furthermore, in this example, the
file mapping would also be a shared kernel object.

There is a difficulty caused by the fact that applications run in a security context separate from that of services, which can run under the system account. Even if no protection is required, it is not adequate to create and/or open the shared kernel objects with a NULL security attribute pointer (see Chapter 15). Instead, a NULL discretionary access control list (see Chapter 15) is required at the very least—that is, the applications and the service need to use a non-NULL security attribute structure. In general, you may want to secure the objects, and, again, this is the subject of Chapter 15.

Also notice that if a service runs under the system account, there can be difficulties in accessing resources on other machines, such as shared files, from within a service.

Event Logging

Services frequently run "headless" without user interaction, so it is not generally appropriate for a service to display status messages directly. Some services will create a console, message box,[2] or window for user interaction, but the best technique is to log events to a log file or use the event logging functionality provided with Windows. Such events are maintained in the registry and can be viewed from the event viewer provided in the control panel's Administrative Tools.

The serviceSK.c and SimpleService.c programs on the book's Web site show how to log significant service events and errors to a log file, and commented code shows how to use event logging. There are three functions, all described in the on-line documentation.

1. RegisterEventSource obtains a handle to the log file.

2. ReportEvent is used to register a record in the log file.

3. DeregisterEventSource closes the handle to the log file.

Notes on Debugging a Service

A service is expected to run continuously, so it must be reliable and as defect-free as possible. While a service can be attached to the debugger and event logs can be used to trace service operation, these techniques are most appropriate once a service has been deployed.

---

[2] If a service calls MessageBox, it must specify MB_SERVICE_NOTIFICATION for the message box type. The message is then displayed on the active desktop, even if no user is logged on to the computer.

During initial development and debugging, however, it is often easier to take advantage of the service wrapper presented in Program 13–2.

- Develop the "preservice" version as a stand-alone program. `serverSK`, for example, was developed in this way.

- Instrument the program with event logging or a log file.

- Once the program is judged to be ready for deployment as a service, rename the main entry point and link it with the service wrapper code shown in Program 13–2 (and included on the Web site with two programs: `Simple-Service.c` and `serviceSK.c`).

- Additional testing on a service is essential to detect both additional logic errors and security issues. Services can run under the system account and do not, for instance, necessarily have access to user objects, and the preservice version may not detect such problems.

- Normal events and minor maintenance debugging can be performed using information in the log file or event log. Even the status information can help determine server health and defect symptoms.

- If extensive maintenance is required, the service code can be removed from the wrapper and converted back to a stand-alone program or a console mode program, with either a GUI or character-based interface. Alternatively, you can enhance the *ServiceMain* function to access an additional command line argument used as a debug or trace flag.

Summary

Windows services provide standardized capabilities to add user-developed services to Windows systems. An existing stand-alone program can be converted to a service using the methods discussed in this chapter.

A service can be created, controlled, and monitored using the Administrative Tools or the `ServiceShell` program presented in this chapter. Deployed services are controlled and monitored through the SCM, and all services are entered in the registry.

Looking Ahead

Chapter 14 describes asynchronous I/O, which provides two techniques that allow multiple read and write operations to take place concurrently with other processing. It is not necessary to use threads; only one user thread is required.

In most cases, multiple threads are easier to program than asynchronous I/O, and thread performance is generally superior. However, asynchronous I/O is essential to the use of I/O completion ports, which are extremely useful when building scalable servers that can handle large numbers of clients.

Waitable timers are also described in Chapter 14.

Additional Reading

Kevin Miller's *Professional NT Services* thoroughly covers the subject. Device drivers and their interaction with services were not covered in this chapter; a book such as Walter Oney's *Programming the Microsoft Windows Driver Model, Second Edition*, can provide that information.

Exercises

13–1. Extend serviceSK to accept pause controls in a meaningful way.

13–2. ServiceShell, when interrogating service status, simply prints out the numbers. Extend it so that status is presented in a more readable form.

13–3. Convert serverNP (Program 11–3) into a service.

13–4. Modify serviceSK so that it uses event logging.

C H A P T E R

14 | Asynchronous Input/Output and Completion Ports

Input and output are inherently slow compared with other processing. This slowness is due to factors such as:

- Delays caused by track and sector seek time on random access devices (such as discs and CD-ROMs)

- Delays caused by the relatively slow data transfer rate between a physical device and system memory

- Delays in network data transfer using file servers, storage area networks, and so on

All I/O in previous examples has been *thread-synchronous*, so that the entire thread waits until the I/O operation completes.

This chapter shows how a thread can continue without waiting for an operation to complete—that is, threads can perform *asynchronous* I/O. Examples illustrate the different techniques available in Windows.

Waitable timers, which require some of the same techniques, are also described here.

Finally, and more importantly, once standard asynchronous I/O is understood, we are in a position to use *I/O completion ports*, which are extremely useful when building scalable servers that must be able to support large numbers of clients without creating a thread for each client. Program 14–4 modifies an earlier server to exploit I/O completion ports.

Overview of Windows Asynchronous I/O

There are three techniques for achieving asynchronous I/O in Windows.

- **Multithreaded I/O**. Each thread within a process or set of processes performs normal synchronous I/O, but other threads can continue execution.

- **Overlapped I/O**. A thread continues execution after issuing a read, write, or other I/O operation. When the thread requires the I/O results before continuing, it waits on either the handle or a specified event. Windows 9x supports overlapped I/O only for serial devices such as named pipes.

- **Completion routines (or extended I/O)**. The system invokes a specified *completion routine* within the thread when the I/O operation completes. Windows 9x does not support extended I/O for disk files.

The threaded server in Chapter 11 uses multithreaded I/O on named pipes. `grepMT` (Program 7–1) manages concurrent I/O to several files. Thus, we have already written programs that perform multithreaded I/O to achieve a form of asynchronous I/O.

Overlapped I/O is the subject of the next section, and the examples implement file conversion (ASCII to Unicode) using this technique in order to illustrate sequential file processing. The example is a modification of Program 2–4. Following overlapped I/O, extended I/O with completion routines is explained.

Note: Overlapped and extended I/O can be complex, seldom yield performance benefits, may even harm performance, and, for file I/O, work only on Windows NT. Threads overcome these problems, *so some readers might wish to skip ahead to the sections on waitable timers and I/O completion ports*, referring back as necessary. On the other hand, you will find asynchronous I/O concepts in both old and very new technology, so it can be worthwhile to learn the techniques. For example, COM on NT5 supports the asynchronous method call, and many readers who are using or will be using COM may find this feature useful. Also, the asynchronous procedure call operation (Chapter 10) is very similar to extended I/O, and, while my personal preference is to use threads, others like to use this mechanism.

Overlapped I/O

The first requirement for asynchronous I/O, whether overlapped or extended, is to set the overlapped attribute of the file or other handle. This is done by specifying the `FILE_FLAG_OVERLAPPED` flag on the `CreateFile` or other call that creates the file, named pipe, or other handle.

Sockets (Chapter 12), whether created by `socket` or `accept`, have the overlapped attribute set by default in Winsock 1.1, but the attribute must be set explicitly in Winsock 2.0. An overlapped socket can be used asynchronously in all Windows versions.

Until now, overlapped structures have been used with `LockFileEx` and as an alternative to `SetFilePointer` (Chapter 3), but they are essential for overlapped I/O. These structures are optional parameters on four I/O functions that can potentially block while the operation completes:

`ReadFile`

`WriteFile`

`TransactNamedPipe`

`ConnectNamedPipe`

Recall that when you're specifying `FILE_FLAG_OVERLAPPED` as part of `dwAttrsAndFlags` (for `CreateFile`) or as part of `dwOpenMode` (for `CreateNamedPipe`), the pipe or file is to be used only in overlapped mode. Overlapped I/O does not work with anonymous pipes. *Note*: The `CreateFile` documentation suggests that using the `FILE_FLAG_NO_BUFFERING` flag will enhance overlapped I/O performance. Experiments show a small improvement (about 15 percent, as can be verified by experimenting with Program 14–1), but you must ensure that the read length of every `ReadFile` and `WriteFile` operation is a multiple of the disk sector size.

Overlapped Sockets

One of the most important additions to Windows Sockets 2.0 (Chapter 12) is the standardization of overlapped I/O. In particular, sockets are no longer created automatically as overlapped file handles. `socket` creates a nonoverlapped handle. To create an overlapped socket, call `WSASocket` and explicitly ask for one by setting the `dwFlags` parameter of `WSASocket` to `WSA_FLAG_OVERLAPPED`.

```
SOCKET WSAAPI WSASocket (
    int iAddressFamily,
    int iSocketType,
    int iProtocol,
    LPWSAPROTOCOL_INFO lpProtocolInfo,
    GROUP g,
    DWORD dwFlags);
```

Use WSASocket, rather than socket, to create the socket. Any socket returned by accept will have the same properties as the argument.

Consequences of Overlapped I/O

Overlapped I/O is asynchronous. There are several consequences.

- I/O operations do not block. The system returns immediately from a call to ReadFile, WriteFile, TransactNamedPipe, or ConnectNamedPipe.

- The returned function value is not useful for indicating success or failure because the I/O operation is most likely not yet complete. A different mechanism for indicating status is required.

- The returned number of bytes transferred is also not useful because the transfer may not be complete. Windows must provide another means of obtaining this information.

- The program may issue multiple reads or writes on a single overlapped file handle. Therefore, the handle's file pointer is meaningless. There must be another method of specifying file position with each read or write. This is not a problem with named pipes, which are inherently sequential.

- The program must be able to wait (synchronize) on I/O completion. In case of multiple outstanding operations on a single handle, it must be able to determine which operation has completed. I/O operations do not necessarily complete in the same order in which they were issued.

The last two issues listed above—file position and synchronization—are addressed by the overlapped structures.

Overlapped Structures

The OVERLAPPED structure (specified, for example, by the lpOverlapped parameter of ReadFile) indicates the following:

- The file position (64 bits) where the read or write is to start, as discussed in Chapter 3

- The event (manual-reset) that will be signaled when the operation completes

Here is the OVERLAPPED structure.

```
typedef struct_OVERLAPPED {
    DWORD Internal;
    DWORD InternalHigh;
    DWORD Offset;
    DWORD OffsetHigh;
    HANDLE hEvent;
} OVERLAPPED
```

The file position (pointer) must be set in both `Offset` and `OffsetHigh`, although the high-order portion is frequently 0. Do not use `Internal` and `InternalHigh`, which are reserved for the system.

`hEvent` is an event handle (created with `CreateEvent`). The event can be named or unnamed, but it *should* be a manual-reset event (see Chapter 8) when used for overlapped I/O; the reasons are explained soon. The event is signaled when the I/O operation completes.

Alternatively, `hEvent` can be `NULL`; in this case, the program can wait on the file handle, which is also a synchronization object (see the upcoming list of cautions). The system signals completion on the file handle when hEvent is `NULL`, that is, the file handle becomes the synchronization object. *Note*: For convenience. the term "file handle" is used to describe the handle with `ReadFile`, `WriteFile`, and so on, even though this handle could refer to a pipe or device rather than to a file.

This event is immediately reset (set to the nonsignaled state) by the system when the program makes an I/O call. When the I/O operation completes, the event is signaled and remains signaled until it is used with another I/O operation. The event needs to be manual-reset if multiple threads might wait on it (although our example uses only one thread), and they may not be waiting at the time the operation completes.

Even if the file handle is synchronous (it was created without `FILE_FLAG_OVERLAPPED`), the overlapped structure is an alternative to `SetFilePointer` for specifying file position. In this case, the `ReadFile` or other call does not return until the operation is complete. This feature was used in Chapter 3.

Notice also that an outstanding I/O operation is uniquely identified by the combination of file handle and overlapped structure.

Here are a few cautions to keep in mind.

- Do not reuse an `OVERLAPPED` structure while its associated I/O operation, if any, is outstanding.

- Similarly, do not reuse an event while it is part of an `OVERLAPPED` structure.

- If there is more than one outstanding request on an overlapped handle, use events, rather than the file handle, for synchronization.

- If the OVERLAPPED structure or event is an automatic variable in a block, be certain not to exit the block before synchronizing with the I/O operation. Also, close the event handle before leaving the block to avoid a resource leak.

Overlapped I/O States

An overlapped ReadFile or WriteFile operation—or, for that matter, one of the two named pipe operations—returns immediately. In most cases, the I/O will not be complete, and the read or write returns FALSE. GetLastError returns ERROR_IO_PENDING.

After waiting on a synchronization object (an event or, perhaps, the file handle) for the operation to complete, you need to determine how many bytes were transferred. This is the primary purpose of GetOverlappedResult.

```
BOOL GetOverlappedResult (
    HANDLE hFile,
    LPOVERLAPPED lpOverlapped,
    LPWORD lpcbTransfer,
    BOOL bWait)
```

The handle and overlapped structure combine to indicate the specific I/O operation. bWait, if TRUE, specifies that GetOverlappedResult will wait until the specified operation is complete; otherwise, it returns immediately. In either case, the function returns TRUE only if the operation has completed successfully. GetLastError returns ERROR_IO_INCOMPLETE in case of a FALSE return from GetOverlappedResult, so it is possible to poll for I/O completion with this function.

The number of bytes transferred is in *lpcbTransfer. Be certain that the overlapped structure is unchanged from when it was used with the overlapped I/O operation.

Canceling Overlapped I/O Operations

The Boolean function CancelIO cancels outstanding overlapped I/O operations on the specified handle (there is just one parameter). All operations issued by the calling thread using the handle are canceled. Operations initiated by other threads are not affected. The canceled operations will complete with ERROR_OPERATION_ABORTED.

Example: Synchronizing on a File Handle

Overlapped I/O can be useful and relatively simple when there is only one outstanding operation. The program can synchronize on the file handle rather than on an event.

The following code fragment shows how a program can initiate a read operation to read a portion of a file, continue to perform other processing, and then wait on the handle.

```
OVERLAPPED ov = { 0, 0, 0, 0, NULL /* No event. */ };
HANDLE hF;
DWORD nRead;
BYTE Buffer [BUF_SIZE];
...
hF = CreateFile ( ..., FILE_FLAG_OVERLAPPED, ... );
ReadFile (hF, Buffer, sizeof (Buffer), &nRead, &ov);
/* Perform other processing. nRead is not valid. */
/* Wait for the read to complete. */
WaitForSingleObject (hF, INFINITE);
GetOverlappedResult (hF, &ov, &nRead, FALSE);
```

Example: File Conversion with Overlapped I/O and Multiple Buffers

Program 2–4 (atou) converted an ASCII file to Unicode, processing the file sequentially, and Chapter 5 showed how to perform the same sequential file processing with memory-mapped files. Program 14–1 (atouOV) performs the same task using overlapped I/O and multiple buffers holding fixed-size records.

Figure 14–1 shows the program organization with four fixed-size buffers. The program is implemented so that the number of buffers is defined in a preprocessor variable, but the following discussion assumes four buffers.

First, the program initializes all the overlapped structures with events and file positions. There is a separate overlapped structure for each input and each output buffer. Next, an overlapped read is issued for each of the four input buffers. The program then uses WaitForMultipleObjects to wait for a single event, indicating either a read or a write completed. When a read is completed, the buffer is copied and converted into the corresponding output buffer and the write is initiated. When a write completes, the next read is initiated. Notice that the events associated with the input and output buffers are arranged in a single array to be used as an argument to WaitForMultipleObjects.

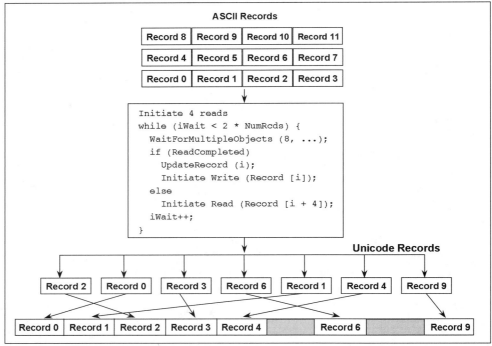

Figure 14-1   An Asynchronous File Update Model

Program 14-1   `atouOV`: File Conversion with Overlapped I/O

```
/* Chapter 14. atouOV
   OVERLAPPED I/O ASCII to Unicode file conversion.
   Windows NT only. */
#include "EvryThng.h"

#define MAX_OVRLP 4 /* Number of overlapped I/O operations. */
#define REC_SIZE 0x8000 /* 32K: Minimum size for good performance. */
#define UREC_SIZE 2 * REC_SIZE
int _tmain (int argc, LPTSTR argv [])
{
    HANDLE hInputFile, hOutputFile;
    /* There is a copy of each of the following variables and */
    /* structures for each outstanding overlapped I/O operation. */
    DWORD nin [MAX_OVRLP], nout [MAX_OVRLP], ic, i;
    OVERLAPPED OverLapIn [MAX_OVRLP], OverLapOut [MAX_OVRLP];
    /* The first event index is 0 for read, 1 for write. */
    /* WaitForMultipleObjects requires a contiguous array. */
```

```
HANDLE hEvents [2] [MAX_OVRLP];
/* The first index on these two buffers is the I/O operation. */
CHAR AsRec [MAX_OVRLP] [REC_SIZE];
WCHAR UnRec [MAX_OVRLP] [REC_SIZE];
LARGE_INTEGER CurPosIn, CurPosOut, FileSize;
LONGLONG nRecord, iWaits;

hInputFile = CreateFile (argv [1], GENERIC_READ,
        0, NULL, OPEN_EXISTING, FILE_FLAG_OVERLAPPED, NULL);
hOutputFile = CreateFile (argv [2], GENERIC_WRITE,
        0, NULL, CREATE_ALWAYS, FILE_FLAG_OVERLAPPED, NULL);

/* Total number of records to process based on input file size. */
/* There may be a partial record at the end. */
FileSize.LowPart = GetFileSize (hInputFile, &FileSize.HighPart);
nRecord = FileSize.QuadPart / REC_SIZE;
if ((FileSize.QuadPart % REC_SIZE) != 0) nRecord++;

CurPosIn.QuadPart = 0;
for (ic = 0; ic < MAX_OVRLP; ic++) {
    /* Create read and write events for each overlapped struct. */
    hEvents [0] [ic] = OverLapIn [ic].hEvent /* Read event/struct.*/
            = CreateEvent (NULL, TRUE, FALSE, NULL);
    hEvents [1] [ic] = OverLapOut [ic].hEvent /* Write. */
            = CreateEvent (NULL, TRUE, FALSE, NULL);
    /* Initial file positions for each overlapped structure. */
    OverLapIn [ic].Offset = CurPosIn.LowPart;
    OverLapIn [ic].OffsetHigh = CurPosIn.HighPart;
    /* Initiate an overlapped read for this overlapped struct. */
    if (CurPosIn.QuadPart < FileSize.QuadPart)
        ReadFile (hInputFile, AsRec [ic], REC_SIZE,
                &nin [ic], &OverLapIn [ic]);
    CurPosIn.QuadPart += (LONGLONG) REC_SIZE;
}

/* All read operations are running. Wait for an event to complete
    and reset it immediately. Read and write events are
    stored contiguously in the event array. */

iWaits = 0; /* Number of I/O operations completed so far. */
while (iWaits < 2 * nRecord) {
    ic = WaitForMultipleObjects (2 * MAX_OVRLP,
            hEvents [0], FALSE, INFINITE) - WAIT_OBJECT_0;
    iWaits++; /* Increment # of complete I/O operations. */
    ResetEvent (hEvents [ic / MAX_OVRLP] [ic % MAX_OVRLP]);

    if (ic < MAX_OVRLP) { /* A read completed. */
        GetOverlappedResult (hInputFile,
                &OverLapIn [ic], &nin [ic], FALSE);
```

```
            /* Process the record and initiate the write. */
            CurPosIn.LowPart = OverLapIn [ic].Offset;
            CurPosIn.HighPart = OverLapIn [ic].OffsetHigh;
            CurPosOut.QuadPart =
                    (CurPosIn.QuadPart / REC_SIZE) * UREC_SIZE;
            OverLapOut [ic].Offset = CurPosOut.LowPart;
            OverLapOut [ic].OffsetHigh = CurPosOut.HighPart;

            /* Convert an ASCII record to Unicode. */
            for (i = 0; i < REC_SIZE; i++)
                UnRec [ic] [i] = AsRec [ic] [i];
            WriteFile (hOutputFile, UnRec [ic], nin [ic] * 2,
                    &nout [ic], &OverLapOut [ic]);

            /* Prepare for the next read, which will be initiated
               after the write, issued above, completes. */
            CurPosIn.QuadPart +=
                    REC_SIZE * (LONGLONG) (MAX_OVRLP);
            OverLapIn [ic].Offset = CurPosIn.LowPart;
            OverLapIn [ic].OffsetHigh = CurPosIn.HighPart;

        } else if (ic < 2 * MAX_OVRLP) { /* A write completed. */
            /* Start the read. */
            ic -= MAX_OVRLP; /* Set the output buffer index. */
            if (!GetOverlappedResult (hOutputFile,
                    &OverLapOut [ic], &nout [ic], FALSE))
                ReportError (_T ("Read failed."), 0, TRUE);
            CurPosIn.LowPart = OverLapIn [ic].Offset;
            CurPosIn.HighPart = OverLapIn [ic].OffsetHigh;
            if (CurPosIn.QuadPart < FileSize.QuadPart) {
                /* Start a new read. */
                ReadFile (hInputFile, AsRec [ic], REC_SIZE,
                        &nin [ic], &OverLapIn [ic]);
            }
        }
    }
    /* Close all events. */
    for (ic = 0; ic < MAX_OVRLP; ic++) {
        CloseHandle (hEvents [0] [ic]);
        CloseHandle (hEvents [1] [ic]);
    }
    CloseHandle (hInputFile);
    CloseHandle (hOutputFile);
    return 0;
}
```

Program 14–1 works only under Windows NT. Windows 9x asynchronous I/O cannot use disk files. Appendix C shows and comments on atouOV's relatively poor performance results. Experiments show that the buffer should be at least 32KB for good performance, but, even then, normal synchronous I/O is faster. Furthermore, the program does not benefit from SMP, because the CPU is not the bottleneck in this example, which processes just two files.

Extended I/O with Completion Routines

There is an alternative to the use of synchronization objects. Rather than requiring a thread to wait for a completion signal on an event or handle, the system can invoke a user-specified completion routine when an I/O operation completes. The completion routine can then start the next I/O operation and perform any other bookkeeping. The completion or callback routine is similar to Chapter 10's asynchronous procedure call and requires alertable wait states.

How can the program specify the completion routine? There are no remaining `ReadFile` or `WriteFile` parameters or data structures to hold the routine's address. There is, however, a family of extended I/O functions, identified by the `Ex` suffix and containing an extra parameter for the completion routine address. The read and write functions are `ReadFileEx` and `WriteFileEx`, respectively. It is also necessary to use one of five alertable wait functions:

- `WaitForSingleObjectEx`

- `WaitForMultipleObjectsEx`

- `SleepEx`

- `SignalObjectAndWait`

- `MsgWaitForMultipleObjectsEx`

Extended I/O is sometimes called *alertable I/O*. The following sections show how to use the extended functions.

Note: Extended I/O will not work with disk files or communications ports under Windows 9x. Windows 9x extended I/O, however, will work with named pipes, mailslots, sockets, and sequential devices.

`ReadFileEx`, `WriteFileEx`, and Completion Routines

The extended read and write functions can be used with open file, named pipe, and mailslot handles if `FILE_FLAG_OVERLAPPED` was used at open (create) time. Notice that the flag sets a handle attribute and, while overlapped I/O and extended I/O are distinguished, a single overlapped flag is used to enable both types of asynchronous I/O on a handle.

Overlapped sockets (Chapter 12) can be used with `ReadFileEx` and `Write-FileEx` in all Windows versions.

```
BOOL ReadFileEx (
    HANDLE hFile,
    LPVOID lpBuffer,
    DWORD nNumberOfBytesToRead,
    LPOVERLAPPED lpOverlapped,
    LPOVERLAPPED_COMPLETION_ROUTINE lpcr)

BOOL WriteFileEx (
    HANDLE hFile,
    LPVOID lpBuffer,
    DWORD nNumberOfBytesToWrite,
    LPOVERLAPPED lpOverlapped,
    LPOVERLAPPED_COMPLETION_ROUTINE lpcr)
```

The two functions are familiar but have an extra parameter to specify the completion routine.

The overlapped structures must be supplied, but there is no need to specify the `hEvent` member; the system ignores it. It turns out, however, that this member is useful for carrying information, such as a sequence number, to identify the I/O operation, as shown in Program 14–2.

In comparison to `ReadFile` and `WriteFile`, notice that the extended functions do not require the parameters for the number of bytes transferred. That information is conveyed to the completion routine, which must be included in the program.

The completion routine has parameters for the byte count, an error code, and the overlapped structure. The last parameter is required so that the completion routine can determine which of several outstanding operations has completed. Notice that the same cautions regarding reuse or destruction of overlapped structures apply here as they did for overlapped I/O.

```
VOID WINAPI FileIOCompletionRoutine (
    DWORD dwError,
    DWORD cbTransferred,
    LPOVERLAPPED lpo)
```

As was the case with `CreateThread`, which also specified a function name, *FileIOCompletionRoutine* is a placeholder and not an actual function name.

`dwError` is limited to 0 (success) and `ERROR_HANDLE_EOF` (when a read tries to go past the end of file). The overlapped structure is the one used by the completed `ReadFileEx` or `WriteFileEx` call.

Two things must happen before the completion routine is invoked by the system.

1. The I/O operation must complete.

2. The calling thread must be in an alertable wait state, notifying the system that it should execute any queued completion routines.

How does a thread get into an alertable wait state? It must make an explicit call to one of the alertable wait functions described in the next section. In this way, the thread can ensure that the completion routine does not execute prematurely. A thread can be in an alertable wait state only while it is calling an alertable wait function; on return, the thread is no longer in this state.

Once these two conditions have been met, completion routines that have been queued as the result of I/O completion are executed. *Completion routines are executed in the same thread that made the original I/O call and is in the alertable wait state*. Therefore, the thread should enter an alertable wait state only when it is safe for completion routines to execute.

Alertable Wait Functions

There are five alertable wait functions, and the three that relate directly to our current needs are described here.

```
DWORD WaitForSingleObjectEx (
    HANDLE hObject,
    DWORD dwMilliseconds,
    BOOL bAlertable)

DWORD WaitForMultipleObjectsEx (
    DWORD cObjects,
    LPHANDLE lphObjects,
    BOOL fWaitAll,
    DWORD dwMilliseconds,
    BOOL bAlertable)

DWORD SleepEx (
    DWORD dwMilliseconds,
    BOOL bAlertable)
```

Each alertable wait function has a `bAlertable` flag that must be set to `TRUE` when used for asynchronous I/O. The functions are extensions of the familiar `Wait` and `Sleep` functions.

Time-outs, as always, are in milliseconds. These three functions will return as soon as *any one* of the following situations occurs.

- Handle(s) are signaled so as to satisfy one of the two wait functions in the normal way.

- The time-out period expires.

- All queued completion routines in the thread finish, and `bAlertable` is set. Completion routines are queued when their associated I/O operation is complete (see Figure 14–2).

Notice that no events are associated with the `ReadFileEx` and `WriteFileEx` overlapped structures, so any handles in the wait call will have no direct relation to the I/O operations. `SleepEx`, on the other hand, is not associated with a synchronization object and is the easiest of the three functions to use. `SleepEx` is usually used with an `INFINITE` time-out so that the function will return only after one or more of the currently queued completion routines have finished.

Execution of Completion Routines and the Alertable Wait Return

As soon as an extended I/O operation is complete, its associated completion routine, with the overlapped structure, byte count, and error status arguments, is queued for execution.

All of a thread's queued completion routines are executed when the thread enters an alertable wait state. They are executed sequentially but not necessarily in the same order as I/O completion. The alertable wait function returns only after the completion routines return. This property is essential to the proper operation of most programs because it assumes that the completion routines can prepare for the next use of the overlapped structure and perform related operations to get the program to a known state before the alertable wait return.

`SleepEx` will return `WAIT_IO_COMPLETION` if one or more queued completion routines were executed, and `GetLastError` will return this same value after one of the wait functions returns.

Here are two final points.

1. Use an `INFINITE` time-out value with any alertable wait function. Without the possibility of a time-out, the wait function will return only after all queued completion routines have been executed or the handles have been signaled.

2. It is common practice to use the hEvent data member of the overlapped structure to convey information to the completion routine because this field is ignored by the OS.

Figure 14–2 illustrates the interaction among the main thread, the completion routines, and the alertable waits. In this example, three concurrent read operations are started, and two are completed by the time the alertable wait is performed.

Example: File Conversion with Extended I/O

Program 14–3, atouEX, reimplements Program 14–1. These programs show how the two asynchronous I/O techniques differ. atouEX is similar to Program 14–1 but moves most of the bookkeeping code to the completion routines, and many variables are made global so as to be accessible to the completion routines. Appendix C shows, however, that atouEX performs competitively with other non-memory-mapped techniques, whereas atouOV is consistently slower.

Figure 14-2 Asynchronous I/O with Completion Routines

Program 14–2   atouEX: File Conversion with Extended I/O

```
/* Chapter 14. atouEX
   EXTENDED I/O ASCII to Unicode file conversion. */
/* atouEX file1 file2 */

#include "EvryThng.h"

#define MAX_OVRLP 4
#define REC_SIZE 8096 /* Block size is not as important for
      performance as with atouOV. */
#define UREC_SIZE 2 * REC_SIZE

static VOID WINAPI ReadDone (DWORD, DWORD, LPOVERLAPPED);
static VOID WINAPI WriteDone (DWORD, DWORD, LPOVERLAPPED);

/* The first overlapped structure is for reading,
   and the second is for writing. Structures and buffers are
   allocated for each outstanding operation. */
OVERLAPPED OverLapIn [MAX_OVRLP], OverLapOut [MAX_OVRLP];
CHAR AsRec [MAX_OVRLP] [REC_SIZE];
WCHAR UnRec [MAX_OVRLP] [REC_SIZE];
HANDLE hInputFile, hOutputFile;
LONGLONG nRecord, nDone;
LARGE_INTEGER FileSize;

int _tmain (int argc, LPTSTR argv [])
{
    DWORD ic;
    LARGE_INTEGER CurPosIn;
    hInputFile = CreateFile (argv [1], GENERIC_READ,
            0, NULL, OPEN_EXISTING, FILE_FLAG_OVERLAPPED, NULL);
    hOutputFile = CreateFile (argv [2], GENERIC_WRITE,
            0, NULL, CREATE_ALWAYS, FILE_FLAG_OVERLAPPED, NULL);
    FileSize.LowPart = GetFileSize (hInputFile, &FileSize.HighPart);
    nRecord = FileSize.QuadPart / REC_SIZE;
    if ((FileSize.QuadPart % REC_SIZE) != 0) nRecord++;
    CurPosIn.QuadPart = 0;
    for (ic = 0; ic < MAX_OVRLP; ic++) {
        OverLapIn [ic].hEvent = (HANDLE) ic; /* Overload the event. */
        OverLapOut [ic].hEvent = (HANDLE) ic; /* Fields. */
        OverLapIn [ic].Offset = CurPosIn.LowPart;
        OverLapIn [ic].OffsetHigh = CurPosIn.HighPart;
        if (CurPosIn.QuadPart < FileSize.QuadPart)
            ReadFileEx (hInputFile, AsRec [ic], REC_SIZE,
                    &OverLapIn [ic], ReadDone);
        CurPosIn.QuadPart += (LONGLONG) REC_SIZE;
    }
```

```
    /* All read operations are running. Enter an alertable wait
       state and continue until all records have been processed. */
    nDone = 0;
    while (nDone < 2 * nRecord)
        SleepEx (INFINITE, TRUE);
    CloseHandle (hInputFile);
    CloseHandle (hOutputFile);
    _tprintf (_T ("ASCII to Unicode conversion completed.\n"));
    return 0;
}

static VOID WINAPI ReadDone (DWORD Code, DWORD nBytes,
        LPOVERLAPPED pOv)
{
    /* A read completed. Convert the data and initiate a write. */
    LARGE_INTEGER CurPosIn, CurPosOut;
    DWORD ic, i;
    nDone++;
    /* Process the record and initiate the write. */
    ic = (DWORD) (pOv->hEvent);
    CurPosIn.LowPart = OverLapIn [ic].Offset;
    CurPosIn.HighPart = OverLapIn [ic].OffsetHigh;
    CurPosOut.QuadPart =
            (CurPosIn.QuadPart / REC_SIZE) * UREC_SIZE;
    OverLapOut [ic].Offset = CurPosOut.LowPart;
    OverLapOut [ic].OffsetHigh = CurPosOut.HighPart;
    /* Convert an ASCII record to Unicode. */
    for (i = 0; i < nBytes; i++)
        UnRec [ic] [i] = AsRec [ic] [i];
    WriteFileEx (hOutputFile, UnRec [ic], nBytes*2,
            &OverLapOut [ic], WriteDone);
    /* Prepare the overlapped structure for the next read. */
    CurPosIn.QuadPart += REC_SIZE * (LONGLONG) (MAX_OVRLP);
    OverLapIn [ic].Offset = CurPosIn.LowPart;
    OverLapIn [ic].OffsetHigh = CurPosIn.HighPart;
    return;
}

static VOID WINAPI WriteDone (DWORD Code, DWORD nBytes,
        LPOVERLAPPED pOv)
{
    /* A write completed. Initiate the next read. */
    LARGE_INTEGER CurPosIn;
    DWORD ic;
    nDone++;
    ic = (DWORD) (pOv->hEvent);
    CurPosIn.LowPart = OverLapIn [ic].Offset;
    CurPosIn.HighPart = OverLapIn [ic].OffsetHigh;
```

```
        if (CurPosIn.QuadPart < FileSize.QuadPart) {
            ReadFileEx (hInputFile, AsRec [ic], REC_SIZE,
                    &OverLapIn [ic], ReadDone);
        }
        return;
}
```

Asynchronous I/O with Threads

Overlapped and extended I/O achieve asynchronous I/O within a single thread, although the OS creates its own threads to support the functionality. These techniques are common, in one form or another, in many older OSs for supporting limited forms of asynchronous operation in single-threaded systems.

Windows, however, supports threads, so the same effect is possible by performing synchronous I/O operations in multiple, separate threads. The multithreaded servers and Chapter 7's grepMT have already illustrated this. Threads also provide a uniform and, arguably, much simpler way to perform asynchronous I/O. An alternative to Programs 14–1 and 14–2 is to give each thread its own handle to the file and each thread could synchronously process every fourth record.

The atouMT.c program, not listed here but included on the book's Web site, illustrates how to use threads in this way. Not only does atouMT work on all Windows versions, but it is also simpler than the two asynchronous I/O programs because the bookkeeping is less complex. Each thread simply maintains its own buffers on its own stack and performs the read, convert, and write sequence synchronously in a loop. The performance is also competitive. *Note*: The atouMT.c program on the Web site contains some comments about several pitfalls that can occur when a single file is accessed concurrently from several threads. In particular, the distinct file handles should all be created with CreateFile rather than with DuplicateHandle.

My personal preference is to use threads rather than asynchronous I/O for file processing. Threads are easier to program, and they provide the best performance in most cases.

There are two exceptions to this generalization. The first exception, as shown earlier in this chapter, is a situation in which there is only a single outstanding operation and the file handle can be used for synchronization. The second, and more important, exception occurs with asynchronous I/O completion ports, as will be described at the end of this chapter.

Waitable Timers

Windows NT supports waitable timers, a type of waitable kernel object.

You can always create your own timing signal by creating a timing thread that sets an event after waking from a `Sleep` call. `serverNP` (Program 11–3) also uses a timing thread to broadcast its pipe name periodically. Therefore, waitable timers are a redundant but useful way to perform tasks periodically or at specified times. In particular, a waitable timer can be set to signal at a specified absolute time.

A waitable timer can be either a *synchronization timer* or a *manual-reset notification timer*. A synchronization timer is associated with a callback function, similar to an extended I/O completion routine, whereas a wait function is used to synchronize on a manual-reset notification timer.

The first step is to create a timer handle with `CreateWaitableTimer`.

```
HANDLE CreateWaitableTimer (
    LPSECURITY_ATTRIBUTES lpTimerAttributes,
    BOOL bManualReset,
    LPCTSTR lpTimerName);
```

The second parameter, `bManualReset`, determines whether the timer is a synchronization timer or a manual-reset notification timer. Program 14–3 uses a synchronization timer, but you can change the comment and the parameter setting to obtain a notification timer. Notice that there is also an `OpenWaitableTimer` function that can use the optional name supplied in the third argument.

The timer is initially inactive, but `SetWaitableTimer` activates it and specifies the initial signal time and the time between periodic signals.

```
BOOL SetWaitableTimer (
    HANDLE hTimer,
    const LARGE_INTEGER *pDueTime,
    LONG lPeriod,
    PTIMERAPCROUTINE pfnCompletionRoutine,
    LPVOID lpArgToCompletionRoutine,
    BOOL fResume);
```

`hTimer` is a valid timer handle created using `CreateWaitableTimer`.

The second parameter, pointed to by `pDueTime`, is either a positive absolute time or a negative relative time and is actually expressed as a `FILETIME` with a resolution of 100 nanoseconds. `FILETIME` variables were introduced in Chapter 3 and were used in Chapter 6's `timep` (Program 6–2).

The interval between signals is specified in the third parameter, but in millisecond units. If this value is 0, the timer is signaled only once. A positive value indicates that the timer is a periodic timer and continues signaling periodically until you call `CancelWaitableTimer`. Negative interval values are not allowed.

`pfnCompletionRoutine`, the fourth parameter, is appropriate when using a synchronization timer and specifies the time-out function (completion routine) to be called when the timer is signaled *and* the thread enters an alertable wait state. The routine is called with the pointer specified in the fifth parameter, `plArgToCompletionRoutine`, as an argument.

Having set a synchronization timer, you can now call `SleepEx` to enter an alertable wait state so the completion routine can be called. In the case of a manual-reset notification timer, wait on the timer handle. The handle will remain signaled until another call to `SetWaitableTimer`. The complete version of Program 14–3 on the book's Web site allows you to experiment with using the four combinations of the two timer types and with choosing between using a completion routine or waiting on the timer handle.

The final parameter, `fResume`, is concerned with power conservation. See the documentation for more information.

Use `CancelWaitableTimer` to cancel the last effect of a previous `SetWaitableTimer`, although it will not change the signaled state of the timer. Use another `SetWaitableTimer` call to do that.

Example: Using a Waitable Timer

Program 14–3 shows how to use a waitable timer to signal the user periodically.

Program 14–3   `TimeBeep.c`: A Periodic Signal

```
/* Chapter 14. TimeBeep.c. Periodic alarm.
/* Usage: TimeBeep period (in milliseconds). */
#include "EvryThng.h"

static BOOL WINAPI Handler (DWORD CntrlEvent);
static VOID APIENTRY Beeper (LPVOID, DWORD, DWORD);
volatile static BOOL Exit = FALSE;
HANDLE hTimer;

int _tmain (int argc, LPTSTR argv [])
{
```

```
    DWORD Count = 0, Period;
    LARGE_INTEGER DueTime;

    /* Catch Ctrl-c to terminate operation. See Chapter 4. */
    SetConsoleCtrlHandler (Handler, TRUE);
    Period = _ttoi (argv [1]) * 1000;

    DueTime.QuadPart = -(LONGLONG)Period * 10000;
            /* Due time is negative for first time-out relative to
               current time. Period is in ms (10^-3 sec) whereas
               the due time is in 100 ns (10^-7 sec) units to be
               consistent with a FILETIME. */

    hTimer = CreateWaitableTimer (NULL,
        FALSE /* "Synchronization timer" */, NULL);
    SetWaitableTimer (hTimer, &DueTime, Period,
            Beeper, &Count, TRUE);

    while (!Exit) {
        _tprintf (_T ("Count = %d\n"), Count);
        /* Count is increased in the timer routine. */
        /* Enter an alertable wait state. */
        SleepEx (INFINITE, TRUE);
    }

    _tprintf (_T ("Shut down. Count = %d"), Count);
    CancelWaitableTimer (hTimer);
    CloseHandle (hTimer);
    return 0;
}

static VOID APIENTRY Beeper (LPVOID lpCount,
        DWORD dwTimerLowValue, DWORD dwTimerHighValue)
{
    *(LPDWORD) lpCount = *(LPDWORD) lpCount + 1;

    _tprintf (_T ("Perform beep number: %d\n"), *(LPDWORD) lpCount);
    Beep (1000 /* Frequency. */, 250 /* Duration (ms). */);
    return;
}

BOOL WINAPI Handler (DWORD CntrlEvent)
{
    Exit = TRUE;
    _tprintf (_T ("Shutting Down\n"));
    return TRUE;
}
```

Comments on the Waitable Timer Example

There are four combinations based on timer type and whether you wait on the handle or use a completion routine. Program 14–3 illustrates using a completion routine and a synchronization timer. The four combinations can be tested using the version of `TimeBeep.c` on the Web site by changing some comments.

I/O Completion Ports

I/O completion ports, supported only on NT, combine features of both overlapped I/O and independent threads and are most useful in server programs. To see the requirement for this, consider the servers that we built in Chapters 11 and 12, where each client is supported by a distinct worker thread associated with a socket or named pipe instance. This solution works very well when the number of clients is not large.

Consider what would happen, however, if there were 1,000 clients. The current model would then require 1,000 threads, each with a substantial amount of virtual memory space. For example, by default, each thread will consume 1MB of stack space, so 1,000 threads would require 1GB of virtual address space, and thread context switches could increase page fault delays.[1] Furthermore, the threads would contend for shared resources both in the executive and in the process, and the timing data in Chapter 9 showed the performance degradation that can result. Therefore, there is a requirement to allow a small pool of worker threads to serve a large number of clients.

I/O completion ports provide a solution by allowing you to create a limited number of server threads in a thread pool while having a very large number of named pipe handles (or sockets). Handles are not paired with individual worker server threads; rather, a server thread can process data on any handle that has available data.

An I/O completion port, then, is a set of overlapped handles, and threads wait on the port. When a read or write on one of the handles is complete, one thread is awakened and given the data and the results of the I/O operation. The thread can then process the data and wait on the port again.

The first task is to create an I/O completion port and add overlapped handles to the port.

---

[1] This problem may become less severe in the future with Win64 and larger physical memories.

Managing I/O Completion Ports

A single function, `CreateIoCompletionPort`, is used both to create the port and to add handles. Since this one function must perform two tasks, the parameter usage is correspondingly complex.

```
HANDLE CreateIoCompletionPort (
    HANDLE FileHandle,
    HANDLE ExistingCompletionPort,
    DWORD CompletionKey,
    DWORD NumberOfConcurrentThreads);
```

An I/O completion port is a collection of file handles opened in OVERLAPPED mode. `FileHandle` is an overlapped handle to add to the port. If the value is `INVALID_HANDLE_VALUE`, a new I/O completion port is created and returned by the function. The next parameter, `ExistingCompletionPort`, must be NULL in this case.

`ExistingCompletionPort` is the port created on the first call, and it indicates the port to which the handle in the first parameter is to be added. The function also returns the port handle when the function is successful; NULL indicates failure.

`CompletionKey` specifies the key that will be included in the completion packet for `FileHandle`. The key is usually an index to an array of data structures containing an operation type, a handle, and a pointer to the data buffer.

`NumberOfConcurrentThreads` indicates the maximum number of threads allowed to execute concurrently. Any threads in excess of this number that are waiting on the port will remain blocked even if there is a handle with available data. If this parameter is 0, the number of processors in the system is used as the limit.

An unlimited number of overlapped handles can be associated with an I/O completion port. Call `CreateIoCompletionPort` initially to create the port and to specify the maximum number of threads. Call the function again for every overlapped handle that is to be associated with the port. Unfortunately, there is no way to remove a handle from a completion port, and this omission limits program flexibility.

The handles associated with a port should not be used with `ReadFileEx` or `WriteFileEx` functions. The Microsoft documentation suggests that the files or other objects not be shared using other open handles.

Waiting on an I/O Completion Port

Use `ReadFile` and `WriteFile`, along with overlapped structures (no event handle is necessary), to perform I/O on the handles associated with a port. The I/O operation is then queued on the completion port.

A thread waits for a queued overlapped completion not by waiting on an event but by calling `GetQueuedCompletionStatus`, specifying the completion port. When the calling thread wakes up, the function returns a key that was specified when the handle, whose operation has completed, was initially added to the port, and this key can specify the number of bytes transferred and the identity of the actual handle for the completed operation.

Notice that the thread that initiated the read or write is not necessarily the thread that will receive the completion notification. Any waiting thread can receive completion notification. Therefore, the key must be able to identify the handle of the completed operation.

There is also a time-out associated with the wait.

```
BOOL GetQueuedCompletionStatus (
    HANDLE CompletionPort,
    LPDWORD lpNumberOfBytesTransferred,
    LPDWORD lpCompletionKey,
    LPOVERLAPPED *lpOverlapped,
    DWORD dwMilliseconds);
```

It is sometimes convenient to have an operation not be queued on the I/O completion port. In such a case, a thread can wait on the overlapped event, as shown in Program 14–4 and in an additional example, `atouMTCP`, on the book's Web site. In order to specify that an overlapped operation should *not* be queued on the completion port, you must set the low-order bit in the overlapped structure's event handle; then you can wait on the event for that specific operation. This is a strange design, but it is documented, although not prominently.

Posting to an I/O Completion Port

A thread can post a completion event, with a key, to a port to satisfy an outstanding call to `GetQueuedCompletionStatus`. The `PostQueuedCompletionStatus` function supplies all the required information.

```
BOOL PostQueuedCompletionStatus (
    HANDLE CompletionPort,
    DWORD dwNumberOfBytesTransferred,
    DWORD dwCompletionKey,
    LPOVERLAPPED lpOverlapped);
```

One technique sometimes used is to provide a bogus key value, such as -1, to wake up waiting threads, even though no operation has completed. Waiting threads should test for bogus key values, and this technique could be used, for example, to signal a thread to shut down.

Alternatives to I/O Completion Ports

Chapter 9 showed how a semaphore can be used to limit the number of ready threads, and this technique is effective in maintaining throughput when many threads compete for limited resources.

We could use the same technique with serverSK (Program 12–2) and serverNP (Program 11–3). All that is required is to wait on the semaphore after the read request completes, perform the request, create the response, and release the semaphore before writing the response. This solution is much simpler than the I/O completion port example in the next section. The only problem is that there may be a large number of threads, each with its own stack space, which will consume virtual memory. The problem can be partly alleviated by carefully measuring the amount of stack space required. Exercise 14–6 involves experimentation with this alternative solution, and there is an example implementation on the Web site.

There is yet another possibility when creating scalable servers. A limited number of worker threads can take work item packets from a queue (see Chapter 10). The incoming work items can be placed in the queue by one or more boss threads, as shown in Program 10–5.

Example: A Server Using I/O Completion Ports

Program 14–4 modifies serverNP (Program 11–3) to allow use of I/O completion ports. This server creates a small server thread pool and a larger pool of overlapped pipe handles along with a completion key for each handle. The overlapped handles are added to the completion port and a ConnectNamedPipe is issued. The server threads wait for completions associated with both client connections and read operations. After a read is detected, the associated client request is processed and the results are returned without using the completion port. Rather, the server thread waits on the event after the write, and the event in the overlapped structure has its low-order bit set.

An alternative and more flexible design would close a handle every time a client disconnected and would create a new handle for each new connection. This would be similar to the way sockets were used in Chapter 12. The difficulty, however, is that handles cannot be removed from the completion port, so these short-lived handles would cause a resource leak.

Much of the code is familiar from previous examples and is omitted here.

Program 14–4   `serverCP.c`: A Server Using a Completion Port

```
/* Chapter 14. ServerCP. Multithreaded server.
   Named pipe version, COMPLETION PORT example.
   Usage: Server [UserName GroupName]. */

#include "EvryThng.h"
#include "ClntSrvr.h"

/* Request and response messages defined here. */
typedef struct { /* Completion port keys point to these structures, */
    HANDLE hNp; /* which represent outstanding ReadFile */
    REQUEST Req; /* and ConnectNamedPipe operations. */
    DWORD Type; /* 0 for ConnectNamedPipe; 1 for ReadFile. */
    OVERLAPPED Ov;
} CP_KEY;
static CP_KEY Key [MAX_CLIENTS_CP]; /* Available to all threads. */
/* ... */
_tmain (int argc, LPTSTR argv [])
{
    HANDLE hCp, hMonitor, hSrvrThread [MAX_CLIENTS];
    DWORD iNp, iTh, MonitorId, ThreadId;
    THREAD_ARG ThArgs [MAX_SERVER_TH];

    /* ... */

    hCp = CreateIoCompletionPort (INVALID_HANDLE_VALUE, NULL, 0,
        MAX_SERVER_TH);
    /* Create an overlapped named pipe for every potential client, */
    /* add to the completion port, and wait for a connection. */
    /* Assume that the maximum number of clients far exceeds */
    /* the number of server threads. */
```

```
     for (iNp = 0; iNp < MAX_CLIENTS_CP; iNp++) {
        memset (&Key [iNp], 0, sizeof (CP_KEY));
        Key [iNp].hNp = CreateNamedPipe (SERVER_PIPE,
           PIPE_ACCESS_DUPLEX | FILE_FLAG_OVERLAPPED,
           PIPE_READMODE_MESSAGE | PIPE_TYPE_MESSAGE | PIPE_WAIT,
           MAX_CLIENTS_CP, 0, 0, INFINITE, pNPSA);
        CreateIoCompletionPort (Key [iNp].hNp, hCp, iNp,
              MAX_SERVER_TH + 2);
        Key [iNp].Ov.hEvent = CreateEvent (NULL, TRUE, FALSE, NULL);
        ConnectNamedPipe (Key [iNp].hNp, &Key [iNp].Ov);
     }

     /* Create server worker threads and a temp file name for each. */
     for (iTh = 0; iTh < MAX_SERVER_TH; iTh++) {
        ThArgs [iTh].hCompPort = hCp;
        ThArgs [iTh].ThreadNo = iTh;
        GetTempFileName (_T ("."), _T ("CLP"), 0,
              ThArgs [iTh].TmpFileName);
        hSrvrThread [iTh] = (HANDLE)_beginthreadex (NULL, 0, Server,
              &ThArgs [iTh], 0, &ThreadId);
     }

     /* Wait for all the threads to terminate and clean up. */
     /* ... */
     return 0;
}

static DWORD WINAPI Server (LPTHREAD_ARG pThArg)

/* Server thread function.
   There is a thread for every potential client. */
{
    HANDLE hCp, hTmpFile = INVALID_HANDLE_VALUE;
    HANDLE hWrEvent = CreateEvent (NULL, TRUE, FALSE, NULL);
    DWORD nXfer, KeyIndex, ServerNumber;
    /* ... */
    BOOL Success, Disconnect, Exit = FALSE;
    LPOVERLAPPED pOv;
    OVERLAPPED ovResp = {0, 0, 0, 0, hWrEvent}; /* For responses. */

    /* To prevent an overlapped operation from being queued on the
       CP, the event must have the low-order bit set. This is strange,
       but it's the documented way to do it. */
    ovResp.hEvent = (HANDLE) ((DWORD) hWrEvent | 0x1);
    GetStartupInfo (&StartInfoCh);
    hCp = pThArg->hCompPort;
    ServerNumber = pThArg->ThreadNo;
```

```
while (!ShutDown && !Exit) __try {
    Success = FALSE; /* Set only when everything has succeeded. */
    Disconnect = FALSE;
    GetQueuedCompletionStatus (hCp, &nXfer, &KeyIndex, &pOv,
            INFINITE);
    if (Key [KeyIndex].Type == 0) {
        /* A connection has completed. */
        /* Open the temporary results file for this connection. */
        hTmpFile = CreateFile (pThArg->TmpFileName, /* ... */);
        Key [KeyIndex].Type = 1;
        Disconnect = !ReadFile (Key [KeyIndex].hNp,
            &Key [KeyIndex].Req, RQ_SIZE, &nXfer, &Key [KeyIndex].Ov)
            && GetLastError () == ERROR_HANDLE_EOF; /* First read. */
        if (Disconnect) continue;
        Success = TRUE;
    } else { /* A read has completed. Process the request. */
        ShutDown = ShutDown ||
            (_tcscmp (Key [KeyIndex].Req.Record, ShutRqst) == 0);
        if (ShutDown) continue;

        /* Create a process to carry out the command. */
        /* ... */

        /* Respond a line at a time. It is convenient to use
           C library line-oriented routines at this point. */

        fp = _tfopen (pThArg->TmpFileName, _T ("r"));
        Response.Status = 0;
        /* Responses are not queued on the completion port as the
           low-order bit of the event is set. */
        while (_fgetts(Response.Record, MAX_RQRS_LEN, fp) != NULL) {
            WriteFile (Key [KeyIndex].hNp, &Response, RS_SIZE,
                    &nXfer, &ovResp);
            WaitForSingleObject (hWrEvent, INFINITE);
        }
        fclose (fp);

        /* Erase temp file contents. */
        SetFilePointer (hTmpFile, 0, NULL, FILE_BEGIN);
        SetEndOfFile (hTmpFile);
        /* Send an end of response indicator. */
        Response.Status = 1; strcpy (Response.Record, "");
        WriteFile (Key [KeyIndex].hNp, &Response, RS_SIZE,
                &nXfer, &ovResp);
        WaitForSingleObject (hWrEvent, INFINITE);
        /* End of main command loop. Get next command. */
        Disconnect = !ReadFile (Key [KeyIndex].hNp,
            &Key [KeyIndex].Req, RQ_SIZE, &nXfer, &Key [KeyIndex].Ov)
            && GetLastError () == ERROR_HANDLE_EOF; /* Next read. */
```

```
            if (Disconnect) continue;
            Success = TRUE;
        }

    } __finally {
        if (Disconnect) { /* Issue another connect on this pipe. */
            Key [KeyIndex].Type = 0;
            DisconnectNamedPipe (Key [KeyIndex].hNp);
            ConnectNamedPipe (Key [KeyIndex].hNp, &Key [KeyIndex].Ov);
        }
        if (!Success) {
            ReportError (_T ("Server failure"), 0, TRUE);
            Exit = TRUE;
        }
    }
    FlushFileBuffers (Key [KeyIndex].hNp);
    DisconnectNamedPipe (Key [KeyIndex].hNp);
    CloseHandle (hTmpFile);
    /* ... */
    _endthreadex (0);
    return 0; /* Suppress a compiler warning message. */
}
```

Summary

Windows has three methods for performing asynchronous I/O. Using threads is the most general and simplest technique and, unlike the other two, works with Windows 9x. Each thread is responsible for a sequence of one or more sequential, blocking I/O operations. Furthermore, each thread should have its own file or pipe handle.

Overlapped I/O allows a single thread to perform asynchronous operations on a single file handle, but there must be an event handle, rather than a thread and file handle pair, for each operation. Wait specifically for each I/O operation to complete and then perform any required cleanup or sequencing operations.

Extended I/O, on the other hand, automatically invokes the completion code, and it does not require additional events.

The one indispensable advantage provided by overlapped I/O is the ability to create I/O completion ports, but, as mentioned previously and illustrated by a program, atouMTCP.c, on the book's Web site, even that advantage is somewhat constrained by the ability to use semaphores to limit the number of active threads in a worker thread pool. The inability to remove handles from a completion port is an additional limitation.

UNIX supports threads through Pthreads, as discussed previously.

System V UNIX limits asynchronous I/O to streams and cannot be used for file or pipe operations.

BSD Version 4.3 uses a combination of signals (`SIGIO`) to indicate an event on a file descriptor and select a function to determine the ready state of file descriptors. The file descriptors must be set in the `O_ASYNC` mode. This approach works only with terminals and network communication.

Looking Ahead

Chapter 15 completes our discussion of the Windows API by showing how to secure Windows objects. The emphasis is on securing files, but the same techniques are applied to other objects, such as named pipes and processes.

Exercises

14–1. Use asynchronous I/O to merge several sorted files into a larger sorted file.

14–2. Does the `FILE_FLAG_NO_BUFFERING` flag improve `atouOV` or `atouEX` performance, as suggested by the `CreateFile` documentation? Are there any restrictions on file size?

14–3. Modify `TimeBeep` (Program 14–3) so that it uses a manual-reset notification timer.

14–4. Modify the named pipe client in Program 11–2, `clientNP`, to use overlapped I/O so that the client can continue operation after sending the request. In this way, it can have several outstanding requests.

14–5. Rewrite the socket server, `serverSK` in Program 12–2, so that it uses I/O completion ports.

14–6. Rewrite either `serverSK` or `serverNP` so that the number of ready worker threads is limited by a semaphore. Experiment with a large thread pool to determine the effectiveness of this alternative. `serverSM` on the Web site is a modification of `serverNP`. As Win64 implementations and large physical memories become available, the trade-offs between this solution and completion ports may shift.

14–7. Use `JobShell` (Program 6–3, the job management program) to bring up a large number of clients and compare the responsiveness of `serverNP` and `serverCP`. Networked clients can provide additional load. Determine an optimal range for the number of active threads.

15 | Securing Windows Objects

Windows supports a comprehensive security model that prevents unauthorized access to objects such as files, processes, and file mappings. Nearly all shareable objects can be protected, and the programmer has a fine granularity of control over access rights.

Windows, as a single system, is certified at the National Security Agency Orange Book C2 level, which requires discretionary access control with the ability to allow or deny specific rights to an object based on the identity of the user attempting to access the object. Furthermore, Windows security is extended to the networked environment.

Security is a large subject that cannot be covered completely in a single chapter. Therefore, this chapter concentrates on the immediate problem of showing how to use the Windows security API to protect objects from unauthorized access. While access control is only a subset of Windows security functionality, it is of direct concern to anyone who needs to add security features to the programs in this book. The initial example, Program 15–1, shows how to emulate UNIX file permissions with NTFS files, and a second example applies security to named pipes. The same principles can then be used to secure other objects. The references list several resources you can consult for additional security information.

Only Windows NT systems can use these security features; they do not apply to the Windows 9x family.

Security Attributes

This chapter explores Windows access control by proceeding from the top down to show how an object's security is constructed. Following an overview, the Windows functions are described in detail before proceeding to the examples. In the case of files, it is also possible to use the Windows Explorer to examine and manage some security attributes of NTFS objects.

Nearly any object created with a `Create` system call has a security attributes parameter. Therefore, programs can secure files, processes, threads, events, semaphores, named pipes, and so on. The first step is to include a `SECURITY_ATTRIBUTES` structure in the `Create` call. Until now, our programs have always used a `NULL` pointer in `Create` calls or have used `SECURITY_ATTRIBUTES` simply to create inheritable handles (Chapter 6). In order to implement security, the important element in the `SECURITY_ATTRIBUTES` structure is `lpSecurityDescriptor`, the pointer to a *security descriptor*, which describes the object's owner and determines which users are allowed or denied various rights.

An individual process is identified by its *access token*, which specifies the owning user and group membership. When a process attempts to access an object, the Windows kernel can determine the process's identity using the token and can then decide from the information in the security descriptor whether or not the process has the required rights to access the object.

The `SECURITY_ATTRIBUTES` structure was introduced in Chapter 6; for review, here is the complete structure definition:

```
typedef struct _SECURITY_ATTRIBUTES {
   DWORD nLength;
   LPVOID lpSecurityDescriptor;
   BOOL bInheritHandle;
} SECURITY_ATTRIBUTES;
```

`nLength` should be set to `sizeof (SECURITY_ATTRIBUTES)`. `bInherit-Handle` indicates whether or not the handle is inheritable by other processes.

The next section describes the security descriptor components.

Security Overview: The Security Descriptor

Analyzing the security descriptor gives a good overview of essential Windows security elements. This section mentions the various elements and the names of the functions that manage them, starting with security descriptor structure.

A security descriptor is initialized with the function `InitializeSecurity-Descriptor`, and it contains the following:

- The owner security identifier (SID) (described in the next section, which deals with the object's owner)

- The group SID

- A discretionary access control list (DACL)—a list of entries explicitly granting and denying access rights. The term "ACL" without the "D" prefix will refer to DACLs in our discussion.

- A system ACL (SACL), sometimes called an audit access ACL

`SetSecurityDescriptorOwner` and `SetSecurityDescriptorGroup` associate SIDs with security descriptors, as described in the upcoming Security Identifiers section.

ACLs are initialized using the `InitializeAcl` function and are then associated with a security descriptor using `SetSecurityDescriptorDacl` or `SetSecurityDescriptorSacl`.

Security descriptors are classified as either *absolute* or *self-relative*. This distinction is ignored for now but is explained later in the chapter. Figure 15–1 shows the security descriptor and its components.

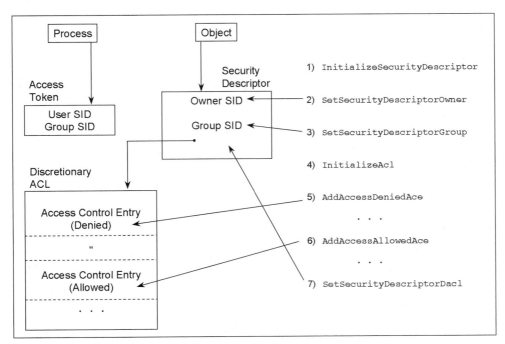

Figure 15-1 Constructing a Security Descriptor

Access Control Lists

Each ACL is a set (list) of access control entries (ACEs). There are two types of ACEs: one for access allowed and one for access denied.

You first initialize an ACL with `InitializeAcl` and then add ACEs. Each ACE contains a SID and an *access mask*, which specifies rights to be granted or denied to the user or group specified by the SID. `FILE_GENERIC_READ` and `DELETE` are typical access rights for files.

The two functions used to add ACEs to discretionary ACLs are `AddAccess-AllowedAce` and `AddAccessDeniedAce`. `AddAuditAccessAce` is for adding to an SACL, causing access by the specified SID to be audited.

Finally, you remove ACEs with `DeleteAce` and retrieve them with `GetAce`.

Using Windows Object Security

There are numerous details to be filled in, but Figure 15–1 shows the basic structure. Notice that each process also has SIDs (in an access token), which the kernel uses to determine whether access is allowed or is to be audited. The access token may also give the owner certain *privileges* (the inherent ability to perform operations that override the *rights* in the ACL). Thus, the administrator may have read and write privileges to all files without having specific rights in the file ACLs.

It is easy to see what happens when a process issues a call to access an object. First, the process has certain privileges by virtue of its user identity and its group membership. These privileges are encoded in the SIDs.

If the user and group IDs do not give access, the kernel scans the ACL for access rights. The first entry that specifically grants or denies the requested service is decisive. The order in which ACEs are entered into an ACL is, therefore, important. Frequently, access-denied ACEs come first so that a user who is specifically denied access will not gain access by virtue of membership in a group having such access. In Program 15–1, however, it is essential to mix allowed and denied ACEs to obtain the desired semantics. A denied ACE for all rights can be the last ACE to ensure that no one is allowed access unless specifically mentioned in an ACE.

Object Rights and Object Access

An object, such as a file, gets its rights when it is created, although the rights can be changed at a later time. A process requests access to the object when it asks for a handle using, for example, a call to `CreateFile`. The handle request contains the desired access, such as `FILE_GENERIC_READ`, in one of the parameters. If the process has the required rights to get the requested access, the request succeeds. Different handles to the same object may have different access. The values used for access flags are the same ones used to allow or deny rights when ACLs are created.

Standard UNIX (without C2 or other extensions) provides a simpler security model. It is limited to files and based on file permissions. The example programs in this chapter emulate the UNIX permissions.

Security Descriptor Initialization

The first step is to initialize the security descriptor using the `Initialize-SecurityDescriptor` function. The `pSecurityDescriptor` parameter should be set to the address of a valid `SECURITY_DESCRIPTOR` structure. These structures are opaque and are managed with specific functions.

`dwRevision` is set to the constant `SECURITY_DESCRIPTOR_REVISION`.

```
BOOL InitializeSecurityDescriptor (
    PSECURITY_DESCRIPTOR pSecurityDescriptor,
    DWORD dwRevision)
```

Security Descriptor Control Flags

Flags within the `Control` structure of the security descriptor, the `SECURITY_DESCRIPTOR_CONTROL` flags, control the meaning assigned to the security descriptor. Several of these flags are set or reset by the upcoming functions and will be mentioned as needed. `GetSecurityDescriptorControl` and `SetSecurityDescriptorControl` (available with NT5) access these flags, but the flags will not be used directly in the examples.

Security Identifiers

Windows uses SIDs to identify users and groups. The program can look up a SID from the account name, which can be a user, group, domain, and so on. The account can be on a remote system. The first step is to determine the SID from an account name.

```
BOOL LookupAccountName (
   LPCTSTR lpSystemName,
   LPCTSTR lpAccountName,
   PSID Sid,
   LPDWORD cbSid,
   LPTSTR ReferencedDomainName,
   LPDWORD cbReferencedDomainName,
   PSID_NAME_USE peUse)
```

Parameters

lpSystemName and lpAccountName point to the system and account names. Frequently, lpSystemName is NULL to indicate the local system.

Sid is the returned information, which is of size *cbSid. The function will fail, returning the required size, if the buffer is not large enough.

ReferencedDomainName is a string of length *cbReferencedDomainName characters. The length parameter should be initialized to the buffer size (the usual techniques are used to process failures). The return value shows the domain where the name is found. The account name Administrators will return BUILTIN, whereas a user account name will return that same user name.

peUse points to a SID_NAME_USE (enumerated type) variable and can be tested for values such as SidTypeWellKnownGroup, SidTypeUser, SidTypeGroup, and so on.

Getting the Account and User Names

Given a SID, you reverse the process and obtain the account name using LookupAccountSid. Specify the SID and get the name in return. The account name can be any name available to the process. Some names, such as Everyone, are well known.

```
BOOL LookupAccountSid (
   LPCTSTR lpSystemName,
   PSID Sid,
   LPTSTR lpAccountName,
   LPDWORD cbName,
   LPTSTR ReferencedDomainName,
   LPDWORD cbReferencedDomainName,
   PSID_NAME_USE peUse)
```

Obtain the process's user account name (the logged-in user) with the `GetUserName` function.

```
BOOL GetUserName (
    LPTSTR lpBuffer,
    LPDWORD nSize)
```

The user name and length are returned in the conventional manner.

It is possible to create and manage SIDs using functions such as `InitializeSid` and `AllocateAndInitializeSid`. The examples confine themselves, however, to SIDs obtained from account names.

Once SIDs are known, they can be entered into an initialized security descriptor.

```
BOOL SetSecurityDescriptorOwner (
    PSECURITY_DESCRIPTOR pSecurityDescriptor,
    PSID pOwner,
    BOOL bOwnerDefaulted)
```

```
BOOL SetSecurityDescriptorGroup (
    PSECURITY_DESCRIPTOR pSecurityDescriptor,
    PSID pGroup,
    BOOL bGroupDefaulted)
```

`pSecurityDescriptor` points to the appropriate security descriptor, and `pOwner` (or `pGroup`) is the address of the owner's (group's) SID. `bOwnerDefaulted` (or `bGroupDefaulted`) indicates, if `TRUE`, that a default mechanism is used to derive the owner (or primary group) information. The `SE_OWNER_DEFAULTED` and `SE_GROUP_DEFAULTED` flags within the `SECURITY_DESCRIPTOR_CONTROL` structure are set according to these two parameters.

The similar functions `GetSecurityDescriptorOwner` and `GetSecurity-DescriptorGroup` return the SID (either owner or group) from a security descriptor.

Managing ACLs

This section shows how to manage ACLs, how to associate an ACL with a security descriptor, and how to add ACEs. Figure 15–1 shows the relationships between these objects and functions.

The first step is to initialize an ACL structure. The ACL should not be accessed directly, so its internal structure is not relevant. The program must, however, provide a buffer to serve as the ACL; the functions manage the contents.

```
BOOL InitializeAcl (
    PACL pAcl,
    DWORD cbAcl,
    DWORD dwAclRevision)
```

pAcl is the address of a programmer-supplied buffer of cbAcl bytes. Subsequent discussion and Program 15–4 will show how to determine the ACL size, but 1KB is more than adequate for most purposes. dwAclRevision should be ACL_REVISION.

Next, add the ACEs in the order desired with the AddAccessAllowedAce and AddAccessDeniedAce functions.

```
BOOL AddAccessAllowedAce (
    PACL pAcl,
    DWORD dwAclRevision
    DWORD dwAccessMask,
    PSID pSid)

BOOL AddAccessDeniedAce (
    PACL pAcl,
    DWORD dwAclRevision,
    DWORD dwAccessMask,
    PSID pSid)
```

pAcl points to the same ACL structure initialized with InitializeAcl, and dwAclRevision is ACL_REVISION again. pSid points to a SID, such as one that would be obtained from LookupAccountName.

The access mask (`dwAccessMask`) determines the rights to be granted or denied to the user or group specified by the SID. The predefined mask values will vary by the object type.

The final step is to associate an ACL with the security descriptor. In the case of the discretionary ACL, use the `SetSecurityDescriptorDacl` function.

```
BOOL SetSecurityDescriptorDacl (
    PSECURITY_DESCRIPTOR pSecurityDescriptor,
    BOOL bDaclPresent,
    PACL pAcl,
    BOOL fDaclDefaulted)
```

`bDaclPresent`, if `TRUE`, indicates that there is an ACL in the `pAcl` structure. If `FALSE`, `pAcl` and `fDaclDefaulted`, the next two parameters, are ignored. The `SECURITY_DESCRIPTOR_CONTROL`'s `SE_DACL_PRESENT` flag is also set to this parameter's value.

The final flag, `fDaclDefaulted`, if `FALSE`, indicates an ACL generated by the programmer. Otherwise, it was obtained by a default mechanism, such as inheritance; `bDaclPresent` should be `TRUE`, however, to indicate that there is an ACL. The `SE_DACL_DEFAULTED` flag in the `SECURITY_DESCRIPTOR_CONTROL` is set to this parameter value.

Other functions delete ACEs and read ACEs from an ACL; we will discuss them later in this chapter. It is now time for an example.

Example: UNIX-Style Permission for NTFS Files

UNIX file permissions provide a convenient way to illustrate Windows security, even though this security is much more general than standard UNIX security. The implementation creates nine ACEs to grant or deny read, write, and execute permissions to the owner, group, and everyone. There are two commands.

1. `chmodW` is modeled after the UNIX `chmod` command. The implementation has been enhanced to create the specified file if it does not already exist and to allow the user to specify the group name.

2. `lsFP` is an extension of the `lsW` command (Program 3–2). When the long listing is requested, the owning user and an interpretation of the existing ACLs, which may have been set by `chmodW`, are displayed.

These two commands are shown in Programs 15–1 and 15–2. Three supporting functions are shown in Programs 15–3, 15–4, and 15–5. These functions are as follows.

1. `InitializeUnixSA`, which creates a valid security attributes structure corresponding to a set of UNIX permissions. This function is general enough that it can be used with objects other than files, such as processes (Chapter 6), named pipes (Chapter 11), and synchronization objects (Chapter 8).

2. `ReadFilePermissions`.

3. `ChangeFilePermissions`.

Note: The programs that follow are simplifications of the programs provided on the book's Web site. The full programs use separate `AllowedAceMasks` and `DeniedAceMasks` arrays, whereas the listings here use just one array. The separate `DeniedAceMasks` array assures that `SYNCHRONIZE` rights are never denied because the `SYNCHRONIZE` flag is set in all three of the macros, `FILE_GENERIC_READ`, `FILE_GENERIC_WRITE`, and `FILE_GENERIC_EXECUTE`, which are combinations of several flags (see the include file, `WINNT.H`). The full program on the Web site provides additional explanation. The full program also checks to see if there is a group name on the command line; here, the name is assumed.

Program 15–1 `chmodW`: Change File Permissions

```
/* Chapter 15. chmodW command. */
/* chmodW [options] mode file [GroupName].
   Update access rights of the named file.
   Options:
       -f Force -- do not complain if unable to change.
       -c Create the file if it does not exist.
          The optional group name is after the file name. */
/* Requires NTFS and Windows NT (won't work under 9x) */

#include "EvryThng.h"

int _tmain (int argc, LPTSTR argv [])
{
    HANDLE hFile, hSecHeap;
    BOOL Force, CreateNew, Change, Exists;
    DWORD Mode, DecMode, UsrCnt = ACCT_NAME_SIZE;
    TCHAR UsrNam [ACCT_NAME_SIZE];
    int FileIndex, GrpIndex, ModeIndex;

    /* Array of file access rights settings in "UNIX order". */
    /* These rights will be different for different object types. */
```

```
/* NOTE: The full program on the Web site uses separate */
/* allowed and denied mask arrays. */
DWORD AceMasks [] =
        {FILE_GENERIC_READ, FILE_GENERIC_WRITE,
            FILE_GENERIC_EXECUTE};
LPSECURITY_ATTRIBUTES pSa = NULL;
ModeIndex = Options (argc, argv, _T ("fc"),
        &Force, &CreateNew, NULL);
GrpIndex = ModeIndex + 2;
FileIndex = ModeIndex + 1;
DecMode = _ttoi (argv [ModeIndex]);

/* The security mode is in octal (base 8). */
Mode = ((DecMode / 100) % 10) * 64    /* Decimal conversion. */
        + ((DecMode / 10) % 10) * 8 + (DecMode % 10);
Exists = (_taccess (argv [FileIndex], 0) == 0);
if (!Exists && CreateNew) {
    /* File does not exist; create a new one. */
    GetUserName (UsrNam, &UsrCnt);
    pSa = InitializeUnixSA (Mode, UsrNam, argv [GrpIndex],
        AceMasks, &hSecHeap);
    hFile = CreateFile (argv [FileIndex], 0, 0, pSa,
        CREATE_ALWAYS, FILE_ATTRIBUTE_NORMAL, NULL);
    CloseHandle (hFile);
    HeapDestroy (hSecHeap); /* Release security structures. */
}
else if (Exists)
{   /* File does exist; change permissions. */
    Change = ChangeFilePermissions (Mode, argv [FileIndex],
        AceMasks);
}
return 0;
}
```

Program 15–2 shows the relevant part of lsFP—namely, the ProcessItem function.

Program 15–2   lsFP: List File Permissions

```
static BOOL ProcessItem (LPWIN32_FIND_DATA pFileData,
      DWORD NumFlags, LPBOOL Flags)

/* List attributes, with file permissions and owner. */
/* Requires NTFS and Windows NT (won't work under 9x). */
{
    DWORD FType = FileType (pFileData), Mode, i;
    BOOL Long = Flags [1];
    TCHAR GrpNam [ACCT_NAME_SIZE], UsrNam [ACCT_NAME_SIZE];
```

```
    SYSTEMTIME LastWrite;
    TCHAR PermString [] = _T ("---------");
    const TCHAR RWX [] = {'r','w','x'}, FileTypeChar [] = {' ','d'};

    if (FType != TYPE_FILE && FType != TYPE_DIR)
        return FALSE;
    _tprintf (_T ("\n"));

    if (Long) {
        Mode = ReadFilePermissions (pFileData->cFileName,
                UsrNam, GrpNam);
        if (Mode == 0xFFFFFFFF) Mode = 0;
        for (i = 0; i < 9; i++) {
            if (Mode >> (8 - i) & 0x1)
                PermString [i] = RWX [i % 3];
        }

        _tprintf (_T ("%c%s %8.7s %8.7s%10d"),
                FileTypeChar [FType - 1], PermString, UsrNam, GrpNam,
                pFileData->nFileSizeLow);

        FileTimeToSystemTime (&(pFileData->ftLastWriteTime),
                &LastWrite);

        _tprintf (_T (" %02d/%02d/%04d %02d:%02d:%02d"),
                LastWrite.wMonth, LastWrite.wDay,
                LastWrite.wYear, LastWrite.wHour,
                LastWrite.wMinute, LastWrite.wSecond);
    }
    _tprintf (_T (" %s"), pFileData->cFileName);
    return TRUE;
}
```

The next step is to show the implementation of the supporting functions.

Example: Initializing Security Attributes

Program 15–3 shows the utility function `InitializeUnixSA`. It creates a security attributes structure that contains an ACL with ACEs that emulate UNIX file permissions. There are nine ACEs granting or denying read, write, and execute permissions for the owner, the group, and everyone else. The actual array of three rights (read, write, and execute for files) can vary according to the object type being secured. This structure is not a local variable in the function but must be allocated and initialized and then returned to the calling program; notice `AceMasks` array in Program 15–1.

Program 15–3   `InitUnFp`: Initializing Security Attributes

```
/* Set UNIX-style permissions as ACEs in a
   SECURITY_ATTRIBUTES structure. */

#include "EvryThng.h"

#define ACL_SIZE 1024
#define INIT_EXCEPTION 0x3
#define CHANGE_EXCEPTION 0x4
#define SID_SIZE LUSIZE
#define DOM_SIZE LUSIZE

LPSECURITY_ATTRIBUTES InitializeUnixSA (DWORD UnixPerms,
      LPCTSTR UsrNam, LPCTSTR GrpNam, LPDWORD AceMasks,
      LPHANDLE pHeap)
{
   HANDLE SAHeap = HeapCreate (HEAP_GENERATE_EXCEPTIONS, 0, 0);
   LPSECURITY_ATTRIBUTES pSA = NULL;
   PSECURITY_DESCRIPTOR pSD = NULL;
   PACL pAcl = NULL;
   BOOL Success;
   DWORD iBit, iSid, UsrCnt = ACCT_NAME_SIZE;

   /* Tables of User, Group, and Everyone Names, SIDs,
      etc. for LookupAccountName and SID creation. */

   LPCTSTR pGrpNms [3] = {EMPTY, EMPTY, _T ("Everyone")};
   PSID pSidTable [3] = {NULL, NULL, NULL};
   SID_NAME_USE sNamUse [3] =
      {SidTypeUser, SidTypeGroup, SidTypeWellKnownGroup};
   TCHAR RefDomain [3] [DOM_SIZE];
   DWORD RefDomCnt [3] = {DOM_SIZE, DOM_SIZE, DOM_SIZE};
   DWORD SidCnt [3] = {SID_SIZE, SID_SIZE, SID_SIZE};

__try { /* Try-except block for memory allocation failures. */
   *pHeap = SAHeap;
   pSA = HeapAlloc (SAHeap, 0, sizeof (SECURITY_ATTRIBUTES));
   pSA->nLength = sizeof (SECURITY_ATTRIBUTES);
   pSA->bInheritHandle = FALSE;
               /* Programmer can set this later. */
   pSD = HeapAlloc (SAHeap, 0, sizeof (SECURITY_DESCRIPTOR));
   pSA->lpSecurityDescriptor = pSD;
   InitializeSecurityDescriptor (pSD,
         SECURITY_DESCRIPTOR_REVISION);

   /* Get a SID for User, Group, and Everyone.
    * See the Web site for additional important details. */
```

```
    pGrpNms [0] = UsrNam; pGrpNms [1] = GrpNam;
    for (iSid = 0; iSid < 3; iSid++) {
        pSidTable [iSid] = HeapAlloc (SAHeap, 0, SID_SIZE);
        LookupAccountName (NULL, pGrpNms [iSid],
                pSidTable [iSid], &SidCnt [iSid],
                RefDomain [iSid], &RefDomCnt [iSid],
                &sNamUse [iSid]);
    }
    SetSecurityDescriptorOwner (pSD, pSidTable [0], FALSE);
    SetSecurityDescriptorGroup (pSD, pSidTable [1], FALSE);
    pAcl = HeapAlloc (ProcHeap, HEAP_GENERATE_EXCEPTIONS, ACL_SIZE);
    InitializeAcl (pAcl, ACL_SIZE, ACL_REVISION);

    /* Add all the access allowed/denied ACEs. */
    for (iBit = 0; iBit < 9; iBit++) {
        if ((UnixPerms >> (8 - iBit) & 0x1) != 0 &&
                AceMasks[iBit%3] != 0)
            AddAccessAllowedAce (pAcl, ACL_REVISION,
                    AceMasks [iBit%3], pSidTable [iBit/3]);
        else if (AceMasks[iBit%3] != 0)
            AddAccessDeniedAce (pAcl, ACL_REVISION,
                    AceMasks [iBit%3], pSidTable [iBit/3]);
    }
    /* Add a final deny all to Everyone ACE. */
    Success = Success && AddAccessDeniedAce (pAcl, ACL_REVISION,
            STANDARD_RIGHTS_ALL | SPECIFIC_RIGHTS_ALL, pSidTable [2]);
    /* Associate ACL with the security descriptor. */
    SetSecurityDescriptorDacl (pSD, TRUE, pAcl, FALSE);
    return pSA;
}   /* End of try-except block. */

__except (EXCEPTION_EXECUTE_HANDLER) { /* Free all resources. */
    if (SAHeap != NULL)
        HeapDestroy (SAHeap);
    pSA = NULL;
}
    return pSA;
}
```

Comments on Program 15–3

Program 15–3 may have a straightforward structure, but its operation is hardly simple. Furthermore, it illustrates a number of points about Windows security that should be reviewed.

- Several memory allocations are required to hold information such as the SIDs. They are created in a dedicated heap, which is eventually destroyed by the calling program.

- The security attribute structure in this example is for files, but it is also used with other objects such as named pipes (Chapter 11). Program 15–4 shows how to integrate the security attributes with a file.

- To emulate UNIX behavior, the order of ACE entry is critical. Notice that access-denied and access-allowed ACEs are added to the ACL as the permission bits are processed from left (Owner/Read) to right (Everyone/Execute). In this way, permission bits of, say, 460 (in octal) will deny write access to the user even though the user may be in the group.

- The ACEs' rights are access values, such as FILE_GENERIC_READ and FILE_GENERIC_WRITE, which are similar to the flags used with Create-File, although other access flags, such as SYNCHRONIZE, are added. The rights are specified in the calling program (Program 15–1 in this case) so that the rights can be appropriate for the object.

- The defined constant ACL_SIZE is large enough to contain the nine ACEs. After Program 15–5, it will be apparent how to determine the required size.

- The function uses three SIDs: one each for User, Group, and Everyone. Three different techniques are employed to get the name to use as an argument to LookupAccountName. The user name comes from GetUserName. The name for everyone is Everyone in a SidTypeWellKnownGroup. The group name must be supplied as a command line argument and is looked up as a Sid-TypeGroup. Finding the groups that a user belongs to requires some knowledge of process handles, and solving this problem is Exercise 15–12.

- The version of the program on the book's Web site, but not the one shown here, is fastidious about error checking. It even goes to the effort to validate the generated structures using the self-explanatory IsValidSecurityDescriptor, IsValidSid, and IsValidAcl functions. This error testing proved to be extremely helpful during debugging.

Reading and Changing Security Descriptors

Now that a security descriptor is associated with a file, the next step is to determine the security of an existing file and, in turn, change it. The following functions get and set file security in terms of security descriptors.

```
BOOL GetFileSecurity (
   LPCTSTR lpFileName,
   SECURITY_INFORMATION secInfo,
   PSECURITY_DESCRIPTOR pSecurityDescriptor,
   DWORD cbSd,
   LPDWORD lpcbLengthNeeded)

BOOL SetFileSecurity (
   LPCTSTR lpFileName,
   SECURITY_INFORMATION secInfo,
   PSECURITY_DESCRIPTOR pSecurityDescriptor)
```

secInfo is an enumerated type that takes on values such as OWNER_SECURITY_INFORMATION, GROUP_SECURITY_INFORMATION, DACL_SECURITY_INFORMATION, and SACL_SECURITY_INFORMATION to indicate what part of the security descriptor to get or set. These values can be combined with the bit-wise "or" operator.

To figure out the size of the return buffer for GetFileSecurity, the best strategy is to call the function twice. The first call simply uses 0 as the cbSd value. After allocating a buffer, call the function a second time. Program 15–4 operates this way.

Needless to say, the correct file permissions are required in order to carry out these operations. For example, it is necessary to have WRITE_DAC permission or to be the object's owner to succeed with SetFileSecurity.

The functions GetSecurityDescriptorOwner and GetSecurity-DescriptorGroup can extract the SIDs from the security descriptor obtained with GetFileSecurity. Obtain the ACL with the GetSecurityDescriptor-Dacl function.

```
BOOL GetSecurityDescriptorDacl (
   PSECURITY_DESCRIPTOR pSecurityDescriptor,
   LPBOOL lpbDaclPresent,
   PACL *pAcl,
   LPBOOL lpbDaclDefaulted)
```

The parameters are nearly identical to those of SetSecurityDescriptor-Dacl except that the flags are returned to indicate whether a discretionary ACL is actually present and was set as a default or by a user.

To interpret an ACL, it is necessary to find out how many ACEs it contains.

```
BOOL GetAclInformation (
    PACL pAcl,
    LPVOID pAclInformation,
    DWORD cbAclInfo,
    ACL_INFORMATION_CLASS dwAclInfoClass)
```

In most cases, the ACL information class, dwAclInfoClass, is AclSize-Information, and the pAclInformation parameter is a structure of type ACL_SIZE_INFORMATION. AclRevisionInformation is the other value for the class.

An ACL_SIZE_INFORMATION structure has three members: the most important one is AceCount, which shows how many entries are in the list. To determine whether the ACL is large enough, look at the AclBytesInUse and AclBytes-Free members of the ACL_SIZE_INFORMATION structure.

The GetAce function retrieves ACEs by index.

```
BOOL GetAce (
    PACL pAcl,
    DWORD dwAceIndex,
    LPVOID *pAce)
```

Obtain the ACEs (the total number is now known) by using an index. pAce points to an ACE structure, which has a member called Header, which, in turn, has an AceType member. The type can be tested for ACCESS_ALLOWED_ACE and ACCESS_DENIED_ACE.

Example: Reading File Permissions

Program 15–4 is the function ReadFilePermissions, which is used by Programs 15–1 and 15–2. This program methodically uses the preceding functions to extract the information. Its correct operation depends on the fact that the ACL was created by Program 15–3. The function is in the same source module as Program 15–3, so the definitions are not repeated.

Program 15–4   ReadFilePermissions: Reading Security Attributes

```
DWORD ReadFilePermissions (LPCTSTR lpFileName,
      LPTSTR UsrNm, LPTSTR GrpNm)
   /* Return the UNIX-style permissions for a file. */
{
   PSECURITY_DESCRIPTOR pSD = NULL;
   DWORD LenNeeded, PBits, iAce;
   BOOL DaclF, AclDefF, OwnerDefF, GroupDefF;
   BYTE DAcl [ACL_SIZE];
   PACL pAcl = (PACL) &DAcl;
   ACL_SIZE_INFORMATION ASizeInfo;
   PACCESS_ALLOWED_ACE pAce;
   BYTE AType;
   HANDLE ProcHeap = GetProcessHeap ();
   PSID pOwnerSid, pGroupSid;
   TCHAR RefDomain [2] [DOM_SIZE];
   DWORD RefDomCnt [] = {DOM_SIZE, DOM_SIZE};
   DWORD AcctSize [] = {ACCT_NAME_SIZE, ACCT_NAME_SIZE};
   SID_NAME_USE sNamUse [] = {SidTypeUser, SidTypeGroup};

   /* Get the required size for the security descriptor. */
   GetFileSecurity (lpFileName,
      OWNER_SECURITY_INFORMATION | GROUP_SECURITY_INFORMATION |
      DACL_SECURITY_INFORMATION, pSD, 0, &LenNeeded);
   pSD = HeapAlloc (ProcHeap, HEAP_GENERATE_EXCEPTIONS, LenNeeded);
   GetFileSecurity (lpFileName, OWNER_SECURITY_INFORMATION |
         GROUP_SECURITY_INFORMATION | DACL_SECURITY_INFORMATION,
         pSD, LenNeeded, &LenNeeded);
   GetSecurityDescriptorDacl (pSD, &DaclF, &pAcl, &AclDefF);
   GetAclInformation (pAcl, &ASizeInfo,
      sizeof (ACL_SIZE_INFORMATION), AclSizeInformation);
   PBits = 0; /* Compute the permissions from the ACL. */
   for (iAce = 0; iAce < ASizeInfo.AceCount; iAce++) {
      GetAce (pAcl, iAce, &pAce);
      AType = pAce->Header.AceType;
      if (AType == ACCESS_ALLOWED_ACE_TYPE)
         PBits |= (0x1 << (8-iAce));
   }
   /* Find the name of the owner and owning group. */
   GetSecurityDescriptorOwner (pSD, &pOwnerSid, &OwnerDefF);
   GetSecurityDescriptorGroup (pSD, &pGroupSid, &GroupDefF);
   LookupAccountSid (NULL, pOwnerSid, UsrNm, &AcctSize [0],
         RefDomain [0], &RefDomCnt [0], &sNamUse [0]);
   LookupAccountSid (NULL, pGroupSid, GrpNm, &AcctSize [1],
         RefDomain [1], &RefDomCnt [1], &sNamUse [1]);
   return PBits;
}
```

Example: Changing File Permissions

Program 15–5 completes the collection of file security functions. This function, `ChangeFilePermissions`, replaces the existing security descriptor with a new one, preserving the user and group SIDs but creating a new discretionary ACL.

Program 15–5 `ChangeFilePermissions`: Changing Security Attributes

```
BOOL ChangeFilePermissions (DWORD fPm, LPCTSTR FNm, LPDWORD AceMsk)

/* Change permissions in existing file. Group is left unchanged. */
{
    TCHAR UsrNm [ACCT_NAME_SIZE], GrpNm [ACCT_NAME_SIZE];
    LPSECURITY_ATTRIBUTES pSA;
    PSECURITY_DESCRIPTOR pSD = NULL;
    HANDLE hSecHeap;

    if (_taccess (FNm, 0) != 0) return FALSE;
    ReadFilePermissions (FNm, UsrNm, GrpNm);
    pSA = InitializeUnixSA (fPm, UsrNm, GrpNm, AceMsk, &hSecHeap);
    pSD = pSA->lpSecurityDescriptor;
    SetFileSecurity (FileName, DACL_SECURITY_INFORMATION, pSD);
    HeapDestroy (hSecHeap);
    return TRUE;
}
```

Comments on the File Permissions

When you're running these programs, it is interesting to monitor the file system using the Windows Explorer. This utility cannot interpret the access-denied ACEs and will not be able to display the permissions. The Windows NT 4.0 Explorer will generate an exception on encountering an access-denied ACE.

Using the access-denied ACEs is necessary, however, to emulate the UNIX semantics. If they are omitted, the Windows Explorer can view the permissions. A collection of permissions set with, for example, 0446 would then allow the user and group members to write to the file because Everyone can write to the file. UNIX, however, does not act this way; it prevents the user and group members from writing to the file.

Also observe what happens when you try to create a secured file on a diskette or other FAT file system and when you run the program under Windows 9x.

Securing Kernel and Communication Objects

The preceding sections were concerned mostly with file security, and the same techniques apply to other filelike objects, such as named pipes (Chapter 11), and to kernel objects. Program 15–6, the next example, deals with named pipes, which can be treated in much the same way as files were treated.

Securing Named Pipes

While the code is omitted in the listing of Program 11–3, the server (whose full code appears on the book's Web site) optionally secures its named pipe to prevent access by unauthorized clients. Optional command line parameters specify the user and group name.

```
Server [UserName GroupName]
```

If the user and group names are omitted, default security is used. Note that the full version of Program 11–3 (on the Web site) and Program 15–6 use techniques from Program 15–3 to create the optional security attributes. However, rather than calling InitUnixSA, we now use a simpler function, InitializeAccess-OnlySA, which only creates access allowed ACEs and puts a final access denied ACE at the end of the ACL. Program 15–6 shows the relevant code sections that were not shown in Program 11–3. The important security rights for named pipes are as follows:

- FILE_GENERIC_READ
- FILE_GENERIC_WRITE
- SYNCHRONIZE (allowing a thread to wait on the pipe)

Alternatively, simply use STANDARD_RIGHTS_REQUIRED, where all rights are required if the client is to connect. You also need to mask in 0x1FF to obtain full access (duplex, inbound, outbound, and so on). The server in Program 15–6 optionally secures its named pipe instances using these rights. Only clients executed by the owner have access, although it would be straightforward to allow group members to access the pipe as well.

Program 15–6 ServerNP: Securing a Named Pipe

```
/* Chapter 15. ServerNP. With named pipe security.
 * Multithreaded command line server. Named pipe version.
 * Usage: Server [UserName GroupName]. */
 . . .
_tmain (int argc, LPTSTR argv [])
{
    . . .
    HANDLE hNp, hMonitor, hSrvrThread [MAX_CLIENTS];
    DWORD iNp, MonitorId, ThreadId;
    DWORD AceMasks [] = /* Named pipe access rights */
            {STANDARD_RIGHTS_REQUIRED | SYNCHRONIZE | 0X1FF, 0, 0 };

    LPSECURITY_ATTRIBUTES pNPSA = NULL;
    . . .
    if (argc == 4)        /* Optional pipe security. */
        pNPSA = InitializeAccessOnlySA (0440, argv [1], argv [2],
            AceMasks, &hSecHeap);
    . . .
    /* Create a pipe instance for every server thread. */
    . . .
    for (iNp = 0; iNp < MAX_CLIENTS; iNp++) {
        hNp = CreateNamedPipe (SERVER_PIPE, PIPE_ACCESS_DUPLEX,
                PIPE_READMODE_MESSAGE | PIPE_TYPE_MESSAGE | PIPE_WAIT,
                MAX_CLIENTS, 0, 0, INFINITE, pNPSA);

        if (hNp == INVALID_HANDLE_VALUE)
            ReportError (_T ("Failure to open named pipe."), 1, TRUE);
    . . .
}
```

Kernel and Private Object Security

Many objects, such as processes, threads, and mutexes, are *kernel objects*. To get and set kernel security descriptors, use GetKernelObjectSecurity and SetKernelObjectSecurity, which are similar to the file security functions described in this chapter. However, you need to know the access rights appropriate to an object; the next subsection shows how to find the rights.

It is also possible to associate security descriptors with private, programmer-generated objects, such as Windows Sockets or a proprietary database. The appropriate functions are GetPrivateObjectSecurity and SetPrivateObjectSecurity. The programmer must take responsibility for enforcing access and must exchange security descriptors with CreatePrivateObjectSecurity and DestroyPrivateObjectSecurity.

ACE Mask Values

The "user, group, everyone" model that InitUnixSA implements will be adequate in many cases, although different models can be implemented using the same basic techniques.

It is necessary, however, to determine the actual ACE mask values appropriate for a particular kernel object. The values are not always well documented, but they can be found in several ways.

- Read the documentation for the open call for the object in question. The access flags are the same as the flags used in the ACE mask. For example, Open-Mutex uses MUTEX_ALL_ACCESS and SYNCHRONIZE (the second flag is required for any object that can be used with WaitForSingleObject or WaitForMultipleObjects). Other objects, such as processes, have many additional access flags.

- The "create" documentation may also supply useful information.

- Inspect the header files WINNT.H and WINBASE.H for flags that apply to the object.

Example: Securing a Process and Its Threads

The OpenProcess documentation shows a fine-grained collection of access rights, which is appropriate considering the various functions that can be performed on a process handle. For example, PROCESS_TERMINATE access is required on a process handle in order for a process (actually, a thread within that process) to terminate the process that the handle represents. PROCESS_QUERY_INFORMATION access is required in order to perform GetExitCodeProcess or GetPriority-Class on a process handle. PROCESS_ALL_ACCESS permits all access, and SYNCHRONIZE access is required to perform a wait function.

In order to illustrate these concepts, JobShellSecure.c upgrades Chapter 6's JobShell job management program so that only the owner (or administrator) can access the managed processes. The program is on the book's Web site.

Overview of Additional Security Features

There is much more to Windows security, but this chapter is an introduction, showing how to secure Windows objects using the security API. The following sections give a brief overview of additional security subjects that some readers will want to explore.

Removing ACEs

The `DeleteAce` function deletes an ACE specified by an index, in a manner similar to that used with `GetAce`.

Absolute and Self-Relative Security Descriptors

Program 15–5, which changed ACLs, had the benefit of simply replacing one security descriptor (SD) with another. To change an existing SD, however, some care is required because of the distinction between absolute and self-relative SDs. The internal details of these data structures are not important for our purposes, but it is necessary to understand why there are two distinct SD types and how to convert between them.

- During construction, an SD is absolute, with pointers to various structures in memory. In fact, `InitializeSecurityDescriptor` creates an absolute SD.

- When the SD is associated with a permanent object, such as the file, the OS consolidates the SD into a compact, self-relative structure. However, changing an SD (changing an ACL, for example) causes difficulties in managing space within the absolute SD structure.

- It is possible to convert between the two forms using Windows functions for that purpose. Use `MakeAbsoluteSD` to convert a self-relative SD, such as the one returned by `GetFileSecurity`. Modify the SD in self-relative form and then use `MakeSelfRelativeSD` to convert it back. `MakeAbsoluteSD` is one of the more formidable Windows functions, having eleven parameters: two for each of the four SD components, one each for the input and output SDs, and one for the length of the resulting absolute SD.

System ACLs

A complete class of functions is available for managing system ACLs; only system administrators can use it. System ACLs specify which object accesses should be logged. The principal function is `AddAuditAccessAce`, which is similar to `AddAccessAllowedAce`. There is no concept of access denied with system ACLs.

Two other system ACL functions are `GetSecurityDescriptorSacl` and `SetSecurityDescriptorSacl`. These functions are comparable to their discretionary ACL counterparts, `GetSecurityDescriptorDacl` and `SetSecurityDescriptorDacl`.

Access Token Information

Program 15–1 did not solve the problem of obtaining the groups associated with a process in its access token. Program 15–1 simply required the user to specify the group name. You use the `GetTokenInformation` function for this; a process handle, covered in Chapter 6, is required. Exercise 15–12 addresses this, providing a hint toward the solution. The solution code is also included on the book's Web site.

Access tokens also contain security privileges so that a process will gain certain access by virtue of its identity rather than by the rights associated with the object. For example, an administrator requires access that will override those specifically granted by an object. Note, again, the distinction between a right and a privilege.

SID Management

The examples obtained SIDs from user and group names, but you can also create new SIDs with the `AllocateAndInitializeSid` function. Other functions obtain SID information, and you can even copy (`CopySid`) and compare (`CompareSid`) SIDs.

Secure Sockets Layer (SSL)

Windows Sockets (Winsock), described in Chapter 12, provides networked communication between systems. Winsock conforms to industry standards, so it is also possible to communicate with non-Windows systems. SSL, an extension, layers a security protocol on top of the underlying transport protocol, providing message authentication, encryption, and decryption.

Summary

Windows implements an extensive security model that goes beyond the one offered by standard UNIX. All objects, and not just files, can be secured. The example programs have shown how to emulate the UNIX permissions and ownership that are set with the `umask`, `chmod`, and `chown` functions. Programs can also set the owner (group and user). The emulation is not easy, but the functionality is much more powerful. The complexity reflects the Orange Book C2-level requirements, which specify the access control lists and object owners with access tokens.

Looking Ahead

This chapter completes our presentation of the Windows API. The next chapter discusses Win64, the 64-bit extension to the Win32 API, and shows how to assure that programs will build and run properly in both 32-bit and 64-bit mode.

Additional Reading

Windows

Microsoft Windows Security Inside Out for Windows XP and Windows 2000, by Ed Bott and Carl Siechert, discusses Windows security administration and security policies. *Programming Server-Side Applications for Microsoft Windows 2000*, by Jeffrey Richter and Jason Clark, also describes security in depth.

Windows NT Design and Architecture

Inside Windows 2000, by David Solomon and Mark Russinovich, describes details of Windows security internal implementation.

Orange Book Security

The U.S. Department of Defense publication *DoD Trusted Computer System Evaluation Criteria* specifies the C2 and other security levels. Windows is C2 certified.

Exercises

15–1. Extend Program 15–1 so that multiple groups have their own unique permissions. The group name and permission pairs can be separate arguments to the function.

15–2. Extend Program 15–4 so that it can report on all the groups that have ACEs in the object's security descriptor.

15–3. Confirm that chmodW has the desired effect of limiting file access.

15–4. Investigate the default security attributes you get with a file.

15–5. What are some of the other access masks you can use with an ACE? The Microsoft documentation supplies some information.

15–6. Enhance both chmodW and lsFP so that they produce an error message if asked to deal with a file on a non-NTFS file system. GetVolume-Information is required.

15–7. Enhance the `chmodW` command so that there is an `-o` option to set the owning user to be the user of the `chmodW` program.

15–8. Determine the actual size of the ACL buffer required by Program 15–3 to store the ACEs. Program 15–3 uses 1,024 bytes. Can you determine a formula for estimating the required ACL size?

15–9. The Cygwin Web site (http://www.cygwin.com) provides an excellent open source Linux-like environment on Windows with a shell and implementations of commands including `chmod` and `ls`. Install this environment and compare the implementations of these two commands with the ones developed here. For example, if you set file permissions using the Cygwin command, does `lsFP` properly show the permissions, and conversely? Compare the Cygwin source code with this chapter's examples to contrast the two approaches to using Windows security.

15–10. The compatibility library contains functions `_open` and `_unmask`, which manage file permissions. Investigate their emulation of UNIX file permissions and compare it with the solutions in this chapter.

15–11. Write a command, `whoami`, that will display your logged-in user name.

15–12. Program 15–3, which created a security descriptor, required the programmer to supply the group name. Modify the program so that it creates permissions for all the user's groups. *Hint*: It is necessary to use the `OpenProcessToken` function, which returns an array with the group names, although you will need to experiment to find out how group names are stored in the array. The source program on the book's Web site contains a partial solution.

15–13. Note in the client/server system that the clients can access exactly the same files and other objects that are available to the server on the server's machine with the server's access rights. Remove this limitation by implementing *security delegation* using the functions `ImpersonateNamed-PipeClient` and `RevertToSelf`. Clients that are not in the group used to secure the pipe cannot connect to the server.

15–14. There are several additional Windows functions that you may find useful and that could be applied to simplify or improve this chapter's examples. Look up the following functions: `AreAllAccessesGranted`, `AreAny-AccessesGranted`, `AccessCheck`, and `MapGenericMask`. Can you use these functions to simplify or improve the examples?

CHAPTER

16 | Win64 Programming

The most significant advance in Windows capability since the introduction of Windows NT and 95 is the advent of 64-bit programming and the extension of Win32 to Win64. The combined API is generally referred to simply as the Windows API, and this has been the practice throughout the book. The Win64 API allows Windows to run the largest and most demanding enterprise and scientific applications. These 64-bit systems allow programs to use huge address spaces, larger than the 4GB limit imposed by 32-bit addresses.

This chapter describes Win64 status and benefits, the programming model, and portability and migration issues. These considerations apply regardless of the actual 64-bit processor or the specific Windows version supporting Win64. Program 16–1 shows the process of porting one of the previous examples.

Current Win64 Status

This section reviews the current situation, as of mid-2004, regarding Microsoft's support of Win64 on different systems and processors. The situation is in flux, and this information is only a snapshot in time. Nonetheless, the programming considerations covered here will not be affected by the evolution of Win64 support.

There is likely to be extensive future progress and change, although Win64 adoption has been slow. The information here is generally taken from vendor Web sites and trade publications, and these same sources can be used to obtain updated information in the future.

Processor Support

Win64 is, or almost certainly will be, supported on as many as three distinct processor families.

- Intel's Itanium Processor family (IPF), which uses an architecture totally different from the familiar Intel x86 architecture. IPF provides large register files (including 128 general-purpose registers), multiple instruction pipelines, large on-chip three-level caches, and numerous other features designed for high performance as well as 64-bit addressing. Itanium 2 processors are currently shipping, and while Itanium, the predecessor, is now obsolete, it is convenient simply to say "Itanium" to refer to the entire family.

- AMD's AMD64 processors, Opteron and Athlon 64, which are targeted at servers and workstations, respectively. The AMD64 architecture can be regarded as being the Intel x86 architecture with extensions to allow for 64-bit virtual addressing with concurrent 32-bit and 64-bit operation.

- Intel's 32/64-bit processors, which are comparable to AMD64. At the time of writing, the 64-bit extension technology will first appear on Xeon processors. These processors are predicted to be available sometime after late 2004.

Windows Support

Microsoft's Win64 API is designed to support 64-bit architectures with minimal impact on existing source and binary code. Specific Win64 versions at this time include the following.

- Windows XP 64-bit Edition is available in at least two versions. A beta test version from Microsoft supports only the AMD Opteron processor. HP markets several Itanium workstations with Windows XP-Itanium 2 already installed.

- Windows Server 2003, Enterprise Edition for 64-bit Extended Systems is also currently in beta testing. It supports the AMD Opteron and the Intel Xeon with 64-bit extension technology.

- Windows Server 2003, Enterprise Edition for 64-bit Itanium-based Systems supports, as the name implies, workstations and servers that use one or more Itanium processors. There is also a Datacenter Edition. HP, for example, markets its Integrity systems equipped with this Windows version.

Third-Party Support

Numerous database, mathematical library, enterprise application, open source, and other systems are available on Win64. Nonetheless, anyone planning a Win64 port should verify the availability of required third-party products.

64-Bit Architecture Overview

From a programmer's perspective, the major issue in migrating from 32-bit to 64-bit programming models is that pointers and system data types such as `size_t` and `time_t` can now be 64 bits long. Therefore, process virtual address space is no longer limited to 4GB (actually, only 3GB is directly available to applications). Thus, Win32 to Win64 migration can be regarded essentially as a "pointer and data stretch" and, within the Windows model, there is very little effect on user data.

The Need for 64-Bit Addressing

Many applications require the ability to access large address spaces. Examples, such as the following, are numerous.

- **Imaging applications**. A system with 4GB yields only about 20 seconds of high-definition television (HDTV) with true color.

- **Mechanical and electronic computer-aided design (MCAD and ECAD)**. Part assemblies for complex components require more than 3GB to be represented, and chip design simulations are extremely memory-intensive.

- **Databases and data warehousing**. It is not uncommon to use files of hundreds of gigabytes, and similar amounts of virtual address space simplify the file processing.

Physical systems can now support this demand for large address spaces. For some time, 64-bit microprocessors have been available, and many systems support large physical memories at reasonable cost.

The same factors that make huge files (larger than 4GB) desirable and necessary also drive the need for 64-bit addressing, and now that sufficiently powerful Itanium, AMD64, and 64-bit extension microprocessors are available, it is only natural that Windows should evolve to meet this need. A 64-bit OS is essential if Windows is to play a significant role in enterprise and high-end computing.

Nonetheless, many 32-bit applications will continue to work well and will not require early migration. Personal productivity applications, such as Microsoft Office and Adobe FrameMaker, will probably not require 64-bit migration for some time. Consequently, Windows will support backward compatibility.

Current 64-bit processors frequently provide performance gains, as would be expected, but these gains do not directly impact programming at the source level.

The UNIX Experience

PC systems have always lagged behind mainframe and UNIX systems in terms of core functionality and scalability. The same is true of 64-bit architectures.

- Major UNIX vendors have provided 48-bit and 64-bit microprocessors since the early 1990s.

- The major UNIX vendors have supported 64-bit APIs during the same time period.

- The UNIX community has standardized on the so-called LP64 model, which is different from Win64's P64 model, as will be described later.

- Migrations from 32 to 64 bits have been relatively straightforward, if not always trivial, and the same can be expected of Win32 to Win64 migration.

The Windows 16-Bit to 32-Bit Experience

The Windows 16-bit to 32-bit migration started in the early 1990s with the introduction of Windows NT, and the migration picked up momentum when Windows 95 became commonplace. Although it is tempting to say that we will see a replay of the same history, there are differences.

- Windows NT and 95 were the first widely used "real" PC OSs—that is, these two systems supported demand paging, threads, preemptive scheduling, synchronization, and many other features described in Chapter 1.

- While Win32 greatly expanded the useful address space, as does Win64, the advance was more than that. Obsolete and awkward, but popular, extended memory models were replaced. Although Windows 2000 introduced one similar extended memory model (not described in this book), the overall change is not as significant.

- Win32 introduced extensive new functionality, whereas Win64 does not.

Are 64 Bits Enough?

Within the PC world where Windows originated, one could argue that the original 16-bit Intel x86 model (which actually provided 20 bits of address space) lasted for more than a decade and that the 32-bit architecture has already lasted as long. However, the move to Win64, and 64-bit programming in general, has been much slower than the move to 32 bits. In both cases, however, minicomputers and servers moved to the next level at least 10 years before PCs made the same move.

It's now natural to ask if there will be a future move of servers or even PCs to 128 bits. I would contend that any such extension is more than 10 years into the future simply because of the sheer magnitude of a 64-bit address space.

Predictions are precarious, however, but we could, only half seriously, invoke the oft-quoted Moore's Law to the effect that cost/performance is halved every 18 months. In turn, speed and capacity approximately double every 18 months. Applying this argument to address space, we need one extra bit of address space every 18 months, implying that the 64-bit model should be good for 48 years (nearly as long as the history of modern computing). Whether or not this informal argument, which I have seen in a formal presentation, will hold remains to be seen. However, PC resource requirements in the past have grown faster than this argument would predict.

The Win64 Programming Model

There are several possible 64-bit programming model choices depending on how the Standard C data types, such as pointers and integers (`long`, `int`, and `short`), are represented and on whether or not nonstandard data types are added. Recall that ANSI Standard C does not strictly define the data type sizes, although it does require that a `long int` have at least as many bits as an `int`, which, in turn, must have at least as many as a `short int`.

The Goal

The objective is to have a single definition for the Windows API (that is, both Win32 and Win64), therefore allowing for a single source code base. Some source code changes may be required to use this single definition, but the changes should be minimized.

Microsoft selected the LLP64 model (long data type and 64-bit pointer), which is usually referred to simply as the P64 model. In particular, for both signed and unsigned data, we have the following definitions for the standard data types, which apply to both signed and unsigned data.

- A `char` is 8 bits, and a `wchar_t` data item is 16 bits.
- A `short int` requires 16 bits.
- An `int` is 32 bits.
- A `long int` is also 32 bits.
- A pointer of any type, such as `PVOID`, is 64 bits.

Additional data types are provided when you need to specify the length. Thus, _int16, _int32, and _int64 are all data types recognized by the Microsoft compiler.

The Data Types

The tables in this chapter are taken directly from the on-line help and represent the Windows Uniform Data Model. The type definitions can be found in BASETSD.H, part of the Visual Studio.NET (Version 7.0) and Version 6.0 systems.

Fixed-Precision Data Types

The fixed-precision data types provide a length suffix to familiar Win32 types such as DWORD and LONG, as shown in Table 16–1.

Table 16–1   The Fixed-Precision Data Types

Type	Definition
DWORD32	32-bit unsigned integer
DWORD64	64-bit unsigned integer
INT32	32-bit signed integer
INT64	64-bit signed integer
LONG32	32-bit signed integer
LONG64	64-bit signed integer
UINT32	Unsigned INT32
UINT64	Unsigned INT64
ULONG32	Unsigned LONG32
ULONG64	Unsigned LONG64

Pointer Precision Data Types

Quoting from a Microsoft paper, "The New Data Types" (available at the Microsoft Web site), "As the pointer precision changes (that is, as it becomes 32 bits with Win32 code and 64 bits with Win64 code), these data types reflect the precision accordingly. Therefore, it is safe to cast a pointer to one of these types when performing pointer arithmetic; if the pointer precision is 64 bits, the type is 64 bits. The count types also reflect the maximum size to which a pointer can refer."

These types, then, allow integer sizes to track pointer sizes and are sometimes called *polymorphic data types* or *platform scaled types*. Table 16–2, from the same paper, shows the pointer precision data types.

SIZE_T is the most important of these data types and is used in Chapter 5 to describe memory block sizes.

Finally, note that a Windows HANDLE is 64 bits in Win64.

Table 16–2   The Pointer Precision Data Types

Type	Definition
DWORD_PTR	Unsigned long type for pointer precision.
HALF_PTR	Half the size of a pointer. Use within a structure that contains a pointer and two small fields.
INT_PTR	Signed integral type for pointer precision.
LONG_PTR	Signed long type for pointer precision.
SIZE_T	The maximum number of bytes to which a pointer can refer. Use for a count that must span the full range of a pointer.
SSIZE_T	Signed SIZE_T.
UHALF_PTR	Unsigned HALF_PTR.
UINT_PTR	Unsigned INT_PTR.
ULONG_PTR	Unsigned LONG_PTR.

Example: Using Pointer Precision Data Types

The thread argument passed to a thread function by CreateThread and _beginthreadex (see Chapter 7) is a PVOID pointer. In some situations, the programmer may wish only to pass an integer value indicating, for example, the thread's number or an index to a global table. The thread function, which interprets the parameter as an unsigned integer, might be written as follows:

```
DWORD WINAPI MyThreadFunc (PVOID Index_PTR)
{
    DWORD_PTR Index;
    ...
    Index = (DWORD_PTR) Index_PTR;
    ...
}
```

Similarly, knowing that the actual argument is an integer, you might write the main parent thread this way:

```
...
DWORD_PTR Ix;
...
for (Ix = 0; Ix < NumThreads; Ix++) {
   hTh [Ix] = _beginthreadex (NULL, 0, MyThreadFunc,
                               (PVOID) Ix, 0, NULL);
   ...
}
```

Notice that existing code should be changed as required. There will be more about this later in the Legacy Code Migration section.

A Caution

Do not expect to have the full virtual address space, at least in initial implementations. Virtual address space may be constrained to values such as 512GB, indicating a limitation of 39 bits. Over time, this upper bound can be expected to change as processors and systems evolve.

Windows and UNIX Divergence

Windows and UNIX have selected different strategies. Most UNIX vendors implement the LP64 model, which means that both long and pointer data types are 64 bits. This is sometimes called the I32, LP64 model to emphasize that int data types are still 32 bits. The divergence, then, is simply the length of long integers. What is more, the data types in Tables 16–1 and 16–2 are unique to Windows.

Both models represent reasonable solutions, and the UNIX choice is justified in the "Aspen" white paper listed in the Additional Reading section. It would be convenient, however, if both OSs used the same conventions.

Legacy Code Migration

The Windows Uniform Data Model is designed to minimize source code changes, but it is impossible to avoid modification altogether. For example, functions that deal directly with memory allocation and memory block sizes, such as HeapCreate and HeapAlloc (Chapter 5), must use either a 32-bit or 64-bit size field, depending on the model. Similarly, you need to examine code carefully to ensure that there are no hidden assumptions about the sizes of pointers and size fields.

API changes, primarily to the memory management functions, are described first.

API Changes

The most significant API changes are in the memory management functions introduced in Chapter 5. The new definitions use the SIZE_T data type (see Table 16–2) in the count field. For example, the definition of HeapAlloc is:

```
LPVOID HeapAlloc (
    HANDLE hHeap,
    DWORD dwFlags,
    SIZE_T dwBytes);
```

The third field, the number of bytes requested, is of type SIZE_T and is therefore either a 64-bit or 32-bit unsigned integer. Previously, this field was defined to be a DWORD (always 32 bits).

SIZE_T is used as required in Chapter 5.

Changes to Remove Assumptions about Data Item Size

There are numerous potential problems based on assumptions about data size. Here are a few examples.

- A DWORD is no longer appropriate for a memory block size. Use SIZE_T or DWORD64 instead.

- Communicating processes, whether on the same system or on different systems, must be careful about field lengths. For instance, the socket messages in Chapter 12 were defined with LONG32 length fields to ensure that a port to UNIX or Win64 would not result in a 64-bit field. Memory block sizes should be limited to 2GB during communication between Windows processes that use different models.

- Use sizeof to compute data structure and data type lengths; these sizes will differ between Win32 and Win64 if the data structure contains pointers or SIZE_T data items). Literal size constants should be removed (this, of course, is always good advice).

- Unions that mix pointers with arithmetic data types should be examined for any assumptions about data item size.

- Any cast or other conversion between a pointer and an arithmetic type should be examined carefully. For instance, see the code fragments in the Example: Using Pointer Precision Data Types section.

- In particular, be wary of implicit casts of 32-bit integers to 64-bit integers in function calls. There is no assurance that the high-order 32 bits will be cleared, and the function may receive a very large 64-bit integer value.

- Pointers are aligned on 8-byte boundaries, and additional structure padding caused by alignment can increase data structure size more than necessary and even impact performance. Moving pointers to the beginning of a structure will minimize this bloat.

- Use the format specifier `%p` rather than `%x` to print a pointer, and use a specifier such as `%ld` when printing a platform scaled type such as `SIZE_T`.

- `setjmp` and `longjmp` should use the `<setjmp.h>` ANSI C header rather than assuming anything about `jmp_buf`, which must contain a pointer.

Example: Migrating `sortMM` (Program 5–5)

`sortMM` (Program 5–5) uses pointers extensively and, in particular, performs pointer arithmetic. Migrating this program so that it will build and run under both Win32 and Win64 illustrates the normal techniques used and also demonstrates how easy it is to make assumptions about pointer size.

Using Compiler Warnings

Code inspection is important to detect and remove Win64 problems, but it is always advisable to use the compiler, or some other tool, to scan the code and issue warnings.

Microsoft's C++ compiler included with Microsoft Visual Studio 7.0 (.NET) can be configured to issue these warnings. Simply set the `-Wp64` and `-W3` options on the compiler command line. Within Visual Studio, set these options as follows.

- Select the Project Properties page.
- Open the C++ folder.
- Click on General.

- Select Detect 64-bit Portability Issues and select Yes (/Wp64). Leave the warning level at 3.

Then, when you build the project, the output window will display relevant warning messages. All the Microsoft Visual Studio 7.0 projects from the book's Web site have this warning set.

Premigration Code

Most of `sortMM.c` is free of warnings but one segment at Step 6 (see Program 5–5) produces several typical warnings. Program 16–1 shows the code fragment along with line numbers. Note that line numbers may change in later versions of this program.

Program 16–1   `sortMM.c`: Before Win64 Migration, Part 1

```
           . . .
54            LPBYTE pXFile = NULL, pX;
55            TCHAR _based (pInFile) *pIn;
           . . .
130
131           if (!NoPrint)
132           for (iKey = 0; iKey < FsX / RSize; iKey++) {
133               WriteFile (hStdOut, &ChNewLine, TSIZE,
                       &nWrite, NULL);
134
135 /* The cast on pX is important, as it is a pointer to a
136 * byte and we need the four bytes of a based pointer. */
137               pIn =
                  (TCHAR _based (pInFile)*) *(LPDWORD) pX;
138
139               while ((*pIn != CR || *(pIn + 1) != LF)
                       && (DWORD) pIn < FsIn) {
140                   WriteFile (hStdOut, pIn, TSIZE,
                       &nWrite, NULL);
141                   pIn++;
142               }
143               pX += RSize;
144           }
```

The compiler warnings are listed next, but, before looking at them, you might want to scan the code for potential warnings. Bear in mind that the objective is for the program to be buildable and to operate correctly in both Win32 and Win64 modes.

Compiler Warnings

The compiler warnings for this code segment clearly show an assumption that a pointer is 4 bytes.

```
SORTMM.C(137) : warning C4312: 'type cast' : conversion from
    'DWORD' to 'TCHAR __based(pInFile) *' of greater size
SORTMM.C(139) : warning C4311: 'type cast' : pointer trunca-
    tion from 'TCHAR __based(pInFile) *' to 'DWORD'
```

The first warning (line 137) is appropriate. Dereferencing pX, after it is cast to a LPDWORD, produces a 32-bit quantity that is then assigned to pIn, a pointer. Dereferencing pIn will almost certainly cause an exception or some other serious error. The correct solution for line 137 is to replace the LPDWORD cast to a LPTSTR pointer, as follows:

```
pIn = (TCHAR _based (pInFile)*) *(DWORD_PTR) pX;
```

The warning for line 139 is interesting because we are comparing a based pointer to the file size. Assuming that the file is not huge, the warning can be ignored. Having said that, the warning for line 137 could also be ignored. However, let's take the long view and prepare for huge files, even though FsSize is currently a DWORD. Allowing for the full pointer range, line 139 becomes:

```
while ((*pIn != CR || *(pIn + 1) != LF) &&
    (SIZE_T)pIn < (SIZE_T)FsIn) {
```

A second segment, in Step 2b, produces additional truncation warnings. Program 16–2 shows the code fragment.

Program 16–2 sortMM.c: Before Win64 Migration, Part 2

```
        . . .
 40    DWORD KStart, KSize;
174 /* Step 2b: Get first key; determine key size & start. */
175
176         KStart = (DWORD) pInScan;
177 /* Computed start of key field. */
178         while (*pInScan != ' ' && *pInScan != '\t')
                pInScan++;
179 /* Computed end of key field */
180
181         KSize = ((DWORD) pInScan - KStart) / TSIZE;
```

The compiler warnings are as follows:

```
SORTMM.C(176) : warning C4311: 'type cast' : pointer
    truncation from 'TCHAR __based(pInFile) *' to 'DWORD'
SORTMM.C(181) : warning C4311: 'type cast' : pointer trunca-
    tion from 'TCHAR __based(pInFile) *' to 'DWORD'
```

The correction is to use `DWORD_PTR` as the date type in line 40 and in the casts on lines 176 and 181.

Additional warnings of the same nature occur in Step 2c at the end of the `CreateIndexFile` function. The book's Web site contains the modified file, `sortMM64.c`, which can be used for both Win32 and Win64, and it eliminates all the warnings.

Warnings and Changes in Other Programs

All the book's example projects on the Web site are set to give 64-bit warnings. Most programs compiled without warnings, and no changes were necessary.

`atouEX` (Program 14–2), however, required several changes to use `DWORD_PTR` for the integer stored in the `hEvent` field of an overlapped structure. This is because the `HANDLE` date type is 64 bits in Win64. The changes are noted in the listing on the book's Web site.

Some warnings can be ignored. For example, functions such as `strlen()` return a `size_t` value. Frequently, a string length will be assigned to a `DWORD`, causing a "loss of precision" warning. This warning can be ignored in all practical situations.

Summary

Windows' 64-bit API will allow the most demanding enterprise, scientific, and engineering applications to run on Windows platforms using the next generation of 64-bit processors. A few simple precautions will help assure that your programs can be targeted at both Win32 and Win64 platforms.

Additional Reading

The best additional information sources are the MSDN library and information posted by Microsoft. Here are some suggestions from Microsoft and elsewhere.

- The Microsoft "New Data Types" article is available at http://msdn.microsoft.com/ library/default.asp?url=/library/en-us/win64/win64/the_new_data_types.asp. Tables 16–1 and 16–2 are from this article.

- "Introduction to Developing Applications for the 64-bit Version of Windows" is a good short introduction that describes the different programming models. The paper is available at http://msdn.microsoft.com/library/default.asp?url=/ library/en-us/dnnetserv/html/ws03-64-bitwindevover.asp. This paper also has a brief Itanium overview, even though Itanium is not the only Win64 host processor.

- The UNIX "Aspen" rationale, which makes a strong case for the LP64 model, is available at http://www.opengroup.org/public/tech/aspen/lp64_wp.htm.

- An article, "Migration Tips," at http://msdn.microsoft.com/library/ default.asp?url=/library/en-us/win64/win64/migration_tips.asp provides good 32-bit to 64-bit porting tips and has additional useful links. A Web search will locate additional advice and information.

If you are interested in computer architecture in general, *Computer Architecture: A Quantitative Approach*, by John L. Hennessy and David A. Patterson, is the standard. For specific Itanium information, see Walter Triebel's *Itanium Architecture for Software Developers*. The Intel and AMD Web sites (http://www.intel.com and http:// www.amd.com/us-en) have extensive architectural information on the 64-bit extension architectures.

Exercises

16–1. Assume that p1 and p2 are pointers with p1 > p2, and you wish to subtract them in order to obtain the distance between two items. Under what conditions would the expression (DWORD)p1 - (DWORD)p2 be valid? Assuming that the distance is not large, is it necessary to change this expression to (DWORD)(p1 - p2)? *Hint*: Consider the properties of two's complement arithmetic.

16–2. Remove all 64-bit compiler warnings, if any, from other pointer-intensive programs such as sortBT (Program 5–1) and ThreeStage (Program 10–5).

16–3. If you have access to a Win64 system, test the 64-bit programs. Also, assure that the 32-bit builds still operate correctly.

A | Using the Sample Programs

The book's support Web site (http://www.awprofessional.com/0321227255) contains a zip file with the source code for all the sample programs as well as the include files, utility functions, projects, and executables. A number of programs illustrate additional features and solve specific exercises, although the Web site does not include solutions for all exercises or show every alternative implementation.

- All programs have been tested while running under Windows 2000, XP, and 2003 on a wide variety of systems, ranging from laptops to servers. Where appropriate, they have also been tested under Windows 9x, although many programs, especially those from later chapters, will not run on Windows 9x or even on NT 4.0.

- The programs have been built and run with and without UNICODE defined. Under Windows 9x, only the non-Unicode versions will operate.

- Nearly all programs compile without warning messages under Microsoft Visual C++ Versions 7.0 and 6.0 using warning level 3. There are a few minor exceptions, such as warnings about "no return from main program" when ExitProcess is used.

- Distinct project directories are provided for Microsoft Visual Studio .NET and Visual Studio C++ 6.0. The two directories are ProjectsV7 and ProjectsV6. The projects build the executable programs in the run7 and run6 directories, respectively.

- The generic C library functions are used extensively, as are compiler-specific keywords such as __try, __except, and __leave. The multithreaded C runtime library, _beginthreadex, and _endthreadex are essential starting with Chapter 7.

- The projects (in release, not debug, form) and make files are included. The projects are all very simple, with minimal dependencies, and can also be created quickly with the desired configuration and as either debug or release versions.

- The projects are defined to build all programs, with the exception of static or dynamic libraries, as *console* applications.

It is also possible to build the programs using open source development tools, such as gcc and g++ in the Gnu Compiler Collection (http://gcc.gnu.org/). Readers interested in these tools should look at the MinGW open source project (http://www.mingw.org), which describes MinGW as "a collection of freely available and freely distributable Windows specific header files and import libraries combined with GNU toolsets that allow one to produce native Windows programs that do not rely on any 3rd-party C runtime DLLs." I have not tested most of the programs using these tools, however, but I have had considerable success using MinGW and have even been able to cross-build, constructing Windows executable programs and DLLs on a Linux system. Furthermore, I've found that gcc and g++ provide very useful 64-bit warning and error messages.

Web Site Organization

The primary directory is named WindowsSmpEd3 ("Windows Sample Programs, Edition 3"), and this directory can be copied directly to your hard disk. There is a subdirectory for each chapter. All include files are in the Include directory, and the Utility directory contains the commonly used functions such as ReportError and PrintStrings. Complete projects are in the Projects6 and Projects7 directories (Visual C++ 6.0 and 7.0, respectively). Executables and DLLs for all projects are in the run6 and run7 directories. The TimeTest directory contains files required to run the performance tests described in Appendix C. Before describing the individual WindowsSmpEd3 subdirectories, other Web site contents should be mentioned.

Instructional Overheads (Slides)

The Overheads directory contains a set of PowerPoint slides. The slides are included for the convenience of college and university faculty who might wish to use the book in a course. The slides are not intended for commercial purposes.

The `Utility` Directory

The `Utility` directory contains seven source files for utility functions required by the sample programs.

1. `ReprtErr.c` contains the functions `ReportError` (Program 2–2) and `ReportException` (Program 4–1). Every program executed as a process by other sample programs requires this file, except for the `grep` and `wc` programs and those in Chapter 1.

2. `PrintMsg.c` contains `PrintStrings`, `PrintMsg`, and `ConsolePrompt` (Program 2–1). `ReprtErr.c` calls these functions, so this source file is also required in nearly every project.

3. `Options.c` contains the function that processes command line options and is used frequently starting in Chapter 2. Include this source file in the project for any program that has command line options. The listing is Program A–7.

4. `Wstrings.c` contains the source code for the `wmemchr` function used by `Options.c`. Include this file as necessary. You may find it convenient to add other generic string processing functions.

5. `SkipArg.c` processes a command line by skipping a single argument field with each call. It is listed in Program A–8.

6. `GetArgs.c` converts a character string into the `argc`, `argv []` form. This function is useful when parsing a command line into individual arguments, such as the command line obtained from the `GetCommandLine` function introduced in Chapter 6. The listing is Program A–8.

7. `Version.c` implements the `DllGetVersion` function for the DLL built from these modules.

The functions can be compiled and linked with the calling program. You will find it easiest, however, to build them as a library, either static or dynamic. The `Utility_3_0` project builds a DLL from these source files, while `utility-Static` is the project that creates a static library.

The `Include` Directory

Numerous header files are defined in the `Include` directory. Some of these files are used by nearly all the examples, whereas others are specific to one or two programs. The most important files are the following.

1. `EvryThng.h`, as the name suggests, brings in nearly everything required for normal programs, whether single-threaded or multithreaded. In particular, it includes the files `Envirmnt.h` and `Support.h`. The listing is Program A–1.

2. `Exclude.h` defines a number of preprocessor variables that exclude definitions not required by any of the programs in this book. This arrangement speeds compilation and reduces the size of the precompiled header files.

3. `Envirmnt.h` defines the UNICODE and _UNICODE preprocessor variables consistently as well as the language and sublanguage used by `ReportError`. Program A–2 lists this file.

4. `Support.h` defines many of the common functions, such as `ReportError`, as well as a variety of frequently used symbolic constants. Program A–3 shows this file.

5. `ClntSrvr.h` is used beginning in Chapter 11. It defines the request and response message structures, client and server named pipes and mailslots, time-out values, and so on. See Program A–5.

6. `JobMgt.h` is used in the job management programs at the end of Chapter 6. See Program A–4.

Programs by Chapter

Each chapter directory contains all the programs in that chapter (except for the programs in the `Utility` directory) as well as miscellaneous additional programs. The programs are listed here, with brief descriptions of the additional programs. You will also find a number of programs with an x suffix; these programs contain deliberate defects that illustrate common programming errors.

Note: Many programs, such as `tail` and `touch` in Chapter 3, have names that are identical to the UNIX utilities they mimic. You may wish to rename them with names such as `tailW` and `touchW` to avoid confusion. Several programs have already been renamed; `lsW` and `cpW` are examples.

Chapter 1

- `cpC.c` is Program 1–1.

- `cpW.c` is Program 1–2; `cpwFA.c` shows the code modified for better performance. See the results in Appendix C.

- `cpCF.c` is Program 1–3.

- Other programs include a UNIX version (`cpU.c`) and one (`cpUC.c`) built to use the UNIX compatibility library provided with Visual C++. `CpwFA.c` is a `cpW.c` variation designed to be faster using large buffers, sequential scan flags, and other techniques introduced in Chapter 2.

Chapter 2

- Programs 2–1 and 2–2 are in the `Utility` directory, which was described earlier.
- `cat.c` is Program 2–3.
- `atou.c` is Program 2–4.
- `Asc2Un.c` is Program 2–5; `Asc2UnFA.c` and `Asc2UnNB.c` are performance-enhanced versions. All three files implement the `Asc2Un` function called by Program 2–5.
- `pwd.c` is Program 2–6; `pwda.c` is modified to allocate the required memory for the pathname.
- `cd.c` is an implementation of the UNIX directory change command; it is not an example in Chapter 2.

Chapter 3

- `RandomAccess.c` is Program 3–1.
- `lsW.c` is Program 3–2. `rmW.c` is a similar program to remove files.
- `touch.c` is Program 3–3.
- `getn.c` is an additional program that reads a specified fixed-size record, illustrating file access and computing file positions.
- `lsReg.c` is Program 3–4.
- `FileSize.c` is an exercise solution that determines whether or not file space is allocated sparsely.
- `TestLock.c` exercises file locking.
- `tail.c` is required as part of Exercise 3–3.

Chapter 4

- Program 4–1 is part of `ReprtErr.c` in the `Utility` directory.
- `toupper.c` is Program 4–2. `toupperX.c` has several intentional errors; fixing them would be a good exercise.

- `Excption.c` is Program 4–3 and contains a filter function, Program 4–4.

- `Ctrlc.c` is Program 4–5.

Chapter 5

- `sortBT.c` represents Programs 5–1 and 5–2; `sortBTSR.c` omits the no-serialization option on memory management calls to determine whether there is any performance impact in a simple application. The reader can verify that there is very little effect.

- `Asc2UnMM.c` is the function for Program 5–3.

- `sortFL.c` is Program 5–4, and `sortHP.c` is a similar program except that it reads the file into an allocated memory buffer rather than using mapped memory.

- `sortMM.c` is Programs 5–5 and 5–6.

- `atouEL.c` is Program 5–7, and `Asc2UnDll.c` and `Asc2UnmmDLL.c` are the source files for the required DLLs. `Asc2Unmmfl.c` is yet another variation that flushes memory on completion, which may slow overall execution but leaves the system in a safe state.

- `HeapNoSr.c` is a test program that measures the effect of memory allocation with and without the `HEAP_NO_SERIALIZE` flag. This program can be used with Exercise 5–1.

- `RandFile.c` generates randomly keyed text files of any specified size; these files are suitable for testing the sorting functions and are also used to generate large text files for many of the timing tests.

- `clear.c` is a simple program that allocates and initializes virtual memory in large units, continuing until failure. This program is used between timing tests to ensure that data is not cached into memory, which could distort the measurements.

Chapter 6

- `grepMP.c` is Program 6–1. `grep.c` is the source for a C library–based pattern search program to be invoked as a process by `grepMP.c`.

- `timep.c` is Program 6–2.

- `JobShell.c` is Program 6–3, and `JobMgt.c` provides the support functions of Programs 6–4, 6–5, and 6–6.

- `catHA.c` and `grepMPha.c` are modified versions of other programs designed to show how to pass a handle on the command line, solving Exercise 6–2.

- `version.c` obtains information, including the version number, about the operating system.

Chapter 7

- `grepMT.c` is Program 7–1. `grepMTx.c` is intentionally defective; fixing it is Exercise 7–7.

- `sortMT.c` is Program 7–2. `sortMTx.c` is intentionally defective.

- `wcMT.c` solves Exercise 7–6. There are two versions with intentional defects, and another version that serializes file processing for timing comparison.

The corresponding projects all use the multithreaded C library, as described in the chapter.

Chapter 8

- `simplePC.c` is Program 8–1.
- `eventPC.c` is Program 8–2.

Chapter 9

- `statsMX.c` is Program 9–1. Variations are `statsNS.c`, `statsCS.c`, and `statsIN.c`.

- `TimedMutualExclusion.c` is used for timing studies suggested in the text and the exercises.

Chapter 10

- Program 10–1 contains part of `SynchObj.h`, which is in the `Include` directory. Program 10–3 contains the rest.

- `ThbObject.c` is Program 10–2. `testTHB.c` is the associated test program.

- `QueueObj.c` is Program 10–4, and variations include `QueueObjCS.c` (uses a `CRITICAL_SECTION`), `QueueObjSOAW.c` (uses `SignalObjectAndWait`), and signal model versions.

- `ThreeStage.c` is Program 10–5, and its project requires `Messages.c` and `QueueObj.c`.

- `QueueObjCancel.c` is Program 10–6, and it works in conjunction with `ThreeStageCancel.c`.

- `MultiSem.c`, along with the test program, `TestMultiSem.c`, is the solution to Exercise 10–11.

- `MultiPCav.c` uses Pthreads; converting it to use the Windows API, or, alternatively, using the open source Pthreads library, would be a useful exercise.

Chapter 11

- `pipe.c` is Program 11–1. `wc.c` is used as a convenient command to demonstrate its operation. `pipeNP.c` is a variation using a named pipe.

- `clientNP.c` is Program 11–2.

- `serverNP.c` is Program 11–3.

- `SrvrBcst.c` is Program 11–4.

- `LocSrver.c` is Program 11–5.

Chapter 12

- `clientSK.c` is Program 12–1.

- `serverSK.c` is Program 12–2.

- `command.c` is Program 12–3.

- `SendReceiveSKST.c` is Program 12–4, and `serverSKST.c` and `clientSKST.c` are slight modifications of `serverSK.c` and `clientSK.c` for streaming I/O. `SendReceiveSKST.c` should be built as a DLL, and the DLL should be implicitly linked with the client and server projects.

- `SendReceiveSKHA.c` is Program 12–5, and `serverSKHA.c` is the corresponding server that uses the DLL. `ClientSKST.c` will work with this server.

Chapter 13

- `SimpleService.c` is Program 13–2 and includes all of Program 13–1.

- `ServiceShell.c` is Program 13–3.

- `serviceSK.c` is `serverSK.c` (Program 12–2) converted to a service.

Chapter 14

- `atouOV.c` is Program 14–1.

- `atouEX.c` performs the same task with extended I/O and is Program 14–2.

- `atouMT.c` performs the same task with multiple threads rather than with Win32 asynchronous I/O. `atouMT_dh.c` is an incorrect version included to illustrate an interesting and risky feature of handle duplication.

- `atouMTCP.c` uses I/O completion ports.

- `TimeBeep.c` is Program 14–3.

- `serverCP.c`, Program 14–4, is a version of `serverMT` that uses I/O completion ports and overlapped I/O.

Chapter 15

- `chmodW.c` is Program 15–1, with features added to distinguish allowed and denied ACEs properly (as described in the text). `chmodBSD.c` is a variation that uses the `BuildSecurityDescriptor` function.

- `lsFP.c` is Program 15–2.

- `InitUnFp.c` is the code for Programs 15–3, 15–4, and 15–5. Programs 15–1 and 15–2 require these functions. The source module also contains code showing how to obtain the name of an owning group, which is Exercise 15–12.

- `TestFp.c` is an additional test program that was useful during testing.

- `serverNP_secure.c` is Program 15–6.

- `JobShell_secure.c` and `JobMgt_secure.c` are enhancements to the Chapter 6 job management system.

Chapter 16

There is only one source file, `sortMM64.c`, which is Chapter 5's `sortMM.c` enhanced to work under both Win32 and Win64.

Include File Listings

EvryThng.h

Program A–1   EvryThng.h Include File

```
/* EvryThng.h -- All standard and custom include files. */
#include "Exclude.h"
      /* Excludes definitions not required by sample programs. */
#include "envirmnt.h"
#include <windows.h>
#include <tchar.h>
#include <stdio.h>
#include <io.h>
#include "support.h"
#ifdef _MT
#include <process.h>
/* DWORD_PTR (pointer precision unsigned integer) is used for integers
 * that are converted to handles or pointers.
 * This eliminates Win64 warnings regarding conversion between
 * 32-bit and 64-bit data, as HANDLEs and pointers are 64 bits in
 * Win64 (see Chapter 16). This is enabled only if _Wp64 is defined.
 */
#if !defined(_Wp64)
#define DWORD_PTR DWORD
#define LONG_PTR LONG
#define INT_PTR INT
#endif
```

Envirmnt.h

Program A–2   Envirmnt.h Include File

```
/* Envirmnt.h -- define UNICODE and _MT here. */
/* It is best and easiest to define UNICODE within the project. */
/* Use Project...Settings...C/C++. Then, in the "Project Options" */
/* window on the bottom, add /D "UNICODE". */
/* Do the same for _MT, and _STATIC_LIB. */

//#define UNICODE
#undef UNICODE
#ifdef UNICODE
#define _UNICODE
#endif

#ifndef UNICODE
#undef _UNICODE
```

```
#endif


//#define _STATICLIB
           /* Define _STATICLIB if you are either building a */
           /* static library or linking with one. */
#define LANG_DFLT LANG_ENGLISH
#define SUBLANG_DFLT SUBLANG_ENGLISH_US
```

Support.h

Program A–3 Support.h Include File

```
/* Support.h */
/* Definitions of all symbolic constants and common
   utility functions used throughout the example programs. */

/* IT IS BEST TO DEFINE UTILITY_EXPORTS AND _STATICLIB WITHIN THE
   PROJECT RATHER THAN HERE, BUT THE DESCRIPTIONS ARE INCLUDED. */
/* The name "UTILITY_EXPORTS" is generated by Dev Studio when you
   create a DLL project named "Utility" and it is defined on the
   C command line. */

//  UTILITY_3_0_EXPORTS is defined within the UTILITY_3_0 project.

#if defined(UTILITY_3_0_EXPORTS)
#define LIBSPEC _declspec (dllexport)
#elif defined(__cplusplus)
#define LIBSPEC extern "C" _declspec (dllimport)
#else
#define LIBSPEC _declspec (dllimport)
#endif

#define EMPTY _T ("")
#define YES _T ("y")
#define NO _T ("n")
#define CR 0x0D
#define LF 0x0A
#define TSIZE sizeof (TCHAR)

/* Limits and constants. */
#define TYPE_FILE 1            /* Used in ls, rm, and lsFP. */
#define TYPE_DIR 2
#define TYPE_DOT 3

#define MAX_OPTIONS 20         /* Max # of command line options. */
#define MAX_ARG 1000           /* Max # of command line arguments. */
#define MAX_COMMAND_LINE MAX_PATH+50/* Max size of a command line. */
```

```
/* Commonly used functions. */
LIBSPEC BOOL ConsolePrompt (LPCTSTR, LPTSTR, DWORD, BOOL);
LIBSPEC BOOL PrintStrings (HANDLE, ...);
LIBSPEC BOOL PrintMsg (HANDLE, LPCTSTR);
LIBSPEC VOID ReportError (LPCTSTR, DWORD, BOOL);
LIBSPEC VOID ReportException (LPCTSTR, DWORD);
LIBSPEC DWORD Options (int, LPCTSTR *, LPCTSTR, ...);
LIBSPEC LPTSTR SkipArg (LPCTSTR);
LIBSPEC VOID GetArgs (LPCTSTR, int *, LPTSTR *);

/* Collection of generic string functions modeled after string.h.
   Created as required -- there was only one! Implementation is
   derived from Plauger: The Standard C Library. */

LIBSPEC LPCTSTR wmemchr (LPCTSTR, TCHAR, DWORD);

#ifdef _UNICODE /* This declaration had to be added. */
#define _tstrrchr wcsrchr
#else
#define _tstrrchr strrchr
#endif

#ifdef _UNICODE /* This declaration had to be added. */
#define _memtchr wmemchr
#else
#define _memtchr memchr
#endif

/* Security functions. */
LPSECURITY_ATTRIBUTES InitializeUnixSA (DWORD, LPTSTR, LPTSTR,
   LPDWORD, LPHANDLE);
LPSECURITY_ATTRIBUTES InitializeAccessOnlySA (DWORD, LPTSTR, LPTSTR,
   LPDWORD, LPHANDLE);
DWORD ReadFilePermissions (LPTSTR, LPTSTR, LPTSTR);
BOOL ChangeFilePermissions (DWORD, LPTSTR, LPDWORD, LPDWORD);
/* Simpler forms available with Visual C++ Version 5.0. */
//PSECURITY_DESCRIPTOR InitializeSD (DWORD, LPTSTR, LPTSTR, LPDWORD);

/* Constants needed by the security functions. */
#define LUSIZE 1024
#define ACCT_NAME_SIZE LUSIZE
```

JobMgt.h

Program A–4 JobMgt.h Include File

```
/* JobMgt.h -- Definitions required for job management.
   Chapter 6. */
/* Job management exit code for killed jobs. */

#define JM_EXIT_CODE 0x1000

typedef struct _JM_JOB
{
    DWORD ProcessId;
    TCHAR CommandLine [MAX_PATH];
} JM_JOB;
#define SJM_JOB sizeof (JM_JOB)

/* Job management functions. */
DWORD GetJobNumber (PROCESS_INFORMATION *, LPCTSTR);
BOOL DisplayJobs (void);
DWORD FindProcessId (DWORD);
BOOL GetJobMgtFileName (LPTSTR);
```

ClntSrvr.h

Program A–5 ClntSrvr.h Include File

```
/* Definitions for client/server communication. */
/* Request and response messages. Messages are in ASCII as
   the request may be coming from a Windows 95 system. */

#define MAX_RQRS_LEN 0x1000

typedef struct {
    DWORD32 RqLen;   /* Request length, not including this field. */
    CHAR Command;
    BYTE Record [MAX_RQRS_LEN];
} REQUEST;

typedef struct {
    DWORD32 RsLen;   /* Response length, not including this field */
    CHAR Status;
    BYTE Record [MAX_RQRS_LEN];
} RESPONSE;

#define RQ_SIZE sizeof (REQUEST)
#define RQ_HEADER_LEN RQ_SIZE-MAX_RQRS_LEN
#define RS_SIZE sizeof (RESPONSE)
```

```
#define RS_HEADER_LEN RS_SIZE-MAX_RQRS_LEN

/* Mailslot message structure. */
typedef struct {
    DWORD msStatus;
    DWORD msUtilization;
    TCHAR msName [MAX_PATH];
} MS_MESSAGE;

#define MSM_SIZE sizeof (MS_MESSAGE)

#define CS_TIMEOUT 5000
                /* Time-out period for named pipe
                    connections and performance monitoring. */

#define MAX_CLIENTS 10
#define MAX_SERVER_TH 4 /* Max num of server threads for serverNPCP.*/
#define MAX_CLIENTS_CP 16 /* Max num of clients for serverNPCP.*/

/* Client and server pipe & mailslot names. */
#define SERVER_PIPE _T ("\\\\.\\PIPE\\SERVER")
#define CLIENT_PIPE _T ("\\\\.\\PIPE\\SERVER")
#define SERVER_BROADCAST _T ("SrvrBcst.exe")
#define MS_SRVNAME _T ("\\\\.\\MAILSLOT\\CLS_MAILSLOT")
#define MS_CLTNAME _T ("\\\\.\\MAILSLOT\\CLS_MAILSLOT")
#define MX_NAME _T ("ClientServerMutex")
#define SM_NAME _T ("ClientServerSemaphore")

/* Commands for the statistics maintenance function. */
#define CS_INIT                         1
#define CS_RQSTART                      2
#define CS_RQCOMPLETE                   3
#define CS_REPORT                       4
#define CS_TERMTHD                      5

/* Client/Server support functions. */

BOOL LocateServer (LPTSTR);
```

Exclude.h

Program A–6 defines numerous variables that will exclude definitions not
required by the programs in the book. Rector and Newcomer (1997) discuss this in
detail.

Program A–6 `Exclude.h` Include File

```
/* Exclude.h -- Define variables to exclude selected header files.
   For a complete explanation, see Rector & Newcomer, Win32
   Programming, pp 25ff. */

#define WIN32_LEAN_AND_MEAN
     /* This has the largest impact, halving the precompiled
        header (pch) file size. */

/* These definitions also reduce the pch and improve compiling
   time. All the programs in the book will still compile with
   these definitions. You can also eliminate security with
   #define NOSECURITY. */

#define NOATOM
#define NOCLIPBOARD
#define NOCOMM
#define NOCTLMGR
#define NOCOLOR
#define NODEFERWINDOWPOS
#define NODESKTOP
#define NODRAWTEXT
#define NOEXTAPI
#define NOGDICAPMASKS
#define NOHELP
#define NOICONS
#define NOTIME
#define NOIMM
#define NOKANJI
#define NOKERNEL
#define NOKEYSTATES
#define NOMCX
#define NOMEMMGR
#define NOMENUS
#define NOMETAFILE
#define NOMSG
#define NONCMESSAGES
#define NOPROFILER
#define NORASTEROPS
#define NORESOURCE
#define NOSCROLL
#define NOSERVICE
#define NOSHOWWINDOW
#define NOSOUND
#define NOSYSCOMMANDS
#define NOSYSMETRICS
#define NOSYSPARAMS
#define NOTEXTMETRIC
```

```
#define NOVIRTUALKEYCODES
#define NOWH
#define NOWINDOWSTATION
#define NOWINMESSAGES
#define NOWINOFFSETS
#define NOWINSTYLES
#define OEMRESOURCE
```

Additional Utility Programs

Three additional utility programs—Options, SkipArg, and GetArgs—are sufficiently useful to list here. None, however, is dependent on Win32.

Options.c

This function scans the command line for words with the "-" (hyphen) prefix, examines the individual characters, and sets Boolean parameters. It is similar to the UNIX getopt function, but it is not as powerful.

Program A-7   Options Function

```
/* Utility function to extract option flags from the command line. */

#include "EvryThng.h"
#include <stdarg.h>
DWORD Options (int argc, LPCTSTR argv [], LPCTSTR OptStr, ...)

/* argv is the command line. The options, if any, start
    with a '-' in argv [1], argv [2], ....
    OptStr is a text string containing all possible
    options, in one-to-one correspondence with the addresses of
    Boolean variables in the variable argument list (...). These
    flags are set if and only if the corresponding option character
    occurs in argv [1], argv [2], .... The return value is the argv
    index of the first argument beyond the options. */
{
    va_list pFlagList;
    LPBOOL pFlag;
    int iFlag = 0, iArg;

    va_start (pFlagList, OptStr);
```

```
    while ((pFlag = va_arg (pFlagList, LPBOOL)) != NULL
            && iFlag < (int) _tcslen (OptStr)) {
        *pFlag = FALSE;
        for (iArg = 1;
            !(*pFlag) && iArg < argc &&
                    argv [iArg] [0] == '-';
            iArg++)
            *pFlag = _memtchr (argv [iArg], OptStr [iFlag],
                    _tcslen (argv [iArg])) != NULL;
        iFlag++;
    }
    va_end (pFlagList);
    for (iArg = 1; iArg < argc && argv [iArg] [0] == '-'; iArg++);
    return iArg;
}
```

SkipArg.c

This function processes a command line string to skip over a white-space-delimited field. It is first used in timep, Program 6–2.

Program A–8 SkipArg Function

```
/*  SkipArg.c
    Skip one command line argument -- skip tabs and spaces. */

#include "EvryThng.h"

LPTSTR SkipArg (LPCTSTR targv)
{
    LPTSTR p;
    p = (LPTSTR) targv;
                /* Skip up to the next tab or space. */
    while (*p != '\0' && *p != TSPACE && *p != TAB) p++;
                /* Skip over tabs and spaces to the next arg. */
    while (*p != '\0' && (*p == TSPACE || *p == TAB)) p++;
    return p;
}
```

GetArgs.c

This function scans a string for space- and tab-delimited words and puts the results in a string array passed to the function. It is useful for converting a command line string into an `argv [ ]` array, and it is used initially with `JobShell` in Chapter 6. The Win32 function `CommandLineToArgvW` performs the same function but is limited to Unicode characters.

Program A–9   GetArgs Function

```
/* GetArgs. Put command line string in argc/argv form. */
#include "EvryThng.h"

VOID GetArgs (LPCTSTR Command, int *pArgc, LPTSTR argstr [])
{
    int i, icm = 0;
    DWORD ic = 0;

    for (i = 0; ic < _tcslen (Command); i++) {
        while (ic < _tcslen (Command) &&
                Command [ic] != TSPACE && Command [ic] != TAB) {
            argstr [i] [icm] = Command [ic];
            ic++; icm++;
        }
        argstr [i] [icm] = '\0';
        while (ic < _tcslen (Command) &&
                (Command [ic] == TSPACE || Command [ic] == TAB))
            ic++;
        icm = 0;
    }
    if (pArgc != NULL) *pArgc = i;
    return;
}
```

B | Windows, UNIX, and C Library Comparisons

The tables in this appendix show the Windows (Win32 and Win64) functions described in the main text along with the corresponding UNIX/Linux[1] and ANSI Standard C library functions, if any.

The tables are arranged by chapter (some chapters are combined). Within each chapter, they are sorted first by functionality area (file system, directory management, and so on) and then by the Windows function name.

Each table row gives the following information:

- The functionality area (subject)

- The Windows function name

- The corresponding UNIX function name. In some cases, there are more than one.

- The corresponding C library function name, if any

- Comments as appropriate

The notation used in the tables requires some explanation.

- The Microsoft Visual C++ library contains some UNIX compatibility functions. For example, _open is the compatibility library function for UNIX open. If the UNIX function is in italics, there is a compatibility function. An asterisk next to the name indicates that there is also a wide character Unicode version. For example, there is a _wopen function.

---

[1] More precisely, "UNIX" means the POSIX functions specified in *The Single UNIX Specification* (http://www.opengroup.org/onlinepubs/007908799/). UNIX and Linux implement this specification. In turn, the specification has its historical origins in UNIX.

- A program that uses just the Standard C library, and no Windows or UNIX system functions, should compile, build, and run on both systems if normal precautions are taken. Such a program will, however, be limited to file and I/O operations.

- Commas separating functions indicate alternatives, often using different characteristics or emulating one aspect of the Windows function.

- Semicolons separating functions indicate that you use the functions in sequence to emulate the Windows function. Thus, `fork; exec` corresponds to `CreateProcess`.

- An underlined entry indicates a global variable, such as `errno`.

- In a few cases, the UNIX equivalent may be stated imprecisely in terms such as "terminal I/O" for Windows functions such as `AllocConsole`. Often, "Use C library" is the appropriate comment, as in the case of `GetTempFileName`. In other cases, the situation is reversed. Thus, under the UNIX signal management functions (`sigaddset` and so on), the Windows entry is "Use SEHVEH" to indicate that the programmer should set up structured or vectored exception handlers and filter functions to get the desired behavior. Unlike UNIX, Windows does not support process groups, so the Windows entries are "N/A," although job management, as done by the programs in Chapter 6, could emulate process relationships.

- There are numerous "N/A" entries, especially for the C library, if there is no comparable function or set of functions. This is the case, for example, with directory management.

- The POSIX threads (Pthreads) functions are the UNIX equivalents shown in the tables for Chapters 7–10, even though they are not properly a part of UNIX. Furthermore, even though many UNIX implementations have their own synchronization objects similar to events, mutexes, and semaphores, there is no attempt to list them here.

Generally, the correspondence is more precise in the earlier chapters, particularly for file management. The systems tend to diverge with the more advanced functionality and, in many cases, there is no C library equivalent. For example, the UNIX and Windows security models differ significantly, so the relationships shown are, at best, approximations.

These functional correspondences are not exact. There are many differences, small and large, among the three systems. Therefore, these tables are only for guidance. The individual chapters discuss many of the differences.

Chapters 2 and 3: File and Directory Management

Subject	Windows	UNIX	C Library	Comments
Console I/O	AllocConsole	terminal I/O	N/A	
Console I/O	FreeConsole	terminal I/O	N/A	
Console I/O	ReadConsole	*read*	getc, scanf, gets	
Console I/O	SetConsoleMode	ioctl	N/A	
Console I/O	WriteConsole	*write*	putc, printf, puts	
Directory Mgt	CreateDirectory	*mkdir**	N/A	Make a new directory
Directory Mgt	FindClose	*closedir**	N/A	Close a directory search handle
Directory Mgt	FindFirstFile	*opendir**, *readdir**	N/A	Find first file matching a pattern
Directory Mgt	FindNextFile	*readdir**	N/A	Find subsequent files
Directory Mgt	GetCurrentDirectory	*getcwd**	N/A	
Directory Mgt	GetFullPathName	N/A	N/A	
Directory Mgt	GetSystemDirectory	Well-known pathnames	N/A	
Directory Mgt	RemoveDirectory	*rmdir*, *unlink**	remove	
Directory Mgt	SearchPath	Use opendir, readdir	N/A	Search for a file on a specified path
Directory Mgt	SetCurrentDirectory	*chdir**, fchdir	N/A	Change the working directory
Error Handling	FormatMessage	strerror	perror	
Error Handling	GetLastError	<u>errno</u>	<u>errno</u>	Global variable
Error Handling	SetLastError	<u>errno</u>	<u>errno</u>	Global variable
File Locking	LockFile	fcntl (cmd=F_GETLK, ..)	N/A	
File Locking	LockFileEx	fcntl (cmd=F_GETLK, ..)	N/A	
File Locking	UnlockFile	fcntl (cmd=F_GETLK, ..)	N/A	

Chapters 2 and 3: File and Directory Management (cont.)

Subject	Windows	UNIX	C Library	Comments
File Locking	`UnlockFileEx`	`fcntl` `(cmd=F_GETLK, ..)`	N/A	
File System	`CloseHandle` (file handle)	`close`*	`fclose`	`CloseHandle` is not limited to files
File System	`CopyFile`	`open; read;` `write; close`	`fopen; fread;` `fwrite; fclose`	Duplicate a file
File System	`CreateFile`	`open`*, `creat`*	`fopen`	Open/create a file
File System	`DeleteFile`	`unlink`*	`remove`	Delete a file
File System	`FlushFileBuffers`	`fsynch`	`fflush`	Write file buffers
File System	`GetFileAttributes`	`stat`*, `fstat`*, `lstat`	N/A	
File System	`GetFileInformation-` `ByHandle`	`stat`*, `fstat`*, `lstat`	N/A	Fill structure with file info
File System	`GetFileSize`	`stat`*, `fstat`*, `lstat`	`ftell, fseek`	Get length of file in bytes
File System	`GetFileTime`	`stat`*, `fstat`*, `lstat`	N/A	
File System	`GetFileType`	`stat`*, `fstat`*, `lstat`	N/A	Check for character stream device or file
File System	`GetStdHandle`	Use file desc 0, 1, or 2	Use `stdin`, `stdout`, `stderr`	
File System	`GetTempFileName`	Use C library	`tmpnam`	Create a unique file name
File System	`GetTempFileName`, `CreateFile`	Use C library	`tmpfile`	Create a temporary file
File System	`GetTempPath`	`/temp path`	N/A	Directory for temp files
File System	`MoveFile`, `MoveFileEx`	Use C library	`rename`	Rename a file or directory
File System	`CreateHardLink`	`link`, `unlink`*	N/A	Windows does not support links
File System	N/A	`symlink`	N/A	Create a symbolic link
File System	N/A	`readlink`	N/A	Read name in a symbolic link
File System	N/A, `ReadFile` returns 0 bytes	N/A, `read` returns 0 bytes	`feof`	Rest for end of file
File System	N/A, use multiple `ReadFiles`	`readv`	N/A, use multiple `freads`	Scatter read

Chapters 2 and 3: File and Directory Management (cont.)

Subject	Windows	UNIX	C Library	Comments
File System	N/A, use multiple `WriteFiles`	`writev`	N/A, use multiple `fwrites`	Gather write
File System	`ReadFile`	*read*	`fread`	Read data from a file
File System	`SetEndOfFile`	*chsize**	N/A	
File System	`SetFileAttributes`	`fcntl`	N/A	
File System	`SetFilePointer`	*lseek*	`fseek`	Set file pointer
FileSystem	`SetFilePointer` (to 0)	`lseek (0)`	`rewind`	
File System	`SetFileTime`	*utime**	N/A	
File System	`SetStdHandle`	`close`, *dup**, *dup2**, or `fcntl`	`freopen`	dup2 or fcntl
File System	`WriteFile`	`write`	`fwrite`	Write data to a file
System Info	`GetDiskFreeSpace`	N/A	N/A	
System Info	`GetSystemInfo`	`getrusage`	N/A	
System Info	`GetVersion`	`uname`	N/A	
System Info	`GetVolume-Information`	N/A	N/A	
System Info	`GlobalMemoryStatus`	`getrlimit`	N/A	
System Info	Various defined constants	`sysconf`, `pathconf`, `fpathconf`	N/A	
Time	`GetSystemTime`	Use C library	`time`, `gmtime`	
Time	See `ls` program, Program 3–2	Use C library	`asctime`	
Time	`CompareFileTime`	Use C library	`difftime`	Compare "calendar" times
Time	`FileTimeToLocal-FileTime`, `File-TimeToSystemTime`	Use C library	`localtime`	
Time	`FileTimeToSystem-Time`	Use C library	`gmtime`	

Chapters 2 and 3: File and Directory Management (cont.)

Subject	Windows	UNIX	C Library	Comments
Time	GetLocalTime	Use C library	time, localtime	
Time	See touch program, Program 3–3	Use C library	strftime	
Time	SetLocalTime	N/A	N/A	
Time	SetSystemTime	N/A	N/A	
Time	Subtract file times	Use C library	difftime	
Time	SystemTimeToFile-Time	Use C library	mktime	

Chapter 4: Exception Handling

Subject	Windows	UNIX	C Library
SEH	`_try - _except`	Use C library signals	Use C library signals
SEH	`_try - _finally`	Use C library signals	Use C library signals
SEH	`AbnormalTermination`	Use C library signals	Use C library signals
SEH	`GetExceptionCode`	Use C library signals	Use C library signals
SEH	`RaiseException`	Use C library signals	`signal, raise`
Signals	Use `_finally` block	Use C library	`atexit`
Signals	Use C library or terminate process	`kill`	`raise`
Signals	Use C library	Use C library	`signal`
Signals	Use SEH, VEH	`sigemptyset`	N/A
Signals	Use SEH, VEH	`sigfillset`	N/A
Signals	Use SEH, VEH	`sigaddset`	N/A
Signals	Use SEH, VEH	`sigdelset`	N/A
Signals	Use SEH, VEH	`sigismember`	N/A
Signals	Use SEH, VEH	`sigprocmask`	N/A
Signals	Use SEH, VEH	`sigpending`	N/A
Signals	Use SEH, VEH	`sigaction`	N/A
Signals	Use SEH, VEH	`sigsetjmp`	N/A
Signals	Use SEH, VEH	`siglongjmp`	N/A
Signals	Use SEH, VEH	`sigsuspendf`	N/A
Signals	Use SEH, VEH	`psignal`	N/A
Signals	Use SEH, VEH, or C library	Use C library	`abort`

Note: Many UNIX vendors provide proprietary exception handling capabilities.

Chapter 5: Memory Management, Memory-Mapped Files, and DLLs

Subject	Windows	UNIX	C Library
Mapped Files	CreateFileMapping	shmget	N/A
Mapped Files	MapViewOfFile	mmap, shmat	N/A
Mapped Files	MapViewOfFileEx	mmap, shmat	N/A
Mapped Files	OpenFileMapping	shmget	N/A
Mapped Files	UnmapViewOfFile	munmap, shmdt, shmctl	N/A
Memory Mgt	GetProcessHeap	N/A	N/A
Memory Mgt	GetSystemInfo	N/A	N/A
Memory Mgt	HeapAlloc	sbrk, brk, or C library	malloc, calloc
Memory Mgt	HeapCreate	N/A	N/A
Memory Mgt	HeapDestroy	N/A	N/A
Memory Mgt	HeapFree	Use C library	free
Memory Mgt	HeapReAlloc	Use C library	realloc
Memory Mgt	HeapSize	N/A	N/A
Shared Memory	CloseHandle (map handle)	shmctl	N/A
Shared Memory	CreateFileMapping, OpenFileMapping	shmget	N/A
Shared Memory	MapViewOfFile	shmat	N/A
Shared Memory	UnmapViewOfFile	shmdt	N/A
DLLs	LoadLibrary	dlopen	N/A
DLLs	FreeLibrary	dlclose	N/A
DLLs	GetProcAddress	dlsyn	N/A
DLLs	DllMain	pthread_once	N/A

Chapter 6: Process Management

Subject	Windows	UNIX	C Library	Comments
Process Mgt	CreateProcess	fork (); execl ()*, system()	N/A	There are 6 execxx functions
Process Mgt	ExitProcess	_exit	exit	
Process Mgt	GetCommandLine	argv []	argv []	
Process Mgt	GetCurrentProcess	getpid*	N/A	
Process Mgt	GetCurrentProcessId	getpid*	N/A	
Process Mgt	GetEnvironmentStrings	N/A	getenv	
Process Mgt	GetEnvironmentVariable	N/A	getenv	
Process Mgt	GetExitCodeProcess	wait, waitpid	N/A	
Process Mgt	GetProcessTimes	times, wait3, wait4	N/A	
Process Mgt	GetProcessWorkingSetSize	wait3, wait4	N/A	
Process Mgt	N/A	execl*, execv*, execle*, execve*, execlp*, execvp*	N/A	Windows does not have a direct equivalent
Process Mgt	N/A	fork, vfork	N/A	Windows does not have a direct equivalent
Process Mgt	N/A	getppid	N/A	No parent/child relationships in Windows
Process Mgt	N/A	getgid, getegid	N/A	No process groups in Windows
Process Mgt	N/A	getpgrp	N/A	
Process Mgt	N/A	setpgid	N/A	
Process Mgt	N/A	setsid	N/A	
Process Mgt	N/A	tcgetpgrp	N/A	
Process Mgt	N/A	tcsetpgrp	N/A	
Process Mgt	OpenProcess	N/A	N/A	

Chapter 6: Process Management (cont.)

Subject	Windows	UNIX	C Library	Comments
Process Mgt	`SetEnvironmentVariable`	`putenv`	N/A	putenv is not part of the Standard C library
Process Mgt	`TerminateProcess`	`kill`	N/A	
Synch: Process	`WaitForMultipleObjects` (process handles)	`waitpid`	N/A	
Synch: Process	`WaitForSingleObject` (process handle)	`wait, waitpid`	N/A	
Timers	`KillTimer`	`alarm (0)`	N/A	
Timers	`SetTimer`	`alarm`	N/A	
Timers	`Sleep`	`sleep`	N/A	
Timers	`Sleep`	`poll` or `select`, no file descriptor	N/A	

Chapter 7: Threads and Scheduling

Subject	Windows	UNIX/Pthreads	Comments
Thread Mgt	`CreateRemoteThread`	N/A	
TLS	`TlsAlloc`	`pthread_key_alloc`	
TLS	`TlsFree`	`pthread_key_delete`	
TLS	`TlsGetValue`	`pthread_getspecific`	
TLS	`TlsSetValue`	`pthread_setspecific`	
Thread Mgt	`CreateThread, _beginthreadex`	`pthread_create`	
Thread Mgt	`ExitThread, _endthreadex`	`pthread_exit`	
Thread Mgt	`GetCurrentThread`	`pthread_self`	
Thread Mgt	`GetCurrentThreadId`	N/A	
Thread Mgt	`GetExitCodeThread`	`pthread_yield`	
Thread Mgt	`ResumeThread`	N/A	
Thread Mgt	`SuspendThread`	N/A	
Thread Mgt	`TerminateThread`	`pthread_cancel`	`pthread_cancel` is safer
Thread Mgt	`WaitForSingleObject` (thread handle)	`pthread_join`	
Thread Priority	`GetPriorityClass`	`pthread_attr_getschedpolicy, getpriority`	
Thread Priority	`GetThreadPriority`	`pthread_attr_getschedparam`	
Thread Priority	`SetPriorityClass`	`pthread_attr_setschedpolicy, setpriority, nice`	
Thread Priority	`SetThreadPriority`	`pthread_attr_setschedparam`	

Note: Pthreads, while a part of all modern UNIX offerings, are available on non-UNIX systems as well.

Chapters 8–10: Thread Synchronization

Subject	Windows	UNIX/Pthreads	Comments
Synch: CritSec	`DeleteCriticalSection`	Use mutexes to emulate critical sections. Some systems provide proprietary equivalents.	C library is not applicable
Synch: CritSec	`EnterCriticalSection`		C library is not applicable
Synch: CritSec	`InitializeCriticalSection`		
Synch: CritSec	`LeaveCriticalSection`		
Synch: Event	`CloseHandle` (event handle)	`pthread_cond_destroy`	
Synch: Event	`CreateEvent`	`pthread_cond_init`	
Synch: Event	`PulseEvent`	`pthread_cond_signal`	Manual-reset event
Synch: Event	`ResetEvent`	N/A	
Synch: Event	`SetEvent`	`pthread_cond_broadcast`	Auto-reset event
Synch: Event	`WaitForSingleObject` (event handle)	`pthread_cond_wait`	
Synch: Event	`WaitForSingleObject` (event handle)	`pthread_timed_wait`	
Synch: Mutex	`CloseHandle` (mutex handle)	`pthread_mutex_destroy`	
Synch: Mutex	`CreateMutex`	`pthread_mutex_init`	
Synch: Mutex	`ReleaseMutex`	`pthread_mutex_unlock`	
Synch: Mutex	`WaitForSingleObject` (mutex handle)	`pthread_mutex_lock`	
Synch: Sem	`CreateSemaphore`	`semget`	
Synch: Sem	N/A	`semctl`	Windows does not directly support all these options
Synch: Sem	`OpenSemaphore`	`semget`	
Synch: Sem	`ReleaseSemaphore`	`semop (+)`	
Synch: Sem	`WaitForSingleObject` (semaphore handle)	`semop (-)`	Windows can wait for only one count

Chapter 11: Interprocess Communication

Subject	Windows	UNIX	C Library	Comments
IPC	CallNamedPipe	N/A	N/A	CreateFile, WriteFile, ReadFile, CloseHandle
IPC	CloseHandle (pipe handle)	close, msgctl	pclose	Not part of the Standard C library—see Stevens
IPC	ConnectNamedPipe	N/A	N/A	
IPC	CreateMailslot	N/A	N/A	
IPC	CreateNamedPipe	mkfifo, msgget	N/A	
IPC	CreatePipe	*pipe*	popen	Not part of the Standard C library—see Stevens
IPC	DuplicateHandle	*dup*, *dup2*, or *fcntl*	N/A	Or use file names CONIN$, CONOUT$
IPC	GetNamedPipeHandleState	*stat*, *fstat*, lstat64	N/A	
IPC	GetNamedPipeInfo	*stat*, *fstat*, lstat	N/A	
IPC	ImpersonateNamedPipeClient	N/A	N/A	
IPC	PeekNamedPipe	N/A	N/A	
IPC	ReadFile (named pipe handle)	read (fifo), msgsnd	N/A	
IPC	RevertToSelf	N/A	N/A	
IPC	SetNamedPipeHandleState	N/A	N/A	
IPC	TransactNamedPipe	N/A	N/A	WriteFile; ReadFile
IPC	WriteFile (named pipe handle)	write (fifo), msgrcv	N/A	
Misc.	GetComputerName	uname	N/A	
Misc.	SetComputerName	N/A	N/A	
Security	SetNamedPipeIdentity	Use directory sticky bit	N/A	

Chapter 14: Asynchronous I/O

Subject	Windows	UNIX	C Library	Comments
Asynch I/O	GetOverlappedResult	N/A	N/A	
Asynch I/O	ReadFileEx	N/A	N/A	Extended I/O with completion routine
Asynch I/O	SleepEx	N/A	N/A	Alertable wait
Asynch I/O	WaitForMultipleObjects (file handles)	poll, select	N/A	
Asynch I/O	WaitForMultipleObjectsEx	N/A	N/A	Alertable wait
Asynch I/O	WriteFileEx	N/A	N/A	Extended I/O with completion routine
Asynch I/O	WaitForSingleObjectEx	waitpid	N/A	Alertable wait

Chapter 15: Securing Windows Objects

Subject	Windows	UNIX	Comments
Security	AddAccessAllowedAce	chmod, fchmod	C library does not support security
Security	AddAccessDeniedAce	chmod, fchmod	
Security	AddAuditAce	N/A	
Security	CreatePrivateObjectSecurity	N/A	
Security	DeleteAce	chmod, fchmod	
Security	DestroyPrivateObjectSecurity	N/A	
Security	GetAce	*stat*[*], *fstat*[*], lstat	
Security	GetAclInformation	*stat*[*], *fstat*[*], lstat	
Security	GetFileSecurity	*stat*[*], *fstat*[*], lstat	
Security	GetPrivateObjectSecurity	N/A	
Security	GetSecurityDescriptorDacl	*stat*[*], *fstat*[*], lstat	
Security	GetUserName	getlogin	
Security	InitializeAcl	N/A	
Security	InitializeSecurityDescriptor	*umask*	
Security	LookupAccountName	getpwnam, getgrnam	
Security	LookupAccountSid	getpwuid, getuid, geteuid	
Security	N/A	getpwend, setpwent, endpwent	
Security	N/A	getgrent, setgrent, endgrent	
Security	N/A	setuid, seteuid, setreuid	
Security	N/A	setgid, setegid, setregid	
Security	OpenProcessToken	getgroups, setgroups, initgroups	

Chapter 15: Securing Windows Objects (cont.)

Subject	Windows	UNIX	Comments
Security	SetFileSecurity	*chmod*[*], fchmod	C library does not support security
Security	SetPrivateObjectSecurity	N/A	
Security	SetSecurityDescriptorDacl	*umask*	
Security	SetSecurityDescriptorGroup	chown, fchown, lchown	
Security	SetSecurityDescriptorOwner	chown, fchown, lchown	
Security	SetSecurityDescriptorSacl	N/A	

APPENDIX

C | Performance Results

The example programs have shown a variety of alternative techniques for carrying out the same tasks, such as file copying and ASCII to Unicode file conversion, and it is natural to speculate about the performance advantages of these techniques. Application design requires knowledge of, rather than speculation about, the performance impacts of alternative implementations and the potential performance advantages of various Windows versions, hardware configurations, and Windows features, such as threads and asynchronous I/O. The timep program, Program 6–2, measures the real (elapsed) time, user time, and system (kernel) time required to execute a program and provides a convenient way to measure performance and determine the effects of alternative programming techniques and designs.

Test Configurations

Testing was performed with a representative variety of applications, based on examples in the book and a range of host systems.

Applications

The tables in this appendix show the times measured with timep for the test programs running on several different systems. The five functionality areas are as follows.

1. **File copying**. Several different techniques, such as using the C library and the Windows CopyFile function, are measured to determine the performance impact. File copying stresses file I/O without any data processing.

2. **ASCII to Unicode conversion**. This shows the effect of memory mapping, larger buffers, the Windows sequential scan flags, and asynchronous I/O. Conversion stresses file I/O with a small amount of data processing as the data is moved, and converted, from one buffer to another.

3. **Pattern searching**. This uses the `grep` program in its multiprocess and multi-threaded forms. Simple sequential processing is also tested and turns out to be competitive with the two parallel search methods on a single processor. Pattern searching increases the amount of data processing required and minimizes the output.

4. **File sorting**. This shows the effect of memory mapping, in-memory techniques, and multithreading. Sorting, at least for large files, emphasizes CPU processing speed over file I/O.

5. **Multithreaded producer/consumer system**. This shows the effects of different synchronization techniques for implementing a multithreaded queuing system in order to evaluate the trade-offs discussed in Chapters 8–10 among `CRITICAL_SECTION`s, mutexes, `SignalObjectAndWait`, and the signal and broadcast condition variable models.

All application programs were built with Microsoft Visual C++ 7.0 and 6.0 as release versions rather than debug versions. Running in debug mode can add significant performance overhead. Nearly 80 percent overhead was observed in one CPU-intensive test, and the debug executable images can be two or three times larger than the release versions.

Host Systems

Performance was measured on four current (as of 2004) systems with a wide variety of CPU, memory, and OS configurations. All use the NTFS file system. Data from some older systems is also provided in several cases.

1. A 1GHz Pentium laptop running Windows 2000 Professional.

2. A 2GHz Intel Celeron laptop running Windows XP.

3. A Windows 2000 PC with a Pentium processor.

4. A four-processor Windows 2000 Server system, with NT 5.0. It uses four 1.8GHz Intel Xeon processors. This system shows the effects of a high-performance CPU and multiple processors.

The file processing examples also show results on an older NT 500 MHz Pentium III PC to contrast FAT and NTFS performance, although FAT is no longer as common as it once was. All file systems were less than 50 percent full and were not significantly fragmented.

In addition, the systems were all idle, except for running the test programs. The CPU-intensive applications—the sort programs in particular—gave a good indication of relative processing speeds.

Performance Measurements

Each application was run five times on the host system. Physical memory was cleared before each run so that performance figures would not be improved as the files and programs became cached in memory or the swap file. The averages are shown in the tables in the following sections. Times are in seconds.

Comments are listed after the tables. Needless to say, generalizations about performance can be perilous because numerous factors, including test program characteristics, contribute to a program's time performance. These tests do, however, show some of the possibilities and show the potential impacts of various file and operating systems and different programming techniques. Also bear in mind that the tests measure the time from program start to end but do not measure the time that the system might take to flush buffers to the disk. Finally, there was no attempt to exploit specific system features or parameters, such as stripped disks, disk block sizes, multiple disk partitions, and so on.

The Windows performance monitor, available under the control panel's Administrative Tools, displays CPU, kernel, user, and other activities graphically. This tool is invaluable in gaining insight into program behavior beyond the measurements given here.

The results show that performance varies widely based on the CPU, file system, disk configuration, program design, and many other factors. The timing programs are all on the book's Web site so that you can perform these tests on your own system.

File Copying

Five file copy implementations were used to copy a 25.6MB file (400,000 64-byte records, generated with the `RandFile` program from Chapter 5). The first two columns of Table C–1 show results from an older 500MHz Pentium laptop in order to contrast NTFS and FAT performance.

1. `cpC` (Program 1–1) uses the C library. This test measures the effect of an implementation layered on top of Windows, although the library has the opportunity to perform efficient buffering and other techniques.

2. `cpW` (Program 1–2) is the straightforward Windows implementation with a small buffer (256 bytes).

3. `cpwFA` is a "fast" implementation, using a large buffer (8,192 bytes, a multiple of the sector size on all host systems) and the sequential scan flags on both the input and output files.

4. `cpCF` (Program 1–3) uses the Windows `CopyFile` function to determine whether the implementation within a single system call is more efficient than what can be achieved with other techniques.

5. `cpUC` is a UNIX implementation using a small buffer (similar to `cpW`). It is modified slightly to use the Visual C++ UNIX compatibility library.

While the results are averages of five test runs, the elapsed time can vary widely. For example, `cpUC` (last row), with an average of 7.71 seconds in the third column (W2000 laptop), had a minimum elapsed time of 1.87 seconds and a maximum of 11.71 seconds. This wide variation was typical of nearly all the cases on all the systems.

Comments

1. The NTFS does not necessarily give better performance than the FAT file system. On the contrary, the FAT can be faster, as can be seen by comparing columns 1 and 2.

2. The C and UNIX compatibility libraries give competitive performance that is superior to the simplest Windows implementation in many cases.

3. CPU time, both kernel ("System") and user, are minimal. Consequently, processor speed has very little impact on the elapsed time performance.

Table C-1 File Copy Performance

	CPU	Pentium III	Pentium III	Pentium LT	Celeron LT	Xeon	4 x Xeon
	OS	W2000	W2000	W2000	XP	W2000	W2000
	File System	FAT	NTFS	NTFS	NTFS	NTFS	NTFS
cpC	Real	8.62	14.69	12.75	7.23	6.03	2.67
cpC	User	0.12	0.12	0.10	0.10	0.09	0.06
cpC	System	0.24	0.52	1.39	0.39	0.25	0.36
cpW	Real	8.49	13.35	25.48	7.10	8.94	2.95
cpW	User	0.13	0.12	0.06	0.04	0.04	0.13
cpW	System	0.88	1.37	4.61	0.62	0.56	0.13
cpwFA	Real	8.35	12.59	7.35	8.25	9.10	2.36
cpwFA	User	0.01	0.02	0.03	0.01	0.01	0.02
cpwFA	System	0.40	0.50	0.82	0.29	0.20	0.19
cpCF	Real	8.00	11.69	2.57	6.50	7.62	2.97
cpCF	User	0.02	0.01	0.02	0.02	0.01	0.02
cpCF	System	0.19	0.25	0.53	0.19	0.12	0.17
cpUC	Real	7.84	13.14	21.01	9.98	7.77	3.53
cpUC	User	0.72	0.66	0.47	0.34	0.34	0.42
cpUC	System	0.40	0.67	3.12	0.34	0.36	0.41

4. High-end SMP server systems do produce fast file processing compared to laptops and PCs, as would be expected. Informal tests on a faster W2003 system produced even better results (not shown here), with elapsed times about half those of the right-most column.

5. There are no consistent or significant elapsed time performance advantages obtained by using large buffers, sequential scan flags, or a function such as CopyFile. However, the very small user times for cpwFA and cpCF are interesting and potentially helpful in some situations, even if they do not improve elapsed time. One system, the Pentium laptop, is an exception to this generalization. As mentioned earlier, CPU time is a small part of the elapsed time.

6. Elapsed time results are highly variable, with as much as a 10:1 difference between identical tests run under identical circumstances.

ASCII to Unicode Conversion

Eight programs were measured, all converting the same 12.8MB file to a 25.6MB file. Table C–2 shows the results.

1. `atou` is Program 2–4 and is comparable to `cpW` using a small buffer.

2. `atouSS` is the first "fast" implementation based on `atou`. It uses the sequential scan flags but a small buffer. This program, along with the next two, is generated from the same project, `atouLBSS`, by defining different combinations of macros.

3. `atouLB` uses a large buffer (8,192 bytes) but does not use the sequential scan flags.

4. `atouLSFP` uses both a large buffer and sequential scan flags, and it also presizes the output file to the length required. This turns out to be very effective.

5. `atouMM` uses memory mapping for file I/O and calls the functions in Program 5–3.

6. `atouMT` is a multithreaded implementation of Chapter 14's multiple buffer scheme without asynchronous I/O.

7. `atouOV`, Program 14–1, uses overlapped I/O and does not run on the two Windows 9x systems.

8. `atouEX`, Program 14–2, uses extended I/O and does not run on the two Windows 9x systems.

Comments

1. These results show that there is a small advantage to using large buffers and the sequential scan flags, possibly in conjunction.

2. Presizing the output file (`atouLSFP`) is very effective, giving dramatic performance improvements on all the single-processor systems. The SMP benefits, however, were marginal. This technique could also be used with the previous file copying examples.

3. CPU time is insignificant in these tests.

4. Overlapped I/O, in addition to being limited to Windows NT and very difficult to program, gives poor performance. Notice that the time is predominantly real time and not user or system time. Using NT4, it appears that the system has difficulty scheduling the disk access, and experiments with different buffer sizes (larger and smaller) did not help until 65K buffers were used. NT5 has eliminated this problem.

5. Extended I/O and multiple threads do not provide any significant benefit.

6. Memory-mapped I/O can give very good performance, usually about 30 percent faster than the other versions. The SMP server results were even better.

Table C-2 ASCII to Unicode Performance

	CPU	Pentium III	Pentium III	Pentium LT	Celeron LT	Xeon	4 x Xeon
	OS	W2000	W2000	W2000	XP	W2000	W2000
	File System	FAT	NTFS	NTFS	NTFS	NTFS	NTFS
atou	Real	3.24	7.16	33.53	6.27	5.77	2.77
	User	0.31	0.33	0.01	0.06	0.06	0.08
	System	0.46	0.72	3.55	0.54	0.63	0.63
atouSS	Real	3.77	6.21	43.53	10.12	5.68	2.48
	User	0.20	0.23	0.11	0.07	0.04	0.14
	System	0.52	0.81	3.17	0.04	0.35	0.81
atouLB	Real	4.38	6.41	28.51	5.95	4.75	2.47
	User	0.10	0.07	0.05	0.03	0.03	0.08
	System	0.26	0.34	0.63	0.19	0.21	0.187
atouLSFP	Real	N/A	N/A	5.17	1.38	1.28	2.03
	User	N/A	N/A	0.07	0.05	0.09	0.06
	System	N/A	N/A	0.61	0.16	0.10	0.11
atouMM	Real	4.35	2.75	3.46	3.90	3.74	0.77
	User	0.27	0.29	0.09	0.07	0.05	0.14
	System	0.19	0.19	0.16	0.14	0.10	0.09
atouMT	Real	4.84	6.18	5.83	6.61	5.99	3.55
	User	0.14	0.15	0.26	0.04	0.06	0.02
	System	0.45	0.46	0.66	0.33	0.15	0.31
atouOV	Real	9.54	8.85	32.42	6.84	5.63	3.17
	User	0.14	0.12	0.21	0.06	0.06	0.06
	System	0.24	0.23	0.42	0.18	0.21	0.17
atouEX	Real	5.67	5.92	30.65	6.50	5.19	2.64
	User	1.10	1.50	0.29	0.35	0.41	0.64
	System	1.19	1.74	0.77	0.69	0.59	1.91

Pattern Searching

Three pattern searching methods were tested to compare the efficiencies of multiple threads and processes as well as sequential processing (see Table C–3).

1. grepMP, Program 6–1, searches with parallel processes, each processing a separate file. The system and user times are not given, because timep measures only the parent process.

2. grepMT, Program 7–1, uses parallel threads.

3. grepSQ is a DOS batch file that searches each file in sequence. Again, only the real time is available.

The 20 target files used in the test vary in size from a few kilobytes to more than one megabyte.

Comments

1. In most cases, all three techniques provide similar results on single-processor systems. The Pentium laptop is an exception, where grepMP version was consistently slow.

2. Multithreading offers a slight advantage over multiple processes, even on single-processor systems.

3. User and system times are only meaningful in the multithreaded version.

4. SMP systems show the performance gains that are possible using threads or multiple single-threaded processes. Notice that the total user time exceeds the real time because the user time represents all four processors.

5. The fact that the sequential processing gave such similar results on single-processor systems indicates that the simplest solution is sometimes the best.

Table C-3 Pattern Searching Performance

	CPU	Pentium LT	Celeron LT	Xeon	4 x Xeon
	OS	W2000	XP	W2000	W2000
	File System	NTFS	NTFS	NTFS	NTFS
grepMP	Real	14.72	3.95	10.58	0.63
	User	N/A	N/A	N/A	N/A
	System	N/A	N/A	N/A	N/A
grepMT	Real	7.08	3.61	8.09	0.73
	User	0.30	0.41	0.27	2.23
	System	0.09	0.47	0.13	0.28
grepSQ	Real	6.71	3.86	6.71	0.97
	User	N/A	N/A	N/A	N/A
	System	N/A	N/A	N/A	N/A

File Sorting

A target sort file of 100,000 64-byte records (6.4MB) was used to test four sort implementations from Chapter 5, as shown in the first four rows in Table C–4. The sorted file output was suppressed in all cases to emphasize the time required to perform the sorting itself. Then a multithreaded sort, Program 7–2, of a 25MB file with 400,000 64-byte records was tested with one, two, and four threads. Each individual run used a different file, created by the `RandFile` program that is in the Chapter 5 directory. There was considerable variation from one run to the next.

1. `sortBT` is Program 5–1, which creates a binary search tree, requiring a memory allocation for each record. This program is CPU-intensive.

2. `sortFL` is Program 5–4, which maps the file before using `qsort`. `sortFLSR` (heap access was serialized) was also tested but showed no measurable difference.

3. `sortHP` is not listed in the text. It preallocates a buffer for the file and then reads the file into the buffer for sorting rather than mapping the file as `sortFL` does.

4. `sortMM` is Program 5–5, which creates a permanent index file.

5. `sortMT` is Program 7–2, the multithreaded sort-merge. The results are shown as `sortMT1`, `sortMT2`, and `sortMT4`, according to the number of parallel threads. Results can differ significantly depending on the nature of the data in the file to be sorted, although the size and randomness of the data minimizes this variation, which, in general, is a characteristic of the underlying quick-sort algorithm used to implement the `qsort` C library function.

Comments

1. The binary tree implementation, `sortBT`, is CPU-intensive; it must allocate storage for each record one at a time.

2. Memory mapping and reading the file into a preallocated buffer yield similar performance, but the memory mapping was not as good in these tests, and, in several cases, was considerably worse. However, `sortFL` and `sortHP` gave some excellent results.

3. The total of user and system times sometimes exceeds the elapsed time, even when using a single thread.

4. `sortMT` demonstrates the potential of SMP systems. Additional threads also helped, in some cases, on single-processor systems.

Table C-4 File Sorting Performance

	CPU	Pentium LT	Celeron LT	Xeon	4 x Xeon
	OS	W2000	XP	W2000	W2000
	File System	NTFS	NTFS	NTFS	NTFS
sortBT	Real	N/A	9.61	N/A	N/A
	User	N/A	1.84	N/A	N/A
	System	N/A	7.44	N/A	N/A
sortFL	Real	11.15	0.78	1.74	5.38
	User	4.81	0.41	0.26	5.19
	System	0.15	0.09	0.09	0.02
sortHP	Real	1.76	0.34	1.52	1.30
	User	1.62	0.22	0.15	1.28
	System	0.11	0.05	0.03	0.04
sortMM	Real	0.99	1.44	1.92	1.39
	User	0.31	0.18	0.15	0.38
	System	0.68	0.47	0.36	1.03
sortMT1	Real	3.18	3.58	6.80	0.14
	User	0.01	0.95	0.01	0.05
	System	0.46	0.16	0.16	0.11
sortMT2	Real	2.10	1.22	6.70	0.13
	User	0.01	1.05	0.01	0.02
	System	0.40	0.16	0.16	0.13
sortMT4	Real	2.20	1.49	6.22	0.13
	User	0.01	1.18	0.01	0.12
	System	0.16	0.15	0.16	0.09

Multiple Threads Contending for a Single Resource

This test sequence compares different strategies for implementing the queue management functions of Program 10–4, using Program 10–5 (the three-stage pipeline) as a test application. The tests were run on a four-processor (1GHz) Intel Xeon Windows 2000 Server using 1, 2, 4, 8, 16, 32, and 64 threads, but in all seven cases each thread was asked to perform 1,000 units of work. Ideally, we would then expect real time to increase linearly with the number of threads, but contention for a single mutex (or CS) can cause nonlinear degradation as the number of threads increases. Note that these tests do not exercise the file system.

Six different implementation strategies were used, and the results are shown in separate columns in Table C–5. The comments following Program 10–4 discuss the results and explain the merits of the different implementations, but notice that the signal model does scale with the number of threads, while the broadcast model does not scale, especially with 32 and 64 threads. Also notice how the broadcast model results in large amounts of system CPU time as multiple threads run, test the predicate, and immediately return to the wait state.

1. Broadcast model, mutex, event, separate release and wait calls. The tunable time-out was set to 5 milliseconds, which optimized the 16-thread case.

2. Broadcast model, CRITICAL_SECTION, event, separate release and wait calls. The tunable time-out was set to 25 milliseconds, which optimized the 16-thread case.

3. Broadcast model, mutex, event, atomic SignalObjectAndWait call.

4. Signal model, mutex, event, separate release and wait calls.

5. Signal model, CRITICAL_SECTION, event, separate release and wait calls.

6. Signal model, mutex, event, atomic SignalObjectAndWait call.

Table C-5 Multithreaded Pipeline Performance on a Four-Processor Server

Number of Threads		Broadcast Model	Broadcast Model	Broadcast Model	Signal Model	Signal Model	Signal Model
		Mtx, Evt	Crit Sec, Evt	Mtx, Evt	Mtx, Evt	Crit Sec, Evt	Mtx, Evt
		5-ms T/O	25-ms T/O	`SigObjWait`	Time-out N/A	Time-out N/A	`SigObjWait`
1	Real	0.03	0.03	0.05	0.05	0.03	0.05
	User	0.03	0.06	0.03	0.05	0.08	0.05
	System	0.06	0.02	0.09	0.08	0.02	0.06
2	Real	0.14	0.27	0.09	0.08	0.06	0.08
	User	0.13	0.05	0.14	0.17	0.11	0.08
	System	0.11	0.06	0.16	0.09	0.11	0.17
4	Real	0.39	0.59	0.23	0.19	0.16	0.20
	User	0.18	0.17	0.22	0.26	0.17	0.19
	System	0.30	0.22	0.41	0.31	0.22	0.31
8	Real	0.83	0.92	0.73	0.36	0.34	0.36
	User	0.34	0.36	0.55	0.52	0.45	0.45
	System	0.98	1.00	1.00	0.69	0.39	0.75
16	Real	2.42	2.30	2.38	0.75	0.69	0.75
	User	1.17	1.31	1.22	0.81	0.81	0.88
	System	3.69	3.05	3.39	1.45	1.08	1.33
32	Real	7.56	7.50	7.98	1.50	1.50	1.50
	User	3.33	3.73	2.56	1.75	1.69	1.78
	System	12.52	10.72	11.03	3.13	2.00	2.69
64	Real	27.72	26.23	29.31	3.14	2.95	3.20
	User	7.89	10.75	7.22	3.73	3.69	3.47
	System	46.70	40.33	36.67	6.28	3.89	5.47

Running the Tests

The `TimeTest` directory on the book's Web site includes the following batch files for both Windows 2000/NT and Windows 9x operation:

- `cpTIME.bat`
- `cpTIME.bat`
- `atouTIME.bat`
- `grepTIME.bat`
- `sortTIME.bat`
- `threeST.bat`

The program `RandFile` creates a large ASCII file used for all but the last test sequence.

Bibliography

Beveridge, Jim, and Wiener, Robert. *Multithreading Applications in Win32: The Complete Guide to Threads*, Addison-Wesley, Reading, MA, 1997. ISBN: 0-201-44234-5.

Bott, Ed, and Siechert, Carl. *Microsoft Windows Security Inside Out for Windows XP and Windows 2000*, Microsoft Press, Redmond, WA, 2002. ISBN: 0-735-61632-9.

Box, Don. *Essential COM*, Addison-Wesley, Reading, MA, 1998. ISBN: 0-201-63446-5.

Box, Don (editor), et al. *Effective COM: 50 Ways to Improve Your COM and MTS-Based Applications*, Addison-Wesley, Reading, MA, 1999. ISBN: 0-20-1-37968-6.

Brain, Marshall, and Reeves, Ron. *Win32 System Services: The Heart of Windows 98 and Windows 2000, Third Edition*, Prentice Hall, Englewood Cliffs, NJ, 2000. ISBN: 0-13-022557-6.

Butenhof, David. *Programming with POSIX Threads*, Addison-Wesley, Reading, MA, 1997. ISBN: 0-201-63392-2.

Cohen, Aaron, Woodring, Mike, and Petrusha, Ronald. *Win32 Multithreaded Programming*, O'Reilley & Associates, Sebastopol, CA, 1998. ISBN: 1-565-92296-4.

Comer, Douglas E., and Stevens, David L. *Internetworking with TCP/IP, Volume III: Client-Server Programming and Applications, Windows Sockets Version*, Prentice Hall, Upper Saddle River, NJ, 1997. ISBN: 0-13-848714-6.

Custer, Helen. *Inside Windows NT*, Microsoft Press, Redmond, WA, 1993. ISBN: 155615-481-X. *Second edition by David Solomon replaces this book, which in turn is replaced by Solomon and Russinovich (both in this bibliography).*

———. *Inside the Windows NT File System*, Microsoft Press, Redmond, WA, 1994. ISBN: 155615-660-X.

Department of Defense. *U.S. Department of Defense Trusted Computer System Evaluation Criteria*, formerly known as *DoD Trusted Computer System Evaluation Criteria*, DoD 5200.28-STD, DoD Computer Security Center, 1985. Available at http://www.radium.ncsc.mil/tpep/library/rainbow.

Donahoo, Michael, and Calvert, Kenneth. *TCP/IP Sockets in C: Practical Guide for Programmers*, Morgan Kaufmann, San Francisco, CA, 2000. ISBN: 1-55860-826-5.

Eddon, G., and Eddon, D. *Inside Distributed COM*, Microsoft Press, Redmond, WA, 1998. ISBN: 1-57231-849-X.

Feuer, Alan. *MFC Programming*, Addison-Wesley, Reading, MA, 1997. ISBN: 0-201-63358-2.

Gilly, Daniel, and the staff of O'Reilly & Associates, Inc. *UNIX in a Nutshell*, O'Reilly & Associates, Inc., Sebastopol, CA, 1992. ISBN: 1-56592-001-5.

Hennessy, John L., and Patterson, David A. *Computer Architecture: A Quantitative Approach, Third Edition*, Morgan Kaufmann, San Francisco, CA, 2003. ISBN: 1-55860-596-7.

Hipson, Peter D. *Expert Guide to Windows NT 4 Registry*, Sybex, 1999. ISBN: 0-7821-1983-2.

Josutis, Nicolai M. *The C++ Standard Library: A Tutorial and Reference*, Addison-Wesley, Reading, MA, 1999. ISBN: 0-20-137926-0.

Kano, Nadine. *Developing International Applications for Windows 95 and Windows NT*, Microsoft Press, Redmond, WA, 1995. ISBN: 1-55615-840-8.

Kernighan, Brian W., and Ritchie, Dennis M. *The C Programming Language, Second Edition*, Prentice-Hall, Englewood Cliffs, NJ, 1988. ISBN: 0-13-110370-9.

Miller, Kevin. *Professional NT Services*, WROX, Indianapolis, IN, 1998. ISBN: 1-86100-130-4.

Naik, Dilip. *Inside Windows Storage—Server Storage Technologies for Windows 2000, Windows Server 2003, and Beyond*, Addison-Wesley, Boston, MA, 2003. ISBN: 0-321-12698-X.

Nottingham, Jason P., Makofsky, Steven, and Tucker, Andrew. *SAMS Teach Yourself Windows CE Programming in 24 Hours*, SAMS, Indianapolis, IN, 1999. ISBN: 0-6723-1658-7.

Oney, Walter. *Programming the Microsoft Windows Driver Model, Second Edition*, Microsoft Press, Redmond, WA, 2002. ISBN: 0-735-61803-8.

Petzold, Charles. *Programming Windows, Fifth Edition*, Microsoft Press, Redmond, WA, 1998. ISBN: 1-572-31995-X.

Pham, Thuan, and Garg, Pankaj. *Multithreaded Programming with Win32*, Prentice-Hall, Englewood Cliffs, NJ, 1998. ISBN: 0-130-10912-6.

Plauger, P. J. *The Standard C Library*, Prentice-Hall, Englewood Cliffs, NJ, 1992. ISBN: 0-13-131509-9.

Quinn, Bob, and Shute, Dave. *Windows Sockets Network Programming*, Addison-Wesley, Reading, MA, 1996. ISBN: 0-201-63372-8.

Raymond, Eric S. *The Art of UNIX Programming*, Addison-Wesley, Boston, MA, 2003. ISBN: 0-131-42901-9.

Rector, Brent, and Newcomer, Joseph M. *Win32 Programming*, Addison-Wesley, Reading, MA, 1997. ISBN: 0-201-63492-9.

Richter, Jeffrey. *Programming Applications for Microsoft Windows* (formerly *Advanced Windows NT: The Developer's Guide to the Win32 Application Programming Interface* in previous editions), Microsoft Press, Redmond, WA, 1999. ISBN: 1-57-231996-8.

Richter, Jeffrey, and Clark, Jason. *Programming Server-Side Applications for Microsoft Windows 2000*, Microsoft Press, Redmond, WA, 2000. ISBN: 0-73-560753-2.

Robbins, Kay A., and Robbins, Steven. *Practical UNIX Programming: A Guide to Concurrency, Communication, and Multithreading*, Prentice-Hall, Englewood Cliffs, NJ, 1995. ISBN: 0-13-443706-3.

Sedgewick, Robert. *Algorithms in C*, Addison-Wesley, Reading, MA, 1990. ISBN: 0201-51425-7.

Silberschatz, Abraham, Gagne, Greg, and Galvin, Peter B. *Operating System Concepts, Sixth Edition*, Wiley Textbooks, Hoboken, NJ, 2002. ISBN: 0-471-25060-0.

Sinha, Alok K. *Network Programming in Windows NT*, Addison-Wesley, Reading, MA, 1996. ISBN: 0-201-59056-5.

Solomon, David. *Inside Windows NT, Second Edition*, Microsoft Press, Redmond, WA, 1998. ISBN: 1-57-231677-2.

Solomon, David, and Russinovich, Mark. *Inside Windows 2000*, Microsoft Press, Redmond, WA, 2000. ISBN: 1-73-561021-5.

Standish, Thomas A. *Data Structures, Algorithms and Software Principles in C*, Addison-Wesley, Reading, MA, 1995. ISBN: 0-201-59118-9.

Stevens, W. Richard. *Advanced Programming in the UNIX Environment*, Addison-Wesley, Reading, MA, 1992. ISBN: 0-201-56317-7.

———. *TCP/IP Illustrated, Volume 3: TCP for Transactions, HTTP, NNTP, and the UNIX Domain Protocols*, Addison-Wesley, Reading, MA, 1996. ISBN:0-201-63495-3.

———. *UNIX Network Programming—Networking APIs: Sockets and XTI, Volume I*, Prentice-Hall, Upper Saddle River, NJ, 1998. ISBN: 0-13-490012-X.

Sutton, Stephen A. *Windows NT Security Guide*, Addison-Wesley, Reading, MA, 1997. ISBN: 0-201-41969-6.

Triebel, Walter A. *Itanium Architecture for Software Developers*, Intel Press, 2000. ISBN: 0-970-28464-0.

Unicode Consortium, The. *The Unicode Standard, Version 2.0*, Addison-Wesley, Reading, MA, 1996. ISBN: 0-201-48345-9.

Weiss, Mark Allen. *Data Structures and Algorithm Analysis in C*, Addison-Wesley, Reading, MA, 1993. ISBN: 0-8053-5440-9.

Williams, Robert, and Walla, Mark. *The Ultimate Windows Server 2003 System Administrator's Guide*, Addison-Wesley, Boston, MA, 2003. ISBN: 0-201-79106-4.

Index